T0348617

The Private Sector's Role in Poverty Reduction in Asia

CHANDOS
ASIAN STUDIES SERIES
CONTEMPORARY ISSUES AND TRENDS

Series Editor: Professor Chris Rowley,
Centre for Research on Asian Management, Cass Business School,
City University, UK; HEAD Foundation, Singapore
(email: *c.rowley@city.ac.uk)*

Chandos Publishing is pleased to publish this major Series of books entitled *Asian Studies: Contemporary Issues and Trends*. The Series Editor is Professor Chris Rowley, Director, Centre for Research on Asian Management, City University, UK and Director, Research and Publications, HEAD Foundation, Singapore.

Asia has clearly undergone some major transformations in recent years and books in the Series examine this transformation from a number of perspectives: economic, management, social, political and cultural. We seek authors from a broad range of areas and disciplinary interests covering, for example, business/management, political science, social science, history, sociology, gender studies, ethnography, economics and international relations, etc.

Importantly, the Series examines both current developments and possible future trends. The Series is aimed at an international market of academics and professionals working in the area. The books have been specially commissioned from leading authors. The objective is to provide the reader with an authoritative view of current thinking.

New authors: we would be delighted to hear from you if you have an idea for a book. We are interested in both shorter, practically orientated publications (45,000+ words) and longer, theoretical monographs (75,000–100,000 words). Our books can be single, joint or multi-author volumes. If you have an idea for a book, please contact the publishers or Professor Chris Rowley, the Series Editor.

Dr Glyn Jones
Chandos Publishing
Email: *gjones@chandospublishing.com*
www.chandospublishing.com

Professor Chris Rowley
Cass Business School, City University
Email: *c.rowley@city.ac.uk*
www.cass.city.ac.uk/faculty/c.rowley

Chandos Publishing: Chandos Publishing is an imprint of Woodhead Publishing Limited. The aim of Chandos Publishing is to publish books of the highest possible standard: books that are both intellectually stimulating and innovative.

We are delighted and proud to count our authors from such well-known international organisations as the Asian Institute of Technology, Tsinghua University, Kookmin University, Kobe University, Kyoto Sangyo University, London School of Economics, University of Oxford, Michigan State University, Getty Research Library, University of Texas at Austin, University of South Australia, University of Newcastle, Australia, University of Melbourne, ILO, Max-Planck Institute, Duke University and the leading law firm Clifford Chance.

A key feature of Chandos Publishing's activities is the service it offers its authors and customers. Chandos Publishing recognises that its authors are at the core of its publishing ethos, and authors are treated in a friendly, efficient and timely manner. Chandos Publishing's books are marketed on an international basis, via its range of overseas agents and representatives.

Professor Chris Rowley: Dr Rowley, BA, MA (Warwick), DPhil (Nuffield College, Oxford) is Subject Group leader and the inaugural Professor of Human Resource Management at Cass Business School, City University, London, UK, and Director of Research and Publications for the HEAD Foundation, Singapore. He is the founding Director of the multi-disciplinary and internationally networked Centre for Research on Asian Management (*http://www.cass.city.ac.uk/cram/index.html*) and Editor of the leading journal *Asia Pacific Business Review* (*www.tandf.co.uk/journals/titles/13602381.asp*). He is well known and highly regarded in the area, with visiting appointments at leading Asian universities and top journal Editorial Boards in the UK, Asia and the US. He has given a range of talks and lectures to universities, companies and organisations internationally with research and consultancy experience with unions, business and government, and his previous employment includes varied work in both the public and private sectors. Professor Rowley researches in a range of areas, including international and comparative human resource management and Asia Pacific management and business. He has been awarded grants from the British Academy, an ESRC AIM International Study Fellowship and gained a 5-year RCUK Fellowship in Asian Business and Management. He acts as a reviewer for many funding bodies, as well as for numerous journals and publishers. Professor Rowley publishes extensively, including in leading US and UK journals, with over 370 articles, books, chapters and other contributions.

Bulk orders: some organisations buy a number of copies of our books. If you are interested in doing this, we would be pleased to discuss a discount. Please email *wp@woodheadpublishing.com* or telephone +44(0) 1223 499140.

The Private Sector's Role in Poverty Reduction in Asia

SCOTT A. HIPSHER

CHANDOS
PUBLISHING

Oxford Cambridge New Delhi

Chandos Publishing
Hexagon House
Avenue 4
Station Lane
Witney
Oxford OX28 4BN
UK
Tel: +44(0) 1993 848726
Email: *info@chandospublishing.com*
www.chandospublishing.com
www.chandospublishingonline.com

Chandos Publishing is an imprint of Woodhead Publishing Limited

Woodhead Publishing Limited
80 High Street
Sawston Cambridge CB22 3HJ
UK
Tel: +44(0) 1223 499140
Fax: +44(0) 1223 832819
www.woodheadpublishing.com

First published in 2013

ISBN: 978-0-85709-448-3 (print)
ISBN: 978-0-85709-449-0 (online)

© S. Hipsher, 2013

British Library Cataloguing-in-Publication Data.
A catalogue record for this book is available from the British Library.

The publisher makes no representation, express or implied, with regard to the accuracy of the information contained in this publication and cannot accept any legal responsibility or liability for any errors or omissions.

The material contained in this publication constitutes general guidelines only and does not represent to be advice on any particular matter. No reader or purchaser should act on the basis of material contained in this publication without first taking professional advice appropriate to their particular circumstances. All screenshots in this publication are the copyright of the website owner(s), unless indicated otherwise.

Project management by Neil Shuttlewood Associates, Gt Yarmouth, Norfolk, UK
Printed in the UK and USA

Contents

List of figures

List of abbreviations

ASEAN	Association of South East Asian Nations
BJP	Bharatiya Janata Party
BOP	Bottom Of the Pyramid
CP	Charoen Pokphand
FDI	Foreign Direct Investment
FUNCINPEC	Front Uni National pour un Cambodge Indépendant, Neutre, Pacifique, Et Coopératif
GATT	General Agreement on Tariffs and Trade
HCMC	Ho Chi Minh City
HR	Human Resources
HRM	Human Resource Management
HRP	Human Rights Party
HUL	Hindustan Unilever
IMF	International Monetary Fund
KMT	Kuomintang
LDCs	Less and least Developed Countries
LTTE	Tamil Tigers
MNC	MultiNational Corporation
MOUs	Memorandums Of Understanding
NIEs	Newly Industrialized Countries
OEM	Original Equipment Manufacturer
PAD	People's Alliance for Democracy
PPP	People's Power Party
PRC	People's Republic of China
RD	Research and Development
RLG	Royal Lao Government
SLORC	State Law and Order Restoration Council
SMEs	Small and Medium-sized Enterprises
SPDC	State Peace and Development Council
SRP	Sam Rainsy Party
UNTAC	United Nations Transitional Authority in Cambodia
USAID	United States Agency for International Development

USULS	US University Language School
VNQDD	Việt Nam Quốc Dân Đảng (Vietnamese Nationalist Party)
VOC	Dutch East India Company (*Vereenigde Oostindische Compagnie*)
WTO	World Trade Organization

Acknowledgements

A book project is a major undertaking and requires considerable assistance to complete. Due to limited linguistic skills and limited travel funds, assistance was required in gathering much of the data for the project. It is impossible to acknowledge everyone who has assisted in this project, and also some individuals interviewed have preferred to remain anonymous.

However, I would like to give special acknowledgements to the following individuals for providing information and assistance in completing this work: Ms. Achhara Som, Prof. Ana Liza Ragos, Ms. Amy Hipsher, Mr. Bounleung Veunvilaong, Dr. Candace Mehaffey-Kultgen, Ms. Dang Thai Phuoc, Ms. Huynh Thi Thu Phuong, Mr. Jeffery Hipsher, Mr. Lu Yitian, Ms. Meena Nuega, Mr. Orgil Balgansuren, Ms. Quynh Huong, Ms. Rosemarie Quilacio, Mr. Scott Johnson, Ms. Souvita Phaseut, Ms. Tran Nhi, Ms. Wilawan Chanajaranwit, Ms. Zheng Lu and Ms Zhu Haibo.

Without the assistance of the individuals listed above, and many others, the completion of this work would not have been possible. For the help given, I heartily give my most sincere appreciation and thanks.

Notes

There are a variety of techniques to compile statistics on economic growth and levels of poverty in less and least developed countries. The difficulty in compiling these statistics is compounded by the large number of individuals in these countries engaging in the informal economy and/or subsistence agriculture. Furthermore, much of the data used to compile these statistics often come from governments which may or may not have motivations to report accurately. Therefore, different agencies often report slightly different numbers and as a consequence one will encounter some inconsistencies in the statistics reported in this book. One should consider numbers and statistics reported on poverty reduction and economic growth to be only approximates.

While having lived in Asia for nearly 20 years and having working knowledge of a few Asian languages, the author is not a linguist and made the decision to rely only on English language sources as references. Spellings used for names and places are generally the spellings used by the authors of the original sources, with a few changes for consistency's sake. In cases of individual names the English spellings have usually been supplied by the individuals who were interviewed and only in a few rare cases has the author used his own translation of an individual's name.

About the author

Scott A. Hipsher has a wide range of experience in the private sector, academia and non-profit organizations. Amongst various occupations, he has worked as a horse racing trainer, farm hand, factory worker, English teacher, member of the US Navy, general affairs manager of an NGO working with refugees along the Thai/Burmese border, area manager of an export company in northeast Thailand and in various positions in academia. The author earned his bachelor's degree in Japan, MBA in Thailand and did the research for his PhD in Cambodia. The author has taught at universities in Thailand, Vietnam and China and has conducted research in a number of other Asian countries. Dr. Hipsher is currently a visiting professor for Fort Hays State University's program in China, but retains a residency in Bangkok, Thailand. The author has written a number of book chapters, academic journal articles and conference papers as well as being the author of the books, *Business Practices in Southeast Asia: An Interdisciplinary Analysis of Theravada Buddhist Countries* (Routledge Publishing), *Expatriates in Asia: Breaking Free from the Colonial Paradigm* (Chandos) and the lead author of *The Nature of Asian Firms: An Evolutionary Perspective* (Chandos).

Asia

Private sector's role in poverty reduction

Abstract: Poverty reduction is one of the world's most important challenges, and it is proposed the private sector has an important role to play in creating the economic growth, employment and purchasing options needed for significant poverty reduction. Poverty is highly correlated with many negative measurable aspects of standards of living and therefore reducing poverty can have a positive impact on the lives of millions of people around the world. There is much to learn about poverty reduction through examining examples in Asia, as it is the region of the world which has both the most people currently living in poverty and has had the most success in reducing poverty.

Key words: poverty reduction, wealth creation, GDP, private sector, LDCs, globalization, privativization, Asia.

Poverty reduction

Words matter and how an issue or problem is framed will influence the steps taken to fix the problem or change the situation. Poverty has been a scourge of mankind throughout history and therefore poverty reduction has become a widespread goal throughout most societies in the world. The word 'poverty', while having a negative connotation, is often associated with victimhood. 'A victim of poverty' is a common phrase used to refer to individuals living in dire economic circumstances. And 'victims' are often thought of as needing the assistance of outsiders, heroes, to come to the rescue. But is having outsiders coming to the rescue the most effective way to combat this enemy of mankind? Or is poverty reduction more likely to come due to the efforts of the individuals in poverty themselves? Has the trillions of dollars spent as foreign aid and in charities in an effort to directly reduce poverty been highly effective in achieving the goal of reducing poverty in the world?

The opposite of poverty is wealth, while the opposite of reducing is increasing. Therefore, the term 'increasing wealth' might be able to be used synonymously with the term 'reducing poverty'. Reducing poverty implies the increasing of the wealth of individuals currently in poverty. However, the term 'wealth' is often associated with elitism and selfishness, and therefore the positive term 'increasing wealth' does not usually produce the same feelings of warmth and charity that the negative term 'poverty reduction' does. However, looking at the creation of wealth in areas where poverty is present as an approach to poverty reduction might produce a different perspective with which to examine and tackle the problem. A wealth creation approach lessens the sense of victimization found in many approaches to poverty reduction. Wealth creation does not require outside heroes to come to the rescue, it can be created by individuals themselves, but it does require creating opportunities. Can we assume extremely few people will willingly choose to live in poverty, if other alternatives are available, and therefore will lift themselves out of poverty if provided the opportunity? Can a shift from thinking the outside world can create solutions to reduce poverty to a focus on creating opportunities which allows individuals to increase their own wealth and therefore lift themselves out of poverty increase the amount of poverty reduction seen around the world?

While it may be true that money cannot buy happiness, severe poverty is normally accompanied by suffering, high rates of infant mortality and relatively short average life-spans, all of which limit the quality of a human's life.

> Poverty doesn't only condemn humans to lives of difficulty and unhappiness; it can expose them to life threatening dangers. Because poverty denies people any semblance of control over their destiny, it is the ultimate denial of human rights. When freedom of speech or religion is violated in this country or that, global protests are often mobilized in response. Yet when poverty violates the human rights of half the world's population, most of us turn our heads away and get on with our lives.
>
> (Yunus and Weber, 2007: 104–5)

There are many economists, development specialists, intergovernmental agencies, and politicians working tirelessly to lessen the impact of poverty. However, it is proposed the private sector and business educators and researchers also have important roles to play in the global struggle against poverty. Yet for the most part, business researchers and large businesses have ignored the 'bottom-of-the-pyramid' markets which consist of the majority of the planet's citizens (Ricart et al., 2004: 194; Habib and Zurawicki, 2010). While the need for further research on business conditions in areas where poverty is widespread has been heartily acknowledged (London and Hart, 2004; Meyer, 2004; Ramamurti, 2004; Choi et al., 2010), there remain many opportunities for further increasing knowledge by business researchers and the use of this knowledge by the private sector operating in the bottom-of-the-pyramid (BOP) markets. These efforts could have the effect of increasing the wealth of those most in need which could lessen the negative impact poverty has on the lives of millions of individuals.

There has been considerable discussion about how private-sector businesses can impact poverty reduction by engaging in for-profit business activities in the BOP markets (e.g., Prahalad and Hart, 2002; London and Hart, 2004; Ramamurti, 2004; Ricart et al., 2004; Prahalad, 2005). C.K. Prahalad has been at the forefront of academic researchers in the drive to increase the private sector's role in poverty reduction and his vision of how private enterprises bring benefits to the poorest in the world is to bring the market's discipline and innovation to the less and least developed countries (LDCs). He believes the market creates additional choices for consumers and employees while respecting the decisions made by the world's poor (Gouillart, 2008). Choice is the key feature in Prahalad's vision. In an interview with Wooten et al. (2005: 170) he shared the following thoughts:

> The most important thing for me—you should not play God or be elitist. A lot of development people decide what poor people should or should not have. We simply have no right to tell poor people what they should have. Give them the same choice you want given to you. Let them decide. Will they make some bad decisions? Yes. So we make bad decisions? Yes. So the rich have as much liberty to make bad decisions as the poor. But give them the information; don't decide for them.

Serving the BOP markets creates a number of challenges. Operating in the BOP markets, and more specifically servicing individuals living in rural areas of LDCs as consumers, can be costly as infrastructure in LDCs is poor and transportation costs are high. Also as individuals living in poverty generally spend the majority of their income on food for subsistence, most have very limited amounts of discretionary income. This lack of discretionary spending ability makes these BOP markets unattractive to many businesses, especially those which produce items that are not considered necessities. In addition, there are many marketing challenges in creating awareness of products and designing products so they are affordable to BOP consumers. Furthermore, creating jobs in the BOP sectors of developing economies requires overcoming challenges due to most of the workforce living in these areas having a lack of access to education and skill development opportunties (Anderson and Billou, 2007; Habib and Zurawicki, 2010).

Moreover, there are critics of this view that free markets and free choice will lead the poor out of poverty. For example, Karnani (2010) feels much of the BOP literature portrays a romantic image of the poor while the author feels in reality the poor are generally not capable of making the best decisions for themselves and need support from governments, NGOs and international organizations to bring a positive change in their circumstances. Karnani expresses the opinion the emphasis on markets and free enterprises providing additional employment and purchasing choices deemphasizes the role of the state and other actors in poverty reduction.

In addition, there have been concerns expressed over ethical issues encountered by international companies when serving BOP markets. BOP markets generally operate in environments with relatively less formal legal systems and more relationship-based business deals. These features can create conflicts with complying with the ethical standards expected of multinational companies which are used to operating in developed economies with stronger legal systems and more developed market-based economies (Choi et al., 2010). Davidson (2009) raised concerns over the ethical decisions a company faces in the BOP markets when designing products, selecting prices and in ensuring honesty in advertising, as consumers in these markets may lack the sophistication to understand the nuances and biases found in a modern marketing campaign. Operating businesses ethically and profitably in areas of the world where poverty is widespread is a challenge, yet it is felt it is possible and individuals and firms are encouraged to take up this challenge.

It is important to avoid stereotypes and not assume those in poverty all have similar problems and will respond the same way to similar poverty reduction approaches. While there are some common features found in the economies and business environments in the LDCs around the world, it should be kept in mind 'The poor are not a homogeneous group' (Caspary, 2008: 92) and therefore the temptation to propose one-size-fits-all specific strategies while ignoring specific local, political, economic and cultural conditions should be avoided.

Private sector's role in poverty reduction

The positive role of the private sector in poverty reduction has been widely acknowledged and increasing the extent of this role has often been advocated. A few examples:

Nowadays the development of the private sector in developing countries is regarded as essential. The logic behind this statement is simple: poverty reduction is the main objective of development co-operation and a target of development policies. Economic growth is essential for development, and growth is best achieved through the private sector ...

(Pietrobelli, 2007: 21)

A dynamic private sector is crucial for sustainable economic growth, a necessary condition for poverty reduction.

(Chino, 2004: 10)

The private sector has a central role to play in the war on poverty and mobilising private investment is imperative for promoting the broad-based and sustained growth that will help drive poverty reduction.

(OECD, 2006: 11)

There is increasing recognition that private sector development has an important role to play in poverty reduction. The private sector, including small enterprises, creates and sustains the jobs necessary for poor people to work and earn the income needed to purchase goods and services.

(Vandenberg, 2006: vii)

Private sector development is an essential component of economic growth and poverty reduction in developing countries, as it is a very important source of innovation and employment generation. A vibrant and competitive private sector can also empower poor people by providing them with better goods and services at more affordable prices.

(Fukasaku, 2007: 11)

Poverty reduction is an important part of any program aimed at improving standards of living. A recent study by Son (2010) demonstrated the strong correlation between economic growth and improved living standards with economic growth in LDCs being more effective in improving the standards of living than economic growth is in more economically developed societies. Increases in GDP per capita were shown to be associated with increasing life expectancy, lowering rates of infant mortality, increasing the percent of women giving birth with qualified medical care, and higher levels of education and literacy. However, Son's study also showed the correlations between economic growth and improvements in standards of living varied from nation to nation indicating that, while economic growth has proven necessary for significant poverty reduction, other factors such as government policies and average levels of education influence the effectiveness of economic growth in lessening the negative conditions associated with poverty.

Economic growth would appear to be a necessary condition for sustained and substantial poverty reduction and it requires improved efficiencies within an economy. The private sector has a very important role to play in increasing the efficiency of an economy. For example, in the People's Republic of China (PRC), where the world has seen the greatest and fastest poverty reduction in the history of mankind, private enterprises and especially fully foreign-owned ones have been shown to be much more productive in their use of resources and are more efficient users of capital than are state-owned firms (Dougherty and McGuckin, 2008). Privatization and increasing the role of the private sector have been key features in improving the performance of the economy and reducing poverty in China. Vandenberg (2006: 27) pointed out an additional benefit as private enterprises in LDCs often step in to fill the needs for vital services such as communications, education and transportation when governments fail to meet the needs of their populations.

Improving the performance of the private sector is important in improving economic performance in LDCs and 'we can all agree that achieving sustained poverty reduction around the world will be practically impossible unless economic growth is achieved in poor countries' (Rodrik, 2005: 201). The former president of Tanzania, Mkapa (2010: 53) wrote, 'There can be no poverty reduction without growth—long-term and sustainable growth.' And growth generally is driven by the private sector.

The private sector's importance in poverty reduction does not indicate that other actors such as governments and non-profit organizations do not have a role, yet governments and other non-profits will have a more difficult time achieving goals in environments where economic growth is slow or non-existent. Yunus and Weber (2007: 8) argued, while governments and government policies have a large role in addressing social problems, some of the fundamental characteristics of a government such as size and need to meet the needs of different sectors of society limit a government's effectiveness and if governments could alone solve the problems of poverty the problems would have been solved long ago. Charities and other non-profit organizations have also proven to have limited ability to solve the world's major problems:

> Nonprofits alone have proven to be an inadequate response to social problems. The persistence and even worsening of global poverty, endemic disease, homelessness, famine, and pollution are sufficient evidence that charity by itself cannot do the job. Charity too has a significant built-in weakness: It relies on a steady stream of donations by generous individuals, organizations, or government agencies. When the funds fall short, the good work stops.

> (Yunus and Weber, 2007: 10)

Globalization

The positive impact of the private sector in poverty reduction does not have to solely come from home-grown businesses. Foreign investment and international businesses can be important sources of funds, innovation and jobs in LDCs. The literature has consistently shown a strong correlation between increases in and openness to international trade and investment with economic growth which is a key factor in poverty reduction (Masson, 2001; Farrell, 2004; Walde and Wood, 2004; Anderson, 2005; Arora and Varnvakidis, 2005; Berggren and Jordahl, 2005; Langenfeld and Nieberding, 2005; Stark, 2005; Winters, 2006; Yao, 2006; Hasan et al., 2007). Sen (2002: 12) saw no advantage to the world's poor of a government using protectionist measures and 'by withholding from them the great advantages of contemporary technology, the well established efficiency of international trade and exchange and the social as well as economic merits of living in open rather than closed societies.' Srinivasan (2009: 15) reported on positive effects of international trade by writing, 'cross-country studies that use appropriate econometric techniques, do find a strong association, not only between trade and growth, but also between growth and poverty reduction.'

There are claims globalization, economic growth and an increased role for the private sector can lead to increases in inequality (Bourguignon and Verdier, 2003; Son, 2007). Yet as discovered by Williamson (2005: 149)

'According to history, globalization has never been a necessary condition for widening world income gaps. It happened with globalization and it happened without it.' Moreover, there is debate over whether it is government policies which distort market conditions or the direct results of market forces themselves which have the most impact on increasing inequality while an economy grows (Morley, 2003; Mugerwa, 2003; Lin and Liu, 2008; Lin et al., 2008). It has been proposed that a trade-off between growth, with its accompanying poverty reduction, and increased inequity is not automatically necessary and poverty reduction and lessening of inequity can happen simultaneously with good governmental policies (Ali, 2007; Ali and Son, 2007; Zhuang, 2008). Hasan et al. (2007) have found the evidence showing international trade benefits the rich at the expense of the poor very weak, instead the evidence indicates benefits of increased wealth from trade are most likely to be shared by all segments of society, although not necessarily equally. At times increases in international trade may lead to increased inequality but in absolute terms the poor seem to benefit from living in open societies which are part of global trading networks. For example:

> The experience of Thailand over the past half-century confirms the importance of sustained economic growth, at least in poor countries, for the achievement of basic social objectives of poverty reduction, improved education, and public health. Life expectancy, infant and maternal mortality and literacy have all improved dramatically. Absolute poverty incidence has declined markedly, but inequality has increased.
>
> (Warr, 2007: 162)

Mugerwa (2003) proposed the idea that inequality in Africa can be attributed to rural–urban divisions, which are a legacy of colonialism, more than it is a result of globalization; in fact, it was found trade liberalization has actually improved rural incomes as a result of increased access to markets for exporting agricultural products which has helped to reduce inequality. Central and South America generally have very high levels of inequality, but it can be claimed these inequalities are not due to globalization as this region is less integrated in the global trading system than are other areas, specifically Asia. Instead the inequality is more likely due to internal factors such as limited access to land and education by the poorer segments of society (Morley, 2003; Robinson, 2003).

While most people would agree the benefits from economic growth should be shared throughout all segments of society, too much concern over equality should not result in pursuing actions and policies which limit growth and therefore the ability of individuals to pull themselves out of poverty. In practice, in a variety of countries around the world, restricting the role of the private sector and decreasing the amounts of international trade have not resulted in either poverty reduction or lessening of income inequality. For example, the case in Myanmar/ Burma where withdrawal from global trading networks has resulted in both increasing poverty and increasing inequality (Alamgir, 2008). Therefore, while it would be overly simplistic to assume the private sector can solve all of the world's problems, the track record in Asia of economies increasing the role of the private sector and opening up to foreign investment and trade is much better than the track record of countries which have chosen to go in the opposite direction of mostly closing off their economies from international investment and trade while increasing the role of the public sector.

Critics of globalization often point to the use of 'sweatshop' jobs and the difficult working conditions many workers face in developing economies. However, sweatshops have to compete for workers and in order to attract a workforce they need to provide better opportunities than the workers have elsewhere. Jeffrey Sachs (2005: 11) commented, 'the sweatshops are the first rung on the ladder out of extreme poverty' and pulling these jobs out of areas where extreme poverty is widespread is unlikely to improve the lives of the workers who would then have fewer employment choices.

> Multinational companies naturally take advantage of a less-developed country's abundance of unskilled workers at a wage less than what they would have to pay similar workers in their home countries. However, the more relevant comparison is that these wages are often higher than the wages paid by domestic companies in the host countries.

> (Srinivasan, 2009: 66)

Globalization in itself does not end poverty and many of the world's trade agreements do not in reality promote free or even fair trade, and all advocates of poverty reduction should work to improve the international trading regime to create fairer and freer trade agreements which could significantly improve the market's ability to create economic growth and poverty reduction. But it makes no sense to throw out the baby (the benefits coming from economic integration) with the bathwater (the unfair trade practices that put many developing economies at a disadvantage under the current system).

Wealth and poverty

Acquiring wealth and the avoidance of poverty are important goals for most individuals and families around the world. However, neither wealth nor poverty are terms which are easily defined and it can be a difficult task in classifying individuals as being wealthy, middle class, working class or in poverty. The average working class family in developed economies, such as the USA or UK, has better access to health care, entertainment, transportation, quality food and other products that the world's richest citizens had 150 years ago. Moreover, this same working-class family has a life-style far removed from the life-style of those living today with the lowest levels of income in LDCs. Is this average working-class family in a developed economy 'rich?' It would seem so if compared to others in a historical context or by a global average, or is this family 'struggling?' This would seem to be the case if these individuals are compared to individuals at the top end of the income scale in the same society.

It has become generally accepted that a definition of poverty should not only include lack of access to material and tangible possessions but also to the intangible components of insecurity, powerlessness and indignity (Vandenberg, 2006). Therefore, poverty reduction programs should not only focus on increasing access to material possessions, but also focus on empowering individuals. The private sector is vital in creating employment and purchasing options and having a job; access to more purchasing options and making one's own decisions can empower individuals to a greater extent than is normally found in the dependence often generated by government assistance or charity programs.

There are different definitions of poverty, and a distinction should be made between absolute poverty and relative poverty. Beaudoin (2007: 4) defines absolute poverty as 'the lack of the basic elements needed for human survival, food, water, proper clothing, and shelter.' Absolute poverty is often measured by caloric intake or ability to maintain proper nutrition. Relative poverty is a comparison to a society's average in regards to access to items and services a community values while a third definition of poverty is the absence of choices (Beaudoin, 2007: 5–6).

It is felt the primary purpose of poverty reduction programs and efforts should be in lessening, and hopefully eventually coming close to eliminating, the presence of absolute poverty. The private sector generally addresses absolute poverty indirectly through its contribution to economic/GDP per capita growth. On the other hand, the private sector's impact will not automatically address issues of relative poverty as there are many factors which go into creating inequality. However, as far as the third definition goes the private sector does directly address the lack of choices by providing additional employment and purchasing options for individuals in all sectors of a society.

Poverty not only creates problems for individuals but for societies as a whole. Poverty often leads to a feeling of hopelessness which can lead individuals to take desperate measures, which can affect all segments of society. Poverty creates desperate individuals who have little to lose and much to gain through illegal and often violent activities. Furthermore, poverty can lead to economic refugees as individuals migrate to seek ways to escape poverty which results in large influxes of individuals into societies with different cultural values, which can put a strain on the societies receiving the refugees (Yunus and Weber, 2007).

Increases in income generally have a much bigger impact on the quality of life of individuals in LDCs than it does in more economically developed areas. One important measure of quality of life is life expectancy. On average, a 1% increase in GDP per capita results in a 0.11% increase in life expectancy around the world. However, the impact in sub-Saharan Africa is much greater with a 1% increase in GDP per capita resulting in an increase of life expectancy by 0.27% while industrial societies see much lower gains of only 0.03% (Son, 2010). Son also found per capita GDP growth, which is mostly driven by private enterprises, improves many other objective measures of quality of life in LDCs including lowering infant mortality, increasing the number of births attended to by qualified personal, improving ratios for literacy and primary school attendance, and overall better health.

Increased income has only minor impacts on objective measures of quality of life in more developed economies, but for those with the least income in LDCs, even small increases in income have been found to have significant positive impacts on the measurable aspects of quality of life such as infant mortality, life expectancy and literacy (Laplante, 2010).

Poverty in Asia

The concept of Asia is in many ways a Western construct which is an attempt to lump extremely different cultures and linguistic groups together. Any study of Asia should acknowledge the limitation of combining the individuals from a region with such diversity and one which encompasses the majority of the world's population into a single grouping. However, alongside the vast differences within the region, there are also some aspects of life that make Asia a different region of the world than the regions of Europe, the Middle East, and North and South America.

The earliest known evidence of human habitation in Asia has been found in Java, Indonesia, which depending on the interpretation of the evidence is thought to indicate humans were living there from between 0.5 to 1.3 million years ago (Bellwood, 1992: 67). East Asia developed to some extent differently than did Central and South Asia. Due to difficulties of traveling between geographical regions, human culture and genetics evolved and developed in East Asia mostly independent from the rest of humanity (Fairbanks et al., 1989: 5).

Most attempts to classify those from Southeast and East Asia into ethnic groups that can be traced into antiquity have been unsuccessful due to the integration and interactions within ethnic groups throughout history (Keyes, 2002), although most East and Southeast Asians share some biological features that some think can be traced to populations which originated in what is today southern China (Bellwood, 1992).

Asia is often thought of the land where 'Asians', a racial category, live. This use of race as a defining characteristic in classification of the region might not be the most useful. Instead, it might be better to think geographically and culturally. Culturally, East and Southeast Asia can be primarily thought of as the land where wet-rice agricultural techniques are used. Wet-rice agricultural techniques and the collectivist cultures needed to ensure irrigation channels were built and maintained to service the whole community spread from the lands of China south of the Yangtze River throughout East and Southeast Asia (Kim, 1982; O'Connor, 1995; Takamiya, 2001), thus creating some common features seen in societies throughout the region. Tudor et al. (1996) felt the traditions and culture of using wet-rice agricultural techniques are still being seen in the business practices found in Asia. Along the same lines, Hipsher et al. (2007: 20) believed the experience of generation after generation working in the rice fields was what made East and Southeast Asia unique and distinguished the regions from other locations around the world.

The countries and areas generally referred to as South and Central Asia have distinctly different histories and cultures than do the lands of East and Southeast Asia; however, looking at Hofstede's (1980, 1983) dimensions of culture we see India and Pakistan (the only two countries from South Asia included in the original research) having scores in the areas of collectivism, power distance and uncertainty avoidance which would be closer to the scores of countries in the rest of Asia than to the scores of countries in the West. Therefore, it can be assumed there are both some similarities and many unique differences between different countries and regions of Asia.

The great success Asia has had recently in poverty reduction has been well recorded (e.g., Pangestu, 2003; Ali and Son, 2007; Warr, 2007; Lin and Liu, 2008; Ravallion, 2009; Zhuang, 2008; Asian Development Bank, 2010). Nevertheless, there continues to be more people living in poverty in Asia than in any other continent (Chino, 2004; Hasan et al., 2007). Bauer and Thant (2010: 2) reported 'Despite sustained growth, 1.6 billion Asians live on less than $2 a day and about 20% in extreme poverty under the international $1.25 poverty line.' Son (2007) reported that while economic growth in Asia has generally resulted in poverty reduction, the extreme poor living well below the $1 a day poverty line have not been benefiting to any considerable extent by the rapid economic growth seen around the region, while those who were already close to the $1 a day poverty line have benefited to a substantial extent by the region's economic development. Therefore, while there are many lessons to be learned from Asia's success in poverty reduction, there continues to be much work needing to be done to meet poverty reduction goals and see improvements in the quality of life of millions of individuals in Asia.

Persistent poverty has been especially a problem in South Asia which has lagged behind much of the rest of the world in improving the indicators of poverty such as life expectancy, adult literacy, primary school enrollment rates, survival rates for children under the age of five and percentage of mothers giving birth in the presence of qualified medical personnel (Son, 2010).

Poverty thoughout the region is more pronounced in rural areas than in urban areas. In China, poverty reduction has been slower in rural than in urban areas (Pangestu, 2003; Lin et al., 2008; Zhuang, 2008). While in the emerging economies of the Greater Mekong Subregion (Cambodia, Lao PDR, Myanmar/Burma), close to 90% of the poor are small-scale farmers who depend on agriculture for their living (Setboonsarng, 2008). Therefore, in order to reduce poverty in the region special attention should be given to expanding employment and entrepreneurial opportunities in the private sector in the rural areas of LDCs.

Some of the gains Asia has had in poverty reduction may be under threat from the recent global economic downturn. Hurst et al. (2010) reported on some troubling signs around the region: growth has slowed in the manufacturing sectors resulting in millions of workers leaving urban areas and returning to their rural homes and some employment is shifting away from the better paid formal sectors of the economy to the less well-paid informal sectors. The authors also point out the global economic downturn is having some unexpected results, higher paid non-production workers have been more likely to lose their jobs and have their wages cut than lower paid production workers, and skilled workers have been more likely to have lost their jobs and have wages reduced than non-skilled workers.

However, workers throughout Asia have shown resilience and have found ways to cope with the difficulties they face. Workers who have seen their hours cut in the formal sector often supplement their income with work in the informal sector; also, many laid-off workers in urban areas are not migrating back to their homes, but instead are staying in the urban area and switching to working in the informal sectors of the economy; and some employees have used their unemployment as a motivation to return to school and gain further qualifications (Turk and Mason, 2010). In India, Sinha (2010) found the slowing of worldwide demand was causing a lowering of world prices which potentially can

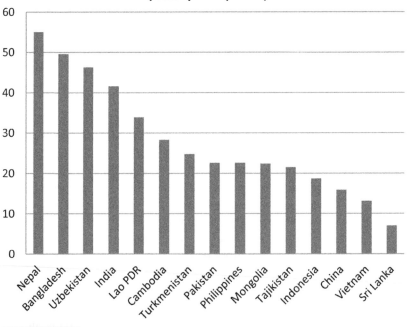

Percentage of population living on less than $1.25 a day (latest year reported)

Figure 1.1

Source: Asian Development Bank (2011b: 68).

result in downward pressure on wages and a shift from more formal to more informal employment. As women make up the majority of the informal sector, they have less to fall back upon during tough economic times and may be more likely to slide back into absolute poverty than men during the global economic downturn (Horn, 2010).

Another challenge Asia faces in the twenty-first century is a rapidly aging population, especially in China, and the smaller size of modern families and the current lack of social programs for the elderly cast doubt on how the countries of the region will cope with the shifting demographic trends (Asher, 2010).

Reducing poverty

There are many strategies and practices which can be used to consolidate gains made in Asia in poverty reduction and pull even more individuals out of poverty. Some of these can only be implemented by individual governments or cross-governmental cooperation while others are more likely to be implemented by non-profit organizations while still others need to be carried out by individuals and organizations in the private sector.

Cross-border trade has helped fuel Asia's economic growth and further liberalization of trade rules within the region may be helpful in continuing economic prosperity and poverty reduction. Over time, Asia's international trade has been growing in value but reducing in volume as the weight per unit value ratio has increased. Also intraregional trade within Asia continues to grow at a faster pace than Asia's trade with other regions; therefore, moves by governments in the region to boost export competitiveness should include improvements which facilitate the ease of cross-border trade within the region (Brooks and Stone, 2010).

There are other strategies that governments can use in the fight against poverty. In order for private businesses to perform efficiently the physical infrastructure of roads, bridges, electricity grids, ports and other public utilities is necessary. However, physical infrastructure alone is not enough, there also needs to be an economic infrastructure which includes legal and judicial systems which help to facilitate trade by promoting the trust of suppliers in getting paid for services and products supplied (Beattie, 2009: 216–7). Governments and intragovernmental organizations have an important role to play in developing both the physical and economic infrastructure needed to facilitate economic growth.

Economic reforms and encouraging private investment are other ways governments can combat poverty. Ospina and Schiffbaer (2010) reported on the correlation between economic reforms aimed at increasing competition and increased productivity and, as productivity is needed to improve economic growth and national competitiveness, these types of reforms can be expected to aid in poverty reduction. Hill and Jongwanich (2009) encouraged governments to promote long-term foreign direct investments which create jobs, knowledge transfers and stability over seeking short-term foreign portfolio investments which can be brought in and pulled out of a country with few transaction costs which can lead to instability.

The private sector also has a very important role to play in poverty reduction and can even produce gains in the quality of the lives of individuals while governments are doing less than a perfect job. For example, Ear (2009: 1) pointed out 'Cambodia has grown rapidly in recent years despite lackluster governance' and this growth and resulting reductions in poverty have been mostly driven by private industry's moves to create successful businesses despite a less than ideal business environment. Operating in the environments found in LDCs can be a challenge for private-sector companies, but finding ways to overcome these challenges can have a major impact on economic growth and poverty reduction.

Many governments have been criticized for failing to curb corruption, and corruption is often used as a justification for lack of investment by foreign companies. While it is impossible to argue corruption helps to promote private-sector investment, its presence doesn't automatically make it impossible to create sustainable win–win situations for a company in an area where it is commonly practiced.

If corruption is stable and predictable enough, it essentially simply becomes a tax. And as the performance of Western European social democracies shows, having substantial rates of taxation, as long as they are collected efficiently and predictably, is no block to getting rich.

(Beattie, 2009: 230)

Beattie (2009: 226) further pointed out that many East Asian countries have had economic growth and seen poverty reduction despite business environments where corruption, as defined by Western standards, is common and 'the most astonishing reduction of poverty in recent history has taken place in another East Asian country, China, which achieves no better than a so-so grade in any international rating of incorruptibility.' Prahalad (2005: 77) warned against failing to recognize the existence of local customs and the need for relationship building in many collectivist developing economies and not automatically assuming these practices which are labeled corruption by Western benchmarks are necessarily undesirable just because these practices are different from what is the norm found in more economically developed, individualistic and egalitarian societies.

Yunus and Weber (2007) proposed one way for private enterprises to bring their energy and expertise into the world of poverty reduction is through the creation of social businesses. Their concept of a social business is one in which the owners eventually are returned their initial investments but no profits are made by the owners of the company, instead the profits are invested back into the social business to better serve those the business was designed to serve. Although the distinction between a social business and a charity on the surface seems slight, Yunus and Weber (2007: 115) make it clear business principles should apply to social businesses and explained:

> In general, I am opposed to giveaways and handouts. They take away initiative and responsibility from the people. If people know that things can be received 'free,' they tend to spend their energy and skill chasing the 'free' things rather than using the same energy and skill to accomplish things on their own. Handouts encourage dependence rather than self-help and self-confidence.

Although the concept of a social business is intuitively appealing, it may be neither necessary nor optimal for private enterprises to abandon the pursuit of profits, which is normally thought to be the source of their dynamism and innovation, when operating in areas where poverty is widespread. Prahalad (2005: 61–2) pointed out serving the 80% of humanity currently underserved by the global economy creates opportunities for both international businesses and people living in poverty. As well as economic flows, knowledge flows may be equally important and the lessons learned by international companies in serving bottom-of-the-pyramid customers can often be used to create more efficient business practices that will help in serving customers in developed markets as well. It may be difficult for a private enterprise to sustain the desire to engage in non-profit activities during an economic downturn or when its stock price is sliding; however, engaging in activities that provide profits, which can only be accomplished through voluntary engagement with customers and employees, will always be attractive and will never fall out of fashion or favor. Therefore, instead of social businesses where no profits are earned, it is proposed more sustainable win–win situations be sought where investors as well as local workers and customers benefit.

Even more important than the availability of additional products for consumers in LDCs, creating the availability of jobs and work opportunities might be the most important impact businesses can have in poverty reduction.

> Central to the problem of poverty is the availability of work. Work allows people to produce for themselves (i.e. food) and earn the money needed to buy goods and services. It is also from work that wealth is created which, through taxation, allows government to fund pro-poor services such as health care, clean water and education. Work, more specifically decent work, is not easily created, however, it develops out of a complex and balanced system of economic, social and political activity. Work is central to poverty reduction . . . .

> (Vandenberg, 2006: 1)

The creation of jobs in environments where poverty is widespread does not come easily. Many developing economies and emerging markets have low rates of investment, low productivity, inadequate incentives for innovation, and returns on investment are often unpredictable (OECD, 2006). Therefore, private enterprises have a challenging, although far from impossible, task in creating sustainable for-profit organizations in developing and emerging economies. Yet these organizations can have an extremely important role to play in reducing poverty and improving the lives of millions of individuals living in areas where employment and purchasing options are limited.

In addition, researchers and those in academia have a role to play. 'If reducing poverty by using economic analysis to accelerate growth and therewith pull people up into gainful employment and dignified sustenance is not moral, and indeed a compelling imperative, what is?' (Bhagwati, 2005: 80). In addition to economic analysis it is proposed business and international business researchers can also play a role in identifying practices and strategies which can be implemented by real companies working to create sustainable businesses in the areas of the world most affected by poverty.

Less developed and least developed economies

There are various classifications used to group countries together by income. Some of the labels for the groupings used by the United Nations include least developed countries, transition economies and less developed countries. The following are considered least developed countries in Asia: Afghanistan, Bangladesh, Bhutan, Cambodia, Lao People's Democratic Republic, Myanmar/Burma, Nepal, and Yemen (UNCTAD, 2011). However in the business and economics literature, clear distinctions are not always made between categories of countries which have lower levels of economic development than seen in the most developed nations where the vast majority of international business research originates. Less developed countries, transition economies, developing countries, emerging markets, least developed countries, bottom-of-the-pyramid markets, and other terms are often used

Figure 1.2   **A day at work in Aranyaprathet, Thailand**

somewhat interchangeably by a variety of writers and scholars to refer to various groupings of nations with comparatively lower economic development.

One of the features of these classifications is they imply a hierarchy of nations with rich on the top and poor on the bottom; which is not necessarily a problem if one sticks to thinking only in terms of economic development and not think in terms of social, moral or other forms of development. People living in the least developed and less developed countries have lives that are as full, interesting, complicated and important as those of peoples living in any other part of the world. While accepting the limitations and for simplicity's sake, in this book the term LDCs will generally be used to refer to both the least developed and less developed countries, as poverty is found in substantial quantities in both categories and making a distinction between categories is not always necessary when discussing general principles.

2

Development:
one size does not fit all

Abstract: Huge sums of money and countless hours have been spent by development agencies to eliminate poverty; however, the results have been less than hoped for. Many specific development programs including microfinance and import substitution have gone through periods of being fashionable, although the results of these programs have been either limited or negative. Yet, there have been many recent stories of economic growth and poverty reduction. These examples of poverty reduction have happened in a variety of different contexts but also have some common features. Most studies of economic development and poverty reduction focus on macroeconomic policies, but it is proposed economic growth and poverty reduction are as much the results of microeconomic decisions made by private enterprises and individuals as they are the results of macroeconomic decisions made by governments.

Key words: development, NGO, microfinance, import substitution, macroeconomics, microeconomic, private sector.

Limitations of traditional development programs and foreign aid

It has often been proposed it is better to teach a man to fish than to give a man a fish. If you give a man a fish he will only eat for a day while if you teach a man to fish he can eat for a lifetime. While this piece of conventional wisdom is hard to argue with, it makes the assumption the man wants fish, which in reality may or may not be accurate. Most top-down development programs make assumptions about what people want. But questions one can ask include: are these two, giving specific items or teaching specific skills, the only options available? And, is the best form of development for some individuals to decide what other individuals need? Would it be better not to assume the man wants fish and provide opportunities which allow the man the choice whether to seek ways to get fish or use his time and energies for other purposes?

The world consists of individuals, each unique with differing goals and motivations in life. What is valuable for one person can be worthless to another. For example, some individuals might be willing to work many hours to afford to see a concert by a particular pop star, while other individuals wouldn't go to the concert if paid to do so. Value is something each of us attaches to various items and services and the value of an item or service differs from individual to individual. Moreover, life goals and motivations differ. Some individuals might be searching for opportunities to work hard and become wealthy. Other individuals might prefer to work just enough to make a decent living and spend the majority of their time with family or pursuing non-monetary goals. Some individuals will be willing to take on work which is unpleasant if it pays more than other options, while others will choose to give up financial gain for more attractive working conditions. The individualistic nature of humans may limit the effectiveness of many top-down development programs which attempt to determine and meet the needs of those living in poverty.

Wealth is not primarily about material possessions, it is about options. It is not unusual for a wealthy individual to fast or eat limited amounts of food for either religious or health reasons, but going hungry is often not an option for one in poverty, but a necessity. Both the wealthy and poor individual might go to bed hungry, but for one it is by choice while for the other there is no choice. While in emergency situations it makes sense to provide those in need with specific material possessions, long-term and sustainable poverty reduction may be more effective if focusing on increasing opportunities for individuals and allowing each person the freedom to make his or her way in the world. Private-sector transactions, which are voluntary exchanges amongst individuals with equal power to engage or not in a transaction, might be better in providing options for individuals than are top-down development and charity programs.

Overall, traditional development programs, foreign aid and charities do not appear to have had a significant impact on reducing poverty. 'Aid cannot, and has not, contributed to the solution of economic problems and therefore economic growth' (Skarbek and Leeson, 2009: 392). Yet the need for economic growth for driving poverty reduction has been well established and explored in Chapter 1. C.K. Prahalad expressed the idea 'Development aid might have made very few people in those developing countries very rich because of corruption. In fact, I think, most of the development aid has been a process of taking taxes from poor people in the developed world and help the very rich in the developing world' (Wooten et al., 2005: 170). Yunus and Weber (2007: 116) also acknowledged foreign aid handouts encourage corruption, which often have had a negative effect on political institutions and motivations of politicians in LDCs.

Easterly (2007: 34) noticed, 'Development ideology has a dismal record of helping any country actually develop. The regions where the ideology has been most influential, Latin America and Africa, have done the worst.' Easterly goes on to point out the countries that have had the most success in economic development and poverty reduction have followed a variety of different paths based on home-grown solutions to each country's unique problems as opposed to importing 'the correct' way advocated by international experts. However, while each success story involves different government policies, all the economic success stories in significantly reducing poverty have included in the recipe the ingredient of dynamic growth in the private sector.

Kihara (2012: 4) found the correlation between foreign aid and economic growth is very weak and not well understood, although foreign aid seems to have a higher correlation with growth in countries which have 'good' polices and institutions. However, correlation does not imply causation. It is highly likely these countries with 'good' policies would have seen economic growth and poverty reduction without the assistance of significant foreign aid, as has been seen in many Asian economies, most notably China. While intuitively the idea that foreign aid can speed up economic development and poverty reduction when used wisely is appealing, the empirical evidence of this actually happening is not as convincing.

Since the end of World War II, developed countries have given an estimated $2 trillion in development aid to LDCs (Werlin, 2009: 501). Yet there is little evidence this money has had a major impact on reducing poverty. Former president of Tanzania Benjamin William Mkapa (2010: 66–7) admitted that aid coming into Africa has not been effective in promoting economic growth and poverty reduction, but insists there is plenty of blame to go around for the results. He acknowledged corruption and inefficiencies within Africa has contributed to the problem, but donor countries have also to shoulder some of the responsibility as many projects have been poorly planned, implemented without local participation and had little oversight. Moreover, the huge budgets spent on expatriate salaries and foreign experts disguised as foreign aid have prevented much of the money from reaching those it was targeted to help. Easterly (2010: 1087) pointed out aid given for such things as health care and education in non-democratic and authoritative states often allow the governments to use more of their own resources on increasing the number of security forces and devising other means to suppress opposition and retain political control, and therefore foreign aid can under some circumstances actually prevent economic and political development as opposed to stimulating it.

Hanlon et al. (2010: 8) made the claim, 'Aid has not failed; what has failed is an aid and anti-poverty industry that thrives on complexity and mystification, with highly paid consultants designing ever more complicated projects for 'the poor' and continuing to impose policy conditions on poor countries.' Therefore, the authors propose foreign aid would have a bigger impact on poverty reduction if donor countries just gave money away to poor people and let the poor decide for themselves how to spend it instead of the current top-down approaches where governments and aid agencies decide what is good for the recipients of aid.

Instead of aid, others have advocated trade as a means to lessen poverty. Trade is conducted between voluntary partners. In every business transaction each party can accept or decline any offer. Therefore, trade is a voluntary exchange which can only go forward when all parties involved feel it is of benefit and therefore all parties have some power in the relationship. Foreign aid, on the other hand, often creates a dependence relationship in which the givers of aid can impose their ideology and values on the dependent party.

> Charity creates a one-sided power relationship. The beneficiaries are favor-seekers rather than claimants of something they deserve. As a result, they have no voice, and accountability and transparency disappear. All such one-way relationships are inequitable and only make the poor more vulnerable to exploitation and manipulation.
>
> (Yunus and Weber, 2007: 116)

Giving away money is fairly easy, but getting aid to the actual poor who are in need is a very complicated and expensive endeavor, and aid donors from developed countries rarely understand the political and social implication of selecting recipients for their programs. As local governments or others in positions of power are usually involved in the distribution of aid, large amounts of aid 'disappear' and both the distribution to and identification of the truly needy is known to be both difficult and expensive (Mirrlees,

2011: 3). Hanlon et al. (2010: 101–20) also acknowledged the difficulties in devising ways to select recipients of aid and proposed that some political trade-offs will have to be made and, to get money into the hands of the truly needy, an organization wanting to give away money to the poor will probably require its programs to give money to some of those who may not be in real need as well.

While claiming that aid and development programs have not been successful can be seen as pessimistic:

> It is easy to forget we have just witnessed half a century of the greatest mass escape from poverty in human history. The proportion of the world's population living in extreme poverty in 2008 (those earning less than a $1 a day) was a fifth of what it was in 1960.
>
> (Easterly, 2009: 77)

The lessons of successful poverty reduction teach us economic growth and poverty reduction come from 'the pragmatic use of time-tested economic ideas – the benefits of specialization, comparative advantage, gains from trade, market-clearing prices, trade-offs, budget constraints – by individuals, firms, governments, and societies as they find their own success' (Easterly, 2007: 35).

Over the past decades, trade and a growing and productive private sector have led to economic growth and poverty reduction, while aid and foreign development programs have not. As the past is often the best guide to the future it is expected further significant reductions in poverty will be primarily the result of economic growth driven from the bottom-up by private investment and private innovation and not from top-down redistribution approaches led by the World Bank, the IMF or other development agencies.

However, Skarbek and Leeson (2009) pointed out that while aid has not done much to eliminate poverty not all aid programs have been failures. The authors argue aid can be beneficial when specifically targeted to achieve a singular and predetermined goal, such as reducing malaria or eliminating small pox. The authors make the case top-down approaches like those used by aid and development agencies can help achieve well-defined and limited goals, much like how a centralized top-down system can help a nation in a time of all-out war where there is only a single goal, victory, which is trying to be achieved. However, the top-down centralized planning approach does not work in systems requiring the complexity and interconnectivity of approaches while simultaneously achieving multiple different, elusive and often conflicting objectives which are needed to create sustained economic growth and poverty reduction.

Therefore, it is proposed foreign aid continue; however, the focus should be on achieving specific concrete goals which can improve the lives of individuals living in poverty in very tangible and measurable ways, such as improving health and education, or creating specific infrastructure projects, which can have an indirect effect by creating the conditions needed for poverty reduction. The choice should not be between aid or trade, but each (aid or trade) should focus on what it is best at achieving. The private sector and trade are good at creating the economic conditions needed for significant poverty reduction; aid agencies can be good at improving the lives of individuals in ways that have a more indirect economic impact.

Aid agencies often acknowledge their past failures and are recently trying to associate themselves with market-based approaches. There has been a shift in thinking in development circles and now 'there is a consensus among development agencies on the need to move towards more market-based and sustainable approaches to providing support to firms' (OECD, 2006: 27). However, it is questioned whether a top-down approach from foreign aid and development organizations will be effective in supporting local firms, and the selection of specific firms or industries to support, which also implies putting other firms and industries at a disadvantage, can cause market distortions. The concept of non-profit organizations directly assisting profit-making firms would appear to have the potential to create as many problems as it would solve.

'Developing the capacity of people, organizations and society to manage their affairs better is a central and cross-cutting element of all development efforts' (OECD, 2006: 26). Is this really happening in development efforts? Or do most development efforts often lead to dependences? In many communities where poverty is widespread, the best paid employment is often with aid and development agencies and the best educated and most ambitious workers of the local community are often pulled into this type of employment. Moreover, while there is no doubt individuals working in these international aid and development organizations gain some very valuable general skills, such as in computer usage and languages, the specific skills gained might not be very transferable to the private sector.

From personal experience while working in an agency providing support for the education of refugees and their children, primarily ethnic Karens, along the Thai–Myanmar/Burmese border it was observed getting a job in an NGO was a very highly sought-after position for the best educated members of the Karen community. It was also observed much NGO and development work involved very specific administrative tasks designed to meet specific reporting requirements which were designed by bureaucrats in donor organizations such as the UN, USAID or the EU, and there was little emphasis on efficiency and productivity. It was rare to see anyone from the local Karen community in northern Thailand, a community whose members have often been discriminated against and have much lower average incomes than those in the majority population, make a successful move from the NGO sector into the private sector. While there is no doubt the families of the NGO employees enjoyed improved living standards due to these employment opportunities, it is questioned whether taking the vast majority of the best and brightest members of an oppressed minority group or other community where poverty is common out of the private sector and into learning bureaucratic tasks and systems helps in developing the skills needed to develop entrepreneurs and private-sector managers within a community. What is more, entrepreneurs and good private-sector management are needed to create economic growth and jobs, both of which are necessary to create more broad-based reductions in poverty.

Microfinance

One type of poverty reduction program, microfinance, has become very trendy since the success of Grameen Bank in Bangladesh and the winning of the Nobel Peace Prize in 2006 by the bank's founder, Muhammad Yunnas. But, despite all the hype and good intentions, the actual success of microfinance in poverty reduction has been somewhat limited (Karnani, 2010: 13). While the goal of microfinancing programs is to be self-sustaining, the majority of microfinance programs in India have remained dependent on funds from donors to cover operating costs. Prahalad (2005: 295–308) feels commercial banks, motivated by the example of microfinance organizations, might be in a better position due to economies of scale and expertise to turn microfinance programs into sustainable sources of credit for microentrepreneurs than are those programs run as non-profit entities.

Newa (2010) felt microfinancing, if adjusted for local conditions, could have a positive impact on small businesses and economic growth in sub-Saharan Africa while Tedeschi (2010) believed microcredit to be helpful in assisting small informal retail firms in Central America to expand. The most famous and imitated microfinance institution, Grameen Bank in Bangladesh, has proved under certain circumstances microfinancing can be sustainable and even profitable while helping individuals move across to the positive side of the poverty line (Yunus and Weber, 2007: 52).

While few disagree that microfinance has a role to play in poverty reduction, it does appear to have limitations which even its most vocal supporters acknowledge. Mkapa (2010: 59) pointed out that, while microfinance has its uses, without the rule of law and a fairly stable environment the poor cannot take advantage of market opportunities even at a microlevel. Microfinancing is not available to most of the world's poor and 'microfinance organizations (MFOs) have found it hard to establish viable programs where populations are dispersed and economies are stagnant,' and the extreme poor are usually excluded from microfinancing programs as often they are considered outsiders and don't fit into programs designed for the majority (Hanlon et al., 2010: 80).

It also appears the system of microfinance might fit some environmental conditions better than others. For example, while the perception of stakeholders of the effectiveness of microfinance in India is strong, the opposite is true in South Africa. The model used in South Asia is based on group cohesion and accumulated social capital, and the social networks in South Asia are quite different from those in other locations which may explain the less positive views of microfinance programs in South Africa (Lerpold and Romani, 2010).

Microfinance programs have normally focused primarily on helping women become more independent and have used group membership and group pressure to ensure repayment. This focus on helping only one gender and using group membership as a criterion for receiving loans can cause problems. Romani and Lerpold (2010) found the underlying assumptions used in microfinance programs are based on certain values including the power of individualism (individuals can control their destiny if given an opportunity), women are more responsible and caring for family than are men (gender stereotyping) and modernism (woman are being held down by the 'bad' traditional culture where woman are downtrodden and microfinance helps to break down these bad traditions). While the focus on providing loans mostly to women can empower them, this focus can also upset and change traditional social relationships in the communities which are targeted by microfinance programs.

Peer pressure and group cooperation are cornerstones of most microfinancing programs but, while these can be useful in ensuring repayment, they can also exclude minorities based on ethnicity, caste or other characteristics as well as those who don't otherwise conform to community norms (Hanlon et al., 2010: 80). For example, Chan (2010) discovered in a microfinancing program in northern Malaysia any woman married to an ethnic Thai was excluded from receiving loans as this behavior was considered to deviate from village norms.

Despite the problems, microfinancing programs appear to have a role to play in an overall approach to poverty reduction, but looking beyond all the hype this role appears to be quite limited. The main problem with microfinancing programs is they encourage small-scale entrepreneurship in the informal economy. The informal economy is notoriously inefficient and the prospect these small-scale businesses started by those in poverty of ever growing into businesses that are innovative and employ a significant number of non-family members and drive real economic growth is somewhat unlikely. What the informal economy and microfinance can do is provide a safety net in areas where quality paid employment is not available so individuals can support themselves. But microfinance and the small-scale informal entrepreneurship it encourages are not substitutes for a dynamic and innovative private sector in the formal economy which provides quality employment opportunities and greater economic growth.

In many rural poor communities in LDCs there is already an over-abundance of microentrepreneurs who add little value and compete with each other for the limited number of purchases possible within the community. Many individuals have turned to microentrepreneurship due to lack of options for paid employment. Unless microfinance creates new businesses that sell or are connected to markets outside the local community, microfinance will normally increase the current over-abundance of supply of sellers within the community without raising demand. However, new paid employment opportunities in firms connected to the wider economy outside the village or community not only help the workers who gain employment, but also increases the demand for existing entrepreneurs operating within the community.

'It is important to bear in mind that it is perceptions as much as reality that is relevant to outcomes' (Steward, 2005: 112) and the perception of success may be what is mainly driving the expansion of microfinance programs as opposed to any measurable results.

Import substitution

One government policy that has often been tried to protect small local businesses in LDCs from being overwhelmed by large foreign firms is the use of the concept of import substitution. The idea of import substitution is to initially close a country from imports which will allow local firms in new 'infant industries' room to grow and then eventually, as the local firms grow strong enough in the protective environment, markets would be opened to competition. After time to grow and develop, it has been claimed the local firms would be mature enough to compete on an equal footing with foreign competition. However, these programs have rarely resulted in strong home-grown industries and the evidence would seem to indicate these programs have done more to retard economic growth and poverty reduction than to improve the situation.

Some of the 'Asian tigers' in the post World War II period did protect their domestic markets while growing rapidly and it is likely in the very early stages in the industrialization process the import substitution policies allowed firms in these countries to grow to some extent. However, it quickly became evident to the leaders of these countries that import substitution was not leading to quick growth, and therefore they switched to export-oriented policies. Although export-oriented strategies worked well for the initial newly industrialized countries (NIEs) of Asia, they have been less successful for those developing later as the world cannot be filled with nations only exporting while no one is importing (Owen, 1992: 495). Inward-looking import substitution strategies generally lead to overall inefficiencies in an economy and higher transaction costs which lead to slower growth than does the use of more outward-looking strategies (Sachs and Yang, 1999).

The track record of import substitution programs has not been very impressive. There have been many studies showing in the long run outward-oriented development strategies have consistently produced higher growth rates than have import substitution programs (OECD, 2011: 21).

Yet in the years following World War II, these programs were very popular in many developing countries, many newly independent and eager to shed off ties and ideas associated with the colonial system. Many leaders of developing countries in the 1950s and 1960s felt the presence of large multinational firms infringed on the nations' sovereignty and it was felt the leaders of large multinational enterprises would be as exploitative as were previous colonial rulers.

The original GATT (forerunner of the WTO) agreements allowed LDCs to maintain high trade barriers, which seemed to have resulted in most of the international trade in the first few decades after World War II to be between different developed countries with few LDCs being connected to the global trading system to any significant extent. These trade patterns seemed to have resulted in fast growth in the developed countries during this time while the economies of LDCs stagnated and poverty was not reduced. The economies of LDCs did start to see economic growth and poverty reduction gain speed as the shift away from important substitution to more open policies became more common (Williamson, 2005; Srinivasan, 2009: 94–5).

Important substitution has been tried in many places in the world. The Philippines was one of the first to attempt to use import substitution in the 1950s and became the 'slowest-growing capitalist state in the region' (Owen, 1992: 476). Important substitution was common in Latin America in the 1960s and 1970s, and the economies of the region did not have anywhere near the success of the more open Asian economies, although the opening up of the economies of Latin America in the 1990s did not bring immediate improvements to Latin American economies either (Rodrik, 2005: 203; Stiglitz, 2005: 30). Many African countries have also used import substitution strategies with poor results. For example, in Ghana the period when import substitution polices were used was a time of low economic growth rates, but the growth rates have improved greatly after more open policies have been implemented (Aryeetey and McKay, 2007). Important substitution was also tried in South Asia, including India, and as Srinivasan (2009: 63) pointed out this policy was especially hard on individuals in the rural areas where most of those in poverty live as the rural poor did not have access to jobs in the protected industries but had to pay higher prices for goods due to the closed markets and lack of purchasing options. Inglehart and Welzel (2009) claimed important substitution strategies have generally failed to produce the desired results and that countries the least involved in global trade, such as Cuba, North Korea and Myanmar/Burma, have also had the least successful economies.

Beattie (2009: 28–35) made the case that, while the United States had high tariffs during its initial industrial development, the size of its overall economy led to domestic competition which forced firms to develop or die; yet when a import substitution program was implemented in Argentina, a smaller economy, competition slowed, the economy stagnated and no world-class industrial producers emerged. After implementing an import substitution strategy Argentina went from being considered one of the world's richer countries to a less developed one. While there are a few cases of growth being correlated with important substitution strategies, it would appear there were special circumstances in these incidents that allowed growth to happen despite the policies – not because of them.

Important substitution policies limit competition which reduces the incentives of firms to improve their products and prices. These types of policies also raise prices for all consumers, which is a hardship for those who are not employed in the protected industries, which include most of the poor. In addition, import substitution raises the costs of imported supplies making it more difficult for local businesses to become competitive internationally. Moreover, it should not be forgotten important substitution policies restrict access to new technologies and knowledge, and this takes away opportunities for these new technologies and knowledge to create positive spillover effects into other firms and industries.

'There is simply no evidence whatsoever that trade protectionism or the absence of multinational companies does a whit to end extreme poverty' (Sachs, 2005: 357).

Development in different environments: one size does not fit all

'It is widely recognized today that a 'one-size-fits-all' approach is not conducive to development and will eventually fail to deliver results. While the ingredients are common across different growth experiences, the recipes need to be very country specific' (OECD, 2011: 57).

Success in creating economic growth and poverty reduction has been found in a variety of different contexts. Success can even be found in countries where initial environmental conditions were not very conducive to growth and where few experts predicted success (Cord, 2007). Economic development and poverty reduction have taken place in both large and small countries, indicating size of the economy alone does not drive or impede success (Srinivasan, 2009: 80). While the geography of a country has an impact on development, being a land-locked country or not having natural resources are not impossible barriers to overcome. In fact, often having natural resources, such as oil or diamonds, has been associated with slower economic growth and less reduction in poverty (Beattie, 2009: 110: Ying et. al., 2010).

There has also been economic development under a variety of political systems and histories. While there is a very strong correlation between being a democracy and having a high standard of living, there is a question about which comes first, 'Is democracy a precondition for economic growth and social development or will democracy only be viable and sustainable when a certain level of development has been attained?' (Van Beuningen, 2007: 50). There does not seem to be a consensus on the answer. Acemoglu and Robinson (2010: 144) have pointed out that some 'dictatorships' in Asia, such as was previously found in South Korea and Taiwan, presided over economic growth and poverty reduction yet there are no concrete explanations why dictatorships have never led to economic development in Latin America or sub-Saharan Africa.

Inglehart and Welzel (2009) made the point development appears to lead to democracy, and in recent decades all middle and high-income countries that have made the transition to democracy from authoritarian rule have been able to sustain a democracy, while low-income countries have often slid back into authoritarian rule after attempts at democracy.

While economic development in sub-Saharan Africa has generally been slower than in other regions, there have been some success stories as well. Since the mid-1980s, Ghana has seen moderate economic growth and some reductions in poverty. There were a number of government policies implemented prior to and associated with this growth including the elimination of import substitution policies and increasing the levels of investments in education and infrastructure. While the country has seen increases in development aid there has not been significant increases in foreign investment into the private sector. Much of the growth has been driven by falling birth rates, increases in informal employment and spending in the public sector. Although Ghana has been not able to attract much private investment and the moderate growth has led to increases in inequalities, there have also been some reductions in poverty, although the poorest of the poor have not generally been helped. Increases in public-sector spending have been mostly fueled by increases in foreign development aid (Aryeetey and McKay, 2007).

Uganda has seen average economic growth of around 2% per capita or 4.5% overall since the mid-1980s which has resulted in some poverty reduction. Similar to what was seen in Ghana, growth came after the government made significant policy changes which liberalized the economy, but unlike in Ghana during the period of moderate growth the private sector grew substantially and the percentage of people employed in the public sector declined. During the 1990s the country saw a fairly stable political environment, and it has been reported poverty reduction was almost entirely driven by economic growth and not by redistribution policies (Okidi et al., 2007).

In 1994 Rwanda experienced a horrific genocide which alongside the terrific cost in human lives also devastated the economy. In a single year GDP was halved and 80% of the population was thrust into poverty, and the country's infrastructure and political systems were nearly destroyed. While the genocide is well known around the world, less well known is the country's recovery. While it took some time, after the country's political environment was stabilized many progressive policy initiatives were undertaken. The central bank was made independent, state-owned enterprises were privatized and price controls were lifted. Rwanda was the recipient of significant international aid, but instead of using the money for short-term projects and redistribution efforts it was mainly used for long-term investments in developing education and building infrastructure. Economic growth was slow to non-existent before the genocide, but from 1995 to 2003 the country saw annual growth of around 5%, and then from 2003 to 2007 the prior investments began to bear fruit and the growth rate averaged nearly 15% for each of these 4 years (Kigabo, 2010) Rwanda is still a poor country where the level of political freedom is less than ideal according to the political opposition, but considering what the country went through in 1994 the recent economic development of the country has to be considered a success.

Another African country that has seen significant economic growth and poverty reduction after liberalizing its economy, moving away from import substitution policies and finding political stability has been Tanzania. Mkapa (2010), the former President of Tanzania, believed the move towards socialist policies in the early years of independence was driven by the fact capitalism was associated with the former colonial rulers and these political moves helped Tanzania and other African countries move towards greater political independence and helped create a feeling of national unity where often there was not one previously. However, during Mkapa's time in office many economic reforms were made and the country experienced respectable economic growth and poverty reduction.

In Asia, Indonesia is another country which has seen market reforms leading to both increases in economic growth and decreases in poverty. A policy seen in Indonesia has been to heavily invest in transportation infrastructure which has had the dual effect of providing immediate employment, often including many non-skilled laborers, and reducing transportation costs which helped the rural poor who are primarily in the agricultural sector of the economy increase their productivity and profits by providing opportunities to connect to new markets. It was felt the market reforms would not have been as effective if the infrastructure was not in place to allow people to take advantage of the new opportunities (Timmer, 2007).

Vietnam has seen both rapid growth and rapid poverty reduction over the past few decades, but unlike many other countries it was able to achieve these objectives without a radical widening of the income gap. In the early 1990s the poverty rate was at 58.1% and it had effectively been cut in half to 28.9% a decade later. Vietnam, retaining a non-elected Communist government, began its market reforms in 1986 (*Doi Moi*) which included shifting away from a primarily centrally planned economy to a market-based economy. Moreover, land reforms and the boom in the worldwide market for coffee, a major Vietnamese export in a sector in which many rural poor worked, contributed to the effectiveness of the economic growth in reducing poverty which like in most countries is concentrated in rural areas (Klump, 2007).

It is generally thought economic growth requires capital accumulation and the economies of scale and efficiencies which come as firms grow. However, in Wenzhou, located in the southeast section of Zhejiang Province in China, economic growth through the efforts of very small firms has occurred. During the early days of Communist rule, Wenzhou was mostly passed over by the central planners for large-scale industrial projects, but as the shift towards a market-based economy started in the 1970s, Wenzhou was one of the first areas which experienced economic liberalization. The central government neither assisted the region nor did it interfere much in the affairs of the individual entrepreneurs in the area. A large number of very small businesses sprang up without any government or foreign investment. Most of these businesses were in mature industries which made low-end products, and since the technology was neither exclusive nor cutting edge firms were able to easily borrow ideas and technologies from abroad. While innovation is often preached as the secret to success in business, businesses in Wenzhou showed borrowing and adapting can also be an appropriate strategy, especially in LDCs where the conditions to create cutting edge innovation do not exist. While Wenzhou has continued to be a region of entrepreneurs and small-scale businesses, some of the firms have grown quite large and are now employing significant numbers of people and are moving up the value chain. In the 1970s the average income in Wenzhou was about half the national average, today average incomes in Wenzhou are about double the national average (Strauss et al., 2010).

While South Asia remains one of the poorest regions in the world, there have also been some recent successes in this part of the world. Poverty reduction in India has been spotty, with some states seeing significant drops in levels of poverty and other states having less success. The states which have more open economies have generally reduced poverty more than have those states with more regulations and legal protections for workers. Moreover, in areas where property rights are better protected and where women make up a higher proportion of the labor force, poverty reduction has been greater (Besley et al., 2007).

Although poverty is still a major issue in Bangladesh, some progress in poverty reduction has been seen. Like in most countries, poverty reduction in Bangladesh has been strongly correlated with economic growth. Liberalization and deregulation 'have influenced both the rate of overall growth and the pro-poor pattern of growth in Bangladesh' and the changes in market conditions have especially been beneficial to the rural poor (Sen et al., 2007: 97). Along with poverty reduction, since independence in 1971, Bangladesh has seen average life expectancy go from 44 years to 62 years, and the infant mortality rate has also seen dramatic reductions (Sachs, 2005: 10).

We also see from a historical viewpoint the developed economies of today reached the developed state in quite different ways. Wright (2003: 338) believed the national development of the USA was likely 'in many ways special and quite possibly non-reproducible' and was as much a result of the limitations placed on the role of the state, what the state couldn't do as much as what the state actually did do. Easterly (2007: 35) pointed out the USA was a relatively poor country upon independence, yet it was able to develop without any foreign aid and without any advice from development experts. O'Brien (2003) showed how the British were able to grow their economy from within while their businesses had to shoulder huge tax burdens to pay for its massive military forces and while some government expenditures went to the development of infrastructure, very little was spent on education. Norway, and to a lesser extent Sweden, had more outward-looking practices and used extensive FDI from abroad and imported technologies to help build their industries and economies (Sejersted, 2003).

Economic development and poverty reduction have taken place under a variety of different conditions and government policies, yet across geographical and time boundaries we normally see the private sector playing an important role wherever substantial economic development and poverty reduction have occurred.

Macroeconomics and government policy

While not the only ingredient in an effective poverty reduction program, government policies do matter. 'Countries do not get rich by accident. They make choices that determine the path their economies take' (Beattie, 2009: 6). While some of the various different paths to economic development were explored in the previous section, there are also some common themes seen in successful poverty reduction cases. One common theme is liberalizing of economies which encourages competition and allows the private sector to take the lead role in economic development.

'In general, trade liberalization is an ally in the fight against poverty; it tends to increase average incomes, providing more resources with which to tackle poverty' (McCulloch et al., 2001: xxiii).

Economic growth is the most powerful means of reducing poverty, moreover, although debated, a large body of empirical literature provides ample evidence that trade liberalization and trade openness have a positive impact on economic growth. No country has successfully developed its economy by turning its back on international trade and long-term foreign direct investment.

(OECD, 2011: 14)

A successful pro-poor growth strategy would thus need to have, at its core, measures for sustained and rapid economic growth. These measures include macroeconomic stability, well-defined property rights, trade openness, a good investment climate, an attractive incentive framework, well functioning factor markets, and broad access to infrastructure and education.

(Cord, 2007: 19)

Simply privatizing as much of the nation's activities as possible and expecting the private sector to work miracles has not always resulted in great success, as any nation's economy is complex and requires government-sponsored or supported institutions as well as actions by the private sector (North, 2005). However while there is near consensus on the importance of the private sector in economic growth, the specific responsibilities and the extent of the role of the government is often debated, although the notion the government does have a role has been widely acknowledged.

Stiglitz (2005) advocated the idea governments should attempt to become a complement to the market and work to correct market failures and act as a catalyst to get markets moving when the economy slows down. Yet at the same time it was felt governments should limit their roles to indirect actions and not directly run or interfere with the market. Pinaud (2007) proposed the use of public–private dialogue where members of the private sector regularly interact with public officials over the creation of government policy, although this policy would seem likely to result in increases in crony capitalism and opportunities for corruption. Laird (2007: 55) has found, due to shifts in thinking about development, many government development programs now work to provide financing and training for specific firms in LDCs. However, it is felt these types of programs can interfere with natural competition. Moreover, these programs require governments to choose which industries and firms to promote, but as noticed by Easterly (2009: 81) 'private entrepreneurs are far better than the government at picking industries that can be winners in the global economy.' Fukasaku (2007) believed giving direct assistance to firms without addressing the overall business environment was not very productive and therefore countries should simultaneously give direct assistance to its SMEs, such as management training, and indirect assistance by creating a better overall economic and legal environment in which the SMEs operate. Pietrobelli (2007) agreed the private sector is needed for economic growth and poverty reduction and advocated governments and development programs get more directly involved in helping firms in developing economies by assisting in establishing linkages with international and multinational firms and providing financial resources and investments while also helping firms gain access to export markets.

However, the experience of direct government assistance to private firms has led to mixed results. It has been suggested the best policy is to 'follow the market' and provide assistance to firms which have demonstrated the ability to be competitive in markets and have already been identified by the private sector as winners. Governments should not try to 'lead the market' and pick which industries or firms to promote (OECD, 2010).

Despite some debate over how best to implement policies, and with the acknowledgement policies need to be tailored to fit each individual situation, there remains quite a lot of consensus over the general principles governments should follow to create economic growth and poverty reduction. Cord (2007: 13) found the following five general guidelines help to relive poverty in rural areas: (1) improve market access and the lowering of transactions costs, (2) strengthen property rights, (3) create incentives which benefit the poor, (4) improve access to technology and (5) help small-scale entrepreneurs and agricultural workers cope with risk.

Rodrik (2005) has found common principles being followed in successful economies include (1) providing effective property rights protection, (2) macroeconomic stability, (3) effective regulations of the financial sector, (4) providing a supportive environment for the private sector and (5) integrating with the global economy. However, the author also explained it is easier to come up with a list of the desirable end results than make specific recommendations on how to make these results become a reality.

Yet despite all the knowledge and experience the world has gained in economic development, there still continues to be individuals and governments making decisions that are inconsistent with the empirical evidence and theories about how to grow an economy. For example, ignoring property rights, the Zimbabwe government embarked on a massive program of expropriation and redistribution of agricultural land that has led to the collapse of the economy which has fallen by around 50% since the program started. This economic downturn has led to both increases in poverty and the exodus of many individuals in search of work and a better life (Acemoglu and Robinson, 2010: 145). Between 1960 and 2000, the Nigerian economy grew at a dismal rate of 0.43% annually resulting in increases in both absolute numbers and percentage of people living in poverty despite having huge oil reserves. During this time the succession of Nigerian governments heavily engaged in redistribution policies which were designed to shore up political support, although political instability, military coups and constant corruption showed the distribution policies generally had no better political results than they had economic results. However, after moving towards increased levels of economic liberalization the country has experienced much better economic growth and some reductions in poverty since 2000 (Iyoha, 2010).

In addition, inconsistent policy decisions are not solely seen in LDCs. In developed economies, protectionism, especially in agriculture, is widespread and has been felt to have had a negative effect on economic growth and poverty reduction both at home and in LDCs. These policies create barriers for firms in LDCs in exporting agricultural products as well as raising costs for the developed country consumers. While at the same time these same countries, whose protectionist policies are commonly believed to slow economic growth, increase poverty in LDCs and raise prices for domestic consumers, are also sending foreign aid paid for by taxpayers to the same LDCs to stimulate economic growth and poverty reduction (Srinivasan, 2009: 74). The only possible explanations for these types of lose–lose decisions are politics and the self-interest of those making the decisions.

It would appear politics and special interests are often obstacles to implementing policies that foster economic growth and poverty reduction. Free markets and trade help entire societies in an abstract and indirect manner, while redistribution policies and protectionism help specific individuals in very visible and direct ways. The market rewards individuals for productivity, which is needed to create economic growth and poverty reduction, redistribution strategies reward people for non-productive behaviors, which can help individuals but does not create overall economic growth, which is needed for large-scale reductions in poverty. Trade liberalization may indirectly help the majority of people to some limited degree over a relatively long period of time. However, removal of protectionism can cause quick and very direct negative effects for the minority of individuals who benefit from the protectionism. What is more, not surprisingly those individuals directly benefiting from protectionism will fight passionately to keep the specific protectionist measures in place while the majority who only benefit indirectly from a removal of any specific protectionism measure will often take only a nominal interest.

For example, in most developed economies including the USA, Western Europe and Japan, agricultural protectionism is widespread. These protectionist measures raise food prices for consumers, but expenditures on food as a percentage of total income for the majority in these countries is relatively small. Therefore, few consumers will push politicians or governments to liberalize the markets to lower prices. On the other hand, the relatively small number of farmers and agricultural workers who benefit from protectionism will put all the pressure they can muster on politicians and the government to retain it. Protectionism almost always benefits the few at the expense of the many, yet the intense attention of the interested minority often wins out politically over the apathy of the majority.

Good economic policies take time to pay off, and there are short-term costs and trade-offs a country has to make to establish conditions in which growth will occur (Ying et al., 2010). For example, many Nigerians were initially very disappointed when democracy and market reforms did not lead to immediate results, but slowly these reforms began to pay off and considerable growth and poverty reduction began to take hold after time was given to these policies (Iyoha, 2010). However, the recent riots over the removal of gasoline subsidies in Nigeria show decisions that make economic sense do not always make political sense. Moreover, one only has to pay attention to any American presidential campaign to realize politicians pandering to populist sentiments and willing to sacrifice one's country's economic growth for one's personal political ambition is not restricted to LDCs. 'One should not try to understand or manipulate economic institutions without thinking about the political forces that created or sustain them' (Acemoglu and Robinson, 2010: 145).

Economics, like most of the social sciences, is better at explaining after the fact than it is in predicting the future. Many of the economies that grew rapidly from 1960 to 1980 and were expected to continue to grow, such as Ecuador and Paraguay, failed to live up to expectations while other countries, such as Vietnam and China, which had little expectation of growth from the experts, have taken off. 'Clearly, past growth does not necessarily translate to future growth, although resources and institutions inherited from past growth do appear to feed into an economy's endowment in the next cycle' (Ying et al., 2010: 105). It should also be acknowledged countries do not make economic decisions in a vacuum, and external factors not under the control of the leadership of any specific country can drive policy decisions and also affect the success or failure of economic policy decisions (Cardoso and Graeff, 2010: 195–6).

It is possible too much attention is paid to macroeconomic policies and decisions of governments and not enough attention is paid to microeconomic policies and decisions of firms in the private sector. It is fairly easy to measure and analyze the relatively few macroeconomic decisions made by governments but it is practically impossible to measure and analyze the daily microeconomic decisions made by a multiple of organizations throughout the various industries in the private sector (Wennekers and Thurik, 1999: 27; Foster, 2011: 13). But, as has been well established, it is the private sector which actually drives growth – not governments and their macroeconomic policies. Van Praag and Versloot (2007) concluded entrepreneurs were important in creating employment, productivity growth and commercializing innovations; the authors also found new ideas are created and knowledge spillover occur to other parts of the economy due to the actions of individual entrepreneurial firms. Business cycles have long been thought to go through their growth stages as a result of technological or business process innovation created by the private sector. Moreover, there is debate on whether private-sector innovation leads changes in macroeconomic policies and the creation of new legal institutions or follows them (Kingston, 2006).

It is likely not all economic activities by firms have the same impact, a study conducted by Tang and Koveos (2004) suggested the creation of new enterprises is more highly correlated with economic growth than new innovations coming from existing firms. Wennekers and Thurik (1999: 51) believed, 'Entrepreneurship matters. In modern open economies it is more important for economic growth than it has ever been.' Foster (2011) pointed out the fact economic growth is the aggregate of the growth of all industries in an economy, yet different industries will simultaneously be at different stages of the growth cycle and growth in one industry does little overall good if it takes away growth from other industries.

'Growth remains the essential measure of national economic success ... and governments continue to assume responsibility for managing macroeconomic tools to achieve conditions favorable to growth' (O'Bryan, 2009: 180). Yet should all focus of poverty reduction be on governments and their policies at the national level while individual business leaders and companies are overlooked in their collective role in economic growth?

An interesting question is: Did the USA become the world's largest economy primarily due to the macroeconomic decisions made by politicians or was the growth driven mostly by business decisions made by Thomas Edison, George Westinghouse, Henry Ford, Bill Gates, Steve Jobs and millions of other less well-known entrepreneurs, investors, managers and private-sector workers on a daily basis? Can good business decisions made in the private sector have as much of an impact on economic growth and poverty reduction as the decisions made by politicians and government officials?

Figure 2.1 **Higher education in a refugee camp along the Thai/ Burmese border**

While it is acknowledged macroeconomic policies have a major role to play in poverty reduction, most individuals have limited abilities to change these policies. However, this does not imply private citizens cannot have a direct impact on poverty reduction. Private citizens in developed economies can always consider purchasing products and services produced in the LDCs and pressure their government to eliminate barriers to trading with LDCs, specifically eliminating agricultural subsidies. Individual citizens in LDCs can also contribute though their individual efforts to improve productivity and government performance.

However, there may be a special role for private-sector businesses, both international and local, in poverty reduction. Businesses drive economic growth and innovation as well as produce goods and services which can be voluntarily chosen to be purchased in order to improve the lives of consumers. It is believed creating business strategies and engaging in productive business operations in LDCs, sometimes with the need to overcome obstacles imposed by less-than-perfect macroeconomic policies created by governments, can have a significantly positive impact on the lives of those living in poverty.

3

Environmental conditions in Asian developing economies

Abstract: Business practices need to be adapted to the internal and external environments a firm operates in, and firms operating in LDCs in Asia operate in different environments than do firms in more developed economies. Firms operating in the LDCs of Asia need to take into account the economic, political, legal, cultural and technological environments they will encounter. Some of the unique features found in firms in LDCs in Asia include smaller size of companies, few firms with a separation between ownership and management, lack of a highly educated and experienced workforce and more of an entrepreneurial orientation. While many business principles are universal, specific practices will often have to be adjusted for local conditions.

Key words: less developed economies, Hofstede, economics, ethics, democracy, culture.

Environmental conditions

It is fairly easy to advocate additional private investment into areas where poverty is widespread, yet it is quite difficult for individual firms to create businesses which are sustainable, profitable and provide quality employment opportunities in the areas of the world most affected by poverty. Before diving in head first and begin developing strategies and writing up business plans, a firm should first review the environmental conditions it will be operating under.

Businesses are open systems and business practices need to be aligned with both the internal and external environments the firms operate in. Most business academic research has been conducted through the study of business practices of firms operating in North America and Europe, where firms operate within specific types of environments. On the other hand, firms operating in LDCs face substantially different challenges as they operate under distinctly different environmental conditions (Peng et al., 2008: 928). Many of the theories used in studying business practices are based on the underlying assumptions of firms working within the specific types of political-legal, social-cultural and economic environments found in developed economies. Before developing business strategies and practices for use by firms operating in areas where poverty is widespread, it might be a good idea to examine some of the underlying assumptions individuals have of running a business and how some of these underlying assumptions might or might not apply when operating a business in the LDCs of Asia.

When looking at firms from the LDCs of Asia, the temptation should be avoided to assume the business practices used are automatically inferior, due to the less developed economic environment, to those used by firms operating in more developed economies. Moreover, it should not be assumed all firms in the LDCs would be improved by adapting all the commonly used business practices found in more economically developed regions. Firms around the world must compete, and competition will normally drive out inferior practices. Business practices always need to be aligned with the specific environmental conditions under which they are practiced. Environmental conditions in Asia and especially in the LDCs can be distinctly different from environmental conditions found in more economically advanced economies. Therefore, it would be natural to see unique practices evolving in these specific environments (Hipsher et al., 2007). On the other hand, there is an abundance of business knowledge which can be transferred from one geographical region to another, and the art of international business includes a feel for knowing what practices from the home country can be duplicated in a new location, which practices will need to be adjusted for the new conditions, which practices will need to be abandoned and which practices should be copied from local examples.

Political and legal environments

The political environments found in the more developed countries, where most academic business theories originate, can be significantly different from what is found within LDCs in Asia. Amongst the political systems found in the LDCs of Asia, there are a wide range of systems: from vibrant democracies with fiercely contested elections in countries such as found in India and the Philippines, to single party control found in China and

Vietnam to a variety of systems that fit in between these extremes. While the actual definition of democracy and its impact on economic development are often debated (Van Beuningen, 2007; Werlin, 2009; Mizuno, 2010), the political environments found in many LDCs in Asia are distinctly different from what is normally found in the more mature democracies of the more developed economies. These differences often result in governments taking a more direct role in the business environments through state ownership of business and controlling access to markets while, on the other hand, there is often less indirect involvement with fewer rules and regulations aimed at controlling the activities of private enterprises, at least fewer that are actually enforced (Hipsher et al., 2007). An example of less government indirect intervention can be found in the fact that, in general, Asian countries have fewer state-controlled or government-mandated social protection systems which private firms engage in and usually have much less developed unemployment insurance schemes than is the norm in Western societies (Scholz et al., 2010). This lack of government-directed intervention in determining working conditions often allows Asian firms considerable flexibility in making employment and other business decisions.

Legal environments in the LDCs in Asia are also often different from what one would find in more developed economies. Business practices in Asia and especially in the LDCs often rely less on formal regulations and instead rely more on arbitrary decision making by leaders and personal relationships. Organizations in Western cultures usually rely heavily on the use of contracts, written rules, regulations and formal agreements, and this formality applies to interactions with both internal and external stakeholders. However, in most of Asia, as well as in most developing economies, there is much more reliance on informal agreements and personal relationships in developing business agreements (Hitt et al., 2002; Hallen and Johanson, 2004; Kim et al., 2004; Wu and Choi, 2004; Nguyen et al., 2005; Peng and Zhou, 2005; Young, 2005). While this preference for informal relationships as opposed to formal contacts can be explained by Hall's (1976) identification of most of Asia and most developing economies as having a preference for using high-context communication styles. The preference for the use of personal relationships can also be attributed to the fact the countries of the region normally have legal systems which are less reliable in enforcing contracts than is the norm found in Western societies. Therefore, in LDCs in Asia there is a need to enforce one's own contracts and one of the most efficient ways to do this is through trust and personal relationships as opposed to relying strictly on formal written contracts, as it is unlikely one could be sure of having a formal contract enforced through the legal system.

It should not be automatically assumed legal systems in which parties are expected to enforce their own contracts are inferior to most of the formal legal systems found in the West. Alongside some obvious disadvantages, the use of relationship contracting and informal contacts has the advantage of reducing the tax burden for everyone. Moreover, instead of having to spend so much time and energy negotiating to create an acceptable agreement that tries to foresee all possible contingencies before any actual exchanges take place, relationship contracting can often allow the negotiations to continue on after business relationships have begun and therefore both parties have better information with which to negotiate, which can often result in more equitable distribution of profits and more sustainable business partnerships (Van de Ven, 2004; Wu and Choi, 2004; Peng et al., 2005; Young, 2005).

Economic environment

A nation's level of economic development has important implications for businesses operating within any country. Economic factors directly impact the level of purchasing power of consumers, availability of financing, growth potential for firms and labor costs. Economic factors also have many indirect effects; for example, there is generally a correlation between the level of economic development and the effectiveness and development of a nation's institutions, such as its legal system (Peng et al., 2008; Shinkle and Kriauciunas, 2010). Hipsher (2007) made the case the level of economic development will have a major impact on a firm's strategic decisions. In countries with lower levels of economic development one sees much less use of differentiation strategies in firms selling consumer products, especially those aimed at the top of the market. Instead, one sees firms using fewer varieties of strategies and most companies work to supply basic needs with prices and costs being major considerations in most firms' overall strategies. Wealth gives consumers a greater ability to make choices in purchases, allowing firms to devise multiple ways to encourage customers to spend their money, while the opposite is true with poverty. Poverty limits customers' ability to spend and firms have fewer opportunities to sell products and services that are not considered necessities in less economically developed regions.

The news media often focuses on GDP growth rates and overall size of an economy; however, this can be quite misleading. For example, in recent years China's economic success and moving to become the world's second biggest economy have been making headlines. However, this hides the fact China, despite its admirable recent success, remains on average quite a poor country with per capita GDP statistics, with or without using the Purchasing Power Index, showing the average Chinese life-style and purchasing power is much closer to those found in sub-Saharan Africa than to those found in developed economies (World Bank, 2010). In most LDCs within Asia the average ability to purchase is far lower than the average in most Western and developed countries.

While the forecasts for growth in LDCs in Asia are generally positive, the starting level remains low and future growth in the LDCs of Asia is not expected to come at the expense of growth in the more developed economies, instead it is expected economic growth in developing Asia can have a positive effect on the USA and Europe's economic recovery (OECD, 2010). Most companies originating within the LDCs within Asia operate at different levels of the global value chain than do most companies from developed economies and therefore can be thought of as being complementary to companies and economies of developed nations and not necessarily competitors.

Despite all the positive economic news and forecasts coming out of Asia there are concerns over increasing levels of inequality (Ali, 2008). Persisting inequality can limit future growth potential. Growing inequalities limit the amount of poverty reduction gained from economic growth and can cause political instabilities. China, despite its amazing record of growth and poverty reduction, has seen increasing inequalities in incomes between the rural and urban areas as well as between the coastal and inland areas resulting in failure to maximize the amount of poverty reduction it gets from its economic growth (Liang, 2008; Lin and Liu, 2008; Tsui, 2008).

The level of economic development a nation has obtained can have significant effects on the business practices a company employs. For example, in comparing business practices in Hong Kong v. mainland China, Luk et al. (2008) found the application of social capital differs considerably even though both locations are Chinese in culture. In the more economically advanced region of Hong Kong, firms concentrated more on using connections and social capital to improve productivity while, on the mainland, connections and social capital were used more often to gain access to markets and other political favors. Along the same lines, Danis et al. (2010) reported that in transition economies, such as found in many developing countries in Asia, managers working in the earlier stages of the transition period spend a large percentage of their time building and maintaining personal networks, but as the transitions to more market-based economies continue there has been a shift of managerial time and energy away from networking in order to gain political connections to more activities that focus on improving market competitiveness.

If one travels to Shanghai, Bangkok or Ho Chi Minh City and stays in a downtown hotel, it is easy to assume from the immediate surrounding environments the levels of incomes in the LDCs of the region are much higher than they actually are. However, business practitioners should keep in mind the relatively lower levels of economic development in the LDCs of Asia will have a major impact on how business is conducted within these countries and locations.

Social-cultural environment

In managing a business, 'cultural does count' (Moran et al., 2007: 3). Culture is a complex phenomenon which has multiple definitions, although most definitions find culture to be shared values of a specific group, which are man-made, passed on by communication, associated with increasing the probability of group survival and increasing the satisfaction of members of the society (Kelly et al., 2006: 68). Culture has an impact on nearly every aspect of one's life, yet most of the time its impact goes unnoticed as cultural influences are normally thought of as normal aspects of human life and interpersonal interactions. It is only when exposed to different cultural environments that the influence of one's own culture become apparent. While not the only culture individuals are influenced by, national culture does appear to have an important impact and will be the primary culture examined.

However, one needs to be careful when studying cultures and cultural differences as these differences are averages and no individual will exactly meet the criteria of being a typical member of their society. While each person is a product of multiple cultures and subcultures to which they have been exposed, each person is also an individual with their own unique individual characteristics. Therefore, while being aware of cultural differences is important, this awareness can lead to thinking in stereotypes and ignoring the individual differences found within people within each society.

There is considerable debate on whether a global convergence of cultures is happening or not. Friedman (2005) famously made the claim the world is flat while Kelly et al. (2006) made the case culture is not static and the interaction between cultures results in 'crossvergence' of cultures and globalization is decreasing the distance between different national cultures.

There is a considerable amount of evidence which shows cultures are not static and are constantly changing, but this does not imply all differences are disappearing. Smith-Speck and Roy (2008: 1213–14) in their study found, 'The results thus indicate that we are not moving towards a single global culture, but rather towards multiple cultures' and 'in many ways this research further demonstrates that, while global economies continue to converge, cultures continue to diverge.' Cultural differences are often reflected in the selection of specific business practices. For example, Metcalf et al. (2007) found distinct differences in the negotiation styles of individuals from different cultures. In addition, bridging cultural divides can create challenges while trying to close a business deal. To illustrate, Dikova et al. (2010) reported increased cultural differences between partners increased the likelihood announced international mergers and acquisitions would not reach completion.

Most people have a strong sense of right and wrong. However, often it is not realized one's sense of right and wrong is strongly influenced by one's own cultural background. Forsyth et al. (2008) used a four-category framework in which to compare ethnical approaches in different cultural contexts. The first category identified was exceptionism. Exceptionism cultures place a high value on consistently following universal moral rules, but with a realization exceptions are allowed on occasion. Countries that fall into the exceptionism quadrant include New Zealand, the USA, Canada, Belgium, Austria, Australia and Russia.

The second category found by Forsyth et al. (2008) was absolutism. Absolutism cultures are those where universal moral rules are expected to be consistently followed with extremely few exceptions. Absolutism cultures include South Africa, Saudi Arabia, Poland, Egypt, Korea and the UAE.

The third category found by Forsyth et al. (2008) was subjectivism. Subjectivism cultures place a high value on individual values and perception guiding decision making as opposed to the use of universal moral values. Subjectivism cultures include Thailand, Hong Kong, Japan, China and Ireland.

The fourth category identified by Forsyth et al. (2008) was situationism. Situationism cultures prize moral decisions which secure the best possible outcome even if the decision violates more traditional rules and ethics. Situationism cultures include Lebanon, Malaysia, India, the UK, Brunei, the Ukraine, Turkey and Spain.

Thus, foreign managers operating in the LDCs of Asia may find themselves operating in cultural environments where their own values might not always be perfectly aligned with the local environment and their ideas about deciding what is right or wrong might be challenged.

Hofstede's dimensions of culture

When studying cultural environments, one of the most commonly used tools is the dimensions of culture framework created by Geert Hofstede. While there has been criticism of the methodology used in the research to create the dimensions and Hofstede himself acknowledges the limitations of these dimensions to explain cultural differences, the framework has stood the test of time and continues to be the foundation for much cross-cultural education and research.

When starting a new class on culture, Hofstede (2002: 1359) used to write on the board, 'CULTURE DOESN'T EXIST.' He went on to explain, 'In the same way values don't exist, dimensions don't exist. They are constructs, which have to prove their usefulness by their ability to explain and predict behavior.' Hofstede has consistently pointed out the limitations of the use of these dimensions of culture, but this framework has proven its usefulness in explaining and predicting human behavior for over 30 years. Although it is not the only model that has been introduced which can be used to classify, measure and compare the abstract and difficult-to-define phenomenon called culture.

Power distance

Despite proclamations such as 'all men are created equal', all societies and lasting organizations are built upon recognized hierarchies. However, not all of these hierarchies have the exact same number of layers nor is the 'distance' between layers the same. In some societies, hierarchies are fairly rigid with little opportunity to move upward, while in other societies the distances between levels of the hierarchies are much lower and there are more opportunities to move upward, or downward for that matter, in society. Hofstede (1983: 80) classified this difference as the cultural dimension of power distance and explained this dimension:

The fundamental issue involved is in how society deals with the fact that people are unequal. People are unequal in physical and intellectual capacities. Some societies let these inequalities grow over time into inequalities in power and wealth; the latter may become hereditary and no longer related to physical and intellectual capacities at all. Other societies try to play down inequalities in power and wealth as much as possible. ... In organizations, the level of Power Distance is related to the degree of centralization of authority and the degree of autocratic leadership ....'

In general, the countries of the LDCs of Asia have higher power distance scores than those found in Western countries, which will have an impact on relationships between managers and workers and the effectiveness of many business practices that deal with people and how they interact on the job. For example, Gallo (2011: 66) noted that, unlike in the West, leaders and managers in China are not expected to explain their actions to their subordinates; in fact, too much explaining can make the leader look weak and managers are expected to maintain some distance from their subordinates.

The power distance of a culture will affect many business practices, especially those which involve personal interactions. The power distance score of a society is likely to affect how a company uses empowerment, performance appraisals (use of a 360 system or other means for subordinates to evaluate superiors are much less commonly found in high power distance cultures), centralized as opposed to decentralized decision making, and many other management and leadership practices.

Individualism

People are both individuals and members of many different groups, such as family, nation, tribe and school. The emphasis on the importance of individuality v. membership in various groups differs between societies. The individualism v. collectivism scale has been used in many studies of cultural differences and cross-cultural management. Hofstede (1983: 79) explained this dimension:

At one end of the scale we find societies in which the ties between individuals are very loose. Everyone is supposed to look after his or her own self-interest and maybe the interest of his or her immediate family. This is made possible by a large amount of freedom that such a society leaves individuals. At the other end of the scale we find societies in which the ties between individuals are very tight. People are born into collectivities or ingroups which may be their extended family (including grandparents, uncles, aunts, and so on), their tribe, or their village. Everyone is supposed to look after the interest of his or her ingroup and to have no other opinions and beliefs than the opinions and beliefs in their ingroup. In exchange, the ingroup will protect them when they are in trouble. We see that both the Individualist and Collectivist society are integrated wholes, but the Individualist society is loosely integrated, and the Collectivist society tightly integrated.

In comparison to Western societies, Asian societies score as being more collectivist and this affects the way people relate to each other. 'Anyone trying to stand out as in the West will be hammered down in China' (Gallo, 2011: 119).

This dimension is probably the most well known of Hofstede's dimensions of culture and often used to distinguish Eastern from Western business practices. Hiring decisions, promotions, decision making, management style and even marketing practices can take on quite different characteristics in a collectivist culture when compared to a more individualistic one.

Masculinity

Hofstede's third dimension is labeled masculinity as opposed to femininity. Hofstede (1983: 83–4) described this dimension in the following way:

> The fundamental issue involved is the division of roles between the sexes in society. All societies have to deal with the basic fact that one half of mankind is female and other male . . .. All social role divisions are more or less arbitrary and what is seen as a typical task for men or for women can vary from one society to the other. We can classify societies on whether they try to minimize or to maximize the social sex role division. Some societies allow both men and women to take many different roles. Others make a sharp division between what men should do and what women should do . . ..

In addition to more distinct gender roles, masculinity refers to

> the degree to which values like assertiveness, performance, success and competition, which in nearly all societies are associated with the role of

men, prevail over values like the quality of life, maintaining warm personal relationships, service, care for the weak, and solidarity, which in nearly all societies are associated with the role of women.

(Hofstede, 1994: 6)

Unlike in some of the other dimensions of culture, there is not a typical Asian tendency found in this dimension, although Japan ranks as the most masculine country of all nations in the original study. Of the developing countries of Asia some such as Thailand and Indonesia fall on the feminine side, others fall on the masculine side, such as India and the Philippines, and still other Asian countries fall pretty close to the middle, such as Singapore (Hofstede, 1983).

Uncertainty avoidance

Hofstede's fourth dimension of culture is labeled uncertainty avoidance. However, it is not exactly the opposite of risk taking. Hofstede (1983: 81) describes this dimension as follows:

The fundamental issue involved here is how society deals with the fact that time runs only one way; that is, we are all caught in the reality of past, present and future, and we have to live with uncertainty because the future is unknown and always will be. Some societies socialize their members into accepting this uncertainty and not become upset by it.

A high uncertainty avoidance score would indicate a society prefers structured over unstructured situations. One would expect to see more rules, either written or unwritten, used in societies with higher levels of uncertainty avoidance. One would expect societies with lower uncertainty scores to be generally more flexible than societies with higher scores (Hofstede, 1994: 5–6). Uncertainty avoidance is not the same as being risk averse. For example, one may see a very high rate of entrepreneurship in countries with high uncertainty avoidance; however, many of the new businesses would most likely be in existing industries. Therefore, it can be speculated in societies with high levels of uncertainty avoidance people may take as many chances as in societies with lower scores in this dimension, but the scale of the risks may be lower. Most advances in pure science come from societies with low uncertainty avoidance scores, while advances in applied science are common in societies with both high as well as lower levels of uncertainty avoidance.

One sees both high and weak uncertainty avoidance scores in the developing economies of Asia. For example, Pakistan has a fairly high score for uncertainty avoidance while the Philippines and India have lower scores (Hofstede, 1983). China is considered a country with a high level of uncertainty avoidance and it appears to have an effect on the behavior of the workers in the country.

> While nearly every Chinese firm today wants people to take risks and encourages them to do so, there is still this deep-seated cultural fear that sometimes undermines people's desire to do so. This is very different in the West where people are taught from an early age to be always willing to try something new.
>
> (Gallo, 2011: 36)

Long-term orientation

The fifth dimension of Hofstede's framework came later and was based on research specifically designed by researchers working in Asia. Hofstede and Bond (1988) labeled this dimension 'long-term versus short-term orientation'. 'Long Term Orientation means valuing, for example, persistence and thrift' (Hofstede, 2007: 418). There is a clear cultural divide with East Asia countries such as Japan, China, Korea having more of a long-term focus while Western and African societies are more short-term orientated (Hofstede, 2007: 418).

This dimension has primarily focused on the uniqueness of East Asian societies, and the high scores in long-term orientation are often associated with Confucian values and are found in countries such as China, Korea and Vietnam.

Size

In business, size matters, although bigger is not always better. In general, there are fewer large corporations originating from the LDCs of Asia as are seen in North America, Europe, Australia and the more developed economies of Asia such as Japan and South Korea. There are some exceptions but many of these are state-owned or state-supported companies often in the energy sector such as PTT in Thailand, Sinopec and China National Petroleum in China, and Petronas in Malaysia (CNN Money, 2011). In most LDCs, small firms play a bigger role in the nation's economy and in employment creation than in more developed economies (London and Hart, 2004; Luthans and Ibrayeva, 2006). Access to capital is important for small firms to have the ability to grow and most firms in LDCs lack the access to capital required to grow rapidly (Angelini and Generale, 2008), resulting in many successful firms staying small and having limited growth potential.

Griffin and Putsay (2005: 309) wrote, 'To survive in today's global marketplace, firms must be able to quickly exploit opportunities presented to them anywhere in the world.' Yet how many firms from Nepal can exploit an opportunity that arises in Iceland? How many firms from Laos PDR can take advantage of opportunities presented in Des Moines, Iowa? Is it possible for most firms originating from Mongolia to open operations throughout the EU? If firms from developing economies lack the resources to go global, does that imply none of them will survive? Or is there an important place in the world's economy for small national or regional companies originating and solely operating in the LDCs of Asia?

In their textbook, Daft and Marcic (2004: 83) proclaimed, 'business is becoming a unified global field as trade barriers fall, communication becomes faster and cheaper, and consumer tastes in everything from clothing to cellular phones converge.' Is this really an accurate description of business environments found in the LDCs in Asia? While an argument that tastes have converged to some extent can be made, convergence of the ability to purchase has not occurred. Can convergence of business practices happen without convergence of economic development and purchasing power? The relatively lower purchasing power of consumers and lower levels of economic activity limit the growth potential of firms in the LDCs in Asia, therefore the assumption most important major business activities are controlled by very large global firms doesn't normally apply when looking at business conditions in areas in Asia which are heavily affected by poverty.

Are some of the assumptions, or at least hype, about the size, scope and the need for all firms to be global in orientation inappropriate when looking at businesses operating within the LDCs of Asia?

Ownership structures

Most studies of business practices use as a foundation the 'theory of the firm' which assumes 'the primary goal or objective of a firm is to maximize the wealth or value of the firm' (Salvatore, 2007: 12). This assumption seems to hold when looking at most large corporations. Yet, in many developing economies family ownership is the principal form of business ownership (Suehiro and Wailerdsak, 2004; Luthans and Ibrayeva, 2006; Peng et al., 2008). In a firm, usually a corporation, where there is a clear separation between management and ownership, an underlying assumption is the managers have been hired to maximize profits for shareholders while appeasing other stakeholders. Corporate managers are generally considered successful when they increase shareholder value and unsuccessful when they fail to increase shareholder value. Yet in family-owned and small entrepreneurial firms, the firms are often managed to maximize intangible as well as tangible benefits, which can result in trade-offs where intangible benefits, such as independence, providing jobs for family members and time off are sometimes gained at the expense of the goal of profit maximization (Pinfold, 2001; Hatcher and Terjesen, 2007; Southiseng and Walsh, 2008).

Family ownership and entrepreneurial ownership structures should not be considered a deficiency in an economy that will cease to exist as economic development occurs. Instead it should be considered a logical response to business conditions found in the LDCs in Asia (Suehiro and Wailerdsak, 2004). Having no separation between ownership and management provides a number of advantages. In areas of the world with less developed and formal legal traditions than those found in Western societies, trust and personal connections are used to bind business agreements together instead of using impersonal legal documents. Having no separation between the ownership and management facilitates this type of relationship contracting (Tsang, 2001; Shapiro et al., 2003; Suehiro and Walerdsak, 2004). In addition, relationship contracting allows for firms to be able to spread out the transaction costs associated with contracting and enforcing of contracts across numerous transactions thus lowering overall costs (Kim et al., 2004; Van De Ven, 2004; Wu and Choi, 2004; Peng et al., 2005; Young, 2005). Therefore, relationship contracting provides family-owned and entrepreneurial firms a competitive advantage over corporations under certain environmental conditions.

Moreover, state ownership of firms remains common in some of the LDCs in Asia and the behaviors, objectives and practices of state-owned firms are not always aligned with the theory of the firm and the idea of profit maximization (Zou and Adams, 2008).

In addition, the informal sectors of the economy play a very important role in the economies in many areas of the world, especially those areas where poverty is widespread. While business education and theories mostly assume business activities are being conducted in formal sectors of the economy, the fact is the majority of the world's workers work in the informal sector of the world's economies (Jutting and de Laiglesia, 2009: 18). The importance of the informal economy in the LDCs in Asia is significant with around 70% of all workers in South and Southeast Asia being in the informal sector of the economy (Charmes, 2009). While there is a strong correlation between having a large percentage of workers in the informal sector of the economy and high rates of poverty, it does not appear in the short to medium term that economic growth reduces the percentage of people in the informal sector of the economy and there remains debate over whether or not moving workers from the informal to the formal sectors should be a goal in helping reduce poverty (Gagnon, 2009; Jutting and de Laiglesia, 2009; Kucera and Xenogiani, 2009; Hasan and Jandoc, 2010). Furthermore, there are indications that firms/individuals in the informal sector do not always follow business practices which are intended to maximize profits and often exchange some intangible benefits, such as independence and quality of life, for the additional profits which could have been gained through additional hours of labor and additional efforts (Hipsher, 2010c).

Therefore, some of the assumptions that firms have a corporate ownership structure where there is a clear separation between ownership and management and firms normally attempt to maximize profits might have to be modified when examining and designing business practices for use in the LDCs of Asia.

Entrepreneurial orientation

In most developed countries, the economies are heavily impacted by the actions of large corporate firms and, for many individuals, climbing the corporate ladder is both a possibility and a preferred career path. This path is rarely available to workers in LDCs.

Family ownership in the LDCs in Asia is not restricted to small firms, but many large firms are also controlled by a single family (Tsang, 2001; Postma, 2002; Shapiro et al., 2003; Suehiro and Wailerdsak, 2004; Yan and Sorenson, 2004). Moreover, it is common for most family-owned firms to restrict entry into top management positions to members of the family making it difficult for one to achieve fame and fortune in someone else's family-owned firm.

Therefore, one sees more of an entrepreneurial orientation in the most ambitious individuals in the LDCs in Asia, as there are fewer opportunities for success while working for a salary than there are in Western countries. But entrepreneurship in the LDCs in Asia can take on somewhat different characteristics than the expectation of the risk-taking innovative entrepreneur glamorized in the West (Hipsher, 2010c). Lu et al. (2010) claimed entrepreneurs are driven by opportunities and build the capacity of their firms in response to the opportunities found in the environment in which they operate and since the environments in the LDCs of Asia are quite different than those found in developed economies it is not surprising entrepreneurs respond differently in these different environments.

Entrepreneurship in Asia might have some different characteristics than it generally does in Western societies. Moy et al. (2003) reported the perceptions of entrepreneurship as a career in Hong Kong were perceived as a fairly conventional career path and chosen by fairly conventional individuals while in the West entrepreneurship as a career was more likely to be pursued by individuals who possess more non-conforming attitudes. This result is aligned with the findings of Bjerke (2000), who reported becoming an entrepreneur in Asia is less about following the path of rugged individualism and usually involves becoming part of an interdependent network and having the right connections in the network can be as important as the skills and daring one brings into the business. In addition, Shapiro et al. (2003) found established family-owned firms in Asia often followed less risky strategies aimed at wealth preservation and ensuring the ability to pass the business on to the next generation, while in Western societies the expectation of entrepreneurs is more likely to be to take new risks and try to expand the enterprise and constantly increase wealth.

Workforce

The labor force available to firms operating in the least developed economies is quite different from the available labor force found in both developing and developed economies. Srinivasan, (2009: 112) reported workers in the least developed economies can be as much as five times less productive than workers in developing economies and nearly 100 times less productive than workers in developed economies. Moreover, the productivity gap may be increasing.

One of the factors associated with the lower productivity of workers in areas where poverty is widespread is the lack of education. To demonstrate, Lee (2008) reported there were higher levels of education in the workforce in the more prosperous coastal regions of China while there were lower levels of education found in the inland areas of the country where poverty remains more widespread.

Alongside the lack of education, the workforce in the poorest regions of the world often lack the opportunities to gain the work experience needed to develop the skills valued in a modern society. Godo (2010) made the case the amount and specific type of human capital affects how effective new technology imported from abroad can be adapted and used to create jobs and reduce poverty. Pre-existing human capital was given by the author as a primary reason Japan and Germany were able to rebuild after the countries and economies were devastated by World War II with relatively little financial aid and why they were able to use borrowed technology so effectively. In contrast, financial aid and the importation of new technologies have not always had the same positive effects on economic growth and poverty reduction in areas where the levels of education and quality work experience are lower.

The workforce available in areas where poverty is common will generally not have the same education or training as the workforce in more developed areas. In addition, the members of a workforce coming from a more traditional society have mostly grown up in a culture preparing individuals to work in subsistence agriculture, where there is less emphasis on punctuality and conformity. If one stops on the way to one's farm for 15 minutes to either help out or chat with a neighbor, this is not a problem as the effort can be easily transferred to another time and the person can make up the missed work by staying 15 minutes later in the evening or taking shorter breaks. However, arriving 15 minutes late at a factory using an assembly line production method could cause the entire production process to fail. A lack of attention to time and punctuality can reduce the efficiency in an assembly line or other modern work system, where work is more interdependent. In the more developed economies the workforce has been programmed through schooling and other social functions to value punctuality and conform to standardized practices, as these traits are valuable in an industrial society. Workers in many agrarian societies have not had the same cultural conditioning that instills these traits, and it generally takes considerable time for the cultural transformation from an agrarian to industrial society to occur (Godo, 2010).

Adapting to specific work practices which seem natural in environments where the population has been conditioned for punctuality and conformity is often difficult for workers coming from cultures with more agrarian values.

Many of the fundamental principles of business are universal. Providing good value for price was understood as a solid business principle during the Roman Empire. Gaining reputation and having first-time customers become repeat customers are as important in Vientiane as they are in New York. However, selection of many of the specific business practices used to achieve these universal principles will need to be aligned with the specific environmental conditions under which they are used. What is more, the specific environmental conditions found in most LDCs in Asia can be substantially different from the environments assumed one will encounter by the authors of most business textbooks.

Figure 3.1 **Family business in Siem Reap, Cambodia**

4

Business strategies and practices in developing economies

Abstract: Strategic business principles apply worldwide; however, practices will vary and often be influenced by the level of economic development found in a specific location. Interpersonal business practices will vary across locations and need to be aligned with the specific cultural environment in which a firm operates. Choice of operational business practices is often influenced by the technological environment and need for efficiencies, and thus is more likely to be able to be used across geographical and industrial boundaries with relatively little need for adaptation.

Key words: strategy, national competitiveness, innovation, human resource management, leadership, operational management.

Business practices and principles

As mentioned in the previous chapter, most business principles can be considered universal; however, the practices needed to be used to implement these principles will vary and need to be aligned with environmental conditions. Business practices come in a wide variety of types, some designed to ensure long-term success while others are used for increasing efficiency in day-to-day operations. While there is no one set of practices which will lead to success in every situation, internal consistency is often required. For example, a firm using a low-cost strategy will need to use practices which are helpful in creating efficiencies and will have to make some trade-offs and avoid most practices which increase costs, even if these practices provide some different forms of benefit. A three-level framework where business practices are broken down and examined into strategic, interpersonal and operational practices is used to examine business practices. While operating in the LDCs of Asia, some business practices can be imported from different environments, others might need to be adapted for local conditions and still others might have to be designed from the ground up based on local environmental conditions.

Strategic level business practices

There is no single set of business strategies that can be universally applied in every situation which will lead to success. Business strategies are about choices and trade-offs; business strategy is as much about what a company chooses not to do as it is about what a company chooses to do (Porter, 1996; Peng, 2002). Using Porter's (1980) framework of generic strategies there can be found examples of firms succeeding using low-cost leadership, focused and nearly endless variations of differentiation strategies. While there can be found universal best practices in operational business practices which can be used across industrial and national borders, there are no best strategic practices that can be used successfully by all firms. Selection of a business strategy relies on multiple internal and external factors. It has been argued the economic environment of a country in which a company operates is especially important when selecting strategies (Hipsher, 2007, 2010a).

Increased wealth provides consumers and businesses more flexibility in purchasing decisions, which therefore provides companies more strategic options to attempt to capture the purchases of customers. Therefore, one finds more and more varied uses of differentiation strategies in more developed economies, while options for the use of differentiation strategies in less developed economies will be relatively limited.

Porter (1980) felt the primary ways for a company to compete were to use one of the following: cost leadership, differentiation or focus/niche strategies.

Cost leadership is 'a business-level strategy in which the organization is the lowest-cost producer in its industry' (Robbins and Coulter, 2005: 193). Cost leadership strategies provide firms the opportunity to compete on price while maintaining profitability. A firm is able to attain cost leadership through superior access to technology, technological leadership, process innovation, as well as leveraging benefits from the learning curve, economies of scale, creating products that are designed to reduce costs and manufacturing time, and/or through reengineering activities (Allen et al., 2006: 25).

'The differentiation strategy is an integrated set of actions taken to produce goods or services (at an acceptable cost) that customers perceive as being different in ways that are important to them' (Hitt et al., 2005: 118). Product differentiation allows firms to charge a premium price based on 'product characteristics, delivery system, quality of service, or distribution channels' (Allen et al., 2006: 25). The differentiation strategy is often reported to be more sustainable that a cost leadership strategy and has the most potential for profitability (Hitt et al., 2005).

'The focus strategy is an integrated set of actions taken to produce goods or services that serve the needs of a particular competitive segment' (Hitt et al., 2005: 122). Niches can arise from a number of factors, including 'geography, buyer characteristics, product specifications, or requirement' and are segments of the market that are often ignored or found unattractive by large companies in the industry (Allen et al., 2006: 25). Therefore, the use of a focus/niche strategy is often associated with smaller firms.

It has been commonly believed the external environment has a significant impact on the choice of strategies made by firms (e.g., Hagan and Amin, 1995; Kim, 2008; Bach and Allen, 2010). There is also significant evidence that a firm's internal environmental factors such as corporate culture, leadership and organizational structure affect strategic choices (e.g., Franke et al., 2007; Epstein et al., 2010; Kipping and Cailluet, 2010).

However, a clear separation between the internal and external environments is in reality not always easy to identify. Organizations are not closed systems but open ones and internal environmental factors are heavily influenced by the external environment. For example, organizational culture appears to be affected to a considerable extent by both the national culture of the country of origin and the country of operation of an organization (Jung et al., 2008; Prasnikar et al., 2008; Klein et al., 2009). National culture also appears to impact a firm's organizational structure (Walsh, 2004; Li and Harrison, 2008) and choice of leadership styles (Kanungo and Wright, 1983; Chong and Thomas, 1997; Neelankavil et al., 2000; Suutari et al., 2002).

If we accept strategy is the linkage between a firm's internal and external environments (Ensign, 2008: 34) and accept that the internal and external environments of firms in LDCs are different from the environments found in more developed economies (Shenkar, 2009), then it would be expected strategies used and strategy formulation in firms in LDCs will be significantly different from those practiced in the environments found in more developed economies.

Environmental conditions

Theories about business strategy and other business practices have mostly been developed by examining business practices in the most developed economies around the world (Mathews, 2000; Lau, 2006). In general, both the internal environments found in firms from emerging economies and the external environment which influences strategic decisions in LDCs are quite different from the environments found in the firms that were explored when developing most strategic theories.

Most strategic management theories make an assumption the goal of increasing competitiveness within a market is the primary driver of strategic decision making. This assumption may hold in environments with relatively free markets and where the government's primary role in business is regulation, but in many LDCs governments play a more direct role in business and it has been found building relationships is often the primary strategic focus of firms operating in LDCs. This choice of strategic option can be attributed to the fact LDCs are often characterized by informal legal systems and the government's direct involvement in economic activities (Kim, 2008; Luk et al., 2008; Chattananon and Trimetsoontorn, 2009). Instead of focusing on beating the competition, in LDCs the focus of strategy is often on joining a network and cooperating with various business partners and government officials (Tsang, 2001; Suehiro and Wailerdsak, 2004; Aribarg, 2005).

The primary factor differentiating LDCs from developed economies is level of economic development. Firms originating from developed economies operate in environments where financial support, technology and skilled labor are more abundant than what is normally found in LDCs. Strategic theory often makes the assumption that firms have access to the resources necessary to engage in a variety of different strategies. This assumption may not hold in LDCs where the lack of access to vital resources, such as technological innovation, financing and human knowledge and skills, may limit the strategic choices available to a firm.

The social-cultural environments firms operate in also have an impact on the strategic options available to them. For example, for the most part religion is not normally thought of as having a direct influence on business practices mainly due to individuals thinking the values shaped by religions in their home markets are natural and often assume they are universal (Ali and Gibbs, 1998). Yet a linkage between Christian values and business practices in Western countries has been identified (Anderson et al., 2000;

Vinten, 2000; Cornwell et al., 2005). Muslim values have been found to influence the business environments and practices where Islam is widely practiced (Abbasi et al., 1989; Ali and Al-Owaihan, 2008). Confucian values have been thought to influence business practices in much of East Asia (Wang, 2004; Yan and Sorenson, 2004). Additionally, it has been proposed the business environments of Thailand, Laos PDR, Cambodia and Myanmar/Burma have been influenced by Theravada Buddhist teachings and values (Hipsher, 2010a). As religion often has more influence on the lives of individuals in LDCs than on individuals living in countries with higher standards of living (Barro and McCleary, 2003; McCleary and Barro, 2006), the impact of religious values may have a more pronounced impact on business practices and strategy formulation in LDCs than in more developed economies.

The technological environment in LDCs is generally less mature than in environments found in developed economies. The number of patents having been filed in, or from residents of, LDCs is very low is comparison to what is found in more developed economies (WIPO, 2008), which would seem to indicate companies from LDCs are farther removed from the invention of cutting edge technology than are firms in developed economies. Another factor limiting the use of technology is the lower pay scales making some technologies used in developed economies less cost effective in LDCs than using human labor.

Ownership structures also differ in LDCs in comparison to what is seen in more developed economies. In studying strategy in Western societies and, in particular, the USA, there is often an assumption of a separation of ownership and management and the sole purpose of a firm is to maximize profits. However, corporations and the separation between owners and managers are rare in LDCs (Suehiro and Wailerdsak, 2004; Luthans and Ibrayeva, 2006). Owner-managed and entrepreneurial firms in both developed and LDCs have been found to have many non-financial objectives (such as independence and the creation of jobs for family members) in addition to, and sometimes conflicting with, the goal of profit maximization (Befus et al., 1988; Pinfold, 2001; Paulson and Townsend, 2005; Choo and Wong, 2006; Hatcher and Terjesen, 2007). Moreover, in many LDCs state-owned firms are not uncommon and these firms also often have objectives in addition to, and sometimes in conflict with, maximizing profits. Since the ownership structures and objectives of many firms from LDCs differ from the corporate model, often there will be found different approaches taken as regards strategy.

Innovation

Innovation has often been considered a necessary component in gaining strategic competitiveness. For example, Pellicer et al. (2010) proclaimed every organization needs to invest in research and development (R&D); however, it is questioned whether the majority of organizations from countries such as Cambodia, Nepal or Afghanistan have access to the financial and human capital needed to engage in effective R&D. Zhang (2010) found some Chinese manufacturing firms made limited use of R&D while others did not engage in any R&D activities at all, and yet still managed to survive and sometimes thrive. De Valk (2003) in his study of firms in Laos PDR felt that it did not make much sense for firms in this country to engage in R&D in order to reinvent the wheel, but rather it made more sense to adapt technology and ideas generated elsewhere for use locally. Instead of expecting firms from emerging economies to either think of innovation and R&D in the same terms as firms from developed economies or to strictly copy ideas, innovation in LDCs may often entail adapting ideas, products and processes originally created in other locations in unique ways for use within the specific environment found in each LDC.

Lederman (2010) reported firms which were globally engaged through the use of licensing, foreign investment or involved in exporting activities generally increased the number of product innovations they created, with firms in China being somewhat of an exception. Most firms in LDCs, with the exception of a few firms in the export sector, generally have few opportunities to engage in activities that allow for substantial importing of foreign knowledge which would appear to limit the amount of product innovation possible. Lederman also found at the country level innovation breeds innovation and firms operating in national environments where there is significant global engagement by other firms can use spillover knowledge to enhance their ability to create product innovation even if the firms were not directly engaged globally. Firms from LDCs are less likely to have the opportunity to take advantage of this spillover effect than are firms from more economically developed and globally integrated economies.

Li et al. (2010) broke down innovation into the categories of exploratory and exploitative. Exploratory innovation involves radical changes and is intended to be used in pursuing new opportunities. Exploitative innovation involves incremental changes intended to improve existing processes. The authors found the external environment had some impact on a firm's innovation strategy. In more competitive environments, which are more likely found in developed economies, exploratory innovation has a higher payoff than exploitative innovation, while the reverse is true in less competitive environments, such as found in LDCs.

National culture might also play a role in fostering innovation within a country. Innovation requires change, which is often accompanied by conflict and challenging existing authority. Individualistic societies with relatively lower levels of power distance would be expected to embrace radical change and innovation to a greater extent than would cultures, such as often found in many LDCs, which are more collectivist and have more respect for existing authority (Ty et al., 2010).

Research has shown innovation can give firms what is referred to as a first-mover advantage (Shao, 2011). First-mover advantages come from both product innovation and consumer brand preferences. However, the length of time an innovative company can leverage a first-mover advantage appears to be shortening over time (Poletti et al., 2011). First movers gain advantages by staying ahead of the learning curve; however, most research on first movers has been conducted in developed economies and it is not well understood what it means to be a first mover in LDCs (Rahman and Bhattacharyya, 2003). While firms originating from LDCs could be considered first movers in their own markets in some existing product categories, as markets become more open it becomes more difficult for firms from LDCs to develop the technological and marketing capabilities to compete with firms from developed economies as first movers in new product categories. Instead, we normally see firms originating from LDCs to be following the lead of international firms and learning from the experience of first movers. Without having to bear the cost of product research, educating the market about the new product or developing an internationally recognized brand name, it would appear most firms from less developed economies will follow the second or late-mover strategies and consider ensuring a reasonable price as being an important part of their strategy.

National competitiveness

The country a firm originates from and operates in affect both its chance for international success and choice of strategies. Torrisi and Uslu (2010) found there are three different sources for national competitive advantage for an industry: basic requirements, efficiency enhancers and innovation/sophistication factors and each of these have different impacts on competitiveness. Basic requirements (labor force, natural resources, etc., ...) drive factor-driven economies within a firm, efficiency enhancers are important for cost advantages, and innovation/sophistication factors are used to create competitive advantage through differentiation. It would appear LDCs have varying types and amounts of basic requirements and efficiency enhancers, but mostly lack the innovation/sophistication factors needed to gain an advantage through innovation and differentiation, at least differentiation aimed at top-of-the-pyramid markets. It is expected this lack of innovation/sophistication factors will normally limit the strategic options for firms originating from LDCs.

A common framework used to examine the competitiveness of an industry within a specific nation is the four-pointed 'Porter's Diamond' (Porter, 1990). Porter's framework consists of four categories which can determine the competitiveness of a specific industry within a nation: (1) Factor conditions such as availability of natural resources, skilled work force, etc., ...; (2) demand conditions, if demand is high, and customers are demanding and sophisticated, an industry is more likely to develop world-class producers; (3) related and supporting industries, without easy access to the services these supporting firms perform, an industry will generally be at a disadvantage to firms operating in nations with access to high-quality suppliers and other strategic business partners; and (4) the strategies, structure and rivalries of specific firms within the industry.

In general, according to Porter's framework, it would appear firms from economically developed nations have advantages in the majority of industries, especially those in the higher value-added segments of a value chain. Many firms from LDCs face a number of obstacles in achieving international competitiveness. These include controlled markets, less sophistication of demand and lack of various human capital factors, especially access to skilled workers and the availability of knowledge and the ability to effectively use knowledge that is gained. These problems are often compounded and perpetuated by the high power distance cultures often found in LDCs where top managers maintain tight control (Shenkar, 2009). Moreover, as these difficulties cross industries, this can have a knock-on effect as potential supporting and related industries are likely to be restrained by the same type of limitations.

The amount and the type of innovation an organization can use are greatly affected by the location in which it operates (Porter and Stern, 2001). For example, Subrahmanya (2009) found, in a study comparing Japanese and Indian entrepreneurs, the backgrounds of the entrepreneurs and initial internal environments within the firms in both locations were often similar. The difference in external environment was where Japanese firms gained their competitive advantage in the field of innovation. In addition, it was found reputation mattered and external actors were more likely to support product innovation for firms originating from Japan, a location with a reputation for product innovation, but were less likely to provide similar support for firms from India, a location without the same type of reputation for product innovation. The commonly held belief that innovation does not come from LDCs would appear to limit access to external resources and support that firms from these countries would need for major product innovation.

However, firms in LDCs often have some advantages in addition to the obviously one of lower labor costs. One of these advantages is the ability to act flexibly, which is gained from experience in working in environments without the formal legal systems and availability of suppliers and complementary businesses found in developed economies; and often this knowledge of working within the systems found in one LDC can be leveraged when expanding into other LDCs (Cuervo-Cazurra and Genc, 2008; Shenkar, 2009: 150). Companies from LDCs also have some cost advantages when compared to multinational firms even when operating within the same country with the same labor market. Companies originating from developed economies, even while operating in a LDC, have tighter regulations as they have to meet home country standards and face pressures from NGOs, while local firms normally operate in a less stringent regulatory environment and are usually not targeted by NGOs and the media for scrutiny over business practices (Shenkar, 2009: 157). These additional costs might help explain the tendency of multinational MNCs to focus on the higher profit margins found at the 'top of the pyramid' of the market in LDCs which leaves most of the bottom of the pyramid open to local firms to operate in without direct international competition (London and Hart, 2004).

The environments found in LDCs indicate firms originating from these areas are at a distinct disadvantage when it comes to creating product innovation. Moreover, public opinion in both developed and developing economies would appear to limit the perception of quality of products from LDCs. Consumers often rank product quality by the nation the product comes from. It would be difficult for an Indian-made automobile to compete with a German automaker on perception of quality. Likewise Chinese wines will have a difficult time in replacing French wines in preference for luxury-oriented customers.

Therefore, it would appear firms from LDCs will generally have a difficult time competing in the high end of the market using a differentiation strategy and will normally compete using a low-cost leadership or niche strategy in operations in the home market or in exporting, and occasionally in other developing economies. Firms from LDCs will also have the option of using a differentiation strategy that focuses on the middle to lower areas of the pyramid within the home market, but will generally not compete at the top end of the pyramid, leaving that segment to developed country multinationals. An example of this can be found in the beer markets of some countries in Southeast Asia. Heineken dominates the top-of-the-pyramid market in Thailand and Vietnam, and no local companies attempt to compete with Heineken at the same price level; however, multiple local companies have positioned themselves in the middle using differentiation strategies while others have chosen to compete primarily on price. This proposal is consistent with Shenkar's research (2009: 151) who reported firms from LDCs more often compete on price than on product differentiation.

Interpersonal business level practices

Strategic management is mostly impersonal and analytical. However, there are a number of business practices that require directly working with other people. While the underlying assumptions of strategic management might be universal, even if the application of strategy may differ depending on the level of economic development and other factors found in different locations, the same cannot be said about many interpersonal business practices such as HR management, tactical marketing practices, negotiations and leadership. Hofstede (1980) found many American management practices were founded on assumptions of working with individuals who prized both egalitarianism and individualism, were fairly comfortable with uncertainty and sought success and monetary gains over maintaining good relationships. Yet these conditions are not commonly found outside the USA and therefore interpersonal business practices which work in the environment found in the USA, or other Western countries, might not always be as effective when working in other cultural environments. Therefore, it has been argued the social-cultural environment a firm operates in will have a significant impact on a firm's choice of interpersonal business practices (Hipsher, 2007, 2010a).

There is significant evidence that national differences in interpersonal business practices remain and the international convergence of interpersonal business practices is limited. Van de Vliert et al. (2009) found distinct differences in decision making involving conforming to leadership ideals, handling work motivations and recruitment across cultures. There is also evidence of the lack of convergence of tactical marketing activities in different geographical locations (Suh and Kwon, 2002; Lu and Lee, 2005). Human resource management practices also differ considerably across national borders (Chew and Goh, 1997; McGrath-Champ and Carter, 2001; Beer and Katz, 2003; Chen and Wilson, 2003; Mayrhofer et al., 2004; Claus and Hand, 2009). Additionally, we see ideas about the ideal forms of managerial and leadership styles and behaviors being very culturally specific (Zagorsek et al., 2004; Javidan and Carl, 2005; Sharma et al., 2009). In addition, whereas companies from different cultural environments may have similar objectives while engaging in a negotiation process, the decisions on how to conduct interpersonal negotiations often differ from one nationality to another (Hurn, 2007). Cultural background can also impact on how one is perceived while working internationally. For example, Varma et al. (2009) found willingness to provide support from locals in China to expatriates was determined by a number of factors, including the quality of the personal relationship as well as the perceived cultural similarity of the expatriate to the local staff.

One of the components often claimed as being a positive managerial trait is the possession of emotional intelligence, but Sharma et al. (2009) reported what constitutes emotional intelligence differs from culture to culture and therefore being emotionally intelligent while working in one culture does not automatically imply one will be emotionally intelligent in other cultures.

Interpersonal business activities in LDCs in Asia are often significantly different from those practiced in other locations. Ideas about leadership and leadership practices are often culturally specific. For example, empowering employees is often thought to be a practice management should embrace; however, the concept of empowerment is usually based on assumptions that employees have values normally found in individualistic cultures with moderate to low levels of power distance. Incorporating Western-style empowerment systems into Asia have not always been very successful (Hui et al., 2004; Huang et al., 2006; Newburry and Yakova, 2006). While many Chinese managers realize the importance and value of empowerment, they also know it is more difficult to implement in China than it is in the West. Confucian teachings stress the need for order and respect for authority and 'empowerment upsets the order between the leader and the follower' (Gallo, 2011: 109).

Modern Western business education generally makes a clear distinction between management and leadership and, while leadership is often not well defined, it is usually thought of as being both personal and 'good'. For example, Bass and Avolio (1993) and Bass and Steidlmeier (1999) advocated the use of 'authentic transformational leadership' as a best practice for dealing with subordinates. Authentic transformational leadership is a concept that has influenced much of the teaching of leadership over the last two decades in Western countries. Authentic transformational leadership includes four general components: idealized influence, inspirational motivation, intellectual stimulation and individualized consideration. Although these components are pretty abstract, they are all considered positive and involve the leader's personality and relationship with subordinates more than the leader's intellect or decision-making abilities. These qualities might be considered ideal in individualistic societies with relatively low power distances, but might not be as central to leadership in other cultural contexts. For example, Gallo (2011: 7, 57) finds the expectation of developing a personal relationship is not part of traditional Chinese ideas about leadership and doesn't fit well with the country's higher power distance culture. Hipsher (2010b) found a more top-down and paternalistic style of leadership was preferred by both management and workers in the countries of mainland Southeast Asia, a style that is quite different from the idealized transformational leader normally advocated in the USA and other Western countries.

The business environments in Western societies generally feature many rules and regulations controlling interpersonal business practices, mostly designed to ensure fairness. Moreover, there is a tradition of more bureaucratic organizations where one's loyalty is to the job, the company or even the profession. However, in many LDCs in Asia one sees less use of a bureaucratic style of management and more use of arbitrary decision making by leaders, as there appears to be less pressure to ensure fairness and more emphasis on adapting decisions that involve people to fit specific situations. What is more, loyalty is more likely to be personal and directed towards one's boss or business owner as opposed to an impersonal organization. For example, Holmes et al. (1996: 34) observed in Thailand that, instead of ensuring workers are following specific rules and guidelines, 'The senior is expected to provide direction, control, protection as well as emotional support, looking after the needs of his colleagues and staff, much like a prosperous father might do. This support is strongly personal in nature.' Somewhat ironically in the individualistic societies of the West, impersonal rules and regulations are much more commonly used to ensure fairness, while in the more collectivist LDCs in Asia one often finds fewer impersonal rules guiding leaders and more arbitrary and contextual decision making as regards personnel issues.

The concept of gaining and protecting one's 'face' is often associated with Asian cultures. Although the term is not necessarily used worldwide, the concept of how one is seen by others and the importance of maintenance of one's pride and reputation are probably in reality pretty universal. Nevertheless, this concept is often thought to have additional importance in Asian societies. Persons (2008) found there were five distinct but interrelated phrases used in Thai to refer to 'face', which can be roughly translated as: appearance to the outside world, honor, fame, dignity and virtue. Gallo (2011: 83) found in China many organizations sometimes give the title 'manager' to individuals who do not actually have managerial responsibilities in order to provide face to their employers which gains the companies greater employee loyalty.

In individualistic Western societies, conflict is often thought to be normal and can be constructive when different ideas compete for acceptance. However, in the more collectivist societies found in Asia, conflict is usually thought of as something to be avoided. The preference for avoidance of conflict has an impact on both internal and external business relationships. Avoidance of conflict in Thailand and the use of compromise often take precedence over making the optimal decision to maintain good relationships (Holmes et al., 1996: 21). A similar situation is found in Laos, where Rehbein (2007a: 54) reported how traders in the market did not focus solely on competition and making sales but often cooperated with each other to ensure everyone went home with at least some profits in order to avoid conflicts and hard feelings. Whereas in China, Gallo (2011: 93) reported that while truthfulness is an important virtue, it is generally acceptable to tell white lies if these lies allow everyone to save face and thus avoid a confrontation.

Everyone likes change but everyone also likes stability. There is nothing as exciting as going on vacation to a new location, and nothing more satisfying than returning home to familiar surroundings at the end of the vacation. However, on the continuum between change and stability, one might find in some companies operating in the LDCs of Asia more preference is given to stability than to change. For example, Gallo (2011: 10) noticed Westerners change jobs, homes and even spouses more frequently than do the Chinese, but we should also remember many communities in Asia have gone from agrarian societies to industrial and even post-industrial societies in a much shorter time period than was the case in the West. These successful transitions show workers in LDCs in Asia have the capability to handle rapid change. This preference for stability may not be seen in all LDCs. As Hipsher (2010a) pointed out the Theravada Buddhist teaching of the non-permanence of everything may assist the societies of many countries in mainland Southeast Asia to accept change easier than is the norm in other more traditional societies found in other locations.

Differences in communication styles between cultures have often been reported. Hall's (1976) framework includes high-context cultures, which use less direct and more contextual communication styles, and low-context cultures, where communication is more direct and there is more emphasis on spelling out the meaning. It has been noted, Asian countries generally use more of a high-context communication style while the Anglo-American countries use more of a low-context communication style. The less direct style of communication in Asia can help avoid confrontations and loss of face. Managers from outside the region working in the LDCs of Asia might want to be mindful of their communication style and adapt a slightly less direct style of communication than would be the norm in some other regions.

In Western societies, laws and the legal system are generally thought of as being mostly black and white where there are fairly clear boundaries between following rules or laws and breaking them. While in Asia, one sees more of an acceptance of gray areas and more reliance on personal interpretations in the application of rules and laws. This makes relationships often more important than compliance in meeting legal requirements. For example, in reference to conducting trade between Thailand and Burma/Myanmar, Aribarg (2005: 126) wrote, 'People find personal relations and social networks more efficient than interacting with formal institutions, since laws and regulations are susceptible to authority's discretion.' Hawks (2005: 111) found for small businesses in Cambodia having personal connections with government officials is often considered a form of competitive advantage as without these connections one is susceptible to arbitrary enforcement of the laws by officials who might be more interested in supplementing their meager salaries than objectively enforcing written laws.

This looser interpretation of laws and rules also applies to the use of contracts. In Western societies a contract is normally considered as written in stone and cannot be altered without the consent of both parties while in China, and other countries in Asia as well, a contract is often more like what those in the West call a letter of intent, or a gentleman's agreement with serves as a guideline for an ongoing business relationship that is expected to evolve and change over time as conditions change (Gallo, 2011: 124).

As managers in many LDCs cannot be assured of enforcements of private contracts by the courts, there is much more reliance on building relationships, and trust is often as important as quality and price in selecting suppliers, distributors and other business partners (Hallen and Johanson, 2004; Nguyen et al., 2005; Young, 2005).

Human resource management practices are often influenced by culture. For example, in individualistic societies the main emphasis on hiring is to find the best person for the job; however, in collectivist societies, while individual skills are also important, added importance is placed on how the individual will fit into the organization and work team (Sekiguchi, 2006). Having a worker in a work team in a collectivist society who does not socially mesh with co-workers is a bigger problem than it would be in a more individualistic society.

Another aspect of HR management which can be quite different in different locations is in how companies find new workers. In most LDCs one sees more informal and personal recruitment methods. Local newspapers are not always common and internet access for potential non-managerial workers is far from universal. Therefore, most firms in LDCs in Asia rely mostly on referrals. For example, in the garment industry in Cambodia, Dasgupta and Williams (2010) reported only slightly over 2% of job seekers search for jobs through newspapers, and most of the rest seek and find jobs through their social networks. Strauss et al. (2010) reported in factories in Wenzhou (China), recruitment for labor was generally informal, although a significant number of managers were recruited through more formal means while many others were family or close friends of the principal owner of the firm.

In most Western societies a cornerstone of performance management is the formal performance appraisal. However, these formal appraisals are not used as often in the LDCs of Asia than they are in the West. For example, Saeed and Shahbaz (2011) found formal performance appraisals were rarely used in SMEs in Pakistan; instead, more informal appraisal methods were primarily used. Claus and Hand (2009) reported most MNCs are already aware of the need to localize performance management systems with differences in the dimensions of power distance and masculinity being the primary drivers of different performance management systems.

If formal performance appraisal systems are to be introduced into the LDCs of Asia, one should be aware of how these systems often make it more difficult for all employees to save face, and ranking employees inevitably will result in conflict and confrontation. Performance appraisals are intended to motivate individual performance through competition, but one should consider whether to use or how to use this form of performance management in a collectivist society with relatively high power distance scores.

Operational level business practices

The operational level consists of day-to-day business practices. Operational business practices are where the grand strategies are implemented. Operational level business practices include production and operational techniques, accounting practices, use of communication technology and logistics procedures. Often the selection of a particular operational level practice is greatly influenced by costs and the need for efficiencies. It has been proposed the most important influences on operational business practices are technology and price of labor (Hipsher, 2007). When globalization and convergence of practices in business are discussed, it is often the technologies and operational business practices that are being referred to. Cellphones, computers, shipping containers, bar codes and other technologies have become the tools used at the operational level of businesses throughout the world. While successful firms use a wide variety of strategies and tactics, there is often less variety seen at the operational level and best practices often emerge which cross geographic and industrial boundaries.

There is some research which supports the concept of global convergence of operational business practices. There has been found some level of international convergence in accounting and auditing (Brackney and Witmer, 2005; Horstmann, 2005; Herrmann and Hague, 2006), and in the use of information technology (Van Ark and Piatkowski, 2004; Zhang and Jeckle, 2004) and production technology (Frantzen, 2004). However, differences remain and a total convergence of operational level business practices has not happened and some differences are likely to remain for a considerable length of time (Pagell et al., 2005). One of the drivers of operational level business practice differences is the difference in labor costs. Some technologies that save money in areas where labor costs are relatively high do not bring cost savings in LDCs where labor costs are much lower. Therefore, in countries with relatively lower labor costs, such as those found in the LDCs of Asia, one is likely to see more labor-intensive operational business practices and less use of technology than in locations where labor costs are higher.

Yu and Zaheer (2010) believed new technologies were usually more easily accepted when introduced than were new practices requiring changes in social interactions or conceptual thinking. They also believed changes in one area, such as use of a new technology, sometimes caused misalignments in other business areas which would then need to be realigned. Therefore, introducing a new technology might help in the gradual acceptance of changes in other work practices which are more interpersonal or strategic in nature.

While convergence in the use of technology and operational level business practices is often seen, the use of specific operational tools can still vary across cultures. For example, Han et al. (2010) found, while moves to have a single worldwide accounting system continue, the nuanced application and choices made within emerging frameworks are affected by culture and companies from more individualistic societies often attempt to 'manage' earnings to a greater extent than do companies from more collectivist countries.

It is proposed best practices in operational level business practices can often be transferred across international boundaries with limited need for adaptation to local conditions. In recent years we have seen many technologies and operational business practices, such as the use of cellphones and bar code readers that originated in more economically developed nations, become nearly universally accepted across the globe and it is likely this trend will continue.

An example of how technology can be used efficiently across borders is the use of mobile phones by banana growers in Uganda. Mobile phones have given farmers more control over price, which has resulted in increased production and sales of perishable bananas. Mobile phone ownership in rural Uganda is not widespread, but as long as one was available in a community, information about prices spread rapidly throughout the community. The use of mobile phones significantly reduced the transaction costs of matching buyers and sellers of bananas, making the entire value chain more efficient, and has increased profits and the standards of living of the farmers (Yamano et al., 2010).

Universal standardization of operational business practices also facilitates international trade. Firms using differentiation strategies can easily buy from suppliers using a niche or cost leadership strategy. In addition, there is no need for interpersonal business practices to be aligned between trading partners. However, at the operational level, to ensure smooth and efficient exchanges, some standardization of practices is required. Therefore, we see some uniform protocols in communications, logistics and other operational business practices. Firms trading with each other need to have some integration of operational business practices, and increased international trade pressures firms to adapt more common operational business practices to reduce transaction costs.

Three-level approach

When operating in LDCs in Asia, it is proposed firms can take a three-level approach. The first step is to use universal approaches to strategic management but, because economic and other environmental conditions may be different from what is found in other locations, firms will need to adjust strategies to local conditions. In the LDCs of Asia, there will generally be limited opportunities to use differentiation strategies at the top of the markets. Instead, costs will take on added importance, and most successful business strategies will most often focus on cost leadership, focused strategies or using differentiation strategies aimed at the lower and middle segments of the market.

For interpersonal business practices, in general, a company will need to adjust practices for the social-cultural environment found in each location.

Figure 4.1 **Transportation system, Aranyaprathet, Thailand**

The third level shows firms can often use universal best operational business practices and adapt foreign technology for use in any environment, although a company might use less technology and more human labor than a firm might use in other locations due to lower labor cost and more availability of low-skilled labor in LDCs.

5

Asian success stories

Abstract: A number of Asian economies, including Japan, South Korea, Taiwan and Singapore have achieved substantial economic growth and success in reducing poverty despite having to overcome difficulties. While each success story in Asia is unique, in each case both the private and public sectors were involved in growing the economy. A number of very successful and innovative companies, such as Sony, Samsung and Acer, have played a key role in economic development in each of these countries. There are a number of lessons to be learned from these successful examples.

Key words: Japan, Korea, Taiwan, Singapore, Sony, economics, Samsung, Acer.

Successful poverty reduction in Asia

East Asia has given the world valuable economic lessons on the benefits of trade liberalization, where market forces lead economies toward improved efficiencies and increased productivity. The high economic growth rates of Hong Kong (China), Republic of Korea, Singapore and Taipei (China) were driven by export-led strategies. This paved the way for them to become the newly industrialized economies of the region. When the People's Republic of China launched its reforms in 1978 and opened its doors to foreign trade and investment, it started an increasing momentum of growth, as the nation attracted huge sums of foreign direct investment (FDI). The world watched and learned.

(Asian Development Bank, 2009a: 8)

East Asia has seen the longest period of sustained economic growth and poverty reduction the world has ever seen. On a per capita income basis, Hong Kong has gone from an average GDP of $3,100 in 1960 to $29,900 in 2005, Japan went from $3,500 in 1950 to $39,600 in 2005, South Korea raised its per capita GDP from $1,100 in 1960 to $13,200 in 2005, Singapore experienced per capita GDP growth starting from $2,200 in 1967 and rising to $25,400 in 2005 while in Taiwan the improvement was from $1,500 in 1965 to $16,400 in 2005 (Brady and Spence, 2010: 3).

However, there were few experts predicting in the years following the end of World War II these would be the countries that would have the most success in finding economic growth and poverty reduction. Japan's industries and infrastructure had been devastated from the war. The government of Taiwan had fled from the mainland in defeat and disarray. South Korea was to embark on a brutal civil war. Singapore and Malaysia, like Burma and South Asia, were being hastily given independence from Great Britain with little preparation and planning and Hong Kong was to remain the sole East Asian colony of Great Britain surrounded by a country with a hostile Communist government. Yet these areas were able to develop, prosper and most importantly dramatically reduce the number of their citizens living in poverty.

One thing each success story has in common was each willingly joined the global trading system. Much of this growth has been attributed to Asian firms engaging in global value chains which included a shift in manufacturing capabilities from Western countries to Asia due to labor costs and the expansion of international trade in the post–World War II era (OECD, 2010).

Some Southeast Asian economies have also seen substantial economic growth and poverty reduction. Thailand experienced very high rates of growth over many years in the 1970s and 1980s, while other nearby countries, notably Indonesia and Cambodia, saw much slower economic growth which actually led to increases in poverty and hunger (Owen, 1992: 488–93). Malaysia is another success story and saw its poverty rate fall from 49% in 1970 to 7.5% in 1999 while at the same time seeing inequality decrease (Steward, 2005: 118). This is despite the fact the government in Malaysia has often intervened directly in the economy and has given preference for selecting the ownership of domestic firms based on ethnicity, resulting in discrimination against the large ethnic Chinese and Indian populations in the country (Rasiah, 2007: 153).

Although experiencing poor economic performance in the first years after the end of World War II (and before the war as well) up until the 1980s, China has seen a major shift towards economic growth and poverty reduction in recent decades. The rate of people in poverty in China amazingly fell from 60% of the population in 1990 to 16% in 2005 (OECD, 2010). China, due to its low labor costs and huge potential market, has been able to attract substantial foreign investment, mostly in low value-added activities in global value chains, despite having what most consider a poor institutional environment (Chang, 2007: 25). China's successful trade liberalization included dismantling state-owned monopolies, allowing privately owned businesses to compete and decentralizing economic decisions and giving more authority to local governments (Lu, 2007).

In looking at the success of the East Asian 'tigers' one sees both trade liberalization which spurred the creation of dynamic private enterprises as well as significant amounts of state planning and direct involvement of the governments in business activities. This has led to a number of debates between those advocating free markets and those advocating significant involvement of the state in economic planning (Shin, 2007: 31). Some of these very successful economies have been slowly opened up as they have developed, but have found further growth on becoming developed and more open economies more difficult; therefore, the debates continue (Chang, 2007). However, this focus and debate over the impact of macroeconomic policies may obscure the impact of decisions made within the private sector to the successful economic growth and poverty reduction found in these economies.

Japan

The success of the Japanese economy and the rise of the standard of living of the Japanese people after World War II is one of the great success stories of modern times. But the path to success did not appear obvious in 1945.

Agricultural output had plummeted so precipitously by August 1945 that mass starvation seemed imminent. Production of consumer goods such as clothing and household wares had long before come to a virtual halt. The ranks of the unemployed swelled as soldiers, administrators, and civilians returned from the former empire and as workers at home were idled by the shutdown of military production.

The destruction of the war had laid waste to great swaths of the industrial capacity of the country, and production was at a 'complete standstill.' Intensive wartime production had left decrepit what industrial facilities remained. Because foreign trade had all but ceased and internal infrastructure almost completely broken down, raw materials were hard to come by. Financial markets were in disarray, causing severe shortages in the capital that industry needed to rebuild and retool. Exacerbating all of this was galloping inflation: by December 1945, prices had risen nearly six times above their level at the time of surrender four months before.

(O'Bryan, 2009: 18).

Despite the destruction of the nation's economy with the defeat in World War II, Japan was able to rise from the ashes economically stronger and more stable politically than ever before. With something as complex as an unexpected economic miracle it is difficult to pick out exactly what specific policies and actions actually led to the success. But, as the popularity of centralized economic planning was at its height at this time, the Japanese employed a mixed economy where the central government worked as a partner with large businesses but did not directly take control of actual production. Japan was able to incorporate centralized planning by the state and its bureaucracy into a model that worked successfully while newly independent states in Africa and other parts of Asia followed advice from the experts of the time to have the government more directly involved in the economy. But this more direct involvement strategy failed to achieve substantial economic growth and poverty reduction while Japan prospered.

Japan's recovery and growth was mainly driven by its manufacturing sector. In the early years following World War II, Japanese companies engaged heavily in licensing foreign technology and producing products for both local consumption and export. At this stage the government was heavily involved in regulating which industries companies could go into and assisting companies in making licensing agreements with firms from developed economies. As the manufacturing sector grew and matured, firms used the knowledge gained and with some government support started to develop their own technology. Productivity increased and the total factor productivity of Japan reached 80% of that of the USA by the 1970s (Aoki et al., 2010).

Although a latecomer to the industry, Japan moved into the production of TV sets and using licensing and technological assistance contracts was able to grow the industry rapidly. By 1959 nearly 3 million TV sets were produced and firms were beginning to export some of these products. The steel industry also used foreign technology to modernize and grow. The Fuji Iron Works and Yawata Iron Works signed technological assistance contracts to obtain strip mill technology with Armco Steel in 1951, while Kawasaki Iron Works signed a similar agreement with Republic Steel in 1958. Following the government plan, Nippon Kokan Corporation obtained a license to use the basic oxygen furnace, and this technology was then passed on to other companies through sublicensing agreements. The automobile industry also used licensing and technological assistance contacts to improve production techniques and gain access to the latest knowledge and technology. Nissan, Hino and Isuzu all used their access to foreign technology to develop the automobile industry. Despite the perception the government was actively involved in promoting specific industries, the amount of expenditure on research and development by the government was in reality quite limited, and debates continue over the effectiveness of these government policies in promoting technological adaptation during this time (Aoki et al., 2010).

However, the ability to adapt and adopt foreign technology would not have been possible without the human capital needed to use it effectively. In the late nineteenth century during the Meiji restoration, the educational system in Japan began a major expansion with an emphasis on acquiring engineering and technological skills in order to catch up with the West (Godo, 2010). The war destroyed much of Japan's physical infrastructure but much of the human capital was left intact providing a foundation on which to build a new modern economy in the postwar era.

After the war, economic planning in Japan had to take on totally different characteristics than the colonial framework of importing cheap raw material from conquered lands and selling manufactured products to captive markets that previously prevailed. Moreover, the real growth in the bureaucracy tasked with directing the economy happened during the period of American occupation immediately after the war and was not a traditional part of Japanese society (O'Bryan, 2009: 8–36).

In the postwar period, the use of statistics in both public and private sectors became very popular. Stuart Rice led a task force sent by the US government during the occupation which helped overhaul the economic planning system and his work was widely accepted and appreciated by the Japanese. One member of the Rice Task Force, W. Edwards Demmings, gave a number of lectures on the use of statistical analysis in quality control in the production process which had a major impact on Japanese industries. In this postwar period, the Japanese adopted many American concepts concerning national accounting and other forms of statistical analysis which were popular at the time (O'Bryan, 2009: 69–100).

The common claim of widespread Japanese Government intervention in the economy in the postwar period might have been overstated. While many in academia in Japan favored Keynesian policies to regulate business cycles, those in government agencies were less enamored with these styles of policies and were in fact fairly conservative in outlook. For example, in 1953 the Japanese government was criticized by the World Bank for lacking specific plans to channel funds into various sectors of the economy. While the Japanese government was involved in directing the market to a greater extent than pure free marketers would have liked, the policies always were directed at supporting private businesses as opposed to heavily regulating the private sector. For example, the Ministry of International Trade opened the Japanese Productivity Center in 1955, with the assistance of the US government, in order to help private manufacturing companies to become more internationally competitive. The country also kept taxes on corporations low and generally favored policies that could be considered business friendly (O'Bryan, 2009: 102–75). While Japan was the recipient of considerable foreign aid and assistance, mostly from the USA, in the early years after the war it did not take long for Japan to go from receiving foreign aid to giving it, mostly concentrating on giving assistance within Southeast Asia (Owen, 1992: 480).

Free market systems are generally based on the assumptions of competition and exchanges between independent firms; however, a unique feature found in the traditional Japanese business system is the large-scale inclusion of cooperation between companies which exists alongside competition. During the Meiji Restoration of the nineteenth century, the government privatized many industries and, to encourage large-scale production, allowed monopolies and granted special privileges for very large selected companies, or series of companies, tied together by a holding company. These conglomerates became known as *zaibatsus*. The *zaibatsu* system was made up of family-owned organizations which dominated the Japanese economy from the Meiji period up to World War II. The big four *zaibatsus* were Mitsubishi, Mitsui, Sumitomo and Yasuda, and later a second tier of *zaibatsus* emerged after the Russian–Japanese War, which included Okura, Furukawa, Nakajima and Nissan (Kienzle and Shadur, 1997; Dedoussis, 2001; Miwa and Ramseyer, 2006).

As many of the *zaibatsus* were associated with supporting the wartime Japanese government, the Allied occupation forces worked to disband the system and many of the largest holding companies and firms were banned from operating. However, soon the desire for economic growth and Cold War concerns overrode the desire to punish individuals and companies for their involvement in the war and many of the *zaibatsus* reorganized, now referred to as *keiretsus* although now they were not necessarily family-owned operations. But the same dominant players from the prewar period continued to flourish in postwar Japan. A *keiretsu* can be defined as a system or series and is used to refer to the intricate web of business relationships within Japan's industrial groupings (Gilson and Roe, 1993; Tan, 1997; Dedoussis, 2001).

The cooperation between suppliers and manufacturers and other long-term business relations associated with the *keiretsu* system has led to numerous debates about the pros and cons of the system. Because relationships are long term within the *keiretsu* system, firms can invest in building collaborative competencies which can be shared throughout the entire system. The system leads to creating trust between business partners which can lower transaction costs and facilitate the sharing of knowledge, including confidential knowledge that is normally not shared with those outside the firm (Ito, 1995; Dyer, 1996; Harley and Tan, 1999; Dedoussis, 2001; Ito and Rose, 2005). On the other hand, there are some problems associated with the *keiretsu* system including poor resource allocation due to being in captive relationships and it is also difficult to align strategic direction for each individual unit within the network (Chu and MacMurray, 1993; Dent, 1998; Wong and Maher, 1998).

Another feature found in the large Japanese export-orientated firms was specific Japanese-style human resource management (HRM) practices. Japanese HRM practices of this period in large companies included 'lifelong' employment, a heavy emphasis on seniority as a basis for promotions, extensive training, long orientations and the development of generalists as opposed to specialists (Hall and Leidecker, 1981; Pucik, 1984; Tung, 1984; Pudelko, 2004), although the sustainability of these practices has been questioned as the country developed and a more expensive workforce was created (Mroczkowski and Hanaoka, 1998; Watanabe, 2003; Tokoro, 2005). In addition, Japanese companies operating internationally in the postwar era generally followed 'global' business practices which placed an emphasis on efficiencies in production as opposed to more innovative and specialized strategies (Yip, 1996; Yip et al., 1997; Allen et al., 2006). This choice of using global strategies during this period might have been especially suited to both the changing international market and the size and skills found in these large *keiretsu*-style firms.

Fifty years ago, when Japan was rebuilding its country and starting on the road to becoming an economic superpower, the label 'Made in Japan' indicated that the product was probably a cheap, poorly made copy. Today it is among the leaders in innovation, from automobiles to appliances to high-tech gadgetry.

(Gallo, 2011: 138)

While it is true the Japanese economy has stagnated over the last two decades or so, which might indicate government policies and private enterprise strategies that worked successfully at earlier stages of development might not work as well at more advanced stages. Nevertheless, Japan is a country where its citizens have a very high standard of living and extreme poverty and hunger are very rare. It is true the country currently has its share of economic problems in trying to revive growth, but these are the types of problems the majority of the world's citizens wished they faced.

South Korea

In the aftermath of the Korean War, poverty was widespread on both sides of the border of the divided country, but South Korea (officially called the Republic of Korea) has become one of the most economically successful of the Asian Tigers and today has an average income far above the world's and region's average. South Korea today is a world leader in many industries including automobiles, electronics, steel, shipbuilding and entertainment. Korea was controlled as a colony of the Japanese from 1910 to 1945 and, at the current time, Japan is often seen by many Koreans as their main natural competitor. But in the postwar period Japan has also been both a role model for the South Koreans and the benchmark by which they measure their own economic success (Kienzle and Shadur, 1997; Tan, 1997; Morden and Bowles, 1998; Lee and Han, 2006).

Like in much of East Asia, business networks have played a key role in building the South Korean economy. The term *chaebol* is used to refer to the large business groups that dominate the Korean business environment. A Korean *chaebol* is similar to a Japanese *keiretsu* in some ways, yet there are some differences as well. 'A typical *chaebol* consists of many diversified and legally independent affiliates, all of which are controlled by a controlling shareholder family' (Hwang and Seo, 2000: 361). Samsung, Hyundai and LG are some of the largest and best known of the *chaebols*, and the *chaebols* dominated the private sector in South Korea during the country's growth stage. The *chaebols* generally grew out of the remnants of firms abandoned by the Japanese as they were forced out of the country in 1945. The *chaebols* were often tightly connected with the government and given special privileges during the period when President Park Chung Hee and the military ran the country in the 1960s and 1970s. *Chaebols* are generally very hierarchal in nature and have normally been dominated by a single family, although actual ownership has often been more diversified (Choi and Cowing, 1999; Lee and Kim, 2000; Lee, 2002; Shin, 2002; Lee and Han, 2006).

The South Korean government in the 1960s heavy regulated FDI and used protectionist policies and support for national industries more or less on the Japanese model (Park, 2007). 'Despite the omnipresence of the state in the Korean system, the Korean state entrusted local entrepreneurs to undertake major industrial projects. It relied on public enterprises only when local entrepreneurs were not available' (Shin, 2007: 40). On the negative side of policies during the growth stages, wealth was not always shared with the workers who were instrumental in creating it, and this led to unionization and militancy in some industrial segments of the economy (Wad, 2007).

East Asia in the post–World War II era provided a couple of natural economic experiments where countries sharing the same culture and history were politically separated with one side following centralized planning while the other side followed paths that gave a higher priority to allowing the private sector to dominate, usually under tight direction. Taiwan and mainland China was one such experiment, in which Taiwan grew economically and reduced poverty while mainland China under Communist rule did not until there was a change in economic direction for the country. Korea was another natural economic experiment.

> Under these two highly contrasting regimes, the economies of the Democratic People's Republic of Korea and the Republic of Korea diverged. Although the Republic of Korea has grown rapidly under capitalist institutions and policies, the Democratic People's Republic of Korea has experienced minimal growth since 1950 under communist institutions and policies.
>
> (Acemoglu and Robinson, 2010: 140)

Much like what was seen in Japan, South Korea was able to prosper with significant indirect control of the economy which was dominated by the private sector, yet North Korea chose more direct control over the economy and its citizens have not benefited from growth and its accompanying poverty reduction.

Singapore

> Newly independent, Singapore found itself saddled with a poorly educated population suffering from severe poverty and chronic unemployment. The country had little by way of resources, aside from its natural harbor and its reputation and role as a major entrepôt trade center for Asia.
>
> (Ying et al., 2010: 111)

> Singapore was the great Southeast Asian success story, over the whole postwar period it was second only to Japan ... Singapore had no delusions of economic self-sufficiency. Its leaders realized that it would have to depend on export-oriented industrialization and services financed by foreign investment if necessary ...
>
> (Owen, 1992: 486)

As the British colonial empire in Southeast Asia came to an end, the leaders of Singapore made the decision to join in a political union with Malaysia driven by economic and security concerns. But this union ended abruptly in 1965 and the tiny city state of Singapore under the leadership of Lee Kuan Yew became an independent country. The country quickly turned its economic policies towards creating a business-friendly environment encouraging exports and openness and in 1967 sharply reduced the corporate tax rates (Cheong, 1992: 451; Ying et al, 2010: 112).

The strategy in Singapore, foreshadowing the now common development strategy in this age of globalization, was for local firms to enter into value chain networks with international firms and provide services and production which were considered complementary to major MNCs originating from more developed economies as opposed to trying to create the entire value chain in one location and directly compete. However, the government did not leave everything up to the market and solely rely on the private sector; instead, it invested heavily in industries the government thought were of strategic importance, when private investment could not be found (Shin, 2007: 38–9).

One of the factors which may have helped Singapore develop was the country's political stability and the support of the population for the government. As the country began growing economically, the population gained faith in the government which gave the government enough political room to embark on policies which would take time to pay off. The country provided incentives and support which attracted investment from some of the world's most progressive companies at the time including National Semiconductor, Fairchild, Texas Instruments and Hewlett-Packard. The government focused its attention on attracting investment into higher value-added activities and investment from the USA and Europe and resisted the temptation to encourage investment from other Asian countries as most of the Asian value chains at the time were mostly engaged in lower value-added activities. In the long term this focus on quality of investment helped the country develop the skills of its workforce. As time went by, Singapore also adapted its policies as companies in the Asian region developed and later on encouraged more East Asian investment as Asian companies began to move up the value chain. In addition, the heavy hand of government began to lighten and by the 1990s the direct involvement of the government had lessened considerably and firms in Singapore were able to make the transition to higher value-added activities as the country's economy developed (Ying et al., 2010: 111–19). As opposed to South Korea which used more of a nationalistic model of development, Singapore used more of an internationalist model of development (Shin, 2007: 32).

> Singapore's experience may be rather unique, given its circumstances. The country's small size allows policy to be highly targeted and makes policy execution, coordination, and implementation somewhat easier ... Singapore has learned that resources and ideas are only necessary conditions, which are in and of themselves not sufficient to ensure sustained growth. Holistic implementation is key: there is no point in having first-class strategies and policies with third-class execution.
>
> (Ying et al., 2010: 110)

Private sector in East Asia

Akio Morita and Sony

Less than a year after the end of World War II, Masaru Ibuka and Akio Morita founded a company called Tokyo Telecommunications Engineering Company, which would be renamed Sony Corporation in

1958. The first product the company attempted to make was a rice cooker, but this product didn't work as planned and was considered a failure. Not deterred by the initial failure, the company turned to making tape recorders and expanded from there. From the beginning, Sony looked internationally.

At first the company imported technology from the USA and later looked to the world for markets for its products. One of its first major commercially successful innovations was the invention of the transistor radio. Sony licensed the technology for transistors from Western Electric, but was told the only use for this new technology was in making hearing aids. However, under the leadership of Akio Morita, a new use for this new technology in radios was found and the transistor radio and the Sony brand name would spread around the world. Later inventions include the Trinitron Color TV, Walkman, Compact Disk Player, Betacam, floppy disk, Handycam and Playstation (Beamish, 1999; Greco, 1999; Peterson, 2001; Moon and Lee, 2004).

While Akio Morita was proudly Japanese, he was also very open to learning about the outside world and new ideas. Akio Morita had a privileged background and was the son of the owner of one of Japan's oldest sake breweries but, instead of following the easy path, he set out to make his own way in the world. As the company began expanding he quickly seized upon the importance of globalization long before the word became widely used. In the 1960s Sony opened a showroom in New York and in 1963 Akio Morita moved his family to New York and immersed them in American culture (Greco, 1999; Peterson, 2001).

In the postwar era, Sony and Akio Morita were not content for Sony to be a low-priced producer taking advantage of the low labor costs found in Japan at that time. While Japan could have been considered economically underdeveloped at this time, it did have considerable human capital to use. Sony took the path of innovation, globalization and use of a differentiation strategy, which other Japanese companies would soon emulate. Sony was a Japanese company, but a Japanese company that was open to the wider world and created a culture that was a fusion of traditional Japanese values with new ideas imported from the rest of the world (Beamish, 1999).

Akio Morita was a visionary in all things. He was an inventor of world-changing consumer products, of course, but he was also Japan's greatest ambassador-at-large, and a thoughtful architect and dynamic builder of the new global economy. He could not only dream the big dreams – he could make them come true.

(Peterson, 2001: 220)

While difficult to quantify, the products and jobs created by Akio Morita and Sony obviously played a key role in Japan's economy miracle, but the ideas and examples of what a Japanese company could accomplish not only in Japan but worldwide probably played a bigger role in the Japanese economic miracle which helped to improve the standards of living of millions of individuals in Japan.

Samsung

Samsung Electronics Co. Ltd. (SEC) grew out of a small export company started in 1938 in Taegu, Korea by Byung-Chull Lee. The small company grew quickly and became one of the nation's *chaebols* and in 1969 ventured in the field of electronics. It first product, a black-and-white TV, was sold under the Sanyo name in 1971. Samsung, which literally means three stars in Korean, has since grown into one of the world's best known brand names and manufacturers of consumer electronics (Moon and Lee, 2004; Hipsher et al., 2007: 77).

In the 1970s, following the example of Sony and other Japanese companies, Korean planners advocated the development of a domestic electronics industry as it was felt this industry would help link South Korea with the emerging global economic system and the strategy of producing high-value products would fit into a nation with few natural resources, high-skilled workers and low-priced labor. Korea was very much a developing nation when Samsung embarked on this strategy of entering the consumer electronics industry (Yu, 1999).

Samsung first began producing products which were in the decline stage of the product life cycle and competed on price. But the company systematically and steadily followed a path where it progressively began moving up the ladder of the value chain until it reached the stage where it was competing in areas of emerging technologies. The strategy of starting at the low end was based on the environmental conditions at the time which included limited purchasing power in the domestic market and lack of joint venture partners willing to share high-end technologies. Moreover, there were substantial opportunities to export, primarily to the USA in the low end of the market. Therefore, the company followed the path to first invest in production facilities, gain the knowledge needed to compete and then move to developing its own products and brand names in order to be competitive in world markets (Yu, 1999: 57–9).

Samsung competed using a low-cost strategy in areas that were considered commodities up until the 1990s when it began diversifying and shifting towards more of a differentiation strategy and moved from low-end to more high-end models. At first the company relied on foreign technology and imitation, but was able to climb up the value chain and later develop its own new technologies. The company initially mostly used OEM (original equipment manufacturer) agreements and exported its products under the brand names of the buyers, but over time the company was able to switch to mostly selling its own designed and manufactured products under the Samsung brand name (Yu, 1999: 60–5). Country-of-origin image is something firms from developing countries have to overcome, but Samsung seems to have overcome this problem to a large extent (Kim, 2006) and the label 'made in Korea' is no longer associated with low-end products.

Samsung, as well as many other Korean companies, has been able to grow alongside the economic growth of the country. The private sector in Korea has driven economic growth while at the same time benefiting from this growth as well.

SEC's [Samsung Electronics Corporation] performance is neither a miracle nor a growth distorted by government subsidy. It is the result of a very carefully crafted strategy following an evolutionary learning process from simple to more complex technologies, and taking advantage of synergy effects by synchronizing the strategy variable of different dimensions, all supported by Samsung's highly disciplined corporate culture.

(Yu, 1999: 69)

Acer

Acer started small; it began with a very meager investment by its founder Stan Shih and his wife Carolyn Yeh in 1977 and initially only had a handful of employees. The company's original name was Multitech but the name was changed to Acer in 1998. The original focus of the company was on distributing electronic parts and consulting on microprocessor technology but soon moved into computer manufacturing and became an OEM supplier for ITT in 1982. The company sold its first computer under the Acer brand in 1984 (Hon et al., 2000).

As Acer expanded there was a change in leadership and a move towards a more diversified strategy was attempted; however, this strategy nearly led the company to bankruptcy and Stan Shih, the founder, returned to take charge of the firm. Stan Shih, known for his hard work, intelligence, logical thinking and low-key approach to management, believed there was a fundamental change happening in the computer industry where profits in the middle of the value chain, assembly, were being squeezed and therefore he placed more of the company's strategic focus on the other ends, component manufacturing and marketing and sales. The company also made a number of changes in organizational structure and become more of a decentralized organization in the 1990s (Mathews, 2006).

Acer's initial period of growth came from using a low-cost leadership strategy, but as both the external economic environment in Taiwan and internal knowledge within the country grew the company was able to move into a differentiation strategy in a very competitive and high-tech market. As seen in other Asian manufacturing firms, Acer used licensing and other foreign sources of information and connections to improve its own operational systems, including improving its production processes. Today Acer is one of the symbols of Taiwan's success in economic development and has spun off a number of other companies which have helped drive the economy of the island forward (Chu et al., 2010).

One of the problems Acer had to overcome was the image of Taiwan as a low-cost producer of low-quality products. In building its brand name, Acer might have been helped to some extent by the government's promotional campaigns to upgrade the image of Taiwan's businesses (Amine and Chao, 2005). Nevertheless, overcoming negative country-of-origin images, especially in high-tech products, is something all companies and governments from LDCs need to do jointly to successfully move up international value chains.

Analysis

In looking at the examples of successful Asian economies and companies, we see both differences and a few common threads. In some cases, such as in Japan and South Korea, growth has been mostly driven by domestic firms using imported foreign technology while in other cases, such as Singapore, much of the growth has been driven by foreign firms using FDI. In general, the Asian success stories include more government intervention in the economies than is normally advocated by most free market economists, but intervention has been mostly indirect in nature while specific business decisions were left to business leaders. Moreover, while many economically successful Asian nations benefited in the early stages from protected markets, none of the successful nations isolated themselves from the outside world and many successful Asian firms found ways to integrate themselves into global production and knowledge networks. The overall economies and many individual businesses and industries have risen together, yet determining how much of this growth was due to specific government policies and how much was driven by the private sector despite government interference is open to speculation.

After examining the example of Singapore, Ying et al. (2010: 124–5) made four general suggestions for nations looking to reduce poverty through economic growth: (1) understand the short-term trade-offs, for example, possible greater inequality in the near term, needed to generate long-term economic growth; (2) develop macroeconomic stability, while also realizing there are multiple paths a country can take to achieve this goal; (3) localize policies; and (4) have leadership who are both competent and have a greater desire to see growth and poverty reduction in their nation than to promote their own political and economic interests.

Aoki et al. (2010), after looking at Japan's success in the postwar era, saw the use and adaptation of foreign technology as being a key factor in growth; however, it was also found government policies and local conditions played a critical role. Having a well-educated population with work experience as well as building the necessary infrastructure allowed the productive use of imported new technologies and new ideas from abroad. Without significant human capital and infrastructure, the gains from joining global production and knowledge networks would have been limited.

Brady and Spence (2010: 14) found economic success was not a simple matter of liberalizing and privatizing; instead, governments often have to make trade-offs due to local political conditions and government's fail at times by doing too much and at other times by doing too little.

The amount and type of government involvement and foreign investment in an economy has differed in different situations, yet the one common ingredient in each recipe of economic success and poverty reduction in Asia used to date is a healthy dose of dynamic private sector led by innovative and ambitious business entrepreneurs and leaders.

6

China

Abstract: China is one of the world's oldest civilizations and has a long, varied and fascinating history. Chinese political history is one of various dynasties, which have risen, ruled and eventually fallen. Currently, the country is politically ruled by a single party, the Communist Party, although a shift towards more of a market economy continues. Although still much less economically developed than the most developed economies, China has experienced amazing recent success in economic growth and poverty reduction. Three case studies of manufacturing firms in China are examined.

Key words: China, history, Mao Zedong, Deng Xiaoping, inequality, case studies.

Country background

'Historians may never capture reality, but that is not to say that there is no reality to be captured' (Legge, 1992: 50).

> Rightly the Chinese pride themselves on being the heirs of the world's oldest continuous civilization, stretching back at least to the Bronze Age of the Shang dynasty of 1600 BC. Today there can be no doubt that a new version of China is being born. Yet it cannot exist apart from its country's history. As Confucius is said to have said, understanding what the future holds requires grasping the lessons of the past. In other words, to comprehend the most important new force in today's world, one has to see where China has come from and what has shaped it.
>
> (Fenby, 2008: xvii)

China is one of the world's oldest and largest civilizations, is spread out over a vast area and houses a large number of ethnic groups and native languages. No book length work, let alone a single chapter in a book, can do more than scratch the surface of the history and the cultures found in this fascinating country. What constitutes China has not always been clear, while there has been a general consensus amongst historians that China has traditionally included the area which is called *guannei*, in the heart of the country, while other regions which are politically within the China of today have not always been considered part of the Middle Kingdom. These disputed regions include the areas which have traditionally been called Manchuria, Inner Mongolia, Xinjiang, Tibet, Yunnan and Taiwan. However, the core of China has been ruled by various Chinese governments, have used the Chinese written languages and have followed Chinese traditions for at least 2,000 years (Crossley, 2010: 66). Today political China encompasses many outlying areas which were not part of traditional China and the legitimacy of Chinese control of some of these outlying regions, specifically Tibet and Taiwan, is open to dispute.

Humans have been living in what today is called China for a very long time, the archeological evidence suggests humans, or ancestors of modern humans, have been living in the region near modern day Beijing for at least 200,000 years and probably much longer. Moreover, it has been believed humans with distinctly Asian features have lived in the region for at least 12,000 years (Hucker, 1975: 21–30). Rice and millet cultivation and pottery making are believed to have originated in ancient times in China, with rice cultivation springing up in the region of the lower Yangtze around 6,000 BC (Bellwood, 1992: 92) and pottery making in China could have begun as early as 10,000 years ago (Fairbanks et al., 1989).

Chinese legends contend the earliest civilizations in China were ruled by mythical individuals who were followed by the Hsia dynasty, whose existence according to the legends extended from 2205 to 1766 BC. It is often believed these early civilizations included being ruled by the legendary first emperor, Huangdi, who legend states came from Xinzheng in today's Henan province (Fairbanks et al., 1989: 21), a city where much of this book was written. However, the first dynasty that left written as well as archeological evidence was the Shang dynasty which historians have dated as lasting from 1766 to 1122 BC. However, this political dynasty covered only a tiny fraction of the China of today and probably had limited control of the population (Hucker, 1975: 26–30).

The 'mandate of heaven', as rule over the country would later be called, shifted to the Western Chou (Zhou), 1122–771 BC, when the final ruler of the Shang who was reported to be a despot was overthrown. The Western Chou was replaced by the Eastern Chou dynasty which lasted from 770 to 256 BC. The Chinese state was greatly expanded and much of what is considered as part of traditional Chinese culture arose during this dynasty (Hucker, 1975: 30–40). Next came the 'Warring States' period, which has been the focus of much of Chinese literature, both ancient and modern, and then the short-lived Ch'in (Qin) dynasty, 221–206 BC. The 'first emperor' Qin Shi Huang, who was buried with his terracotta army in modern Xian, consolidated power and reunited China as the founder of the Ch'in dynasty (Fairbanks et al., 1989: 55–9). A nationwide system of laws, rule by an imperial household and the early formulation of Chinese bureaucracy were initiated during the Ch'in period, all of which lasted until 1911 (Ma, 2011: 66). The Han dynasty, 202 BC–AD 220, followed, which is generally thought of as a time of peace and prosperity in which the population grew, the economy expanded and culture blossomed (Hucker, 1975: 121–33).

There is no question about the success of the pre-modern Chinese economy. Higher education, a functioning bureaucracy chosen by merit, large standing armies, growth of large cities and technological inventions all progressed in China centuries before they became widespread in Europe (Deng, 2003: 308).

The Han followed the pattern found in the other dynasties that came before and after; it began under the rule of a dynamic and capable leader, it rose, prospered, got complacent, declined and then lost the mandate of heaven and fell. After the fall of the Han, a long period of political fragmentation ensued, AD 220–589. Yet, all through the centuries of division the concept of a single China under a single ruler endured (Hucker, 1975: 133–7). Although the country lacked political stability during these years, it was a period of substantial cultural growth and the introduction of new religious ideas (Fairbanks, 1989: 83–99). The leaders of the Sui dynasty, AD 581–618, were the ones to eventually reunite the country which was followed by another golden era in Chinese history, the T'ang dynasty which lasted from AD 618 to 907 (Hucker, 1975: 137–47). However, the inevitable dynastic cycle repeated itself and upon the T'ang dynasty's descent from power another period of political fragmentation with many rivals contesting for the mandate of heaven ensued (Hucker, 1975:147–8).

The dynastic cycle began again when the country was once more united under the Sung, 960–1279 and 'as always in times of prolonged domestic stability, China enjoyed great prosperity through the eleventh century' (Hucker, 1975: 272). However, after enjoying early peace and prosperity, the Sung began experiencing attacks from the north with the fiercest of these coming from the followers of Chinggas Khan (Genghis Khan) and the Sung Dynasty began to decline and eventually lost control over the country (Fairbanks et al., 1989: 123–51). Eventually, the Sung were overrun and replaced by foreigners from the north, the Mongols, who created the Yuan dynasty which at its height stretched all the way to the brink of Africa and Europe. However, over time and generations, exposure to Chinese culture began to change the country's Mongol overlords and the Mongols started acting much like the Chinese. The country continued to be ruled through its pre-existing bureaucracy and maintained its Chinese culture and ways of government (Fairbanks et al., 1989: 162–76).

Once again the reins of power proved too slippery to hold indefinitely and, going from the most powerful rulers on the planet, the Mongol empire began to decline and in China the Yuan dynasty was replaced by the Ming. 'The Ming period from 1368 to 1644 is one of the great eras of orderly government and social stability in human history' (Fairbanks et al., 1989: 177). It was during the Ming period that 'traditional Chinese society and culture attained modern maturity' (Hucker, 1975: 288).

Foreign trade has been a central part of Chinese economic life for centuries. The Chinese were well-known traders throughout Southeast Asia and competed with Muslims from India, but in the sixteenth and seventeenth centuries the Chinese were most likely the most active traders throughout Southeast Asia (Reid, 1992).

After a period of decline, the Ming forces were driven from power by another group of foreigners from the north, the Manchus, who created the Ch'ing (Qing) dynasty which lasted from AD 1644 to 1911. Although considered foreigners by most Chinese, the Manchu Empire 'became a great defender of orthodox Confucius ideology and a champion of a centralized political system with a civil bureaucracy' (Ma, 2011: 71). The Ch'ing followed the pattern of other dynasties: starting strong and then gradually weakening. The Ch'ing rulers were able to maintain control for a surprisingly long period, especially considering the pressure coming from European imperial and colonial expansion. Despite pressures from European forces with superior military technology, the Ch'ing were able to hold the country together while losing a few peripheral territories, such as Hong Kong to the British, Macao to the Portuguese and, after conquering and annexing Taiwan in 1683, losing control of the island to the Japanese (Wakeman, 1975).

Early in the twentieth century a movement to end the absolute rule of the emperors and replace it with some form of more democratic rule took shape. The revolution got off to a premature start when the police discovered radicals plotting in and around Wuhan in October 1911. The radicals had little choice, as it was either fight or be executed for treason. After persuading Li Yuanhong, a senior military officer, to lead the fight, defections by the Ch'ing troops soon became common, the rebellion spread unexpectedly from province to province and the weakened Ch'ing forces could not hold the country together (Fenby, 2008: 119–21).

Sun Yat-sen was one of the leaders of the movement to transform China from an imperial dynasty to a modern democracy; however, when the Ch'ing dynasty started to crumble in 1911, due to Sun's lack of support from any existing military troops, he agreed to allow Yuan Shikai to become President of the Chinese Republic with a promise of holding elections and creation of a parliament. After Sun's party, the Guomindang (KMT), dominated in the elections of 1913, Yuan refused to accept the results and had Sun's top aide at the time, Song Jiaoren, killed. Sun fled to Japan and any semblance of an elected government disappeared (Crossley, 2010: 150).

Although China was still officially called a republic, Yuan at first consolidated his power and created an administration made up of members of the former imperial dynasty. In 1915 Yuan declared he was the new emperor in an elaborate ceremony and attempted to create a new dynasty; however, outside his small group of loyal supporters he had no support from other segments of society. After only three months Yuan abdicated the title he had given himself and died shortly thereafter (Fenby, 2008: 135–38).

Upon the death of Yuan Shikai, the former vice president Li Yuan became the official leader of the country. However, his leadership was not accepted by many military leaders and in 1917 Li signed a decree allowing the general Zhang Xun to reestablish the Ch'ing Emperor by placing 11-year-old Puyi, the last emperor, on the throne. However, this did not last and soon the façade of political unity of the country was again broken and a period of rule by various warlords over different sections of society ensued (Fenby, 2008: 139–56).

Sun Yat-sen returned to Southern China in 1922 and attempted with the aid of his chief military aide, Chiang Kai-shek, to reunify the country under the KMT Party based on left-leaning democratic principles. On 12 March 1925 Sun died of liver cancer but the KMT lived on led by Chiang Kai-shek. The KMT along with the Communist Party, which at times it cooperated with while at other times it fought against, turned out to be the dominant contenders to become the next unifiers of the country and gain the mandate of heaven (Fenby, 2008: 157–82).

The beginnings of the Chinese Communist movement are generally thought to have sprung up at Peking University, with much of the earliest organizing and promotion of a Chinese approach to using Marxist/Leninist theories being credited to Li Dazhao, a professor of economics and head librarian at the university (Crossley, 2010: 169).

China fell into a state of constant warfare, a combination of internal civil wars and external wars against Japanese aggression and in support of the Communist regime in North Korea starting around 1926 and not ending until 1953. This period of warfare was devastating in terms of lives lost, economic stagnation and creating a general feeling of fear and insecurity throughout the country (Crossley, 2010). It is most likely this long experience of war and internal strife helps explain the current emphasis in China on the need for stability which sometimes results in lack of tolerance for open disagreement on major policy issues.

The Chinese Communist Party came close to dying in infancy as the KMT's military under the leadership of Chiang Kai-shek nearly crushed the movement and executed many members of the Communist leadership. Mao Zedong emerged as the new leader of the Communist movement and – through gaining popular support in the rural areas for helping the poor, a reputation for fighting the Japanese, exploiting the legend of the Long March and due to the weaknesses of the nationalists, as Chiang Kai-shek and the KMT were often called – the Communist Party eventually gained ascendency and unified the country in 1949 while the nationalists retreated and formed a new government in Taiwan (Fenby, 2008: 217–350; Crossley, 2010: 205).

However, the unification of the country in 1949 under the Communist Party and Mao Zedong did not bring instant stability to the country. Imposition of collectivist agriculture cooperatives and factories, military adventures into Tibet and Korea, the unrealistic policies of the Great Leap Forward and the Cultural Revolution all added to the country's suffering and woes (Chen, 1987: 4; Li and Yang, 2005; Fenby, 2008: 353–495). Friedman (1994) attributed much of extreme nature of many of the nationalistic policies of the Mao era to lingering anti-imperialist sentiment fueled by a feeling of humiliation amongst the Chinese people caused by a series of perceived injustices imposed upon the Chinese by Western powers and the Japanese stretching back to the opium wars of the nineteenth century. The Great Leap Forward, an attempt to collectivize agricultural production and spread collective small-scale industry into the countryside, had especially tragic results. 'The loss of something on the order of 36,000,000 people without a war merely as a result of ideological misguidance and economic mismanagement, in less than three years, is a unique atrocity in human history' (Crossley, 2010: 226). The Chinese invasion of its neighbor Vietnam in 1979, which resulted in what at best can be described as a stalemate, showed the weakness of the Chinese government and its inability to impose its will on individuals and governments outside its borders (Chen, 1987).

China, while attempting to promote socialism abroad, was becoming more isolated. There was open antagonism against the United States and other 'imperial powers' and – with a widening split with the other Communist power at the time, the Soviet Union – most of the Communist world sided with the more powerful Soviet Union. Against this backdrop, the historical trip of the American President, Richard Nixon, who had a reputation of being strongly anti-Communist, occurred and 'opened up' China to the outside world and the mainland Chinese government soon replaced the government of Taiwan as the official representation of China in the United Nations (Fenby, 2008: 496–507).

After the death of Mao, and following a brief period where Hua Guofeng ruled with a similar ideology to Mao's, a reformer who was both a long-standing member of the Communist Party and a victim of the cultural revolution, Deng Xiaoping, led a faction to power which was to change the direction of the country from one with a strict Communist economic system to one which has become known as market socialism (Fenby, 2008: 508–27). For the first three decades of Communist rule, the economy of China stagnated but, since the market-based reforms began by Deng in 1978, the changes have been staggering. GDP per capita has increased 40 fold and, while the country's average income is low by Western standards, the improvements in measurable aspects of standards of living have improved dramatically (Kuhn, 2010: 3).

Since the reforms of Deng have been in place, the Communist Party has retained control by balancing its retention of a political monopoly with more economic and personal openness and freedom, which is a prerequisite for a dynamic market economy. There appears to be an unspoken agreement between the population and the government that, as long as the government continues to produce economic gains and improved standards of living, the population will show patience in expecting political reforms (Reid, 2011: 20). While this balancing act has been successful and the contradiction of having a Communist government with a market economy hasn't seriously been challenged, it would appear this situation cannot remain indefinitely.

After two decades of economic and social transformations, today's China is freer and more prosperous than at any time in its history.

> Yet politically it remains a centrally controlled party-state. Sooner or later, political reform will be pushed onto the national agenda.
>
> (Zhu, 2006: 103)

There is no doubt about China's economic and political rise, and the Chinese can be justifiably proud of their recent accomplishments, but whether China is going to be a regional or global superpower in the future is far from certain. China's military spending is only a small fraction of that of the USA and the country lacks much of the capacity to project its power on a global scale (Kuhn, 2010: 393–404). In addition, China is still a relatively poor country with its ranking on a GDP per capita basis not even in the top 100 countries of the world (World Bank, 2010).

In addition to currently lacking the hard powers of economic muscle or military strength to be considered a superpower, China's soft power is also limited. Li (2009: 22) stated, 'China has few political values to offer to a world dominated by Western philosophies and reveals the reality that China itself is still undergoing a profound social, economic and political transition.' While Zhang (2009) believed, 'If traditional Chinese culture still holds attraction in East Asia, contemporary China's cultural appeal is extremely limited.'

While there are glowing predictions of a powerful China, one should be somewhat careful about assuming growth and prosperity will continue. A developed and prosperous marked-based economy led by a single party which espouses socialist ideology is still an untested theory.

Glowing predictions of China's future did not begin in the twenty-first century. In a speech in 1917 in Shanghai, the American Consul General Victor Murdoch said:

> No one can reach the limits of China. China is the place of the future. I have been impressed by everything I have seen in this country, with its promise of future development, but one thought that lingers longest in my mind is this: China's future development and prosperity lie in her form of government. It must be a republic to obtain results.
>
> (Wheeler, 1919)

In accordance with this prediction, China suffered economically through most of the twentieth century under fragmented but non-democractic and then authoritarian rule. 'In the long term, the PRC regime will probably democratize as South Korea and Taiwan did' (Zhu, 2006: 139).

Business environment

Chinese economic progress in the last few decades has driven the greatest poverty reduction program the world has ever seen. Since 1978, both overall and rural poverty has been greatly reduced (Zhang and Lin, 2010: 203). The Asian Development Bank estimated from 1990 to recently the poverty rate was reduced from 32.5 to 7.1% using the $1 a day benchmark and, if $2 a day was the benchmark, the rate fell from 71.5 to 29.4% (Lin et al., 2008). 'China is ending extreme poverty, and is on its way to reversing centuries of relative decline' (Sachs, 2005: 150). Yet poverty remains a major concern and, due to the country's massive population, 'China still has the second largest share of the poor in the world' (Zhang and Wan, 2008: 33).

In general, the economic news and forecasts for China are bright. Private consumption has risen and growth has been spread out across different sectors of the economy, although inflation remains a concern. Foreign direct investment (FDI) continues to pour into the country, but also Chinese firms have increased investments abroad. The country continues to run a very large accounts surplus and there is an increasing reliance on internal consumption for growth to supplement the export-led growth the country has relied on in the past (Asian Development Bank, 2011a: 119–24). China is also engaging in more trade with developing economies and many supply chains of Chinese firms are linked with suppliers throughout Southeast Asia. Additionally, China has become the main trading partner of some other developing economies including India, Brazil and South Africa (OECD, 2010).

There are a variety of explanations for the success China has had in growing its economy and reducing its levels of poverty. Ma (2011) hypothesized having a stable monopoly on political power allows leaders to take on policies designed for long-term defense of monopoly rents instead of trying to maximize short-run revenues. This shift in focus from short run to long run allows leaders to invest in and share in the political benefits of infrastructure and other long-term projects which can assist in creating conditions for long-term growth. Jeffrey Sachs (2005: 163–4) found five reasons China was better prepared for the transition to a market economy than were Russia and Eastern Europe: (1) China did not have massive foreign debt; (2) China's long coastlines facilitate export-led growth; (3) China had an existing bridge to capitalist economies in the overseas Chinese business networks; (4) China did not experience an initial decline in oil production as happened in the former Soviet Union; and (5)

China had not previously been able to invest highly in technology and large-scale production and therefore it was relatively easier for the Chinese to adopt Western technology and production techniques. Tsui (2008: 81) felt the level of education which was much higher in China upon the start of reforms than in other countries with comparable levels of economic development was also a contributing factor to successful adaptation of a market economy.

Yet despite all the success the country is still a developing economy with considerable challenges ahead of it. China's economy and business environment is often split into two. 'While Chinese exporters are increasingly connected to regional and global production networks, the majority of Chinese firms are still native producers, manufacturing at the lower end of the chain of production networks dominated by large multinational corporations' (Zhang, 2010: 17). Economic growth has been driven by the private sector, and the productivity of private firms is much higher than in state-owned enterprises (Dougherty and McGuckin, 2008; Zou and Adams, 2008). However, for political and propaganda purposes it is unlikely the state will completely privatize all firms and these inefficient state-owned firms could create a drag on future economic growth.

While economic growth has brought improved standards of living and reductions in poverty, it has also significantly increased income inequality. There is significant inequality due to geography with coastal regions doing much better than inland regions, and there is also a growing divide between rural and urban incomes (Aroca et al., 2008; Wan et al., 2010). China's Gini Coefficient score shows it has far more inequality than most developed economies and many developing economies and 'China is being transformed from an egalitarian society to a highly unequal one' (Wang, 2008: 18).

One group that has helped drive China's growth but has not shared equally in the benefits of growth is the vast army of migrant workers mostly coming to the cities from rural regions. These migrants mostly work in low-paid, labor-intensive and often dangerous jobs with little security and no formal protection. These workers are also very vulnerable to even mild slowdowns in economic growth (Wu et al., 2010: 20; Zhang and Lin, 2010).

While levels of rural poverty appeared to have been lowering up until the 1990s, that trend appears to have stopped and might have even reversed with increases in poverty in the rural areas as migrants flock to the cities in search of improved lives leaving the old behind; there has also been a slowing in the reduction of urban poverty in recent years (Zhang and

Wan, 2008). While most attention on poverty in China is on rural areas and the plight of migrant workers, Wu et al. (2010) reminded the public that there is also significant poverty within urban China mostly caused by dislocations of low-skilled older workers as many state-owned businesses have privatized or have had to become more competitive and therefore have shed inefficient workers.

The average income in Shanghai is well over ten times as high as in the western province of Guizhou, and the gap has grown considerably since reforms began and is around eight times as high as in the other western provinces of Gansu, Guangxi and Yunnan (Aroca et al., 2008: 125; Lin and Liu, 2008: 56). The *China Daily* newspaper (2012) reported per capita annual income in rural areas averaged 6,977 yuan compared to 21,810 yuan for individuals living in urban areas.

As regional income inequalities continue to rise, regional inequalities in other areas are also seen. Most foreign investment continues to pour into coastal areas while little FDI has been moving inland (Tsui, 2008: 97). Although levels of educational inequality are declining slightly, students from the less prosperous provinces are at a distinct disadvantage to students from the more prosperous coastal regions. Not only are students in the inland and western regions less likely to have access to quality teaching and educational facilities, they are also forced to score higher on entrance exams than are students from more prosperous regions for placement in universities (Lee, 2008). Eastern China dominates scientific and technological innovation within the country (Fan and Wan, 2008) which would likely give an advantage to firms that are closer to centers of innovation, as they would be more likely to be able to benefit from spillover effects. In addition, the development of financial institutions has been faster in the coastal areas and 'regions with higher level of financial development tend to enjoy faster economic growth' (Liang, 2008: 120).

It is likely that part of the geographic inequality is due to the proximity of firms from the coastal regions to ports allowing companies to engage in international trade and exporting (Liang, 2008). In addition, it is likely misguided development policies also played a role in creating the massive levels of geographical inequality. In an attempt to spur development, during the days of central planning, the central government moved many heavy industries to inland provinces which are now unable to compete due to transportation costs, lack of human capital and lack of financing. It has been proposed this was an ineffective policy but, instead, as inland areas are heavily populated but short in capital, most inland areas subjected to market forces would have specialized in those industries that are labor intensive rather than capital intensive, as this would better fit local circumstances (Lin and Liu 2008; Tsui, 2008).

To reduce poverty and continue to improve the quality of life of the citizens of China the country has many challenges to address including maintaining social stability and reducing the massive amounts of pollution the country is currently producing (Reid, 2011: 28). Chinese industries have abominable safety records and workplace fatalities are far from rare. Because of the country's one-child policy China faces a future with a large percentage of its population being elderly, which is likely to put a heavy strain on the economy (Kuhn, 2010: 168, 199).

'It is folly to generalize too much about Chinese culture and philosophy. China is a huge country with significant geographically-based differences in how people perceive the world' (Gallo, 2011: 41). Although throughout the centuries many ethnic groups have been absorbed into the culture, today less than 10% of the population identify themselves as 'non-Han' minorities (Crossley, 2010: 177).

Many Chinese business practices and cultural influences have received a lot of attention. The use of reciprocal business relations often referred to as *guanxi* in China has been well documented (e.g., Keller and Kronstedt, 2005) as has the influence of Confucian philosophy on Chinese businesses and culture (e.g., Yan and Sorenson, 2004).

Another value found in Chinese culture which affects how Chinese managers run a business is called 'the Mean'.

> The Mean is one of the core values in Chinese culture. The nature of the Mean encompasses the notion of appropriately balanced relationships between man and man, man and society, man and nature, and well-adjusted relations among nations. Carrying out the Mean implies that one is being neutral and is finding a balance between Yin (feminine or negative principle) and Yang (masculine or positive principle), black and white, right and left, good and bad, and them and us.
>
> (Chen, 2009: 86)

Following the Mean implies an avoidance of extremes and finding a middle path. A leader following this principle 'will often move to the center on an issue, rather than decide for or against it' (Gallo, 2011: 60). This principle may be evident in how the Chinese often try to handle conflicts within a company, as Ma (2007) found Chinese managers were more likely to use indirect methods to avoid conflicts and compromise than were Western managers, although Chinese managers could also be direct and very competitive when deemed necessary.

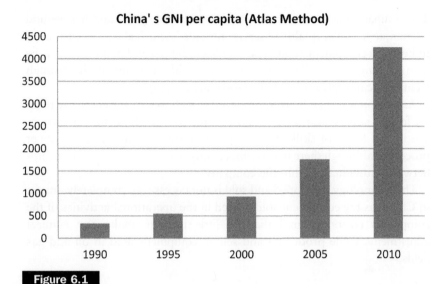

Figure 6.1

Source: Asian Development Bank, 2011b: 163)

China is changing. There has been a shift from employment in state-owned factories and in agriculture to more opportunities in the private sector (OECD, 2010; Wu et al., 2010: 8). Chinese business practices and the relationship of the people to their government are also changing (Gallo, 2011).

> For all the vast economic changes brought about by reform, the greatest change in China has not been economic. The truly greatest change has been the transformation of the *spirit* of the Chinese people – how they think and how they feel – and the sense of confidence they have in their country and their future.
>
> (Kuhn, 2010: 193)

Case studies

Beijing HAMO Energy Technology Co. Ltd.

Beijing HAMO Energy Technology Co. Ltd. sells surface facilities equipment and technical services to extraction companies in the oil and gas industry in China. The company uses a differentiation strategy with higher than average prices but competes on quality of products and service.

The company has been in business for nearly nine years and has around 240 employees. The quality of service provided, which allows its customers to keep the equipment running and to keep the gas and oil pumping, is its main selling point. The company also differentiates itself through technological innovation and new-product development.

As a company in an industry involved in technology, the company relies on formal supervision and, as most of the jobs in the company require specialized levels of skills, the company mostly uses formal recruitment processes, although there is also a lot of emphasis on personal relationships between individuals within the company.

The technology developed and sold is not necessarily completely unique to China, as the equipment sold is used in the operational activities of the company's customers and there is little need to make any cultural adjustments while producing and selling equipment used in oil and gas fields.

Zhongsheng

Zhongsheng is located in Xingxiang, Henan province and is in the industrial supplies industry. The company produces powder coatings and cold-water paints for industrial customers. The company has been in business for around 9 years and has around 40 employees. The company uses a differentiation strategy and, as there are few direct competitors, the company's main competition comes from different, and less expensive, types of metal finishing. The company strives to create new technologies and new uses for its existing processes; therefore, it works with local universities to continue to develop its technologies. The company's products are considered to be more environmentally friendly and of higher quality than more traditional forms of metal finishing.

Henan is located in inland China and is generally not well connected with the export-orientated economies of the coastal region, and therefore Zhongsheng mostly supplies customers in the domestic market.

While skill is an important factor in recruiting new staff, personality and being acquainted with current staff members also play a part. The management style is mostly personal with most instructions given orally and there is a lot of direct contact between the workers and management. The wages paid to employees are around the same level as the industry average.

Operationally, the company uses the basic technologies which were developed outside China, but the company is always looking for ways to make incremental improvements to the technology it uses to better serve its customers.

Beijing Zhongke Zenith Energy-Saving Technology Co. Ltd.

Beijing Zhongke Zenith Energy-Saving Technology Co. Ltd. is an agent of Riello, an Italian company that produces boiler plant and boiler room projects. The company supplies equipment for industrial use. The company has been around for about 9 years and has around 40 employees, most of them technicians. The company's prices are higher than the industry's average but the company differentiates itself primarily through its after-sales service. The company is known to go out of its way to ensure the products it sells match the needs of the customers.

Recruitment of personnel is mostly done through recommendations by others in the business and the management style is mostly personal in nature with few formal written instructions. To get and retain top-quality staff the company pays wages that are higher than the industry average.

The company sells products that are similar to those sold around the world; however, by providing local servicing the company ensures use of the products meets local needs.

Analysis

The three examples provided are all industrial suppliers, and therefore part of the vibrant manufacturing industry which has exploded throughout China. Although China is not a wealthy country and limiting costs is a major concern for most Chinese manufacturers, each of the companies used a differentiation strategy instead of a low-cost or low-cost leadership strategy. When purchasing equipment to be used in operational activities within a company, low price does not automatically mean low cost for the customer. It is speculated that companies can use a differentiation strategy as higher quality and better service can result in lowering manufacturing customers' overall operational costs as opposed to purchasing lower priced products that may have inferior quality and poorer after-sales service.

Although companies might use a slightly more personal management style and more informal recruiting than would be the norm in

Figure 6.2 Xinzheng, Henan, China

Western countries, overall operations would appear to be consistent with internationally accepted best practices. As all three companies produced or sold equipment to be used in operational activities in the companies they were sold to, there was limited need for adjustment to local cultural environmental conditions. Equipment used for oil and gas fields, powder coating and paint, and boilers have basically the same uses in different locations regardless of cultural environment.

7

Vietnam

Abstract: In much of the world, the country of Vietnam is associated with its civil war involving American and international troops, but it has also been influenced by its history both before and after the war. Much like in China, the country has recently moved to more of a market-based economy while retaining a political system where power is monopolized by a single party, the Communist Party. Since the reforms of the late 1980s, Vietnam's economy has become more linked with the global economy, and the subsequent economic growth and poverty reduction have been significant. Four case studies of companies in Vietnam are examined.

Key words: Vietnam, France, colonization, warfare, America, economics, case studies, Ho Chi Minh.

Country background

For many outsiders, especially Americans, the name 'Vietnam' is almost always followed by the term 'war'. But of course Vietnam is a country – not a war – with a long and varied history.

Discoveries of the existence of a group of people often referred to as the *Hoabinhian*, who appear to have been dominant in Southeast Asia from approximately 13,000 BC up until the emergence of an agricultural society around 10,000 years later, have been found in Northern Vietnam, although it is not likely these people were the ancestors of the present day Vietnamese. Evidence has been found of rice cultivation possibly as early as the fifth century BC but definitely from at the latest the late third or early second centuries BC in the Red River Valley just north of present day Hanoi. Evidence shows nearly all residents of the area after the introduction of agriculture were living in the valleys and the 'hill tribes' came into existence at a later date (Bellwood, 1992).

The people living in Northern Vietnam apparently had contacts with the Chinese from an early date. Bronze making appears to have begun in the area in the second century BC and Vietnam became a protectorate of the Han Empire in 111 BC and a full Chinese province in AD 43. However, even before the beginning of political domination by the Chinese, there is evidence of the use of irrigation canals and wet-rice agricultural techniques supporting quite a large population which would have required some form of centralized government (Bellwood, 1992).

Vietnamese legends were promulgated in official court annals during the 15th century to give the Vietnamese a separate history from the Chinese. Legend states that the origin of the Kings of Vietnam can be traced back to a legendary Chinese ruler who was called Than Nong in Vietnamese. The great grandson of Than Nong who was called Emperor Minh had a son, Loc Tuc, who refused to take the throne; instead, he persuaded his older brother to become emperor and went south to reign in a new land. Loc Tuc then had a son called Dragon Lord Lac who lived in a watery kingdom and who with Au Co had 100 sons from which all Vietnamese can claim ancestry (Dror, 2007: 24–5).

By the third century AD, Chinese officials had effectively incorporated Northern Vietnam into the Chinese empire. The area remained under Chinese control although during times of political instability and decentralization in China local rulers in the region often declared their independence; however, there was little resistance when forces from both the Sui and Tang dynasties returned to take back political control (Taylor, 1992: 137). At around this same time the coasts of Central Vietnam were becoming stops on international trade routes and the Kingdoms of Fu-nan and Lin-yi emerged, which were ruled in the Indian Hindu style, from where goods would be carried to Angkor in Cambodia. At the time, Buddhism was taking hold in the Northern areas of Vietnam (Hall, 1992: 263).

The area of central Vietnam become known as Champa, which was probably not a single political entity, although the people in the region appeared to share cultural and linguistic characteristics that made the region distinctly different from the land of the Viets from the North. It would appear the Cham territories had political and cultural connections with Malays also living along the coastal areas of international trade routes, but the connection is not well understood (Taylor, 1992: 153–57).

With Tang (Chinese) dynasty control over Vietnam returning in the seventh century, the site where Hanoi now stands became the center of the political leadership in Vietnam (Hall, 1992: 264; Taylor, 1992: 137). Chinese influence continued while local political elites started to emerge. The kings that ruled from around 960 to shortly before the millennium consolidated power and gained recognition from the Chinese authorities (Taylor, 1992: 139). At this time Vietnamese society had developed at the village level sophisticated systems to control the monsoon-fed waters flowing down the Red River, and the staple foods were fish and rice (Hall, 1992: 261).

In 1009, Ly Cong Uan, who was given the posthumous name Ly Thai To, rose to power and began the Ly dynasty. He was known as a progressive and wise ruler and power was consolidated during his reign through military adventures, building a capital, establishing an effective tax system and a focus on religious, particularly Buddhist, affairs. His son, Ly Phat Ma who was later called Ly Thai Tong reigned from 1028 to 1054 and was known for his enlightened rule and intellectual capacity. Buddhism flourished under the Ly dynasty and it was supplemented with the introduction of worship of native spirits that protected the royal family and developed the idea of the Vietnamese version of the ruler having the mandate of heaven independent of the Chinese emperor (Taylor, 1992: 140–7)

But as each Chinese dynasty also found out, the mandate of heaven can only be held temporarily and Ly power faded and the Tran eventually gained the upper hand and declared a new dynasty in 1225. The Tran instituted a merit-based exam system for its bureaucracy, based on the Chinese model, to broaden and improve the administration of the country. The Tran, who at times allied with various rulers of Champa, were able to resist the invasions of the world's most powerful military force, those of the Mongols who had conquered all of China and much of the rest of the world, on three separate occasions in 1257–8, 1284 and 1287–8 (Taylor, 1992: 148–9). The bravery and success of the defenders of the country during this era are still celebrated in Vietnam to this day. Resistance to Chinese attempts to subdue the country has had a central role in creating Vietnamese culture, and being non-Chinese has been an important element in how the Vietnamese see themselves (Andaya, B., 1992: 415).

The rulers of Champa at the time were heavily dependent on international trade and kept up a series of military raids to gather both plunder and slaves for trade. The Chams were able to sack the Kingdom of Angkor in 1177 and made frequent raids into Northern Vietnam during the decline of the Tran. The Chams, under Che Bong Nga, as he was known to the Vietnamese, in the late fourteenth century sacked the Vietnamese capital three times (Hall, 1992: 259; Taylor, 1992: 155).

In 1406, the armies of the Ming dynasty of China invaded and occupied a politically weakened *Dai Viet* (Vietnam) with the intention of turning it once again into a Chinese province, but Vietnamese resistance to the Chinese occupation gathered around a landowner from Thanh Hoa named Le Loi and, after military victories in 1426 and 1427, the surviving Ming troops were allowed to evacuate and a new dynasty, the Le dynasty, came into existence in 1428 (Taylor, 1992: 150–1).

In 1460, one of the most revered rulers in Vietnamese history Le Thanh Ton ascended the throne and reigned until his death in 1497. His reign is remembered as a time of national progress with the establishment of a system of government that would outlive the dynasty, a period of great scholarship and the creation of works of literature, and military expansion resulting in the final defeat of Champa, whose citizens the Northern Viets felt were culturally and intellectually inferior. The expanded territory of *Dai Viet* became more economically diverse with increased land for agricultural production and control of coastal trade. However, the dynasty fell quickly into decline upon Le Than Ton's death (Andaya, B., 1992: 415; Hall, 1992: 267–69; Taylor, 1992: 150–55).

From 1505 until 1527 the country was in political turmoil with eight different kings taking the throne, six of whom were assassinated by order of rivals for the throne. In 1527 the Le dynasty came to an end and was replaced by the Mac but soon after the Nguyen clan, who claimed to represent the Le, gained control of the south–central area of Vietnam. The Chinese were called in to mediate the dispute and the Chinese decided the Mac should govern the North and the Le with the Nguyen the South, setting a precedence of divided control over the nation which has plagued the country for centuries (Andaya, B., 1992: 415).

The survivors of the Le escaped into the Lao principalities and with the help of the Nguyen and Trinh clans eventually regained power, at least in name if not in reality. Nguyen Kim was the leader of the Nguyen while Trinh Kiem became the leader of what evolved into the rival clan. In 1558 the Nguyen, led at this time by Nguyen Hoang, became the rulers of the southern parts of Vietnam while the North was governed by the Trinh. In 1647 the Trinh from the North launched a military campaign against the Nguyen in the South in order to unite the country, the conflict lasting nearly half a century (Dutton, 2006: 19–21).

After the end of hostilities in which neither side emerged victorious both the North and South concentrated on internal matters although both sides pretended the Le emperor was still the head of state. Despite today's official Vietnamese government policy of focusing on the unity of the Vietnamese throughout history, many historians feel the Trinh and the Nguyen-controlled areas should be thought of as separate nations and this division between North and South created during the time of the two clans has had an influence on the country's subsequent history. The Trinh of the north traded with and were more culturally orientated towards China, and styled their administration on Confucian principles and Chinese models, while the South traded with and had more similarities to the other peoples of Southeast Asia (Andaya, B., 1992: 437; Dutton, 2006: 22–34). Even today, the division remains. The term *mien bac* (north) when uttered by someone from *mien nam* (the south) can be thought of as a derogatory term or just as a description of the origin of an individual, depending on intonation, and the same applies to the use of the term *mien nam* by someone from *mien bac*.

In the latter part of the eighteenth century there emerged a new political movement, called the Tay Son meaning the 'Western Mountain', in central Vietnam and was led by the brothers, Nguyen Nhac, Nguyen Hue and Nguyen Lu and their search for political power engulfed the entire region in warfare. The movement began more or less as a gang of bandits but gathered followers due to frustrations over the economic conditions caused by declining trade, high taxes and the corruption of Nguyen clan leaders. The Tay Son eventually became rulers of a united nation, if only for a short time (Andaya, B., 1992: 447; Dutton, 2006).

The Tay Son leaders formed an alliance with the Trinh and attacked the Nguyen in the South, and in 1777 the Trinh allowed Nguyen Nhac (one of the brothers of the Tay Son movement and not one of the Nguyen clan) political control of the South. After pacifying the South, in 1786 Nguyen Hue (another borther of the Tay Son and again not to be confused with the leaders of the Nguyen clan) led an army to the Northern capital at Thang Long and installed the Le emperor back on the throne, although now it was the Tay Son and not the Trinh leaders who called the shots. However, there was a falling out between Nguyen Hue and his brother Nguyen Nhac and the country was partitioned once again with different brothers ruling different regions. In 1788 the Ch'ing (Qing), who were now ruling China, invaded Northern Vietnam driving out the Tay Son from the capital. Political confusion reached its height at this time: with Le Chieu Thong, backed by the Ch'ing, claiming to be the emperor; with Nguyen Hue, now calling himself the Quang Trung emperor, actually ruling over much of the North; with Nguyen Nhac ruling the central region under the title of the Thai Duc emperor; and with even farther south the remnants of the armies of the Nguyen, led by Nguyen Anh, controlling that area. During *Tet* (Lunar New Year), the armies of the Quang Trung Emperor launched a surprise attack which drove the Chinese out and with them the

Le emperor (Dutton, 2006: 90–107). Soon after taking over control of the throne, the Tay Son leaders resumed the country's tributary relationship with the Chinese (Kathirithamby-Wells, 1992: 588).

However, upon the deaths of Nguyen Hue and Nguyen Nhac and with other problems such as crop failures and economic disruptions as a result of all the fighting, the Tay Son government was much weakened. The armies of the Nguyen – with the help of Chinese pirates, Cambodian mercenaries and backed by the French – 'liberated' and united the country with surprising ease in 1802. The Chinese recognized the legitimacy of the new regime and a chaotic and violent period came to an end (Kathirithamby-Wells, 1992: 589; Dutton, 2006).

However, the period of the Tay Son also resulted in changes to the economic and social systems in the country. The Tay Son rulers liberated trade, increased the supply of money and moved towards more of a cash economy. There were also many improvements and expansions in various sectors of the economy including mining, shipbuilding, paper manufacturing and printing. These advances alongside a generally low overall tax rate led for a time to economic prosperity (Kathirithamby-Wells, 1992: 589).

The French first took an interest in Vietnam in the eighteenth century and a French mission of 1748—51 sought to set up a factory in Danang Bay. Initial French interest was mostly in response to British expansion in South and Southeast Asia as the French considered the British their natural rival (Tarling, 1992: 41).

Numerous Europeans, mostly missionaries, had visited Vietnam in the fifteenth and sixteenth centuries, but one of the first to have a major influence was Alexandre de Rhodea, born in France but representing Portugal, who arrived in 1627. He was the first to transliterate the Vietnamese language into the Western alphabet. Upon returning to Europe his experience inspired the French to explore the commercial and religious missionary opportunities in Vietnam. Although the French impact was slow in materializing due to indifference by much of the French public and Vietnamese opposition to foreigners, the French were eventually granted a number of concessions after assisting Nguyen Anh, who took the title Gia Long after ascending the throne in Hue. However, the French influence only grew gradually (Karnow, 1985: 59–71).

Pressure mounted to expand France's overseas presence to counter British influence, and therefore a decision was made to expand the French presence in Southeast Asia. In 1868 French troops led by Admiral Rigault de Genouilly landed in the area around present day

Danang and a year later Saigon was invaded – the gradual move to colonize Vietnam had begun (Karnow, 1985: 71–5; Ileto, 1992: 220; Chapuis, 2000: 6, 48).

The French invaded Hanoi, which resulted in 200,000 Chinese troops entering Vietnam under the guise of protecting Emperor Tu Duc. Apparently, the plot by the French to colonize Vietnam was conceived locally by three men, Admiral Dupré (who was the first governor of Cochinchina), Jean Dupuis (an adventurer who had spent a decade in China and was probably involved in illicit trade) and Francis Garnier. As a result of French military officers and officials making decisions on their own, political leaders in France had little choice but to support them, but their unauthorized actions drew France deeper into its involvement in the country, a situation that would repeat itself nearly a century later with the Americans. After two years of fighting, in which Garnier, who had previously gained fame for his exploration of the Mekong River and writing about it, was killed, the Chinese and French struck a deal to recognize French rights within Vietnam. Soon the French would divide the country into three regions, Tonkin, Annam and Cochinchina (Chapuis, 2000: 7, 42–3).

At the end of hostilities, the Treaty of Philastre was signed in 1874 which allowed Vietnam to officially retain its sovereignty under French protection. Vietnam became a formal protectorate of France when Emperor Hiep Hoa was forced to sign what became known as the Harmand Treaty (Chapuis, 2000: 60–6).

The Vietnamese had previously repelled numerous Chinese invasions while succumbing to others. When the Vietnamese leadership was united and strong, Chinese military incursions were usually rebuffed. However, when political control was fragmented, there had been few difficulties for the Chinese to assert their control. It is likely a similar situation occurred with the French. While the French obviously had the advantage of superior technology, the main factor allowing the French to colonize Vietnam was most likely the fragmentation and weakness of Vietnam's political leadership at the time (Chapuis, 2000: 93–4).

Vietnamese resistance to French rule did not begin with Ho Chi Minh and the Communist/Nationalist movement he led. Although lacking national support and the means to overthrow the French, Vietnamese military and political opposition to colonization continued throughout most of the French colonial era under a variety of nationalistic leaders including Truong Cong Dinh, Ton That Thuyet, Dinh Cong Trang, Phan Dinh Phung, Phan Boi Chau and Phan Chu Trinh. Many of these men were considered to be 'Confucian scholar activists'. Later, in 1927 a nationalistic party, known by its Vietnamese acronym VNQDD was formed but was brutally suppressed by the French after it was found to have engaged in violence against the foreign colonizers (Karnow, 1985: 107–12; Kratoska and Batson, 1992: 277–9).

The French had a major impact on the economics of the country. In the south, the French used modern technology to dig and dredge irrigation canals that doubled as transportation routes, which had a huge impact on increasing the agricultural productivity of the land. The result was Vietnam at the beginning of the twentieth century had become one of the world's leading producers and exporters of rice (Elson, 1992).

Ho Chi Minh, the man who is most associated with the Vietnamese struggle for independence, was born Nguyen Sinh Cung and spent 30 years away from Vietnam after signing on as a stoker and cabin boy for a French steamer. During this period he used multiple aliases and spent time in New York, London, Paris, Thailand, Hong Kong, Moscow and China (Karnow, 1985: 118–27). Ho left for France on a French steamship and while in France working under the name of Nguyen Ai Quoc (Nguyen the Patriot) he joined and advanced within the French Communist Party, and then in 1934 he entered the Lenin Institute in Moscow. His Communist credentials were further solidified after studying at Eastern Workers University, also in Moscow, in the 1920s. In the late 1920s Ho was sent by the Komintern from Bangkok to Hong Kong, where many left-leaning Vietnamese Nationalists had gathered to consolidate the various factions into a single Vietnamese Communist Party. In 1941, Ho moved the Viet Minh, which was the name of the movement he led and created as a broad-based organization that comprised other Nationalists as well as Communists, back into Vietnam from China. However, Ho returned to China in 1942 where he was arrested and jailed by the Chinese. During his career Ho had used at least 20 aliases which made it difficult at the time for opponents and outsiders to know who he really was (Stockwell, 1992: 338; Chapuis, 2000: 102–6).

In Vietnam, as in so much of the world, World War II had a major impact on the country's future direction. At first the French were allowed to continue to rule after the Vichy government was set up in France. In reality, however, after overcoming initial French resistance, it was the Japanese who were in control (Kratoska and Batson, 1992: 281). Although Japanese control helped speed the end of the colonial system, the Japanese proved to be tougher overlords than the French and life for the average Vietnamese was very difficult and starvation and hardship were common. On 9 March 1945, apparently seeing the end of the war in sight, the Japanese seized direct control from the French, although the pretense that Vietnam was actually independent under Emperor Bao Dai was maintained, which resulted in the Viet Minh, led by the now free Ho Chi Minh, to start attacking Japanese outposts. The day after the first atomic bomb was dropped on Hiroshima, Ho seized the opportunity and converted his forces from guerilla fighters into a liberation army (Chapuis, 2000: 29, 137–40).

On 30 August 1945, the emperor signed away power to the Viet Minh who named Ho Chi Minh as president of the Democratic Republic of Vietnam with its capital in Hanoi. According to the Potsdam Conference of 1945, the Chinese were to accept the surrender of the Japanese in Tonkin in the North while in Cochinchina the British were to take control until the French were able to return. As China itself was not politically unified, General Lu Han ignored orders and showed no interest in allowing the French to return, and the Chinese even attempted to militarily oppose the return of the French in 1946. Fearing the Chinese more than the French, Ho Chi Minh signed an agreement to allow the French to return instead of being dominated by the Chinese (Chapuis, 2000: 140–4).

> Vietnam is not an easy country to understand. Much of what transpired in the society was so enveloped in mystery and secrecy that one could be forgiven for failing to delineate the specific segments of the political structure and give each part its due importance.
>
> (Cheong, 1992: 388)

Traditional regional rivalries, personal ambitions of individuals, Vietnamese and French pride and nationalism and early Cold War concerns by the superpowers all contributed to plunging Vietnam into civil war with the forces of Vietnamese Nationalism led by Ho Chi Minh struggling against the French, who as the war wore on became increasing dependent upon American financial support to fund the war. The Americans initially resisted the return of French colonial rule but Cold War considerations came to override democratic principles. 'Of the three options in Indochina – colonialism, communism or monarchy – the Americans relished none' (Stockwell, 1992: 368).

While the romantic notion is that the Vietnamese Nationalists were just a ragtag group of insurgents who overcame overwhelming odds to defeat the modern French army, in reality the Vietnamese troops, while at a huge technological disadvantage, were well supplied by the Chinese and became a large and well-trained force. Moreover, the French army was attempting to regroup after its humiliation in World War II and was hampered by frequent changes in political leadership which resulted in frequent changes in policies. The war started going bad for the French and by 1951 the North was effectively in the hands of the Nationalists. Total control was achieved as a result of the impressive military victory by Vietnamese nationalists led by General Vo Nguyen Giap at Dien Bien Phu where the French surrendered on 7 May 1954. The Vietnamese victory was carried out through incredible feats of bravery, sacrifice and amazing logistic accomplishments which required the moving of equipment and supplies through very rough jungle terrain (Stockwell, 1992: 370; Chapuis, 2000; 155–70).

The hostilities ended or, more accurately, were delayed long enough for the French to retreat in time for signing of an agreement in Geneva where the countries would be partitioned with a Communist and primarily Buddhist country to dominate in the North while South Vietnam would be turned over to be run by the Catholic elites who rose to prominence during the French colonial era. The agreement was much less than the independent North Vietnamese had wanted and fought for and the North Vietnamese leadership felt betrayed to some extent by the willingness of the Chinese and Russians to compromise, for their own purposes, during negotiations despite the military victory by the Vietnamese Communists (Karnow, 1985: 198–205).

Ngo Dinh Diem, a Catholic, became the head of the South Vietnamese government after the Geneva Conference ended the war with the French. Diem's regime lacked popular support and was riddled with corruption, although Diem himself didn't appear to be directly involved in widespread corruption. Diem's regime had a very centralized leadership structure which contributed to its failure to gain allies and support from the other South Vietnamese elites. Diem, with American backing, won a rigged election in 1954 and became the country's prime minister but refused to hold the nationwide election as stipulated in the Geneva agreement, which would almost certainly have resulted in a Communist victory. In 1955 in another rigged election he became president, the monarchy was abolished, Bao Dai retired to France and the last of the French troops left a year later. During his time as head of the South Vietnamese government the National Front for the Liberation of South Vietnam, called the Vietcong by its opponents and supported by the North Vietnamese government, grew in numbers and organization (Karnow, 1985: 213–39; Turnbull, 1992: 607; Chapuis, 2000: 172).

Ngo Dinh Diem's government was overthrown by South Vietnamese military leaders, and Diem and his brother, Nhu, were killed in November

1963. While the coup was not sanctioned at the highest levels of the US government, the message that the US would not attempt to stop a coup and change in government was sent by some of the American military officers and diplomats on the ground in Vietnam. This message was taken as a green light by those in the South Vietnamese military wanting Diem out (Karnow, 1985: 277–311).

Diem's government was followed by two short-lived military governments, one led by the civilian Nguyen Ngoc Tho who was only a figurehead and another government led by General Nguyen Khanh. These were followed by three fairly short-lived civilian governments led in succession by Tran Van Huong, Nguyen Xuan Oanh and Phan Huy Quat. In 1965 the government led by Nguyen Cao Ky and Nguyen Van Thieu took over and lasted until South Vietnam as an independent political entity ceased to exist (Karnow, 1985: 597; Cheong, 1992). None of these governments were able to gather popular support and all concentrated more on political infighting and maneuvering than on governing and fighting the war. The Americans gave financial and military support regardless of government or policies. It is likely this unconditional support led to each government developing a dependence on foreign aid which allowed inept governments to concentrate on political maneuvering and contributed to the ineffective rule of each government.

American involvement steadily increased after the demise of Diem. Many of the decisions that led to increasing levels of American involvement in Vietnam were driven by American domestic political considerations and the individual pride of individuals making those decisions (Karnow, 1985: 349–426). Although the concept of 'face' is usually considered something associated with Asian societies, the escalation of America's defense of the government of South Vietnam might have been driven more by both the nation's collective desire, as well as that of the individuals directly involved, to 'save face' and maintain national and personal pride as well as reputation as opposed to actually defending America's national interests.

Infrastructure projects, the presence of so many American troops and the infusion of so much money transformed South Vietnamese society from a primarily self-sufficient agricultural economy to one with a dependence on American aid dollars. However, despite all the money that poured into the country a solid basis for manufacturing or other productive activities was not created and later, as the Americans and their money departed, the economy suffered (Karnow, 1985: 436–44).

On 2 March 1965 the US bombing campaign codenamed 'Rolling Thunder' began and on 8 March the first 'combat' troops arrived in

Danang, although American 'advisors' had previously been involved in combat, some actually dying alongside their South Vietnamese allies (Karnow, 1985: 415–16).

So American soldiers went into action in Vietnam with the gigantic weight of American industry behind them. Never before in history was so much strength amassed in such a small corner of the globe against an opponent so apparently inconsequential.

(Karnow, 1985: 435)

During Lunar New Year (*Tet*) of 1968 Communist forces launched a major offensive against nearly every major city controlled by the South Vietnamese government. The brutal treatment the Communists forces inflicted on individuals associated with the South Vietnamese government foreshadowed policies that would come at the end of the war. Militarily, the offensive was a major defeat for the Communist forces which had many of its Vietcong divisions (divisions of troops from the South) wiped out and the number of Communist forces killed was very high. The Communist forces were driven out of each area they had initially captured. However, an unintended consequence was increased dissatisfaction with the war within the USA, although the impact on public opinion of this military campaign has often been overstated. Looking at opinion poll numbers taken during the time shows support for the war amongst the US population had started to decline even before the *Tet* offensive (Karnow, 1985: 515–67).

In 1969 Richard Nixon became president of the United States and, despite tough talk and expanding the bombing campaign into Laos and Cambodia, under his administration troop numbers started to be reduced and a long series of negotiations whose purpose was to allow America to withdraw with its honor intact took place. In the end the Americans pulled out unilaterally with the Communist forces making only superficial concessions that no one ever expected to be fulfilled. The South Vietnamese government which had grown dependent on American troops and money was not able to put up a serious defense of the country. Communist forces marched into Saigon on 30 April 1975, ending the war and uniting the country (Karnow, 1985: 567–671).

The war took a terrible toll on the Vietnamese people. In the 16 years of war, approximately 4 million Vietnamese, soldiers and civilians from the North and South, around 10% of the entire population, were either killed or wounded (Karnow, 1985: 11).

Neither the soldiers nor the population of South Vietnam ever developed the attachment to either their cause or government to create the desire to win at all costs. The Americans were limited in how far they were willing to go in winning the war by the desire not to repeat the experience they had in Korea which brought huge numbers of Chinese troops into the war. Moreover, both domestic and international political considerations prevented the Americans from engaging in all out war. However, the North Vietnamese commitment to winning reached near fanatical proportions. 'The Communists were prepared to accept appalling casualties for the sake of minimal gains' (Karnow, 1985: 643) and this willingness to win at all costs was most likely the deciding factor in the outcome.

Although the war was often thought of at the time as between Communist bloc v. free (or imperialist) countries, the idea of a united Communist front in Vietnam was an oversimplification and did not reflect the actual situation. Despite both the Soviet Union and China supplying considerable aid, weapons and supplies, as the war went on splits became more evident and over time the objectives of the Chinese and Vietnamese diverged and relations between the two Asian Communist countries became strained. Chinese support over the course of the war faded causing the North Vietnamese to become more dependent on the Soviet Union (Chen, 2006; Lien-Hang, 2006).

The end of the war did not immediately result in easing the suffering of the people of Vietnam. While the economy of South Vietnam was already in dire straits before the final Communist victory, the initial policies of the Communists seemed to have made things even worse. Communist-initiated agricultural cooperatives had the result of depressing production to a considerable extent. Cooperatives in the North as well as the South resulted in farmers abandoning their fields, and therefore the country did not have enough rice or other food to feed its population (Ngo, 2006). This resulted in severe malnutrition for many of the children which not only affected them at the time but also in later life (Karnow, 1985: 30). In addition to poverty there were mass reprisals against individuals suspected of having supported the former South Vietnamese government or the Americans and massive repression and violence was used against members of the ethnic Chinese community (Chen, 1987: 54–5, 119).

Nothing has dramatized the revulsion against poverty and repression more vividly than the mass exodus from Vietnam – one of the largest migrations of modern times. Nearly a million people have risked their lives to escape from the country, most by sea. Some fifty thousand of them have died from exposure or drowning, or from attacks by pirates who traditionally maraud the waters off Southeast Asia.

(Karnow, 1985: 34)

For those who stayed behind, life in Ho Chi Minh City (HCMC), which was previously named Saigon, worsened. Inflation ran wild and for most individuals food and other necessities were either hard to find or priced out of reach (Chen, 1987: 60).

Still seemingly not tired of war, the government of the newly united Vietnam launched an attack on Christmas Day 1978 against the murderous Khmer Rouge regime in Cambodia. Backed by the Soviet Union the Vietnamese quickly overran the Khmer Rouge army which was in a state of confusion after being demoralized by constant purges of its members by the government. The Vietnamese government then engaged in its own version of imperialism and installed a puppet government in Cambodia led by Heng Samrin and Hun Sen (Chandler, 2000, 222–5). After the fall of the Berlin Wall and the Soviet Union, Vietnam no longer had the foreign financial support needed to maintain its presence in Cambodia and retreated in the early 1990s (Widyono, 2008).

In 1979, the split between Vietnam and its Communist neighbors in China erupted into yet another war which the Chinese initiated to punish Vietnam for its belligerence and its attack on China's ally, the Khmer Rouge. While both sides afterwards claimed victory, it appears after an initial setback that battle-hardened Vietnamese troops held their own against the Chinese (Chen, 1987). The Chinese invasion did have the effect of driving Vietnam even deeper into the Soviet camp (Turnbull, 1992: 663).

The Vietnamese economy continued to deteriorate and the average annual income in 1984 was only $302: 'this previously economically self-sufficient land has now become one of the twenty poorest nations in the world' (Chen, 1987: 144).

In 1986, after the fall of the Soviet Union and seeing the economic success China was experiencing, the Vietnamese government embarked on a number of reforms, called *doi moi*, which have led to spectacular success.

The story of poverty-reducing growth in Vietnam is the story of the impact that the *doi moi* (renovation) reform process begun in 1986 has had on transforming the country's economy and, in the process, raising the incomes of millions of Vietnamese.

(Klump, 2007: 120)

The 1990s saw both rapid economic growth and rapid poverty reduction. The country saw average per capita growth of 5.7% anually but an even more impressive rate of poverty reduction of 7.8% per year. Poverty rates went from near 60% in the early 1990s to under 25% by 2004. The factors driving economic growth and poverty reduction included international trade liberalization which increased prices for coffee and rice, two of the country's major exports, more productivity in both the agricultural and manufacturing sectors and reforms helped to create a vibrant private sector to supplement state-owned enterprises (Klump, 2007: 119–20).

The Communist Party continues to lead the country with Nguyen Minh Triet as president and Nguyen Tan Dung as prime minister at the time of writing. As the government moves farther away from state ownership of enterprises coupled with the fact that those remaining state enterprises are a drain on the economy, which is being pushed forward by the private sector, the government has an increasingly difficult time in linking its propaganda to the way it actually governs. There is little appetite in the country to reverse course and increase government control of the economy. Government corruption and the public's dissatisfaction with the government's performance has grown. It cannot be claimed there is freedom of the press in the country; yet reporting on corruption and other topics that don't glorify the government is not uncommon. Nevertheless, it is expected the Communist Party will both continue to monopolize policy control and continue to reside over an increasingly market-based economy in the near term (Koh, 2011).

Business environment

Vietnam has been experiencing steady economic growth in recent years with an estimated annual growth rate of 6.8% in 2010 which was an improvement on the rates of 2008 and 2009 but not up to the over 8% annual growth rates seen earlier in the decade. The country's growth rates have gone in tandem with its exports over the past few years; with exports declining due to the global slowdown in 2008 and 2009, the country's growth rate also slowed. As exports have picked up, so has economic growth. Per capita GDP remains under $1,000 and inflation has been a recent problem. Economic growth has been mostly fueled by the construction and manufacturing sectors with slower growth seen in services and agriculture. China is the country's leading trading partner. Incoming FDI continues to increase and there is speculation this increase could be accelerated by rising wages in China (Asian Development Bank, 2011a).

Vietnam has a mixed economy with both private and state-owned firms. Thai and Agrawal (2009) reported private firms are at a disadvantage compared to state-owned firms. The authors also pointed out most private businesses are relatively small, the growth of firms in the export sector is faster than that of the economy as a whole, and the underdeveloped financial sector is an obstacle to firms attempting to grow. However, Thai and Ngoc (2010) reported changes have come to Vietnam and, as the external environment has changed with increased private ownership and foreign investment, all firms including state-owned ones have had to adjust their strategies and rely more on competitiveness and less on government support and protection.

As is the case of operating in many transition economies, for firms operating in Vietnam learning how to deal with bureaucracy and the system is very important, and this can be quite a difficult task for a new business (Troilo, 2010). Firms that do not learn how to work within the unwritten rules of the system, which has both market and command and control features, have been known to have incredibly difficult times in getting projects off the ground (Kim, 2008: 77).

Vietnam has seen economic growth despite generally failing to follow the economic reforms the IMF and World Bank have recommended. Vietnam's institutional environment is generally not aligned with general thinking about what is needed to support a market economy. However, entrepreneurs have emerged who have learned how to make deals and create dynamic and value-adding enterprises in spite of the perceived obstacles found in legal and political environments. Among features of the business environment are a focus on cooperation between firms in the same industry instead of competition, a regional difference with a more dynamic environment found in the South in and around Ho Chi Minh City where the Hanoi-based national government has less control over firms, and blurred lines between private and public enterprises resulting in considerable direct involvement of public officials in private enterprises (Kim, 2008).

The brand name of 'Vietnam' is not generally associated with luxury products or advanced technology. For many Westerners, the name 'Vietnam' may be more associated with the American–Vietnamese war of the 1960s and 1970s than with the present day country. Bui and Perez (2010) reported the image of the brand name of Vietnam might have a negative impact on the country's tourism industry. This perception of the country may make it difficult for Vietnamese firms to convince customers and other business partners of local firms' abilities to compete on brand image or innovation.

'In roughly fifteen years, Vietnam has transitioned from being one of the poorest developing countries to the second fastest growing country in the world' (Kim, 2008: 3). While the country has a large informal sector of the economy, this growth has mostly been the result of the growing and dynamic formal private sector. This growth can be partly attributed to simplification of government regulations, easing of restrictions, increased level of exports and government investment in infrastructure (Klump, 2007). Moreover, since most of the poor were rural agricultural workers, the reduction in poverty has mostly come from increases in agricultural productivity and access to export markets (Cord, 2007: 12).

Since joining ASEAN, Vietnam has significantly increased its share of regional trade (Areethamsirikul, 2008) although Jongwanich et al. (2009) contend the region's exports remain ultimately dependent on markets in developed economies.

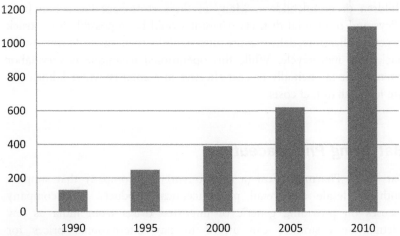

Vietnam's GNI per capita (Atlas Method)

Figure 7.1

Source: Asian Development Bank (2011b: 163)

Case studies

Hoang Viet Beverages

Hoang Viet Beverages (a pseudonym) sells beverages, mostly beer and soft drinks, to both retailers and a few small wholesalers in HCMC. The company is in a fairly competitive industry and competes with a number of similar-sized firms. The company does not have exclusive rights to the brands it sells; therefore, it is competing with other firms that are selling exactly the same products.

The company primarily uses a low-cost strategy which allows it to offer lower than average prices, but the main downside of this strategy is profit margins are quite slim. The company mostly markets through personal relationships, it attempts to build up good relationships with customers and provide friendly and consistent service to build and retain its customer base. The company has found employee turnover can be a problem; therefore, it pays slightly higher than average wages to retain its best employees. The company operates mostly on an informal basis with instructions given orally with very few written or formal rules and regulations.

At the operational level, we see the company using different delivery techniques than would be common in more developed economies. Its customer base is mostly very small family-owned retail outlets, often operated by women who combine running a store with taking care of children or grandchildren. Many of these stores are located in back alleys and residential districts where it would be impossible for a truck to get to. Therefore, deliveries are often made by tying cases of drinks to the back of a motorcycle. While this operational technique is very labor intensive, it can actually be cost-effective in a country where labor costs are lower than fuel costs.

Bat Trang Pharmaceutical

Bat Trang Pharmaceutical (a pseudonym) is a company that supplies both wholesale and retail pharmaceutical products. The company focuses on providing generic or imported drugs from India as few Vietnamese customers can afford to pay international prices for branded pharmaceutical products imported from the US or Europe.

The company keeps its prices fairly low to remain competitive, as price is a deciding factor in purchasing decisions for most Vietnamese consumers.

The company does not do much in the way of traditional marketing; instead, it works with doctors to have them write prescriptions and encourage patients to use the company's services. The company uses the common practice found in Vietnam (and many other countries) of splitting commission for sales with the doctors who write the prescriptions. The business relies on relationships with doctors who have control over which brands are prescribed and where patients buy their medicines. While it is easy to be critical of this practice, seeing the level of money spent by pharmaceutical companies on 'entertainment' and other expenses in encouraging physicians in the USA and some other developed countries to prescribe the company's products, we can see the level of ethics in the industry may be similar across cultures although the specific practices used to encourage doctors to prescribe specific brands or more expensive drugs are somewhat different.

The company uses mostly informal oral communication practices instead of formal written rules and instructions. The firm mostly recruits informally and relies on recommendations from family, friends or current employees. It pays wages at a similar rate to its competitors and mostly uses commissions as encouragement to work hard and increase sales.

Operationally, the firm mostly uses similar techniques to those found in other locations although the move from paper to electronics in fulfilling prescriptions has not been completed.

US University Language School (USULS)

US University Language School (USULS) (a pseudonym) is a prestigious school which focuses on teaching English and operates in Southern Vietnam. USULS is affiliated to a well-known US university and has many foreign teachers and brings in American professors to do workshops in Vietnam as well.

USULS caters for the high end of the market and charges a premium price compared to its local competitors. It uses its foreign image and reputation that result from its international connections as its primary source of competitive advantage. The company has found its affiliation to a recognizable Western institute of higher learning provides the organization with more credibility and status than purely local schools are able to attain. It competes with a number of other foreign operations at the high end of the market, while local schools compete more on price.

This is a highly competitive business as there are few barriers to entry and actual quality is often difficult to determine, therefore branding and reputation are of utmost importance in this industry. It would appear foreign operations, or those with foreign connections and partners, have a natural advantage in the branding and reputation areas over local competitors in Vietnam.

Saigon Shoes

Saigon Shoes (a pseudonym) is a locally owned retail chain operating in Southern Vietnam which sells a variety of styles of shoes. The company is family owned and sells men's, women's and children's shoes. The company does not try to compete with foreign brands, which are usually more expensive and aimed at the lucrative high end of the market.

The company does not use a pure low-cost price strategy; instead, it focuses on the average urban customer who wants good value and is willing to pay for increased quality. The company has a well-respected brand name and has developed a loyal core of customers. The company would appear to be using a differentiation strategy, but one aimed at the middle of the market and not at the high end.

Figure 7.2   **Water distribution shop in Ho Chi Minh City**

The company has been successful in the past, but is currently at a bit of a crossroads. As the economy continues to grow and competition increases, the company will need to gain additional skills and connections to expand the business to take advantage of the country's growing middle class.

Analysis

As seen in the examples, companies in Vietnam use a variety of different strategies, although they must always keep price and costs in mind because of the average income level in the country. We also see interpersonal business practices being aligned with the collectivist nature of society, while operational practices often reflect the low labor costs.

8

Thailand

Abstract: Thailand has seen significant economic growth and poverty reduction in recent decades, yet poverty and income inequality persist. The Kingdom of Thailand has recently experienced considerable political instability, although there has been a surprising amount of social stability. Thailand's cultural environment has been heavily influenced by its main religion, Theravada Buddhism, and this influence is also seen in the business practices used by firms in the Kingdom.

Key words: Thailand, Lannathai, Ayutthaya, Sukhothai, Thaksin Shinawatra, case studies, economics, Theravada Buddhism.

Country background

There is considerable evidence showing people and civilizations have resided in Thailand for a considerable length of time. Although earlier claims that Thailand might have been home to the earliest civilizations to domesticate rice are mostly discounted, there is evidence from the Ban Chiang archeological site which suggests a civilization with elaborate burial rituals has been in the region for thousands of years (Bellwood, 1992; 97–8). Evidence suggests domesticated rice may have been produced in modern day Thailand as early as 2000 BC and the use of technology to produce bronze appeared shortly afterwards with iron production starting around 500 BC (Hall, 1992: 185). However, these people are generally not thought of as being the cultural ancestors of modern day Thais.

Linguistic evidence suggests the geographical origins of the 'Tai' people, which includes the Lao, Shan and other ethnic minorities scattered throughout Southeast Asia as well as the Thais themselves, are in Southeast China. It has been speculated the Tai are the descendents of the ancient Kingdoms of Lung and Pa which were located in the present day province of Sichuan, while others point to the area around Guangdong province as a more likely location of origin. Traditionally, it has been assumed the Tai people eventually created the independent Kingdom of Nan Chao which was located in the modern Chinese province of Yunnan and were forced to flee into Southeast Asia after Nan Chao was overrun by the Mongols who were rulers of China at the time. However, this traditional version is being challenged and many historians now believe Nan Chao was not primarily a Tai kingdom, Tai languages were not commonly used there and the Tai were actually moving into Southeast Asia long before Nan Chao was overrun (Bellwood, 1992: 110; Syamananda, 1993: 614; Jumsai, 2000: 8, 16; Wyatt, 2003: 716; Pholsena, 2004: 237).

What is northern Thailand today was previously under the political control of the Angkor Empire, but in the thirteenth century a new Thai kingdom which was independent emerged. King Mangrai was born and first ruled in Chiang Saen, and then shifted his rule to what is Chiang Rai today before making alliances with other Tai and Shan rulers in the areas and settling in Chiang Mai where he founded the Kingdom of Lannathai. Lannathai can be translated as land of a million rice fields. Much of King Mangrai's life was spent in fighting and fending off Mongol-led forces from China who were attempting to spread Mongol rule into Southeast Asia. Lannathai is usually thought of as the first 'Thai' kingdom but it appears that in the early years the ethnic mark-up of the population was very diverse and included Mons, Lawas, Khmers as well as various differing groups of Tai peoples (Taylor, 1992: 169; Jumsai, 2000: 31; Wyatt, 2003: 33–9).

In the thirteenth century, yet another Thai kingdom emerged to the south of Lannathai which became known as Sukhothai. Sukhothai had previously been an outpost of the Angkor Empire but, as Angkor's influence began to fade, the city and surrounding area became a 'Thai' kingdom as Tais made up the majority of the population. One of the most famous rulers in Thai history, King Ramkhamheang, came to power in Sukhothai and he is known mostly due to the stone inscriptions that have been found which glorified his rule. Apparently, Sukhothai was well integrated into the international trading system of the time, and it was reported King Ramkhamheang sent four different embassies to the court of Kublai Khan, the Mongol ruler who controlled China during this era, and even visited China twice himself. After the death of King Ramkhamheang, which has been reported to have occurred in 1318 by some sources and 1294 by others, the Kingdom of Sukhothai began a slow but steady decline which resulted in eventual incorporation of the kingdom into the Kingdom of Ayutthaya in the early fifteenth century (Syamananda, 1993: 20–33; Jumsai, 2000: 81–3; Jumsai, 2001: 26; Wyatt, 2003: 39–49).

Another Thai state which rose from the ashes left after the decline of the Khmer Empire of Angkor was the Kingdom of Ayutthaya (Ayudhya). This southernmost of the three principal early Thai kingdoms was founded by a wealthy ethnic Chinese from a merchant family named U Thong, who took on the title of King Ramathibodi. King Ramathibodi was less the founder of a new kingdom than the inheritor of an existing population center that was in transition from being predominantly Khmer influenced and pledging allegiance to Angkor to an independent kingdom that was becoming more ethnically Thai. King Ramathibodi married into both the ruling families of Lopburi and Suphanburi and, in bringing these two smaller political units together, was able to found a lasting dynasty which in the fifteenth and sixteenth centuries was a wealthy and important center of international trade with a very cosmopolitan and ethnically diverse population which some Portuguese observers at the time ranked equal to the other major empires of Asia (Andaya, B., 1992: 410–1; Taylor, 1992: 170; Syamananda, 1993: 32; Jumsai, 2001: 28; Wyatt, 2003: 50–85).

Another power was growing to the west, Burma, and a long-lasting competition for dominance over the western part of mainland Southeast Asia ensued. In both 1548 and again in 1549 Burmese troops personally led by King Tabinshwehti invaded the Kingdom of Ayutthaya but were rebuffed. However, the Burmese forces regrouped and launched a major invasion which destroyed nearly all major population centers in the Kingdom including Ayutthaya itself. However, the Burmese were more interested in plunder than in colonizing the land area and, under the leadership of King Naresuan, the Kingdom of Ayutthaya reemerged as a sovereign Thai kingdom. While the Kingdom of Ayutthaya was extremely wealthy and successful as evidenced by its large monuments and temples, it seemed unable to avoid court intrigues and fighting over royal succession after the death of each king, and this feature of dividing the population and elites politically weakened the kingdom leaving it susceptible to foreign invasion. In 1760 the Burmese again attacked and it was only the injury sustained leading to the eventual death of the Burmese King Alaunghpaya that resulted in a withdrawal which kept the Kingdom and city of Ayutthaya from being sacked once again. However, the Burmese once again returned in 1776, overrunning the Kingdom, killed off the entire Thai royal family and took as slaves a large number of citizens of Ayutthaya back to Burma. These wars decimated the Thai population and greatly reduced Thai political power in the region for decades. The later repopulation of the Thai nation was done through the capture and enslavement of Cambodians (Khmers), Mons, Malays and Laotians (Reid, 1992: 462; Wyatt, 2003: 52–121).

The Burmese once again failed to consolidate their military victory and soon found themselves in their own fight for survival due to an invasion by the forces of the Ch'ing (Qing) Chinese dynasty. The Burmese needed all their resources to repel the invaders from the north, leaving Thailand in a power vacuum. The Thais reorganized and were led by the partly ethnic Chinese former governor of Tak named Sin who later became known as Taksin. Taksin rebuilt the Thai army and not only regained the lands that previously belonged to Ayutthaya but also conquered lands previously controlled by the now weakened Kingdom of Lannathai. Taksin decided against reestablishing Ayutthaya as the capital and, instead, created a new capital in Thonburi, across the river from present day Bangkok. Taksin's reign was short lived. It has been reported he grew into an intolerable megalomaniac, went insane and was replaced by his most important general (Young, 1900: 2; Syamananda, 1993: 93–9; Wyatt, 2003: 122–8; Myint-U, 2006: 104).

It appears there is independent verification of the excesses of Taksin. The issue of his insanity was an important factor in establishing the current royal family as saviors of the nation as opposed to being a dynasty founded by a usurper. Despite all of his apparent faults, the modern state of Thailand is most likely a direct result of the political consolidation accomplished by Taksin that occurred in the aftermath of the wars with Burma. Today the bravery of those who opposed the Burmese is glorified in movies and in history lessons that all Thai students attend. The Thai version of the history of this period and Thai resistance against Burmese aggression has been very influential in creating a sense of Thai nationalism and patriotism.

The Chakri dynasty which has endured to the present was founded in 1782 when the former general, who previously held the title of Chaophraya Chakri, took over the throne after the imprisonment and execution of the previous ruler, Taksin. The new king took on the title of King Ramathibodi and was given the title of Phra Phuttahayofa Chulalok (also spelled Pra Buddha Yodfachulaloke) after his death. He is most often referred to now as King Rama I. Under the new king the capital was moved to Bangkok (Young, 1900: 3–4; Syamananda, 1993; Wyatt, 2003: 128–44).

One of the features that set the Chakri period apart from earlier Thai kingdoms was the lack of serious divisiveness over succession, with the smooth transition of Rama II coming to power. Although there was considerable controversy over the succession of Prince Chetsadabodin, who ruled under the title Phrao Nangklao, when he became Rama III. But the divisions were not as severe as those that weakened the Kingdom of Ayutthaya. Rama II (Phra Phutthaloetla Naphalai) is remembered as one of the great Thai poets and patrons of the arts, and the nation grew and consolidated during his reign. Rama III was more aggressive and attacked Laos, destroyed most of the political structures in that country and carried off large numbers of individuals to populate the rice-growing areas of the central plains. During his reign, the Thais also conquered the Malaya area of Kedah, in which the seeds for the long-lasting troubles along the Thai–Malaysian border were sown (Ileto, 1992: 230; Evans, 2002; Wyatt, 2003: 144–65).

Rama IV, also often called King Mongrut, is today one of the most revered figures in Thai history. King Mongrut was known as a scholar and, prior to taking the throne, had been a Buddhist monk for 27 years. During his time on the throne, Thailand (Siam as it was called internationally at the time) began experiencing pressures from the colonial powers in the region, the British to the west and the French to the east. In response, the country opened up to international trade at this time and brought in policies to learn and adapt many Western technologies and ideas. The changes made during King Mongrut's reign, while significant, were also gradual and designed to create incremental change in the country that would enhance stability as opposed to quick and radical change which might have created political and social instability in the country (Wyatt, 2003: 166–74). As the Ch'ing dynasty in China was in decline at this time, trade with China fell considerably and King Mongrut had enough confidence to end the tradition of sending tribute to China (Stuart-Fox, 2003: 119).

Succeeding Rama IV was his son, King Chulalongkorn (Rama V), whose reign consolidated the power and prestige of the dynasty. His reign is portrayed in a very positive light by historians and others in Thailand today. Thailand is very proud of not being colonized and King Chulalongkorn's diplomatic skills are often given credit for keeping the country free as he was able to reform the country while at the same time play both the French and British off one another. After visiting Europe, he felt his country needed to adopt many Western ideas and modernize, but he also realized Europe had not solved all of its own problems and decided on a program of selective borrowing from the West as opposed to attempts to import all aspects of European life into Thailand. During his reign there were considerable educational reforms and slavery was outlawed. King Chulalongkorn was known for his hard work and was personally involved in many of the details of the administration of the country. He mostly relied for advice and implementation of his plans on a small number of relatives, increasingly centralizing government by putting it in the hands of the royal family during his 42-year rule (Tarling, 1992: 78; Trocki, 1992: 121; Wyatt, 2003: 175–209).

King Vajiravudh, Rama VI, came to the throne in 1910 and was less involved in the daily running of the country than were his two predecessors. He supported a number of social changes, in particular the promotion of sports and increasing the social position of women. He was known for his somewhat flamboyant life-style, interest in the theater and other arts, and having little interest in female companionship. He waited until quite late in life to marry and had just one daughter, who was born two days prior to his death. He is today mostly remembered for starting and supporting the Wild Tiger Corps, which could be described as a militaristic version of the Boy Scouts. During his reign government expenditure grew considerably (Wyatt, 2003: 10–21). At this time Chinese immigration increased and the ethnic Chinese community more firmly established its position in dominating economic activities (Trocki, 1992: 123; Montesano, 2005: 185). The country's economy was also becoming more integrated with the larger global economy and, with the opening up of new areas for cultivation in the central plains, Thailand was becoming a world leader is rice exports (Elson, 1992: 146). The country's rule over the Muslim majority in the South was again challenged during this time with a widespread uprising occurring in 1922 (Ileto, 1992: 230).

King Prajadhipok, Rama VII, ascended the throne in 1925 and tried to get royal expenditure under control, which had expanded greatly during the reign of the previous monarch. The world was changing and he believed the country would eventually have to move away from an absolute monarchy to a country with some form of representative aspect to the government, but he hoped to steer the country through gradual changes to ensure survival of the monarchy and stability for the country. However, as in much of the rest of the world, the Great Depression caused both economic and political turmoil which made gradual changes unlikely to succeed. In 1932, led by Pridi Phanomyong (Pridi) and Luang Phibunsongkhram (normally referred to as Phibun), a group called the 'Promoters' staged a coup with the stated goal of implementing democracy. The rule of the absolute monarchy in the country ended and a new chapter in Thai politics began. King Prajadhipok abdicated the throne in 1935 and was replaced by ten-year-old Prince Mahidol (Wyatt, 2003: 222–38). Although the group who seized power called themselves the People's Party, most people took little notice and the small group of around 100 members now running the country had little popular support (Kratoska and Batson, 1992: 297).

The end of absolute political control did not necessarily bring democracy to the country. The years following the end of absolute monarchy witnessed the first of many military coups in the country. Thai politics in the next few decades was mostly a series of political skirmishes between factions led by the more left-leaning Pridi and the more conservative Phibun, with the military actively involved in all aspects of politics in the country. In 1935 a government was formed with Phraya Phahon as Prime Minister, Pridi as Minister of Foreign Affairs and Phibun as Minister of Defense. Having control of the military allowed Phibun to rise to the position of prime minister in 1938 and, rather than openly oppose the Japanese, the country officially sided with Japan against the Allies as World War II pushed itself into Southeast Asia (Wyatt, 2003: 234–50).

Thailand's history had in many ways prepared it for being caught up in the middle of international political struggles. The elites of the country often played both sides, siding with the Japanese early in the war when Japan had the upper hand but never shutting off communications, often secretly, with both the British and Americans. However, the elites had no difficulty in switching alliances as the fortunes of war changed and it became apparent the Japanese Empire would not last (Reynolds, 2004: 411). This flexibility and willingness to bend to the wishes of dominant regional powers was a continuation of the policy used earlier with the British and French to retain formal sovereignty for Thailand (Kratoska and Batson, 1992: 292). While the Japanese pressured the Thai government to economically assist with Japan's war effort, Thailand's willingness to bend and be flexible was likely a contributing factor in Japan not directly interfering in the domestic running of the country during the war (Stockwell, 1992: 334).

At the end of the war, Britain and France were intent on a return to the old colonial system in Southeast Asia and wanted to punish Thailand (one can only speculate whether the intention was expansion of their colonial empires to include Thailand). But the Americans felt the Thais were acting under duress when declaring war on the Allies and should not be thought of as having actually been a real enemy. In 1944, Phibun resigned and a new more neutral government with Khuang Aphaiwong as prime minister and Pridi as regent for King Mahidol was formed. Pridi held the real power and worked towards the end of the war and in its immediate aftermath to align the country and himself closely with the United States. Thailand was admitted to the United Nations in 1946. However, soon afterwards new Cold War concerns overtook past histories in importance and the more militaristic and less left-leaning Phibun made a return to power in 1948 holding on to the top spot in the government until 1957. Phibun instituted some anti-Chinese measures, partially in response to the Communist takeover of China and sent Thai troops to fight in the Korean War (Turnbull, 1992: 590–601; Wyatt, 2003: 250–65). Ethnic Chinese were encouraged to take Thai names and engage in society as Thais. Over time the importance of Sino-Thais as entrepreneurs with a central role in growing the economy and creating jobs was recognized (Owen, 1992: 496–7).

King Bhumibol Adulyadej was not expected to become king. However, when his older brother, King Ananda Mahidol, Rama VIII, was found shot dead under very mysterious circumstances he ascended the throne and has reigned ever since. The King is almost universally respected by the population who consider him almost as semi-divine.

However, the popularity of the monarchy was not always as strong as it is today. The resurgence of the popularity of the monarchy was promoted by the government of Sarit Thanarat which came to power through a military coup in 1957. Sarit's government lacked credibility even though the Phibun government it replaced had become corrupt and unpopular. Sarit sought legitimacy through a strong connection to the King and through increasing the prestige and role of the monarchy both domestically and internationally (Cheong, 1992: 439).

Thailand found it advantageous to ally itself with the USA during the 1960s and early 1970s. In return for the country's willingness to provide bases and support for US troops and military equipment, Thailand received substantial amounts of US foreign aid. After the death of Sarit Thanarat in 1963, a military government led by General Thanom Kittikachorn ruled for ten years until 1973. Student-led demonstrations starting at Thammasat University initially led to a violent crackdown on protesters and the removal of many civil liberties of the people. After the crackdown, many of the student leaders of the protesters joined the Communist movement and fled to the northeast, but in general the Thai population supported the crackdown. International and internal pressures eventually led to the temporary end to military rule, which led to a time of chaotic democracy with a revolving door of leaders, followed by a series of further coups and military rule intermixed with more periods of democratic rule (Cheong, 1992; 442; Wyatt, 2003: 266–304; Ungpakorn, 2007: 83–4).

The elected civilian government of Prime Minister Chatichai Choonhawan was brought down by another military coup d'état under the pretext of removing an intolerably corrupt government (a claim that was reused in 2006 to justify the military takeover of the elected government of Thaksin Shinawatra). The military government led by General Suchinda Kraprayoon proved to be unpopular and another series of large-scale protests occurred in Bangkok with a heavy-handed and bloody response by the government which led to the intervention of King Bhumibol, which resulted in ending the violence as well as taking away all credibility from the government. The now discredited military government was replaced in an election which was won by the Democrat Party with Chuan Leekpai as Prime Minister in 1992 (Chanthanom, 1998: 67–8). It appeared military rule had been discredited and the path to democracy had been completed, but this view turned out to be premature.

Since first winning the election in 2001, Thai political life has been dominated by Thaksin Shinawatra and those in opposition to his rule. Thaksin amassed a fortune through being issued monopoly rights in the mobile phone industry at the time the technology was just beginning to take off. Although one of and initially supported by the Bangkok elites, he began building his own power base primarily through support in the less economically developed north and northeast parts of the country and with the politically awaking working class and rural farmers. His *Thai Rak Thai* (Thais love Thailand) Party initiated a number of populist programs and his increased support from the rural sections of the country alienated many of the country's traditional elites. After being the first prime minister to lead his party to reelection, the tanks rolled through the city in 2006 in a bloodless coup while Thaksin was conveniently out of the country. After a year of increasingly unpopular rule, the military allowed elections to go ahead and, although Thaksin had been convicted of corruption and was in exile, his supporters under the name of the People's Power Party (PPP) won the election. However, Thaksin's opponents did not take their election defeat lying down and swayed the Thai courts to remove the next two prime ministers from office as part of their efforts to remove the elected government, which included taking over and shutting down the country's international airport by the ironically named group, People's Alliance for Democracy (PAD) (Ungpakorn, 2007; Hengkietisak, 2008; McCargo, 2008, 2011; Phongpaichit and Baker, 2008).

After a faction of the ruling party led by a politician for the province of Buriram, Newin Chidchob, was 'persuaded' to switch alliance to the opposition, the Democrat Party was able to form a government in which Abhisit Vejjajiva became the prime minister. The 'Yellow Shirts', a loose coalition of the Democrat Party, royal supporters and Bangkok's middle class, did not seem to see the irony of supporting the overthrow of a corrupt elected government by itself coming to power by, what was an open secret, bribing members of a faction of the party that had won the election to switch sides in parliament. Now it was the turn of the 'Red Shirts', supporters of Thaksin and a coalition of mostly rural politicians and interested parties, to take to the streets in protest which resulted in deadly and destructive battles with the police in 2010. In 2012 another election was called and, not surprisingly, the Red Shirt party once again won, this time renamed the Pheu Thai Party led by Thaksin Shinawatra's sister, Yingluck Shinawatra.

Winning elections in Thailand requires support from the populous regions of the north and northeast, but ruling the country requires cooperation from the traditional elites, mostly from Bangkok, who control the non-elected judiciary and royal institutions. In recent times it has been difficult to align the support needed to both win elections and effectively rule.

Serious political divisions are likely to remain and only time will tell if the Yellow Shirts will again attempt to bring down another elected government through non-democratic means or will bide their time and allow the ruling party to build a record which it will then try to challenge in the next election. Until all factions decide to abide by election results the political stability of the country will remain in doubt.

All the political activities and divisions have tended to overshadow many serious issues Thailand has around its borders. Thailand has been embroiled in controversy with Cambodia over ownership of the land on which the Preah Vihear temple stands which has resulted in sporadic exchanges of gunfire between Thai and Cambodian troops. Violence has continued in the southernmost provinces of Pattani, Narathiwat and Yala, mostly between various factions of Muslim 'separatists' and Buddhist supporters of the Thai government. There also continue to be over 100,000 refugees living in refugee camps along the Thai–Myanmar/Burma border, the majority being ethnic Karens from Myanmar/Burma who support the Karen National Union, which has been engaged in a 60-plus year struggle for some form of self-rule, although there has been some recent indications of a breakthrough. A lasting peace seems for the first time in recent memory to be a possibility.

Despite the superficial turmoil in the history of the country the lives of the people outside the royal family and political factions have been surprisingly less affected than an outside observer would likely think. For example, by the afternoon of the day the military took control of the country from its elected civilian government in 2006 the citizens of Bangkok were back to normal with shops open and people going about their daily business showing seemingly little concern for the change in government. After all, they had been through it many times before and changes at the top usually have had little impact on how the country has actually been run.

Despite the political instability of the country since the end of absolute rule by the monarchy, the country has experienced very high levels of economic growth and from 1987 through 1996 had the world's fastest growing economy. In 1945 the country was quite poor and had life expectancy and infant mortality rates similar to what was seen in sub-Saharan Africa, while today these measurable aspects of quality of life are near developed country levels. Although the country has experienced very high levels of economic growth in recent decades, growth has not been shared equally and inequality between rural and urban areas, as well as other regional variations, continues to be high. It is likely this inequality contributes to the political instability (Warr, 2007; Faulkner, 2011).

Business environment

Despite all the changes in government, economic policies have been quite consistent and Thailand has traditionally had a market-based economy. There have not been many pressures to evolve into a European-style welfare state (Warr and Sarntisart, 2005: 194). Most large-scale businesses are controlled by the Sino-Thai community. As Chanthanom (1998: 272) explained, the ruthless pursuit of wealth often needed for large-scale business success is inconsistent with Buddhist teachings and therefore most educated 'Thais' have traditionally sought careers in the civil service leaving the running of businesses to the ethnic Chinese. In addition, there is a vibrant informal economy and the country has one of the world's highest levels of females engaging in entrepreneurial activities (Hatcher and Terjesen, 2007; Hipsher, 2009).

Thailand's development can be classified somewhere on the continuum between a developed and developing economy. When measuring the country's competitiveness against the other countries of ASEAN, Kao et al. (2008) found Thailand was third in economic performance, behind Singapore and Malaysia; third in technological performance, behind the same two countries; first in human resource performance (with labor costs factored in); third in managerial performance; and third in overall national competitiveness. Wang and Chien (2007), when looking at Thailand's infrastructure and level of technology, ranked the country behind Malaysia and Singapore, but it was seen as being ahead of the rest of the region. It was also felt Thailand had some advantages over Malaysia and Singapore due to the country's abundance of natural resources and supply of low-cost labor.

Thailand's economy started its recovery in 2010 after a sharp recession in 2009 due to the global financial crisis. In 2010 the country saw a sharp increase in investments after a number of slow years and also an increase in demand for the country's exports. Most of the growth was from the manufacturing sector as agricultural production declined in 2010 mostly due to poor weather and flooding. Increasing exports to China, India and the rest of Southeast Asia are becoming more important to the nation's economy. Macroeconomic conditions have been fairly strong as foreign currency reserves have increased and the ratio of public debt to GDP has decreased slightly and is at the fairly manageable level of 42.5% (Asian Development Bank, 2011a). The floods of 2011 will probably have the effect of slowing the country's economic performance, at least in the short term.

Economic forecasts are for moderate growth for the near future of over 4% annually with inflation running around 3%. The country faces many challenges economically, with political stability being the main one. Will the election of Yingluck Shinawatra and the Red Shirts bring stability and reconciliation to the country or will it deepen the divisions? Moreover, the country's wealth is distributed in a highly unequal manner and the country's Gini coefficient is quite high at 0.51 (Asian Development Bank, 2011a). The government is planning and implementing many projects to assist the rural areas to lessen the impact of poverty (Montreevat, 2011), but whether these programs will have a greater impact than previous ones is open to debate.

Thailand is a major trading partner of many of its neighbors including Myanmar/Burma. However, various issues have resulted in the occasional closing of official border crossings between the two countries, which has resulted in increased black market trading between the two countries (Anantarangsi, 2011).

Management styles in Thailand appear to be heavily influenced by the social-cultural environment where Theravada Buddhist values permeate. Management in Thailand often takes on a very personal, hierarchal and paternalistic manner. There is normally a strong emphasis on personal relationships amongst co-workers, and if the work environment is not considered *sanuk* (fun) a firm may have difficulties retaining employees. In general, there may be less separation between one's personal and professional lives than would be considered the norm in Western environments (Hipsher, 2010a).

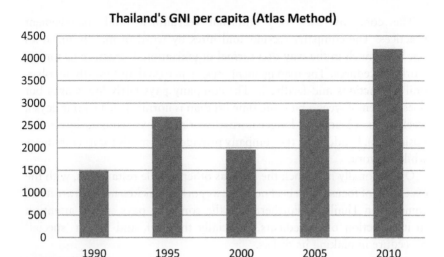

Thailand's GNI per capita (Atlas Method)

Figure 8.1

Source: Asian Development Bank (2011b: 163).

According the Hofstede's (1983) earlier study, Thailand was found to be quite high in power distance and low in individualism as is the norm in Asia. However, it was found that Thailand's scores for uncertainty avoidance were a bit lower than most Asian countries and that it had a slightly more feminine and less masculine society than that found in Japan and most other Asian societies.

Case studies

Roon-a-roong Beef Noodles

Roon-a-roong is a small beef noodle shop operated in Bangkok by the owner-manager. As is the case in many Thai SMEs, there is no separation between ownership and managers. The company uses a low-cost differentiation strategy as it charges approximately the same prices as its nearest competitors but competes on the quality of its product and specific taste that derive from the company's own recipe. Nevertheless, the company needs to keep costs down as it mostly competes as a form of 'fast food' as opposed to being a more formal dining experience, and a reasonable price is important for its target market.

The company uses very informal recruitment and management practices. The company recruits and hires by word of mouth and does not have much in the way of a formal organizational structure or formal work procedures. The management style is personal and mostly involves oral instructions and feedback. The company pays fairly low wages but does give employees a bit more time off than is normal (six 11-hour days a week v. six 12-hour or longer normal working days required by similar businesses). In addition, the company provides free meals for its employees while at work.

Operationally it is much the same as other noodle restaurants, with the exception of focusing on beef noodles, as pork or chicken noodles are more common in Thailand. Furthermore, the company pays special attention to its selection of ingredients, especially the beef, and uses a 'special' procedure in making its dishes.

A-5

A-5 is a company which sells used cars in Bangkok, the nation's capital. The company has been in business for about 20 years but only has a few employees as the owner and owner's family do most of the work involved in running the company. The used car business is a very competitive business in Bangkok as a result of plenty of competitors and increasing use of the internet to bypass used car dealers altogether. Therefore, maintaining competitive prices is important as buyers of used cars in Thailand are both very price conscious and fairly sophisticated in understanding the market. However, the company does not compete solely on price, it also relies on return customers and word-of-mouth advertising. It therefore seeks to stand out in terms of honesty and being straightforward. As the used car business in Thailand is much the same as used car businesses in other countries around the world, being honest and trustworthy could be considered a strategy intended to differentiate the company from the pack.

The company mostly recruits informally and, as is the case in most SMEs in developing economies in Asia, it uses a personalized and informal system of management. Most instructions are given orally and come directly from the owners. However, skills are also important and the company needs to hire workers who have the knowledge and skills to clean and fix used cars to ensure a high-quality product for its customers.

Operationally, the techniques the firm uses to clean, repair and prepare vehicles for sale would appear to be very similar to those used by firms around the world. The firm is also aware of a move toward more shopping online with most customers coming to look at specific cars they have found online as opposed to just stopping by and browsing.

Huang Li Steel Company (Plit-Tapan Nawt Huang Li)

Huang Li Steel Company, like so many medium to large-sized companies in Thailand, is an ethnic Chinese family-owned and operated firm. The firm was started by Khun Tik Seehang, who got his start in business selling noodles on the street around 40 years ago, after first spending time learning the technical side of the steel industry as an employee in another steel company. Today the firm is run by his daughter, Wilawan Chanajaranwit, with three of his sons acting as operational and marketing managers. The company specializes in producing and selling steel for construction projects and was in position to take advantage of the country's construction boom in the 1980s and 1990s. However, the company, after getting established, has taken a rather conservative approach, has not gone in for much diversification and has decided to stay small enough to be managed by the family itself. The company has around 100 employees and a core and loyal set of customers in the construction industry.

As steel is more or less a commodity, keeping prices low and limiting costs through operational efficiency will always be important parts of the strategy within this industry. However, Huang Li Steel Company does not charge the lowest prices and does not follow a low-cost leadership strategy. Instead, the company focuses on a niche market of small and medium-sized construction companies around Bangkok. One of the primary needs of these SMEs is financing, as construction companies are often only paid at the end of a project. Therefore, Huang Li Steel Company has developed relationships and trust with the owners of some of these smaller companies, also usually owned and operated by ethnic Chinese families, and provides quality steel at a reasonable, but not the lowest, price. As a form of differentiation, it provides credit to its customers who are willing to pay the slightly higher price as a result of having to wait to make payments until these SMEe are paid at the end of a construction project.

Being part of a business network of trusted ethnic Chinese business owners in a country where one does not usually want to rely on the legal system to enforce contracts has proven an advantage to the company. The company's current location has no physical room to grow and, as the third generation of the family has mostly gone into other businesses and occupations, there is thus little motivation to grow the business. Instead, the plans are to continue as is and provide quality employment and a decent living for the family owning the company.

The company uses a very paternalistic management style. It provides housing and utilities for many of its employees and, while the basic pay is only average for the industry, employees can expect 'bonuses' on special occasions such as the birth of a child or a marriage in the family. The company uses mostly informal recruitment efforts and most new employees are relatives or close friends of existing employees, making operations almost as much a family affair as is the management of the firm. Turnover is quite low and the company does keep up to date on new operational techniques and technology used in the industry, but as the steel industry is a mature industry and the company focuses on a niche or focused strategy it is not vital it stays at the cutting edge of new technology. It is content to be a follower and learn from international best operational practices.

Figure 8.2   **Street restaurants, Bangkok**

Analysis

While there are a few Thai companies in recent years that have grown internationally and have developed widely known brand names, such as CP (Charoen Pokphand) in agro-business, Red Bull (Krating Daeng) in energy drinks and Chang in beer as well as being the primary sponsor of Everton (an English Premiership football team), most Thai companies remain small, family owned and focused on serving middle and working-class Thais. While economic growth in recent decades has eliminated most extreme poverty, the country remains a developing economy and many of its citizens live fairly close to the bread line; hence, low price and good value for money are important criteria for most businesses operating in the country. Interpersonal business practices often take into account the local cultural environment, which has been heavily influenced by the teachings and philosophies of Theravada Buddhism. The Thais are well known for their openness to new ideas, which allows businesses and individuals to adapt and adopt foreign ideas and technology into their daily lives and operational businesses practices fairly quickly. The three-level approach helps to explain operations in the Thai firms examined.

9

Cambodia

Abstract: Cambodia is a country in Southeast Asia that has received considerable amounts of foreign financial aid in recent years. Modern Cambodia grew out of the ancient Angkor Empire and more recently has gone through a horrific period of genocide while being ruled by the Marxist-inspired Khmer Rouge. Theravada Buddhism is the religion of the majority of the population and it is proposed the religious traditions of the country have an impact on the culture and business practices found within Cambodia. Case studies of SMEs and entrepreneurs in the informal economy are presented.

Key words: Cambodia, Khmer, Angkor Wat, informal economy, Theravada Buddhism, Khmer Rouge.

Country background

Today, Cambodia, land of the Khmer people, is mostly known for the genocide perpetrated by the Khmer Rouge in the 1970s and the poverty that has inflicted the country in the aftermath of this the country's darkest period. However, the country's challenges began long before getting caught up in the international struggle between Communist and non-Communist forces and the country has been caught up in both previous and subsequent regional power struggles.

In the nineteenth century, Adams (1879: 171) expressed the thought, 'Unhappy is the Cambodian! Hemmed in between the Siamese on the one hand, and the Annamites [Vietnamese] on the other.' However, this has not always been the case, in fact the Khmer people and the lands of present day Cambodia were once at the center of one of the world's most advanced civilizations and the main political power in Southeast Asia (Jumsai, 2001: 17–9).

Little is known of the pre-Angkorean period of Cambodia's history, but there did not appear to be a fixed capital or a unified political organization (Taylor, 1992: 158). Archeological evidence indicates humans have lived in the region surrounding the Tonle Sap river and lake for tens of thousands of years and it appears that by the third century BC, the people living in present day Cambodia could be classified as Khmer-Mon and were most probably ancestors of the present day Khmer people (Tully, 2005: 7–8). The Chinese referred to a place called Fu-nan near the current day Cambodian–Vietnam border which was on the sea route between China and points west, although it appears Fu-nan was not ruled by a central authority. Fu-nan appeared to have been the center of the Khmer people from around the first century until the sixth century when power shifted to the people of Zhenla, a name given by the Chinese to a group of Khmer people living farther inland (Hall, 1992: 192–6; Chandler, 2000: 15).

In the latter part of the sixth and then into the seventh century a Khmer nation began forming, partly led by the brothers Bhavavarman and Mehendravarman, yet no single ruler was able to consolidate power until Jayavarman I in the late seventh century (Taylor, 1992: 159). Although there is no consensus amongst historians, the Angkor Period has generally been thought of beginning in AD 802 and ending around 1432 (Chandler, 2000: 29). Although Penny et al. (2007) discovered the sediment profiles found in the moats around Angkor Wat indicate a large population and workforce stayed in the area long after the time generally thought of as the end of one of the world's greatest early civilizations.

Jayavarman II, who it is thought began his political career in the southeast of modern day Cambodia, is credited with founding the Kingdom of Angkor. There are no known inscriptions he authorized still in existence today, nor is his motivation for moving the Khmer Kingdom to the area adjoining the Tonle Sap known. However, it is believed Sanskrit-educated priests conducted a ceremony in 802 which proclaimed him to be a universal monarch. He reigned for 50 years and started a dynasty which would last for over 600 years (Taylor, 1992: 159; Chandler, 2000: 34; Jumsai, 2001: 19; Tully, 2005: 15, 20). Much of the groundwork was laid for the most prosperous age of the Kingdom during the reign of Suryavarman I which lasted from around 1002 to 1050 (Hall, 1992: 234).

The Angkor tradition of building in stone apparently began under the rule of Yasovarman (Taylor, 1992: 160). However, the best known monument of the Khmer Empire, Angkor Wat, was built during the reign of Suryavarman II as a sign of his devotion to the Hindu god,

Vishnu. Suryavarman II's court was known to have had diplomatic relations with the Southern Sung in China and was heavily involved in international trade with the Chinese (Taylor, 1992: 161; Chandler, 2000: 49–50; Tully, 2005: 26).

Around 1150 some type of political upheaval apparently transpired and, in the aftermath, there was fragmentation of political power. By the end of the twelfth century power was again consolidated under Jayavarman VII and a major cultural shift occurred with a new religious focus on Mahayana Buddhism. During Jayavarman VII's reign the empire spread through much of mainland Southeast Asia and the building of the impressive Bayon found at Angkor Thon took place, which was reworked after Jayayavarman's death to make it appear its focus was on Hinduism and hide its Buddhist origins. There has been speculation Angkor might have been the largest city in the pre-industrial world with a population of around one million (Taylor, 1992: 161–2; Chandler, 2000: 56, 61, 67; Tully, 2005: 26–7, 39, 44; Sharrock, 2009).

After a brief return to rulers practicing Hinduism, 'The largest change affecting Cambodia in the thirteenth century was the conversion of most of the people to the Theravada variant of Buddhism' (Chandler, 2000: 68). The inclusion of an increasing number of speakers of Tai languages and Mon missionaries in the vast kingdom is often attributed to contributing to this conversion. The subtle differences between Mahayana and Theravada Buddhism had the result of ending the period of monument and empire building and inscriptions in Sanskrit were replaced by new ones in Pali (Taylor, 1992: 162; Chandler, 2000, 69: Tully, 2005: 39).

The demise of Angkor is a mystery that has not been solved to the satisfaction of all historians. The Siamese (Thais), who had previously been vassals of the Khmers, apparently launched a large-scale and successful assault on Angkor around 1431, which seems to have played a part in moving the capital of the Khmer civilization to Phnom Penh. Other factors given for the decline of Angkor include ecological degradation and the impact of Theravada Buddhism on the population. Although conventional wisdom has been that Angkor was suddenly abandoned, evidence indicates that Angkor Thom was only abandoned in 1629, nearly 200 years after the attacks by the Siamese, and other parts of Angkor were rebuilt as late as 1747 (Taylor, 1992: 163; Vickery, 2004; Tully, 2005: 17, 49).

The period after the demise of Angkor resulted in a more decentralized political structure and less building of monuments in stone, and therefore there is less evidence for historians to gather and analyze for this time frame than for the previous period. Although this post-Angkor period is generally thought of as a period of decline, Chandler (2000: 78–9) cautioned against assuming the periods of centralized political control and massive building projects were actually golden ages for the average individual living at the time. The loss of Saigon (Prey Nokor) and the Mekong Valley in the 1620s to the Nguyen (Vietnamese) cut off the Khmer Kingdom from maritime trade, which weakened the country and may have been one of the factors leading to the Khmer becoming politically and economically weaker and eventually resulting in the country losing some sovereignty to its two neighbors, Vietnam and Thailand. Sharing a religion and many cultural aspects led to Cambodia's relationship with Thailand being significantly closer and different than its relationship with Vietnam, which was culturally more distant (Chandler, 2000: 77, 95, 100, 115; Tully, 2005: 56, 62).

The French colonized Cambodia through Vietnam and established a protectorate in Cambodia in 1863. At first the French planned to rule through puppet kings, but in 1884 when King Norodom attempted to rule the Kingdom in ways the French thought improper, the King was forced to revise the original treaty giving the European colonial rulers complete control over nearly all matters in the country (Chandler, 2000: 137; Tully, 2005: 80–8).

French rule over the country was mostly indirect and had limited impact in the villages. The French administration was a product of its time, took a very paternalistic approach and mostly discounted local opinions. The French often thought it was their duty to bring civilization and modernization to this backward land. The costs of operating the administration in Cambodia were consistently higher than the income the colony produced for the French, and the French imported substantial numbers of Vietnamese to work in the colony's administration. There was resentment over the immigration of so many Vietnamese and anti-Vietnamese sentiment was a factor in developing a stronger feeling of Cambodian nationalism in the 20th century. Even though the French presence in Cambodia was limited, it did have an effect and many changes such as abolishing slavery, limiting corruption, limiting the power of the royal family, creation of a civil service based on merit and improvement in the county's infrastructure all eventually came about under French rule (Chandler, 2000: 139; Clymner, 2004: 2; Tully, 2005: 88, 92, 103).

As in the rest of Southeast Asia, World War II and its aftermath destroyed the image of Western invulnerability and made a return to the type of colonialism found before the war impossible. A young Sihanouk, a figure who would remain at the center of Cambodian political life for decades, was placed on the throne by the French in 1941 as it was felt he could be easily manipulated. In 1945, the King, as directed by the Japanese, who toward the end of the war took direct control from the French, declared independence but the French returned at the war's end with the intention of reimposing its mastery over its colonies. The King proved to be his own man and had his own ideas, and this along with France's increasing military problems in its fight against Communist forces in Vietnam which culminating in the French defeat at Dien Bien Phu in 1954, made it evident the old order was not going to be restored. The Franco-Khmer treaty of 1949 established Cambodia as an independent nation within the French Union, although Cambodia's sovereignty was severely restricted under this treaty. King Sihanouk began his drive for full independence in March 1953. By October the French approved the right of the King to have authority over Cambodia's armed forces, judiciary and foreign affairs. On 9 November 1953, the last French troops left Cambodia and full independence was formally recognized on 21 July 1954 (Chandler, 2000: 167–85; Tully, 2005: 81–121).

While independence probably initially meant little to the majority of people living in the villages, it did give Sihanouk a lot of prestige and power as he was able to take most of the credit for Cambodia's independence; however, soon the country was pulled into the broader Southeast Asian war. At first Sihanouk sided with the US and the US-backed South Vietnamese government. But in 1963 he decided to stop accepting military aid from the USA and declared the country's neutrality, although he did accept some aid from Communist China. Sihanouk's falling out with the USA was over the perceived use of Cambodian territory by the North Vietnamese Communist forces, a few comments by Sihanouk about looking the other way when North Vietnamese troops traveled through Cambodia on their way south and extensive US bombing of areas alongside the Cambodian/Vietnamese border. In 1965 diplomatic relations with the USA were terminated and a year later Sihanouk entered into a secret arraignment with North Vietnam. His grip on power began to loosen as Cambodian Communist forces began to become a bigger threat, and in 1970 a successful military coup occurred and a new government led by Lon Nol came to power (Chandler, 2000: 187–204; Clymner, 2004: 9–17; Tully, 2005: 145–51).

Sihanouk has often been criticized for changing sides and his involvement with different factions. However, political maneuvering and trying to stay neutral while playing more powerful forces off each other has a long tradition in Cambodia and Southeast Asia. Cambodia, located between the two more populous and powerful nations of Thailand

and Vietnam, had used this type of political technique to maintain its independence for centuries and Thai leaders had also skillfully played the French and British off each other to remain the only nation in Southeast Asia not to be colonized by a European power. The Thais also skillfully balanced their support of various factions in World War II to minimize the effect of the Japanese 'occupation' and prevent being considered an enemy by the Americans in the postwar period. Therefore, Sihanouk's strategy was not only consistent with the Theravada Buddhist value of following the middle path, it was also consistent with regional leadership models. However, in this case, moderation and a balanced approach towards two different powerful external forces could not overcome the radicalism of the times.

Although this coup of 1970 is almost always referred to as a CIA-backed coup, the general consensus of experts is there is no evidence of direct involvement by the White House or the CIA while almost certainly there were some US military intelligence officers involved (Clymner, 2004).

Only a week after the military coup, Sihanouk announced the creation of the National United Front of Kampuchea, which joined in partnership with the Khmer Rouge in the battle for control of the country against the new regime. The leadership of the Khmer Rouge was dominated by hardline communists, but most popular support for the removal of the Lon Nol government was due to support for Sihanouk. The Lon Nol government had a number of weaknesses, including possessing an inefficient military leadership. When Lon Nol suffered a stroke the government lacked the leadership needed to give it direction. In the Paris Accords that were signed ending the widespread American involvement in Vietnam, Cambodia's fate was not clearly spelled out and the Lon Nol government was left to fend for itself (Chandler, 2000: 202, 296; Clymner, 2004; 53–62; Tully, 2005: 154–8).

North Vietnamese troops remained in Cambodia after the signing of the Paris Accords and, with the withdrawal of American air support, the war began to go even worse for the Lon Nol government and morale among the government troops sank even lower. After a long and bloody fight, the city of Phnom Penh fell to the rebels on 17 April 1975 and the Khmer Rouge were now in power. Within hours of final victory, the Khmer Rouge ordered the entire population of the city, which had swelled to approximately 2 million, to evacuate the city and go to the countryside and grow rice. Sihanouk was made the first head of state of the country, but was given no real power and was forced to resign the following year. The Khmer Rouge instituted radical policies based on a mix of paranoid nationalism with an imperfect understanding of Marxism that resulted in one of the most genocidal regimes in recent history which has been estimated to have resulted in the deaths of nearly 2 million Cambodians (Chandler, 2000: 208–11; Eanes, 2002; Clymner, 2004; 70–5; Tully, 2005: 172–78).

The brutality and ineffectiveness of the Khmer Rouge regime's misrule of the country has been well documented and included execution of intellectuals and anyone with connections to the country's perceived enemies in either the West or Vietnam. When the first accounts of the atrocities of the regime were initially revealed by the flood of refugees seeking safety these accounts were often dismissed by mainstream academics and former anti-war activists in the West, but over time the evidence of the scale of the tragedies became too great to continue to make excuses for. However, it is unlikely that even if the scale of the tragedies had been known and acknowledged the international community would have been able to react, as it would have been politically very difficult to launch any type of military intervention which could have stopped the bloodshed at that time as the bad taste of America's military adventures in Southeast Asia was still fresh in the mouths of most Americans and others (Ear, 1995; Clymner, 2004: 107–11).

There was a mass exodus of refugees fleeing the country under the Khmer Rouge rule and as time went by this flood of people included members of the regime as the paranoia of the rulers increased and the Khmer Rouge began to turn on its own members and accused many of spying for the regime's enemies. Two prominent members of the Khmer Rouge, Heng Samrin and Hun Sen, fled to Vietnam and became allies of the government of Vietnam. Cambodia's involvement in international political struggles and intrigue continued, and the Soviet-backed Vietnamese launched an attack on the Chinese-backed Khmer Rouge on Christmas Day in 1979. The Khmer Rouge army, which had been weakened by continuous purges and lack of popular support, proved no match for the battle-hardened Vietnamese troops which overran most of the country in a few weeks (Cheong, 1992: 401; Chandler, 2000: 222–5; Stuart-Fox, 2003: 199; Tully, 2005: 192–3; Pribbenow, 2006).

With the overthrow of the Khmer Rouge regime, the country began to wake up from its nightmare; however, concerns over Soviet expansion in Southeast Asia led American, Thai, ASEAN countries and other international actors to support the remnants of the Khmer Rouge which acted as a guerrilla rebel force from its base in western parts of the country. This support had the result of preventing any significant amounts of international aid to reach the country and help it rebuild. While the Vietnamese government actually invested some money in Cambodia at the time, which was a burden as Vietnam was itself in the middle of economic troubles, the new government did not create the conditions needed for significant growth and recovery (Jeldres, 1993: 105; Stuart-Fox, 2003: 201; Tully, 2005: 202–16).

After the end of the Soviet Union and the Cold War, Vietnam's hold over Cambodia began to fade and the UN-led UNTAC mission to allow the country to make the transfer to a democracy was begun in 1992. While the mission was a turning point in Cambodia's history, the mission itself has been heavily criticized for the arrogance of many of the UN personnel, the bureaucratic nature of its organization and lack of Asian and Cambodian experience of much of the mission's leadership. The mission created huge income divisions within society as UNTAC international staff were paid an astonishing $4,350 dollars a month and local staff between $300 and $500 a month while in the local economy teachers were paid $6 and judges $20 a month at this time (Jeldres, 1993; Chandler, 2000: 228; Widyono, 2008).

Although the UN declared the elections it sponsored free and fair, most outside observers did not agree and the outcome did not seem to be consistent with democratic principles. In 1993, Cambodians, over 4 million strong, went to the polls to select the representatives of their new government. While no single party gained a majority of votes, the party with the most votes was FUNCINPEC, a loose coalition with connections to the royal family, while the Cambodian People's Party (CPP), led by Hun Sen and the party of the existing Vietnamese-installed government, received the second highest number of votes. However, after the elections the CPP refused to give up power and, as it controlled the military, none of the parties involved were willing to attempt to force the existing government out. In the end the UN approved a compromise where basically two separate governments – one led by First Prime Minister Ranariddh and FUNCINPEC, and another government led by Second Prime Minister Hun Sen and the CPP – were allowed to exist side by side. After spending millions of dollars the UN pulled out before peace and stability were obtained and left the Khmer to sort out the mess by themselves. The power-sharing arrangement did not last long and since Hun Sen and the CPP controlled the military and police forces they were able to oust the government led by FUNCINPEC and took full control over the government and have governed ever since (Tully, 2005: 221–6; Widyono, 2008).

While Hun Sen's government has justifiably received severe criticism for its lack of democratic values, corruption and treatment of its political opponents, the government has led the country through extremely turbulent times and has presided over it while something resembling peace and stability has been attained (Chandler, 2000: 244; Downie and Kingsbury, 2001; Header, 2005).

Although two major opposition parties, the Human Rights Party (HRP) and Sam Rainsy Party (SRP), have agreed to join together and run against the CPP in 2013, it is unlikely the CPP's domination of the political scene will be seriously challenged. Despite being involved in widespread corruption, the CPP has been able through its funneling of foreign financial aid into building schools, temples and roads and taking credit for the projects, build strong grassroots support, primarily in rural areas. The government continues to tread a fine line between being an authoritarian state having the sole function of holding onto power while limiting freedom of speech in the political arena and having all the outward trappings, such as elections, of a democracy which are needed to give the government enough legitimacy to satisfy the needs of its financial aid donors in the international community. However, China's influence in both investment and as a source of financial aid which is given with no human rights or democratic strings attached has the potential to change the point of balance between authoritarianism and openness (So, 2011).

The country's recent diplomatic relationships with the US have not always been without tensions. Due to political violence against the government's opponents in 1997, the US government placed lasting economic sanctions on trade with the country which were not fully lifted until 2007. However, in more recent times US trade with and financial aid to Cambodia has steadily increased. One of the reasons behind the US's renewed interest in Cambodia is most likely to counter increased Chinese influence in the region (Thayer, 2010).

Business environment

Cambodia is a country with a population estimated to be slightly over 13 million, which is spread out over a considerable land area giving the country a very low population density. An estimate by the World Bank in 2010 for Cambodia indicates the country's has a GDP per capita of only $760 dollars. Cambodia is located between the two far more densely populated nations of Vietnam and Thailand. Although historically linked to Vietnam from being a colony in French Indochina, it is culturally closer linked to Thailand due to sharing similar religious and cultural traditions (Hipsher, 2010a). Cambodia came to the world's attention in the 1970s due to the genocidal regime of the Khmer Rouge whose legacy the country continues to work to overcome.

Like much of the world, the country experienced a significant economic downturn in 2009 but, helped by a growing demand for Cambodian-made garments and an increase in the number of foreign tourists, growth forecasts for the future are estimated at over 6% annually. The majority of the population lives in rural areas and the country has a poverty rate of around 30% with the majority of the poor living in rural areas and engaged in the agricultural sector. Higher food prices and reliance on foreign tourism and garment exports, both of which were hurt by the recent global economic slowdown, have prevented any significant recent reductions in the percentage of individuals living in poverty (Asian Development Bank, 2011a).

Cambodia shares many characteristics with other less developed nations. The country is primarily rural with little heavy industry, high levels of illiteracy, the majority of the population lacking modern skills due to working in the subsistence agricultural sector, corruption, a lack of managerial and technical skills and an underdeveloped educational system (Mahmood, 2005; Tan, 2007; Kao et al., 2008; Ear, 2009). These conditions alongside Cambodia's relative lack of population and their limited spending power have restricted the amount of foreign investment coming into the country.

The US is Cambodia's largest trading partner and nearly all of the exports from Cambodia to the US are in textiles and garments (Thayer, 2010: 450). Much of the country's economic growth has been due to the textile and garment sector, which primarily employs young women from the rural areas of the country. The country's openness to foreign investment, low labor costs and abundance of low-skilled labor has made Cambodia an attractive location for foreign investment in this industry. The industry has grown very rapidly, has contributed to the country's development and is almost entirely controlled by foreign interests, most of whom are ethnic Chinese. Without this option for employment, many of the young women would most likely remain working on the farms or in the informal economy (Dasgupta and Williams, 2010). However, the economic downturn in the US has slowed exports in this sector resulting in significant numbers of layoffs, mostly of woman who make up the majority of the workers in the garment and textile sector (Tong, 2010).

Challenges will need to be overcome in order for continued economic growth and development to occur. Diplomatic tensions with Thailand over the Preah Vihear Temple which straddles the border between the two countries and which both countries lay claim to could result in lessening trade between the two countries as well as Thai investment in the country. Moreover, dollarization of the nation's economy has given the government very few macroeconomic tools to use and inflation has been a problem. Another problem the country needs to overcome to become competitive internationally is the high price of electricity. The country will need to find employment for the large percentage of its population that will be coming of age in the near future, as more than 50% of the population of the country is below the age of 21 (Menon, 2011).

Cambodia may have some unique features that come from its history and the influence of religion on the vast majority of the people, Theravada Buddhism. Hipsher (2010a) proposed the business environment in Cambodia shares the following five characteristics which are a reflection of the religious and traditional values which it shares with its neighbors, Laos, Thailand and Myanmar/Burma: (1) organizations are hierarchical, but paternalistic in nature; (2) emphasis on flexibility with little in the way of long-term planning; (3) both managers and workers have a relatively low level of locus of control; (4) moderation of ambition (taking the middle path); and (5) a greater focus on the individual than found in most collectivist Asian societies.

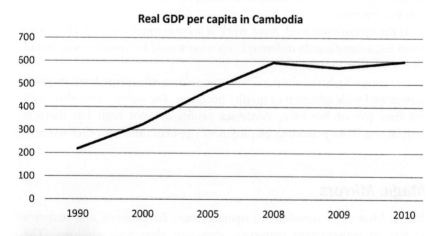

Real GDP per capita in Cambodia

Figure 9.1

Source: UNCTAD (2011: 130)

Case studies

Elegance

The first case is of a shop called Elegance, which is located in the city of Siem Reap. It could be said the shop is using a differentiation strategy as it tries to have a wider selection and stocks some specialized items which other stores don't have. However, while in some cases its prices for specialized items are higher than its competitors, price does matter and because of the relatively low purchasing power of the majority of its customers it makes sure it does not price items outside the normal price range. For non-specialized items which are identical to items found in competitors' shops, it charges approximately the same price which would be found elsewhere.

Elegance sells clothes and underwear for women and competes with similar shops and clothes being sold in stalls at the local markets, which have much lower overheads than for entrepreneurs running a permanent store. Therefore, like most retailers in the formal economy it cannot compete on price with sellers in the informal economy resulting in being forced to use either a differential or niche/focus strategy.

Management style is very informal. There are few written and formal instructions; instead, the company uses a personal and paternalistic style of management. For recruitment we also see the informal nature of the firm as the firm hires workers the owner knows, or who have been recommended by other employees. Pay is in the same range as its competitors, but Elegance offers some additional benefits, like shorter work hours, than other companies.

At the operational level, most work is done manually and would not be considered significantly different from what would be found in other retail stores in other locations.

The owner feels the shop gains a competitive advantage from its good service and wide selection of quality products. The owner, who also has a full-time job of her own, confesses profits are not high but there is satisfaction from providing employment opportunities for other women.

Magic Mirrors

Magic Mirrors (a pseudonym) operates near Battambang and makes a variety of construction materials, including glass and windows. The company was started by an individual who learned the trade while working in another company.

While the company's prices are similar to those found in its competitors, it tries to differentiate itself from its competition by providing quicker and more reliable service. This is very important as its primary customers are construction companies and retail outlets.

The management style is mostly informal and training is done primarily on the job. Hiring is done informally with new employees being mostly those who have been recommended by current employees or are personally known by the owner.

The company tries to learn about new production techniques but still primarily relies on labor-intensive techniques as the cost of new equipment is high while the cost of labor is not.

Puthyrith's Auto Repair

The third case is of a family-owned automotive repair shop, Puthyrith's Auto Repair (a pseudonym) located in western Cambodia. Due to its location away from the city, there is little competition. Therefore, its location and the skill of the owner in doing repairs are its primary competitive advantages. Although there is little competition, the company is limited in what it can charge for its services due to the relatively low average income of its customers.

All employees are family members; therefore, management and HR practices are very informal and based on personal relationships.

Operationally, the company makes limited use of technology, but usually relies on the knowledge and skills of the owner of the company. However, as the technology used to make cars continues to change the owner needs to constantly update his knowledge in order to be able to repair newer cars which incorporate newer technology.

Analysis

In all three cases, each company did not compete primarily on price, but did need to keep their prices in the range their customers could afford. We also see that interpersonal aspects are quite informal and in keeping with the Theravada Buddhist values that are so common in the region. On the operational level, while we see some use of modern technology and worldwide best practices, the full implementation of these are restricted due to lack of economies of scale in small firms, lack of capital available to the firms and the low cost of labor making the retention of labor-intensive technology feasible.

Informal economy and informal entrepreneurs

The majority of Cambodians work in the informal sector of the economy. While visiting Sisophon, a Khmer friend made the astute comment, 'There are too many people selling things.' There are very large numbers of people working as informal entrepreneurs in the country and too little value being added to the economy by most of these efforts. The following cases exam the motivations of some of these individuals.

Ms. Solyna

The first informal entrepreneur examined is Ms. Solyna (a pseudonym) who sells rice and other types of food at the roadside during the mornings in Battambang. Ms. Solyna has been selling rice at the same location for nearly 10 years. She took over from her mother who used to run the same business. Her customers are people traveling on the road in the morning, often going to work, wanting some breakfast. She has a number of return customers who praise the taste of her offerings and appreciate the low price.

Ms. Solyna doesn't really think of what she does as running a business, she thinks of it as a job she goes to nearly every day. She feels selling food at the roadside is a good option for her as she feels she lacks the experience and education needed for more formal types of employment.

Ms. Solyna doesn't have any real plans to change what she does for a living and has no plans to expand or move her business into the formal sector of the economy. While Ms. Solyna might not think and plan strategically, she has learned from her experiences and made adjustments in her pricing and product offerings in response to customer needs and competition.

She feels her business/job makes her a sufficient income but of course there are downsides to running an informal business, including being outside in the tropical sun and having a smelly canal running close to where she works. Her sister helps her out from time to time, but mostly this business in a one-woman show.

Ms. Sreykeo

The second case examined is a restaurant run by Ms. Sreykeo (a pseudonym). Ms. Sreykeo runs the restaurant from her home and has been doing this for a little over a year. Sometimes business is good, other times business is a little slow. Running a restaurant in the informal economy was not her first choice of occupation. She would prefer to have a job with an adequate salary, but good jobs are difficult to come by in western Cambodia. In fact, were she not an entrepreneur in the informal sector of the economy she says she would probably try her luck working in Thailand where jobs are easier to come by.

She started her business because the work was not as strenuous as other activities she could have done and there was a lack of competition in the village she lives in. She gets many of her supplies of vegetables and meat from her sister's family who own a farm. One of the plus sides of this type of business is if she is unable to sell all of the food she makes she can save the leftovers and serve them to her children and family.

Ms. Sreykeo has no plans to expand the business in the future or to move it into the formal economy. However, she does keep trying to improve her business on an operational level. She often reads books on cooking and listens to recommendations and suggestions from her customers. The downsides of running the business include no separation between her professional and personal life because her business is run out of her home and because of the long hours when business is good.

Ms. Raksa

Ms. Raksa (a pseudonym) runs an informal business selling food, mostly rice and other foods that accompany rice, from her home. She has been running this business for about 8 years, but she is disappointed with the overall profits she makes. If given the opportunity, she would prefer to have a full-time job with a steady salary, but good jobs in her village outside Battambang in Cambodia are rare, especially for someone like Ms. Raksa who doesn't have specialized skills or advanced education. She started the business as she was already cooking for her children, and just started to make some extra to sell to her neighbors.

Her primary customers are those in her neighborhood who know her and choose to buy her products due to the convenience, good taste and low prices. She relies on her husband for advice and she has learned about what foods sell and how to manage supplies to ensure profitability while running her business. She started out mostly selling noodle dishes, but she has changed her product offerings to better match the demands of the customers.

She combines selling food at home with taking care of her domestic and child-rearing duties. By being an informal entrepreneur she can earn some extra money for her family while still taking care of her children and family. She dreams of opening a larger restaurant someday, but for the time being that is mostly a dream and she has no solid plans to actually make this dream happen.

Mr. Sopheak

Mr. Sopheak (a pseudonym) owns and operates an informal motorcycle repair business in Battambang. He has been running this business for over 15 years. He started this business as he needed to earn money to support his family and there were few options for paid employment. Mr. Sopheak feels his lack of education made it difficult to find quality paid employment, and therefore his best option was to create his own job. He is good with his hands although at times he gets tired of the dirt, grease and mess that accompany being a motorcycle mechanic in the informal sector of the economy.

On the upside, he has grown used to the flexibility that comes from being self-employed and enjoys being able to set his own hours. He has no real plans for the future and thinks of his work as a job – not really a business to grow and expand. He takes things day by day but for now his work supports his family and he feels it is currently his best option.

Analysis

None of the individuals examined fit the description of a risk-taking innovative entrepreneur trying to start a business to seek wealth. Instead, we see individuals who have been pushed into creating their own jobs because of lack of other opportunities. Each of the individuals has shown flexibility and the ability to respond and adjust to customer demands; however, they have not created employment for others outside their own families and could not be seen as creating new ideas leading to increases in productivity or innovation or to new industries coming about

Figure 9.2   **Poipet, Cambodia**

in the region. The informal economy has a place in poverty reduction, but it does not replace the need for a growing formal sector of the economy where increases in productivity, innovation and transformation of occupational skills are more likely to take place.

10

Laos PDR

Abstract: Laos PDR is a small landlocked country in Southeast Asia where poverty is common. Culturally, linguistically and historically the country is closely linked to Thailand. The country has a government controlled by the Communist Party and was previously a colonial possession of France. Case studies from the country are examined and it is proposed business development in the country will be affected by the small size of the country's market, its cultural heritage and its geographical location.

Key words: Laos, Lao, Tai, case studies, Theravada Buddhism, Vientiane, France.

Country background

The history of Laos is intertwined with the history of the entire region of mainland Southeast Asia, and there is debate over whether Lao is a separate culture with a distinct language and history or whether Lao culture is a part of the greater Tai culture linked too close to Thai culture, language and history to be separable. Within mainland Southeast Asia, the term Lao has been widely used to distinguish both a regional and linguistic subset of Thai citizens, often in a derogatory manner, as well as to refer to citizens of the country of Laos PDR (Burusphat et al., 2011; Ford, 2011: 116). Over 100 years ago, Freeman (1910: 13) observed, 'Laos is the name of a people, not of a political division,' while Stuart-Fox (2002) commented, 'the Lao people have a history, Laos does not,' and Jumsai (2000: 1) expressed the idea, 'One wonders why the Thai and the Lao, though two people of different countries speak the same language? Why are both Buddhist? Why do the two people share the same cultural activities?' Yet, while culturally similar there has also historically been a distinction between the people of Lao and the Thais (previously referred to as the Siamese). 'Though the Laos and the Siamese are both Shans and have much in common, a stranger would note at once many marked differences in natures, habits, and customs of these two peoples' (Curtis, 1903: 8). Chanthanom (1998: 195) reported after doing interviews on both sides of the Thai–Lao border, 'Every interviewee agreed that people in northeastern Thailand are Laotian, not Thai. They are divided by laws, not by culture.'

Despite its historical linkage with the rest of the region, today Laos is an independent country with its own independent government. Much of the recent history of Laos, at least that originating in Laos, has been written from a Marxist viewpoint which has deemphasized the role of royalty and the historical connection with the people of Thailand and has placed more importance on the role of peasant uprisings (Gay, 2002). The government's focus on its socialist nature has not been well accepted by the population and has been replaced to some extent by a more recent attempt to link the government with the country's Theravada Buddhist heritage (Martinez, 2011). Moreover, during the colonial era French historians downplayed the country's historical connection with Thailand to assist in the justification for including Laos in French Indochina (Kratoska and Batson, 1992: 283; Jumsai, 2000: 6).

Traditionally, it has been believed the 'Tai' people – a linguistic group which includes the Lao, Thai and various 'hill tribes' throughout Southeast Asia and Southern China – emigrated from a region which is today located in the southern part of Guangxi province in China, which it was speculated they originated from (Evans, 2002: 2). There is a legend in Laos that prior to the arrival of the Tai the present day land of Laos was inhabited by a race of giants in a kingdom called Sawa (Phothisane, 2002: 83–4). It has long been believed the present day Tai are descendents of the first Tai Kingdom of Nan Chao in the present day Yunnan province of China (Syamananda, 1993: 14; Pholsena, 2004: 237). It has been speculated the Tai were eventually forced out of Nan Chao after a bitter struggle with Mongol-led Chinese forces and moved to conquer much of mainland Southeast Asia.

This traditional theory of the Tai race coming from somewhere in China to conquer the lands of Southeast Asia is being challenged and an alternative theory has emerged which proposes the origins of the Tai people are actually from the region of present day southern China, northern Vietnam and upper Laos (Pholsena, 2004). Jumsai (2000: 8) reminded us that Chinese chronicles referred to the people living in Nan Chao as the

Payi or the *Huans* and not Tai. Regardless of actual location of origin, 'prior to the nineteenth century it makes little sense to use the ethnic terms "Lao" or "Thai," although it is common for national histories to project such entities into the distant past' (Evans, 2002: 2).

King Borum was a legendary ruler of Nan Chao and a central figure in Lao mythology/history who was reported to have ruled from AD 729 to 749. The legend states he, along with Khun Lo, were great and wise rulers who reigned over a prosperous and powerful kingdom. However, the rulers who followed were not of the same caliber and the ensuing decline led to the defeat of the independent kingdom of Nan Chao by the forces of Kublai Khan in 1253 (Jumsai, 2000: 10–26). However, there appears to be a lack of solid evidence to support these legends.

The earlier history of present day Laos is not well known, but it is known the area was inhabited and engaged in international commerce prior to the traditional date for the coming of the Tai. 'Trade routes in the middle Mekong date from prehistoric times and trans Mekong commercial traffic was by no way new in the seventh century' (Hoshino, 2002: 53). Therefore, it appears a complex civilization was active in present day Laos before the time of recorded history of the region, but whether these individuals were 'Lao' or another ethnic group does not appear to be entirely clear.

Lan Xang Hom Khao (a million elephants under a white parasol), or more commonly referred to as Lan Xang, is generally considered the first great Lao kingdom, which was founded by King Fa Ngum, who was most likely a vassal of the then powerful Kingdom of Angkor (Evans, 2002: 9). The rulers of the other *muang* around the area of today's Laos submitted to the overrule of King Fa Ngum with the exception of Phanya Phao, the ruler of Muang Phai Nam, located at the site of present day Vientiane; therefore, King Fa Ngum had to conquer this territory through the use of force (Grabowsky and Tappe, 2011). The territory of the kingdom at its height extended as far west as the area around present day Roi-et in Thailand (Jumsai, 2000: 103–5). King Fa Ngum ruled from 1352 to 1371 and 'was considered by the Lao to be one of their greatest kings. He united the country into a powerful state and the extent of his country was probably the biggest known in Lao history' (Jumsai, 2000: 98). However, the kingdom was never able to create an organization that was efficient at more than recruiting and mobilizing an army (Taylor, 1992: 172). By 1371 the King was driven into exile and in 1374 he died (Evans, 2002: 10; Jumsai, 2000: 108). Today the official government history celebrates Fa Ngum as the founder of the state that is considered the political ancestor of the modern Laos state (Grabowsky and Tappe, 2011: 13).

Un Huan, also called Sam Saen Thai, succeeded Fa Ngum as ruler of Lan Xang and kept the kingdom together until his death in 1416, which was followed by a long period of factional fighting and confusion until the kingdom was reunited by a king named Sainyachakkaphat in 1442 (Taylor, 1992; 172; Grabowsky and Tappe, 2011: 13). During the period of confusion there was a woman named Kaeo Phimphen, commonly known as Maha Thewi, who reigned over much of the country from 1428 to 1438 (Phothisane, 2002: 77–9).

The first Europeans reported to have visited the territories that now comprise the country of Laos were a group of Portuguese mercenaries who accompanied a Burmese envoy in a visit in 1545. Europeans who visited the area in the seventeenth century reported on the extensive trade being carried on in the region and international trade disputes that were ongoing between the kingdoms located in what is today Laos, Thailand and Cambodia. The Europeans in Laos at the same time also noticed the importance the Lao placed on the practice of Theravada Buddhist (Ngaosrivathana and Ngaosrivathana, 2002).

According to the official history of the Laos government, the last great King of Lan Xang was Sulinyavongsa, who died in 1694 and shortly therefore the kingdom went into a state of decline (Grabowsky and Tappe, 2011: 18).

In 1707, Lan Xang was split into two independent kingdoms with one monarch located in Luang Prabang, the capital of Lan Xang, and the other in the present day capital of Vientiane (Phothisane, 2002). Later, the Lao people were further politically divided with the creation of another kingdom called Champasak (Jumsai, 2000: 86). In the late eighteenth century the various Lao kingdoms became embroiled in the Tay-son rebellion in which the Tay-son general Quang Trung invaded and eventually laid waste to Luang Prabang in 1791 before retreating; however, during this time different parts of Laos were also becoming economically connected with the wider world through alliances and were exporting products through ports in Vietnam (Breazeale, 2002; Quy, 2002; Dutton, 2006).

When the Burmese invaded and sacked the Kingdom of Ayutthaya in present day Thailand in 1776, the Kingdom of Vientiane took advantage of the weakness of the Thai Kingdom and began to expand its geographical influence into territory that had previously been under the control of Ayutthaya. However, the Thai recovery began in 1778 under a general named Taksin. After reuniting the Thai kingdom Taksin invaded and conquered Vientiane and later Luang Prabang, setting the stage for Thai dominance over the territories that used to make up Lan Xang until the coming of the French. In the aftermath of the invasions, much of the population of Laos was forcibly moved to areas in present day Thailand (Evans, 2002: 25).

In 1827, Chao Anou, who came to the throne in 1804 with the approval of the Chakri dynasty in Bangkok, launched a rebellion against the control of the monarch in Bangkok. The rebellion was brutally put down and Chao Anou was brought as a prisoner to Bangkok where he was subjected to public humiliation and torture. Today, King Anou is celebrated as a great Lao patriot (Ford, 2011; Grabowsky and Tappe, 2011).

Thai dominance of Laos continued until the coming of the French colonial era. In 1899, France added Laos into its Indochina territories that already included Cambodia, Tonkin, Annam and Cochinchina. The French justified their claim over Laos using vague claims of previous control of the territory by Vietnam. The first French governor of Laos was Auguste Pavie. French control over Laos was quite light and a census in 1907 showed only 189 French citizens living in the country. Nevertheless, changes to the land and its people did come, such as the abolishment of slavery and the heavy immigration of Vietnamese who the French used as administrators of the country (Kratoska and Batson, 1992: 282; Jumsai, 2000: 234; Evans, 2002: 45–7, 59).

Laos, like most of France's other colonies, was an economic burden on France, and it has been suggested the possession and holding on to colonies may have had more to do with French nationalism and pride than it had to do with economic interests. Although initially there were intentions of integrating Laos into the economy of the rest of Indochina, the reality was the majority of international trade in the region remained in the hands of Chinese merchants and was conducted through Thailand – not Vietnam. Prior to World War II, there were a few minor uprisings against the French but nothing that actually threatened French control over Laos (Kratoska and Batson, 1992: 282–3; Evans, 2002: 42, 49–59).

Without becoming a territory of the French, it is unlikely Laos as it is known today would exist. Although current Lao historians have been trying to link the current Laos state with an ancient past, Kratoska and Batson (1992: 283) felt the French 'virtually created Laos in its modern form. Pre-modern "Laos" was composed of a number of rival principalities, often in conflict with one another and all subject to varying external pressures.' Evans (2002: 70) found 'When the French took over Laos there was no sense of a Lao nation among the population.' Even the name Laos as a country or state was invented by the French, 'The term

"Laos" is an arbitrary one, being the French spelling of the name of a single tribe of Laos, namely the Lao tribe. But the Siamese call all the Laos in their kingdom and in French territory Lao' (Curtis, 1903: 5). Jumsai (2000: 2) made the claim 'Prior to the French occupation, the Laos referred to their language as Thai' and the French thought of Laos as 'more a cartographic reality than a social or historical one' (Evans, 2002: 71).

However, Lao nationalism began to emerge and was fueled to a large extent by anti-Vietnamese sentiment due to the large influx of Vietnamese who were used by the French to run the administration of the government (Evans, 2002: 70).

As in most of the rest of Southeast Asia, during World War II Laos fell under the control of the Japanese, which helped to weaken the colonial era concept that Westerners were naturally superior and had a right to rule over other ethnic groups. The Japanese allowed the French to continue their rule until March 9, 1945 when the Japanese forced the French out and the King of Luang Prabang was pressured into declaring independence. However, the end of the war brought a split between the King, who agreed to a return to French rule, and the faction which wanted the declaration of independence to stand, led by Prince Phetsarath. Although often given credit as the father of Lao Nationalism, Prince Phetsarath actually favored joining into a political union with Laos' linguistic and culturally close neighbor, Thailand and opposed the French idea of joining Laos into the Vietnamese-dominated Indochina Federation (Ivarsson and Goscha, 2007). Prince Phetsarath, who was forced to leave his positions in the government upon the return of the French in 1946, was the eldest brother of Prince Souvanna Phouma and Prince Soupanouvong, the leaders of opposing forces who would seek to control an independent Laos in the years to come (Jumsai, 2000: 276).

In response to the French return, a Lao nationalist movement called Lao Issara with close links to Vietnam was formed. While the movement was neither long-lasting nor successful in its goal of achieving independence it did prove to be an effective training ground for many future leaders of the later Lao independence movement including Prince Souphanouvong and Kaysone Phomvihan (Evans, 2002: 85–7). A limited form of democracy was introduced by the French with power staying initially in French hands, but the days of the colonial era were coming to an end and full sovereignty was granted to the Royal Lao Government (RLG) in October 1953 (Evans, 2002: 90–1).

King Sisavangvong, who had reigned for over 50 years and had been very open in his pro-French attitudes, died and a new monarch, King Savang Vatthana, ascended the throne. In the 1960s a short-lived regime led by the neutralist Souvanna Phouma came to power in the aftermath of a coup led by army Captain Kong Le. However, it was not long before a bloody battle ensued with troops loyal to the anti-Communist Phoumi Nosavan overrunning Vientiane resulting in the formation of a government headed by Boun Oum (Evans, 2002: 117–19).

Under pressure from the United States, a compromise in 1962 was reached by the three princes who controlled the political situation in Laos at the time: Boun Oum, Souvanna Phouma and Souphanouvong. Most of the power was held by the elites who were members of the old royal families who had previously been given access to Western education during the French reign. This compromise, called neutralism, ended up playing into the hands of the Communists, the Pathet Lao, who by 1962 had fallen under the control of the North Vietnamese who were seeking control of the north of the country to allow its troops to travel to the south of Vietnam. By the time this second coalition government fell in 1964, the military of the Pathet Lao and the North Vietnmaese had control of around half of the territory of the country (Cheong, 1992: 402–4; Evans, 2002: 123–8).

Laos got caught up in the war centered in Vietnam between Communist forces and the non-Communist world, which few Laotians cared about or understood. The US wanted to limit its military involvement in Laos to preventing the North Vietnamese from using the country as a supply route into the south. While the North Vietnamese Communist forces wanted both access to supply routes into the south as well as increasing the scope of the war to make it more unpopular politically in the US. While there was an international agreement that forbade foreign troops from being stationed in Laos, both sides broke the agreement. The US pretended to be following the agreement and stationed its aircraft, which were used to fly bombing raids into Laos, in Thailand while having a limited number of special forces in the country who concentrated on training local troops, mostly from the ethnic Hmong community led by General Vang Pao, to do the fighting. While the North Vietnamese openly violated the UN agreement by having large numbers of Vietnamese Communist troops continue fighting against the RLG's troops, who were loyal to the government and trained and supplied by the US. After the US decided to pull its military out of Southeast Asia, the RLG quickly collapsed and the Pathet Lao took control of the country in 1975 (Kurlantzick, 2005). The Chinese also sent a large number of non-combat troops to build roads and engage in other activities in Laos to support the Pathet Lao both before and after the Communist victory (Zhang, 2002).

After the last King of Lao abdicated in 1975 and a new Communist government with Souphanouvong as president and Kaysone Phomvihan as prime minister came into existence, economic changes happened in the country. The majority of the ethnic Chinese merchant class and most educated Laotians simply migrated across the easy-to-cross border into Thailand leaving the country with a severe shortage of human capital. Moreover, there was considerable retribution dished out against some of the former leaders of the RLG and against the Hmong population, so much so that it has been described as coming close to being considered 'ethnic cleansing' (Evans, 2002: 178–86).

The new government signed a 20-year Friendship and Cooperation Treaty with Vietnam in 1977 and closely followed Vietnam's example in implementing a socialist economic system. However, socialism never really took hold in Laos and as early as 1979 there were moves towards returning to a market-based economy. By 1980 the final Vietnamese troops left the country. As prior to the Communist takeover, the country continued to rely on foreign aid, at first from other Communist countries but, after the fall of Communism in Eastern Europe, the government of Laos PDR opened up to the rest of the world and became a major recipient of foreign aid from the West and Japan (Evans, 2002, 187–227).

Politically, the country has remained dominated by a few individuals during the years following the Communist takeover. While there have been numerous economic reforms, there has been little in the way of political reforms and the country continues to have a very authoritarian government with corruption rampant (Gunn, 2008; Stuart-Fox, 2011). The current president, Choummaly Sayasone, is well over 70 years of age and is considered part of the more traditional leadership while there is some speculation the vice president, Bounnyang Vorachit, who was previously the prime minister, is more inclined to consider some reforms. Thongsing Thammavong is the current prime minister (at the time of writing).

Although the US has maintained continuous diplomatic relations with Laos since it achieved independence, it is not surprising there have been some disagreements between the two countries. The government of Laos remains leery of the US's focus on human rights and fears the US is plotting a peaceful revolution which will bring down the one-party political system. A bi-lateral US–Laos trade agreement was finally ratified by the US government in 2004 after a 7-year delay (Thayer, 2010).

While the US provides some development aid to Laos, its main donors of financial aid are Japan, France, Sweden, Germany and Australia. The government of Laos may be planning to further engage in the global economic system and is primarily looking for US support in its hope of eventually join the WTO. Nevertheless, Laos' relationship with the US, both politically and economically, is less important than its relationships with its regional neighbors, Thailand and Vietnam, and the government is increasingly looking towards China as a source of investment and political support (Pholsena, 2010).

While there have been some recent changes in economic policy and a shift in focus towards China, it is often difficult to predict the future direction of the country.

Politics is conducted in contemporary Laos, entirely within the upper echelons of the LPRP and with no publicity. Nothing reported in the tightly controlled Lao media will reflect differences in political opinion. There will be no political commentary, let alone speculation. Diplomats may pick up rumours and talk to one another, but what is really going on within the Party, and how decisions are arrived at, will as usual remain almost entirely opaque to outside observers.

(Stuart-Fox, 2011: 33)

Business environment

Laos PDR is one of the most improvised countries in Asia with a per capita GDP under $1,000, although the country has recently been experiencing respectable growth rates and forecasts are for continued significantly positive economic growth rates into the future. Economic growth has been driven largely by exploiting the country's natural resources through mining and the use of the country's rivers to produce hydroelectricity and, to a lesser extent, by tourism. However, the majority of the population continues to work in the agricultural sector which has not seen much growth or improved efficiency in recent years (Asian Development Bank, 2011a). However, Rigg (2005) pointed out in reality many, if not most, rural agricultural families have been engaging in other sectors of the economy while continuing to farm and one should not assume the country's economic growth has not increased incomes in rural farming communities. As the country is fairly insulated from the global economy, the recent global economic crisis has had only a limited impact on the majority of the country's citizens (Phannalangsi, 2011).

While agriculture continues to play a major role in the Laos economy, mining and hydropower are becoming increasingly important. There are well over 100 mining companies operating in the country with the majority being foreign owned and China being the country with the most investment in this sector. Recently, there were 15 hydropower facilities in operation and with the government having signed over 50 other memorandums of understanding (MOUs) to construct additional facilities with most of the power created expected to go to Thailand and Vietnam (Phannalangsi, 2011).

Laos PDR remains one of the most economically underdeveloped nations in Asia and there appears to be opportunities for improvements in the business environment. In a study of the competitiveness of business environments of the ten Southeast Asian nations in ASEAN, Laos came tenth (i.e., last overall). Breaking this down the country was ranked tenth in managerial performance; ninth in human resource performance, ahead only of Cambodia; and tied with Myanmar/Burma for last place in technological performance (Kao et al, 2008). To improve the business environment, Phouphet (2011) suggested the government: (1) improve monetary and fiscal discipline, (2) create additional monetary tools to help create additional stability, (3) continue with market-based reforms especially in the banking sector and privatize more state-owned enterprises and (4) create a better business environment for SMEs to prosper in. As pointed out by Baird (2010), continued central government control over some sectors of the economy have caused numerous problems for some of the country's most disadvantaged citizens as many government-run projects have not taken into account the needs of those being displaced and affected. The author also felt additional reforms which give power to local communities and individuals would be helpful in spreading some of the wealth being created more evenly throughout society.

Tourism has become an increasingly important part of the economy; however, the quality of jobs created in this sector is debatable. Many of the businesses in this sector are family owned and only employ non-family members for non-managerial or non-professional positions. Moreover, much of the work is seasonal with no long-term security and there is little found in the way of skills training or professional development (Southiseng and Walsh, 2011).

Most businesses in the country are relatively small and run by single entrepreneurs or families. Southiseng and Walsh (2010) found most businesses in Laos relied on informal recruiting, selection of personnel, training and managerial procedures. The authors also found Laos firms were lacking in long-term planning, were highly centralized with the owners doing little in the way of delegation and were mostly self-financed.

Laos is connected to the global economy primarily through its membership in the Association of South East Asian Nations (ASEAN).

ASEAN was formed as an anti-Communist organization in 1967 with an original membership consisting of Indonesia, Malaysia, the Philippines, Singapore and Thailand. Laos joined in 1997. Today, ASEAN is characterized by its emphasis on non-interference in the internal matters of its members which is a necessity as its current membership is very diverse in political structure, economic development and social values. Economic integration and agreements started picking up steam in the 1990s and, while the overall level of integration of the region is quite limited if compared to the EU, there has been increasing levels of cooperation and trade within the region. Laos' percentage of trade within the ASEAN region has increased substantially since the country's admission to the organization (Areethamsirikul, 2008).

Culturally, Laos is significantly different from either the West or East Asia. Foreigners have often observed people in Laos have a different attitude towards work, success and ambition than is the norm in the West. 'The Laos are often called lazy, unjustly I think' (Freeman, 1910: 102). During the colonial era the French thought the population was basically lazy and blamed most of Laos's problems on this characteristic (Creak, 2011). Hipsher (2010a) found the influence of Theravada Buddhism – with its emphasis on the middle path, karma and the elimination of desire – has an impact on moderating the ambition of most of the workforce.

This moderation of ambition has often been observed. Rehbein (2007a) pointed out that, while the people of Laos seek out consumer products and increased incomes much like people everywhere, one sees less emphasis on aggressiveness and competition and more emphasis on family, cooperation and moderation of ambition giving the market and workplaces in Laos a softer edge than often seen in other locations. Dana and Barthman (2009) also reported on the impact the Theravada Buddhist value of eliminating desire has had on discouraging the formation of competitive private businesses and entrepreneurship, which has resulted in much of the private sector being controlled by ethnic Chinese entrepreneurs. Owen (1992: 509) found the Southeast Asian tradition of sharing within the community has given the Chinese, who as outsiders have traditionally been free from these obligations to share, an advantage in the market in the modern capitalist system; the domination of ethnic Chinese as merchants in Laos has a long history (Evans, 2002; Hill, 2002; Stuart-Fox, 2003).

Laos is a landlocked country with a small population and has generally not been the recipient of substantial foreign investment except for natural resource extraction.

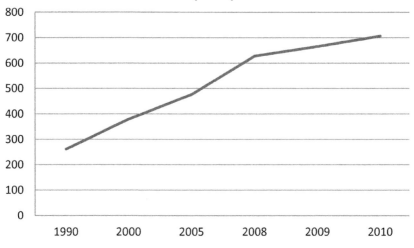

Figure 10.1

Source: UNCTAD (2011)

The small size of the domestic market is inefficient and the low purchasing power of the population itself cannot stimulate economic growth. Therefore, it is clear that Laos is likely to be better off under an outward-looking policy and substantial assistance from international donors; and ASEAN is a clear factor to pull Laos into international economic linkages and resources.

(Areethamsirikul, 2008: 153)

Case studies

Tourism restaurants

Ms. Nattiwapan (a pseudonym) owns two small restaurants in the same general area in the middle of the tourist district of Vientiane. The restaurants appear to using a niche strategy which focuses on foreigners staying in the immediate area. The company prices its food to be competitive with similar competitors targeting the same group of customers. The restaurants serve both Lao and Western food but their prime source of competitive advantage is their near perfect location near both the river and a number of guest houses which cater to tourists.

The company is a family-owned business, which is not unusual in the region. For Ms. Nattiwapan the business is not her sole source of income as she is a government official and her husband works in neighboring Thailand. She employs family members and confesses that part of the reason she keeps the restaurants open is to provide employment for her nieces and other family members. Southiseng and Walsh (2010) have found it is common in Laos for entrepreneurs to employ family members, and family concerns are often as important in decision making as are business concerns. Ms. Nattiwapan keeps her restaurants open when she and her family are available to work, but feels free to keep them closed when other matters come up. Rehbein (2007b) found wealth was generally not an end in itself in Laos and business owners often have additional motivations to run a business in addition to making money. This may be the case here as Ms. Nattiwapan would appear to have personal motivations to being an entrepreneur and business owner in addition to seeking purely financial gains.

Although the restaurants bring in a relatively small income for the family, Ms. Nattiwapan has been offered quite substantial sums to sell the businesses due to their attractive locations. From a purely financial standpoint it would appear selling the restaurants would make sense, yet she has no interest in selling and expects to run the businesses in a more full-time manner when she reaches retirement age, which is still awhile off.

The company does not use formal rules or guidelines and, as a family-owned business, it does not use any formal recruitment, selection or professional development practices.

From an operational standpoint, the restaurants use similar practices to those found in other restaurants of similar size in other parts of the world.

Lao Magic Carpets

Lao Magic Carpets is run by the husband and wife team of Mr. Ismet and Ms. Lani. The company is run as a business with both social and financial objectives that combine elements of private industry with being an NGO training program funded by the German government.

In addition to making products for sale, it also has the goal of training individuals, normally women who are often disabled, to develop skills that they can be used outside the company.

The company uses a niche strategy by selling handmade silk carpets and *kilims* (flat-weave carpets) mostly to foreigner customers. A single carpet can take a group of three or four workers a number of months to complete.

The carpets are made to order and mostly sold to high-end consumers in developed economies, often those who have visited Laos and want both a high-quality work of art as well as helping to provide employment and training to disadvantaged, rural and handicapped women from Laos. Recruitment is mostly done by word of mouth. However, even with the best of intentions managing employees in Laos can be a challenge. Employees often take off to return to homes in the countryside to help with planting and harvesting and to assist with domestic responsibilities. Sometimes employees return after harvesting, planting or handling domestic responsibilities, other times not. The company employs around 30 to 40 workers, and employees need considerable training to be able to produce the carpets and other silk products.

The company uses very labor-intensive practices in the production of its products. First, the silk is selected then spun before being dyed. The company has been moving to exclusively using natural dyes made in Laos instead of using foreign-made synthetic dyes. Finally, the carpets are handmade using approximately 300,000 knots per square meter. However, the company does use modern advertising methods such as the internet to promote and market its products.

Cultural Production Company

The Cultural Production Company, a former state-owned company which was privatized in 1994, is owned by four of the surviving five former managers of the company who worked at the company while it was still state owned. The former managers purchased the company and have continued to run its day-to-day operations. The company has focused on producing authentic and traditional Lao products. The company has five divisions: wood carving, furniture, document supply and printing, traditional Lao musical instruments and sculpture and molding. Traditional Lao culture is inseparable from the Theravada Buddhist religion; therefore, many of the company's products have a religious theme. The company has numerous customers but for its largest and most profitable divisions – furniture, wood carving, and sculpture and molding – its main customers are the government and Buddhist temples (*wats*). In fact, the company has made many of the statues seen in the country's parks, the furniture in the Prime Minister's office and many of the pieces used in renovations of the nation's most famous and revered temples.

Most of the products produced by the company are for domestic sale, although the company has a few foreign customers, usually relatively wealthy ethnic Lao individuals living in developed countries who want a special item for their homes. The company makes a few mass-produced items, such as small Buddha images for individual homes, but the majority of its work is customized and made to order. For example, the company often produces handmade carved wooden doors or other wooden carvings in a specific pattern for a specific temple.

The company does not use formal recruitment or hiring practices; instead, it relies on informal practices. Many of the managers moonlight as instructors at the local college for the arts and choose the best students to become employees; however, as turnover is quite low the need to hire new employees is rather infrequent. The company also uses mostly on-the-job training instead of more formal practices and its purchasing and marketing activities do not appear to be systematic; instead, each situation is handled individually and often the purchaser of the finished product supplies the raw material for the project. The employees and management are not strictly in the business to make money and it would appear they gain considerable satisfaction from producing pieces of art that keep the Lao traditions and the country's primary religion alive.

The company mostly uses traditional by-hand production techniques; however, the use of some modern tools and materials is also seen.

Analysis

In all three cases examined we see the use of a niche or focused business strategy. It would seem these choices of strategy are driven to some extent by the external environment. Due to the country's small domestic market and lack of personnel with technical skills it would be very difficult to compete in the manufacturing sector on cost with companies from China or Thailand. Moreover, without internationally recognized brand names or technological innovation it is difficult for Lao companies to compete using a differentiation strategy targeting top-end consumers in the urban areas.

Both Lao Magic Carpets and the Cultural Production Company use their local knowledge and origins to create products that appeal to customers wanting products that are uniquely Lao in nature, while Ms. Nattiwapan primarily uses her location to advantage in targeting foreign tourists.

The interpersonal business practices of the three firms would appear to be heavily influenced by the social-cultural environment. Hipsher (2011) proposed that firms originating from the Theravada Buddhist countries of Southeast Asia which include Laos PDR are likely to (1) use a paternalistic management style, (2) use informal HR and interpersonal management practices, (3) have few formal rules, (4) are generally more reactive and use little long-term planning and (5) focus more on cooperation and quality of life as opposed to competition and an all out drive for success. The practices of the three companies examined would appear to be consistent with the proposals.

At the operational level, none of the companies are using cutting edge technologies but we do see considerable influence from international practices and technologies. Ms. Nattiwapan's restaurants use 'modern' equipment (including a microwave oven) in producing its food, Lao Magic Carpets uses the internet for its marketing effort and power tools and modern building materials are used to some extent by the Cultural Production Company. However, complete convergence with international operational techniques was not seen in these companies, most likely due to the choice of using a niche strategy and the relatively low cost of labor.

Figure 10.2 Shop selling religious items in Vientiane

While from a strategic standpoint the companies' choices of using niche strategies can be explained using typical strategic management frameworks and choice of operational practices would seem to be consistent with expectations of using a cost–benefit analysis, many of the interpersonal business practices would appear to be shaped by unique local conditions and differ from practices found in different cultural environments.

In Laos, the work ethic differs from what is seen in Western societies or in East Asia. While it would be unfair to claim the owners and managers of the three companies examined are lazy, there does appear to be a moderation of ambition and more of a focus on quality of life that is consistent with the teachings of the middle path which is a central feature of Theravada Buddhism. This moderation of ambition should not be considered an inferior feature of the Laos business environment, but it is a feature which should be understood while developing the most effective and efficient business practices to use within the country.

While managers and business owners in Laos PDR can use the same frameworks for deciding on strategies and operational business practices as managers around the world use, successful interpersonal management practices in Laos will normally require adaptations based on a strong understanding of the unique social-cultural environment found in the country.

11

Island Southeast Asia (Indonesia and the Philippines)

Abstract: Economic development in the island nations of Southeast Asia, the Philippines and Indonesia, takes on some unique characteristics due to each country being an archipelago. The business environment in the Philippines has been influenced by its history of being a colony of both Spain and the USA while Indonesia is the most populous country in the world with a Muslim majority. Case studies are presented and the use of unrelated diversification strategies in LDCs is examined.

Key words: Philippines, Indonesia, Netherlands, Spain, USA, conglomerates, Salim Group, San Miguel, Islam, Catholicism, unrelated diversification.

Area background

The Philippines

'A central paradox in discussing the Philippine past is that the Philippines did not exist as such in the tenth century, or even in the sixteenth century when the archipelago received this name from colonizing Spaniards' (Abinales and Amoroso, 2005: 19). Yet, today the Philippines is a sovereign nation with its own culture. The Philippines is an archipelago which consists of over 7,100 islands and islets with Luzon and Mindanao being the largest (Guillermo and Win, 2005).

Because of the climate and the apparent life-styles of individuals who lived in island Southeast Asia, there is little archeological evidence to give clues about what life was like in prehistoric times. It would seem there were few large settlements and the population in what was to become the Philippines was quite small (Bellwood, 1992).

Archeological evidence suggests the first humans to arrive in the area that is now the Philippines were from Asia and were Aetas or pygmies, yet these are not considered to be the ancestors of modern Filipinos. Later there was an influx of 'Malays' who are considered to be the ancestors of the modern Filipinos (Guillermo and Win, 2005: 2). There does appear to be linguistic links between languages of the Philippines such as Tagalog and Visayan with languages of the peoples who were living in what is now southern China of 4,000 years ago, which provides evidence of the probable ancestral mainland home of the people of the Philippines (Abinales and Amoroso, 2005: 20).

Early civilizations in the regions of island Southeast Asia that today are the Philippines apparently had few large centers of population and lacked central political control. Most of the people lived in small groups under local political leaders whose rule was based on personal loyalty as opposed to living in what would be considered a state or kingdom. However, evidence indicates trade was an important part of life and ocean travel between islands and to mainland Asia appeared to have been a component of life and the economy of the islands from at least the fourth century AD. Sung dynasty chronicles record that in 1001, Butuan, a trading center in northwest Mindanao, sent its first tribute to China through Champa, which was located in present day Vietnam (Abinales and Amoroso, 2005: 23–36).

> The Philippines in early times had less-populated and less-centralized polities than did other parts of Southeast Asia, but was of the same cultural and political realm, sharing the hierarchical yet fluid, ruling practices of the region and contacts organized though the Chinese tribute trade.
>
> (Abinales and Amoroso, 2005: 38)

Sulu, an island group located near northeast Borneo, might have been the first large-scale sultanate in the Philippine archipelago and was recorded as sending several tribute missions to the Ming court in China beginning in 1349. Although Sulu did not have a Muslim ruler until Rajah Baginda and Sayyid Abu Bakr, exiles from Sumatra, arrived around 1450 (Abinales and Amoroso, 2005: 43–4).

Magellan and his crew were the first Europeans and Christians to arrive in the Philippines in 1521 when Magellan's fleet landed in Cebu on their historical trip which circumnavigated the globe. Although Magellan was to die in the islands after getting involved in a local political dispute, his fleet's recording of the visit marked a turning point in the history of the

Philippines. Connecting to Asia from its base in Mexico, the Spanish under leaders such as Ruy López de Villalobos, who named the islands after the then Spanish Crown Prince Felipe, and Miguel López de Legazpi began to make contact with peoples in the archipelago and plant the seeds for colonization and conversion to Christianity (Andaya, B., 1992; Andaya, L., 1992; Abinales and Amoroso, 2005: 49–50; Guillermo and Win, 2005: 5).

During Spanish rule of the Philippines, trade with China increased in importance and there was significant immigration into Manila and other areas from China (Andaya, L., 1992: 367; Abinales and Amoroso, 2005: 65). Much of the work of colonization was done by the Catholic clergy and the Philippines never proved to be profitable for the Spanish; the non-clergy presence of the Spanish was to remain very minimal. In fact, from 1624 to 1634 there were only about 60 Spanish citizens in the country who were not priests (Abinales and Amoroso, 2005: 67). The Spanish 'vision of a united Christian colony owing allegiance to one centre has no precedent in the history of the Philippine archipelago, but it was ultimately to furnish the framework for the modern Philippine state' (Andaya, B., 1992: 418).

However, many Filipinos did not passively accept foreign rule. Manila had to be taken by force and up to 500 people may have been killed (Andaya, B., 1992: 430). There were many attempts, with little success, by the Spanish to conquer and convert the Muslims of Sulu and Mindanao (Abinales and Amoroso, 2005: 69, 96), and in the late nineteenth century the Philippine independence movement was given international attention through the writings of Dr. José Rizal who was eventually executed for his calls for freedom from Spanish rule (Ileto, 1992).

'Spanish rule had two lasting effects on Philippine society: the near universal conversion of the population to Roman Catholicism and the creation of a landed elite.'

(Guillermo and Win, 2005: 5)

Spanish power had steadily weakened and after the US war with Spain in the last years of the nineteenth century, the United States purchased the Philippines and for the first time the US became the master of an overseas colony outside North America; in the early years of American rule there were attempts to militarily defeat the Americans but the uprisings were brutally put down by the new colonial power (Kratoska and Batson, 1992: 260–1; Trocki, 1992: 105; Abinales and Amoroso, 2005: 113–7).

However, there were some major changes which took place under American rule. Filipinos became more involved in the administration of their own country and a system of widespread public education was introduced; in addition, the first elections were held for municipal and then provincial posts including for provincial governors starting in 1901 and 1902 (Kratoska and Batson, 1992: 251, 257; Abinales and Amoroso, 2005: 119, 135; Guillermo and Win, 2005: 7).

In 1934 the US congress passed the Tydings–McDuffie Act which was to make the Philippines into a commonwealth starting in 1935 with full independence scheduled to come in 1946. Manuel Quezon was elected president of the Philippine Commonwealth in 1935. The move towards independence was sidetracked due to the Japanese take-over of the country almost immediately after the attack on Pearl Harbor, but upon the end of the war and the Japanese withdrawal from the country – and the passage of the Bell Act which provided a continuation of free trade between the USA and the newly independent Republic of the Philippines as well as the Tydings Act which provided financial aid from the USA to the Philippines – independence was proclaimed on 4 July 1946 (Kratoska and Batson, 1992: 264; Stockwell, 1992: 349; Abinales and Amoroso, 2005: 149–63). The Philippines paid a heavy price during World War II. Upon the initial Japanese invasion of the islands the Americans led by General Douglas McArthur were defeated, but the Americans later regrouped and retook the islands. In the fighting it has been estimated around one million Filipinos lost their lives (Guillermo and Win, 2005: 8–9).

Even after independence, the ties between the USA and the Philippines remained strong. The Philippines became home to important US military bases and the country received substantial financial aid from the USA for many years (Owen, 1992: 479; Turnbull, 1992: 592, 601).

Manuel Roxas became the president of the newly independent country but he died unexpectedly of a heart attack and was replaced by his vice president, Elpidio Quirino, who was defeated in the next election by Ramon Magsaysay. In 1957, Magsaysay was killed in a plane crash and the Vice President Carlos P. Garcia took office. Garcia later won an election on his own but by the time of his defeat in the election of 1961 by Diosdado Macapagal, Garcia's administration had earned a reputation for corruption. The Macapagel administration's reputation did not fare much better and Macapagel was defeated in the 1965 presidential elections by Ferdinand Marcos (Abinales and Amoroso, 2005: 169–94).

Marcos became the first president of the Philippines to win reelection in 1969; however, using the pretext of battling Communist and Muslim separatists, he declared martial law during his second term. Democracy and elections were suspended and Marcos became a virtual dictator.

After achieving some initial economic success, later in Marcos' reign the country's debt ballooned, corruption increased from already high levels and the economy faltered. Although Marcos began losing popular support he had the backing of the military and was able to retain power for a time through the use of martial law (Cheong, 1992: 425; Abinales and Amoroso, 2005: 198–214; Guillermo and Win, 2005: 11).

One of Marcos' fiercest critics was former senator Benigno Aquino Jr. who was at the time in self-imposed exile. Upon Aquino's return to the Philippines on 21 August 1983, he was assassinated upon leaving the airplane while surrounded by military personnel. The public assumed Marcos ordered the killing and his already fading public support weakened even more (Cheong, 1992: 427; Abinales and Amoroso, 2005: 221; Guillermo and Win, 2005: 12).

In 1986, Marcos inexplicably decided to call a snap election and his challenger was the widow of Benigno Aquino Jr., Corazón (Cory) Aquino. While Cory Aquino clearly won the election, Marcos refused to give up power which led to the 'People Power' movement and more than a million people flooded the streets of Manila demanding Marcos step down. After the military leadership abandoned its support of Marcos and the USA granted him refuge in Hawaii, he and his wife Imelda left the country and the Marcos era came to an end and Cory Aquino became the country's leader (Cheong, 1992: 428; Turnbull, 1992: 636; Abinales and Amoroso, 2005: 224–25).

While the country applauded the return to democracy which came with the Aquino Presidency, the new administration had little success in reversing the country's economic slide and increases in levels of poverty. The new leader was faced with many complex problems which included a number of coup attempts, controversy over renewing the rights of the US to maintain military bases on Philippine soil, agricultural reforms, corruption, heavy foreign debt and renewed violence by leftist and Muslim separatist groups. Despite all the initial optimism, the inability to fix all of these serious problems soon led to a decline in popularity for the new president (Abinales and Amoroso, 2005: 231–43; Guillermo and Win, 2005: 13).

Replacing President Aquino was Fidel Ramos who took a pro-market economic approach and got the budget under control resulting in the Philippines weathering the Asian financial crisis better than most other Southeast Asia nations. His rule of the Philippines is generally considered one of the country's brightest periods and there was general optimism as he left office in 1998 (Abinales and Amoroso, 2005: 244–5; Guillermo and Win, 2005: 13).

In a complete reversal of political direction, the successor of the highly educated and highly experienced Fidel Ramos was the former actor, Joseph Estrada, who won the election through populist promises and appeals to the poorer segments in society. However, Estrada's time in office was plagued by allegations of corruption and cronyism and once again the Philippine people came out in the streets in large numbers in 2001 and the president was forced from office and was replaced by the daughter of former President Diosdado Macapagal, Gloria Macapagal Arroyo. President Arroyo was then reelected by a slim margin in 2004 (Abinales and Amoroso, 2005: 268–83). Although popular when entering the office of the president, upon the end of her time in office her popularity had dramatically declined (Abinales, 2011). In 2010, Senator Benigno Aquino III, the son of former President Corazon Aquino and Benigno Aquino Jr., was elected President.

Philippine society is the product of eastern and western cultural influences, which blend into a distinctive entity. Four cultures and two major religions have shaped the modern Philippines. Early exposure to Chinese cultural and commercial influence, more than three centuries of Spanish colonial rule, and almost 50 years of American tutelage have appreciably altered, but not obscured, the Malayan character of Philippine society.

(Guillermo and Win, 2005: 3)

Indonesia

Hominids and our human ancestors have lived in the islands that today make up Indonesia for a very long time. *Homo erectus* fossils have been found in Java that date from possibly as early as 1.7 million years ago. However, the use of bronze and iron only began around 500 BC, much later than in much of mainland Asia. Another feature of the islands in equatorial Asia was that early varieties of domesticated rice were not well suited to the environmental conditions found in the region and therefore rice cultivation probably played a lesser role in prehistoric Indonesia than it did on Asia's mainland (Bellwood, 1992).

There is limited knowledge of the early kingdoms and political systems in island Southeast Asia. One of the earliest known kingdoms was in central Java in the sixth century, although Chinese records indicate they had visited a thriving civilization called Sitiao in central Java in the third century (Hall, 1992: 202–3). Another important early kingdom was that of the Śailendras, and the scant evidence of these rulers appears to indicate they were not only active in Java but also in Sumatra and along the coast of mainland Southeast Asia in present day Cambodia and Vietnam. Although they were driven out of Java by the Saivite king called amongst other names Pikatan. The Śailendras were Mahayana Buddhists and were known for building the Borobuḍur (Hall, 1992; Taylor, 1992: 177).

The most dominant political force in the region from around the seventh to fourteenth centuries was called Srivijaya. Srivijaya controlled much of the Malay Peninsula, Sumatra and western Java. There had been many smaller kingdoms in the region for centuries but Srivijaya apparently was able to take advantage of its location on international trade routes and through the use of inter-marriage with the royal family of the Śailendras to increase its power (Hall, 1992: 202; Taylor, 1992: 174, 198). Apart from a few historians, the people of the region 'have preserved virtually no memory of what we now call Srivijaya' (Taylor, 1992: 173).

In the late tenth and early eleventh centuries, central Java was in a state of chaos which is generally linked to a military loss to Srivijaya; however, in 1016 Airlangga became the new king and a period of strength and prosperity ensued. Later, the Singhasari ruled from 1222 to 1292 and then the Majapahit from 1293 to 1528. At its peak the Kingdom of Majapahit claimed control over much of the Malay peninsula and most of the islands of Southeast Asia although its true power was probably more limited. Majapahit retained power partially though its control over the spice trade. In 1528 after years of decline due to losing control over trade the ruling family of the Majapahit fled Java and settled in Bali (Hall, 1992: 210–19, 227; Taylor, 1992: 178–9).

As the Majapahit kingdom faded it began being replaced by Muslim rulers. Muslims began to dominate trade and trade routes and the incentive to convert to Islam increased when the king of the important trade center of Melaka (Malacca) converted to Islam around 1400 (De Casparis and Mabbett, 1992: 330). In the sixteenth and seventeenth centuries the spice trade began to economically dominate the region (Andaya, B., 1992: 411; Reid, 1992: 466). In the early seventeenth century Mataram emerged as a regional power under Sultan Agung after it militarily defeated its main rival Surabaya and extended its influence across Java and beyond.

The spice trade brought attention from the Europeans. The Dutch, newly freed from Spanish rule, after taking Melaka from the Portuguese and eliminating other European competition, began expanding their presence in the region through the Dutch East India Company VOC (*Vereenigde Oostindische Compagnie*). The VOC was one of the world's first global trading companies and began expanding its reach throughout the islands until by 1680 it had a near monopoly on the world's supply of nutmegs and cloves. In the eighteenth century the VOC continued to expand its influence mainly through alliances with local rulers (Andaya, B., 1992: 441, 451; Andaya, L., 1992: 339; Reid, 1992: 448). 'For the most part Indonesian states had lost their independence by stages, involving treaties, Dutch pressure, British connivance, others' non-intervention or threats to intervene, their own incapacity; they were gradually subsumed into the Netherlands realm' (Tarling, 1992: 21).

The Dutch retained their holdings in the islands of Asia throughout the eighteenth century but their hold outside its center in Batavia (Jakarta) in Java was limited. In the nineteenth century Dutch rule consolidated and there was some local resistance to Dutch control. The Dutch met resistance in their attempts to expand into Borneo and more serious conflicts erupted in the Dutch attempt to subdue Aceh in Sumatra (Ileto, 1992: 228–9; Tarling, 1992: 13).

By consolidating diverse regions together, the Dutch in many ways created the concept and idea of Indonesia as a single country and culture. Moreover, there were other changes that happened during the colonial period including seeing very rapid and sustained growth in the population, especially in Java where Dutch control was tightest in the early parts of the twentieth century, which was similar to population growth in other parts of Southeast Asia colonized by Western powers. However, Dutch presence in the country was very limited and never rose higher than one tenth to one fifth of 1% of the total population of the Indonesian islands (Elson, 1992: 162, 183).

In the pre–World War II period a spirit of Indonesian nationalism and an embryonic move towards independence began to take shape. As in other European colonies, independence movements were started and led by young students educated in the European home of the colonial ruler. These movements included the organizations Perhimpunan Indonesia, Partai Indonesia and Pendidikan Nasional Indonesia (PNI). One of the leaders of these movements was Sukarno who the Dutch arrested and jailed more than once (Kratoska and Batson, 1992: 266–74).

As in the rest of Southeast Asia, World War II and the temporary military defeat of the European colonial powers turned out to be the turning point which hastened the end of colonial rule in Indonesia. At the end of the war, the Dutch attempted to reassert control over the colony, but after military operations met resistance and brought international condemnation, the Dutch agreed to negotiate a withdrawal from Indonesia and in December

1948 Sukarno became president of an independent Indonesia (Stockwell, 1992: 355–63). After independence the Dutch presence quickly faded, most investments were withdrawn and little foreign aid or guidance was given by the Netherlands (Owen, 1992: 478).

The country held its first national election in 1955 which showed serious political divisions in the country and the political leadership's popularity and support outside Java to be limited. Sukarno's attempt to bring the country together was what he called 'guided democracy'. However, his political opponents saw this as a dictatorship by Sukarno and the Javanese elites and violence erupted which was quickly put down. Afterwards, a power-sharing arrangement between Sukarno and the military came about (Cheong, 1992: 423–32).

'Demokrasi Terpimpin (guided democracy) concentrated power within the executive, particularly the president. Guided democracy was a great contrast to liberal democracy' (Bhakti, 2004: 198).

However, dissent continued and a general named Suharto wrested power away from Sukarno. Suharto was named Acting President in 1967. Suharto had been one of the leaders of the military in a prior bloody crackdown of Communist supporters, including many ethnic Chinese. Suharto created an organization/political party called Golkar and, although a second national election was held in 1971, Suharto and Golkar retained a near monopoly on political power for over three decades (Cheong, 1992: 434–5; Turnbull, 1992: 601–13).

The Indonesian economy was hard-hit by the Asian financial crisis of 1997 and, following riots and mass killings in Jakarta in 1998, military support for Suharto evaporated leading to his downfall and a transition to democracy. As invariably happens in a transition from authoritarian rule to democracy, it was not smooth and did not immediately produce major improvements in the lives of most citizens of the country. In the first five years of democracy in Indonesia the country saw three different presidents, B.J. Habibie, Abdurrahman Wahid and Megawati Sukarnoputri, none of whom could maintain popularity or stay in power long enough to lead major political reforms or economic improvements. The future of democracy at this time was quite uncertain (Bhakti, 2004).

Dr. Susilo Bambang Yudhoyono became president in 2004 and won a resounding reelection victory in 2009. Since becoming president, Dr. Yudhoyono has led many reforms designed to reduce corruption and improve the investment environment of the country. In recent years Indonesia has seen both economic growth and solidification of the democratic system. While the country faces many challenges including those coming from being a multi-ethnic country with a Muslim majority, there are also many encouraging signs which indicate the country might be on the path to developing a mature and stable democratic political system with sustained economic growth which would be expected to have a positive impact on poverty reduction (Platzdasch, 2011).

Culturally, while Indonesia is a Muslim majority country and the form of Islam which came to Indonesia was mostly Sufism in nature, Woodward (2011) makes the case Islam, like all other religions, is a dynamic force and changes and adapts to local conditions and changing times. While the form of Islam practiced in Indonesia might in general have some features which are different from those found in the Arabic world, Woodward believed the Islam religion as practiced in Indonesia is as genuine and authentic as that practiced in any other parts of the world.

Business environments

The Philippines

The Philippines' economic performance has generally been less impressive than that seen in most of East and Southeast Asia. This underperformance has been going on for a considerable length of time. Much of the population works in the relatively inefficient and low-paid informal sector of the economy. However, to some extent the country's weaknesses have shielded it from the recent global economic crisis as it is less dependent on international trade than other countries in the region. The Philippine economy is heavily dependent on remittances from its overseas workers and, unlike in many other countries, the Philippines did not see a major reduction in its overseas workforce in the recent global downturn nor a drop in remittances (Riester, 2010; Weber and Piechulek, 2010), although it is questionable whether sending many of the best, brightest and most ambitious citizens abroad and living on their earnings is the best strategy for long-term economic growth for the country.

While the Philippines remains a poor country with considerable poverty, there has been decent economic growth in recent years. The service sector is the largest sector of the economy and employs about half of the nation's workforce yet manufacturing is increasing in importance. Much of the nation's growth comes from investment in the manufacturing sector and increased consumer consumption, driven by a steady increase in remittances from abroad. Although starting from a low base by regional standards, exports have increased but agricultural output has been pretty stagnant. GDP annual growth projections for the near future are around 5%. However, recent moderate economic growth has not led to growth in employment which is needed for sustained poverty reduction; in fact, the number of people living in poverty has actually increased by over 3 million since 2003. The country has other challenges to face including rising inflation, poor infrastructure and political instability. The lack of opportunities at home continues to drive many Filipinos to seek work abroad (Asian Development Bank, 2011a). The Philippines is a country which appears to have many advantages and strengths but always seems to underperform economically; it is a country where large increases in private investment would appear to be able to have a major impact on economic growth and poverty reduction.

Indonesia

Indonesia's economy, much like that of the Philippines, is less dependent upon international trade than other economies in the region and therefore was not greatly affected by the recent global economic crisis. But, also like the Philippines, the country has not seen much growth in labor-intensive industries forcing a significant portion of its labor force to seek work abroad or remain unemployed or underemployed for long stretches while searching for work. One way in which surplus labor is adsorbed is by having people stay on farms and work in agriculture, even if their labor is not really needed, instead of earning additional income in more productive employment. One of the difficulties Indonesia has had in developing faster growth is the expense of building infrastructure in a nation which is an archipelago. Another problem in building the economic growth needed to reduce poverty is the existence of high levels of corruption and an investment climate filled with bureaucratic procedures which deters foreign investment and lacks incentives to encourage small firms to grow and therefore many small firms stay in the informal economy. In addition, the government's expenditure on social protection programs and programs directly targeting poverty reduction has been limited; most of the country's reduction in poverty has come from economic growth and not government programs (Timmer, 2007; Papanek et al., 2010). Although the country has introduced a cash transfer system for the poorest families which has considerable conditions attached, such as children must attend school (Hanlon et al., 2010: 43), the effectiveness of this program in reducing poverty has yet to be determined.

The economy has been experiencing respectable growth rates of around 6% annually with growth being driven mostly by increases in manufacturing exports, private consumption and private investment. Growth in the service sector has been strong while growth in agriculture has been positive but lagging other sectors of the economy. Inflation and high food prices are concerns and approximately two thirds of the labor force remains in the informal economy. Spending on subsidies has been high but there have been economic reforms, such as lowering the tax rates, which have improved the investment climate. While the economic outlook is generally positive, the projected annual moderate growth of between 6 and 7% is slower than that in other economies in the region and the growth in employment has not been fast enough to provide meaningful jobs for much of the work force. Other challenges include improving the government's handling of the country's finances and continuing to reduce its budget deficits which will lower its borrowing costs (Asian Development Bank, 2011a).

Case studies

Marcelo's Pharmacy and General Merchandise

Marcelo's Pharmacy and General Merchandise store has been serving customers for over 52 years in Makati city and in another branch in Manila in the Philippines. The company sells a wide variety of products including groceries as well as beauty and health care products, but its main business is its pharmacy. The company has significant levels of competition with many other pharmacies in the immediate vicinity of its two locations.

The company follows a low-cost differentiation strategy with the differentiation being targeted at speed and quality of service. As price is always important to customers, especially in a LDC like the Philippines, the company has to keep its costs low to be able to offer low prices and Marcelo's generally offers prices either as low or lower than its main competitors. However, being located in an area with a developing economy does not mean price is everything, and customers are very demanding and expect quick and efficient service to accompany low prices; Marcelo's works to meet these demands of its customers. Having been in business for so long the company's reputation is another one of its competitive advantages.

At the interpersonal levels of business, the company shares many characteristics with other small firms in LDCs. The company normally recruits new employees amongst the friends and relatives of existing employees and supplements its formal written standard operating procedures with personal supervision. Another feature is employees are expected to be flexible and willing to work late to meet the needs of customers if there is a rush. There are no time clocks at Marcelo's and working hours are driven by customer needs. Although the company is not able to pay high wages due to its low-cost strategy, it has been able to retain employees with few leaving due to a personal management style which takes into account the individual needs of its employees.

The company is somewhat limited in its choice of suppliers as many of the drugs the company sells come from distributors with exclusive rights to the products. However, when a choice of suppliers is available the company primarily makes choices based on price, which is consistent with its low-cost strategy.

As a retail outlet, use of modern technology is somewhat limited but the company has learned from experience the most efficient methods to dispense and sell pharmaceutical products and its operational procedures would be considered similar to those found in other locations of the world.

San Miguel

Sam Miguel Brewery (La Fábrica de Cerveza de San Miguel) became the first brewery in the Philippines back in 1890 when the country was still a Spanish colony. The company was founded by Don Enrique María Barretto de Ycaza, with the help of a German brewmaster, and began limited exporting as early as 1913 to Hong Kong and China. The company started diversifying early on and began bottling soft drinks, then produced dairy products in the 1920s and in 1927, in a step that gained the company considerable prestige both nationally and internationally, San Miguel partnered with Coca-Cola and started to produce and bottle Coca-Cola in the Philippines. This move allowed the company to gain a near monopoly on distribution of beverages in the Philippines. The company shut down during the Japanese occupation but regrouped and began expanding in the postwar era (Alley and Stanley, 1993; San Miguel Corp., 2006).

For most of the period from 1918 up until 1998 the company was controlled by the Soriano family, except for a brief period when Eduardo Cojuangco Jr., a crony of former President Marcos, took control of the company. However, Cojuangco Jr. was ousted when his cousin, Corazón Aquino, became president. In another turn of fate, in

1998, Cojuangco Jr. returned from exile to again take control of the company. During the time under the Soriano family, the company continued expanding. Although most of the expansion was initially in the food and beverage fields, more unrelated diversification began under the new management as the company moved into areas such as manufacturing, real estate and insurance (Angeles, 2005). More recently, the company has become more of a corporation, less of a family-owned business and has increased its unrelated diversification which now includes considerable investment in the power-generating industry (San Miguel, 2010).

The company followed a somewhat familiar path from being a small family-owned firm to a large diversified conglomerate in Southeast Asia. Other examples of similar family-owned conglomerates include Charoen Pokphand (CP) in Thailand, run by the Chearavont family, which is at its core an agro-business but also has large stakes in retail (it runs the very successful 7-11 and Lotus franchises in Thailand), telecommunication and other diversified businesses including the manufacturing of motorcycles in Henan province of China. Another example is the Kuok family dynasty in Malaysia which made its initial fortune in sugar and now controls hotels, retail outlets, newspapers and Coca-Cola bottling plants amongst other diversified businesses throughout Asia. These family-owned conglomerates which include San Miguel follow similar patterns as seen in the earlier family-owned conglomerates in Korea and Japan which have grown into modern *chaebols* or *keiretsus*. Hipsher et al. (2007) found the need to operate in the legal and political environments in Southeast Asia, especially when working across borders, often makes social capital and political connections extremely valuable intangible assets which often allows firms to make further use of unrelated diversification strategies than is normal in Western societies where the trend for major corporations in recent years has been to retain focus on core businesses and spin off many unrelated investments. However, whether San Miguel will be able to continue to use its connections and access to capital to grow and diversify as large Asian family-owned companies have in the past as the world becomes more globalized, competitive and the company takes on more of a corporate nature is yet to be decided.

Salim Group

The Salim Group has its headquarters in Jakarta and is a huge conglomerate with a highly diversified portfolio that includes interests in agriculture, food, manufacturing of automobiles, construction materials, chemicals, banking and finance, real estate, hotels and resorts, importing and exporting, communications and the media. Although the various units of the group have a wide variety of ownership structures, the Salim Group itself is a private family-owned concern.

The Salim Group was founded by Liem Sioe Liong, also known by his Indonesian name Soedono Salim. Liem was born in the Fujian province of China in 1916 and emigrated to what was then still part of the Dutch East Indies in 1938. Through a combination of political connections and business savvy he was able to start a business which grew into the country's largest conglomerate (Sato, 1993: 408; Dieleman and Sachs, 2006: 525).

Liem became a supplier to the Army in the 1950s which resulted in becoming well connected to an Army officer who would later become the president, Suharto. Two of the group's earlier companies were P.T. Waringin, an export company, and P.T. Mega which imported cloves. The Salim Group began to take off after Suharto came to power in 1967 and the company benefited from its political and commercial connections. In 1967, P.T. Waringin was granted a license which allowed it to export five times the formal quota in coffee while P.T. Mega joined with a company owned by Suharto's stepbrother and then the partnership was given a monopoly on the importation of cloves. The group also benefited from subsidized loans and access to low-cost resources as part of the government's import substitution policy. The company earned a reputation for being one of the most professionally run ethnic Chinese conglomerates of those which had strong ties to the Suharto government (Sato, 1993: 411; Dieleman and Sachs, 2006; 525–7).

Using the profits from his monopolies and access to credit, Liem expanded his business in the late 1960s and early 1970s with a focus on manufacturing which was assisted by the government's protectionist policies under the theme of import substitution. The Salim Group moved into pulp/paper, aluminum smelting, production of fertilizer, steel and other diversified areas of business. Next came an expansion into banking, followed by a major move into cement which was followed by a move into an increasing variety of diversified businesses. By the mid-1980s the Salim Group was the largest company in Indonesia with the country's largest private bank and was the largest producer of cement in Indonesia. Some of the moves and evolution of the company away from manufacturing was driven by the shift in government policies from important substitution policies to more open and export-orientated priorities (Sato, 1993: 412–22). By the 1990s the company began making a transition to a more modern and market-based struture and many of the company's businesses were placed under the control of professional managers while the core businesses remained under direct control of the family. Moreover, Liem's son, Anthony Salim, began to take over more control of the group's operations (Dieleman and Sachs, 2006: 528).

The Asian financial crisis and the overthrow of the Suharto regime were major challenges for the company. The family was charged with crony capitalism, lost control of Bank Central Asia and violence against the company due to its political connections forced many of the company's top managers to flee to Singapore. The new Indonesian government fined the company $5 billion for a variety of offenses; however, some of the reforms previously begun by Anthony Salim had laid a foundation for the company and it was able to make the transition from one that relied mostly on relationships and a protected environment within Indonesia to one that could operate effectively under market conditions internationally (Dieleman and Sachs, 2006: 229–30).

Business groups using unrelated diversification strategies are found throughout Asia and have evolved due to market imperfections, government intervention and Asian social-cultural environments. It has been proposed, as economies such as those found in the Philippines and Indonesia become more market based, the reason for the existence of business groups will disappear (Chang, 2006). Yet, family-owned business groups, such as the Salim Group, have shown remarkable resilience and have often adapted to changes in the fortunes of politicians and changes in government policies. Therefore, business groups using heavily unrelated diversification strategies are still a major part of the business environment found throughout Asia in the beginning of the twenty-first century.

Analysis

The business environments found in the Philippines and Indonesia share many characteristics with environments found in other LDCs in Southeast Asia, yet because of unique histories, political environments and cultures each nation also has some unique feature which affects how business is conducted in each individual country.

With Marcelo's Pharmacy and General Merchandise Store we see a small business facing many of the same strategic and operational challenges facing many other small businesses found in LDCs in Asia, while the company's interpersonal management style is aligned with the cultural environment its workers operate in.

Both San Miguel and the Salim Group are large conglomerates which have in the past mostly used extreme forms of unrelated diversification strategies. An unrelated diversification strategy requires the ability to leverage a firm's existing capacities into new areas. As business environments become more market based and have less direct government involvement it becomes harder for a company to find synergies between existing capacities, gained in very specific businesses, and the capabilities needed to find competitive advantage in totally unrelated industries. Apple has not ventured into investments outside industries associated with computers and related technologies. General Motors has divested itself of most of its non-automaking ventures and McDonald's confines itself to the fast food industry. However, in Asia, where there is often more direct government involvement, we see far more use of unrelated diversification strategies by large business groups. It is felt unrelated diversification strategies in Asia are successful as firms are often able to leverage the intangible benefits which come from government connections, business connections, and access to capital across operations in different industries. As economies have moved away to some extent from direct government control to more open and market-based economies, the intangible benefits that come from connections are expected to lessen, but past predictions of the demise of business groups in Asia have not been very accurate.

It would be easy to criticize San Miguel and the Salim Group for having previously been involved in 'crony capitalism'. But these companies did not create the business environment they operated in. Is it fair to expect firms in developing economies where there is considerable corruption and direct government involvement in the economy to operate under the same ethical guidelines as firms which operate under environmental conditions where success is mostly based on the market? Can these conglomerates in LDCs evolve into more modern corporations which can compete in the more open markets that seem to be evolving in the twenty-first century? Will they continue to follow unrelated diversification strategies with most focus on domestic markets or will they become more specialized and global firms?

The external environment matters and firms have to operate in the political, legal and cultural environments they find themselves in. Can private businesses still supply quality products, quality employment and help drive economic growth while operating in environments where less than ideal ethics and business practices are rewarded?

12

South Asia

Abstract: The South Asian countries of India, Pakistan, Bangladesh, Sri Lanka and Nepal each have significant portions of its population living in poverty. These countries are generally less integrated into the global economy than are countries in other regions of the world. The large populations of the region and low average incomes make the region both attractive and challenging for firms to operate in. Case studies of firms originating from the region are analyzed.

Key words: India, Pakistan, Sri Lanka, Nepal, Hindustan Unilever, Tata Nano, Nabil Bank.

Area background

South Asia and India

The South Asian region has a fascinating history, although the area has not performed very well economically in the modern world. South Asia

> is home to 40% of the world's poor, with 29.5% of its population living on less than $1 a day. While almost a quarter of the world's population lives in the region, South Asia accounts for only 3% of global gross domestic product (GDP).
>
> (Asian Development Bank, 2009a: 1)

Today, 'South Asia is the region in the developing world that is least integrated with the world economy' (Srinivasan, 2009: 60).

The areas consisting of India and much of modern day South Asia in earlier times were mostly isolated from other areas of human habitation due to the surrounding oceans in the south and mountain ranges in the north, although as civilizations grew more sophisticated more contacts with the outside world were made. Humans have been living in South Asia for over 30,000 years, with indications that suggest the first use of agriculture and domesticated animals began around 6500 BC (Walsh, 2011: 1–6).

One of the earliest civilizations in the region was located in the Indus River Valley in today's Pakistan and the Punjab region of India and has been given the name the Harappan civilization. This civilization was in existence around 4,000 years ago but little is known about it and the civilization had been completely forgotten until rediscovered by archeologists in the nineteenth and early twentieth centuries. Yet the evidence suggests it was one of the major centers of civilization of the ancient world. Around 1500 BC a tribe calling themselves Aryans lived in the Punjab area and their hymns later became known as the Rig-Veda. The Indo-Aryans began consolidating and spreading their power through their use of iron technology in areas that are in today's Pakistan and northern India. As the Indo-Aryans changed from a nomadic to an agrarian lifestyle, they developed the written language now referred to as Sanskrit and the key concepts of Hinduism began to take shape including dividing the population into four *varnas*, or castes. The Indo-Aryans under the Nanda dynasty settled in agricultural communities along the northern Ganges and remained dominant until the fourth century BC. In the fourth century BC, the army of Alexander (the Great) invaded the Punjab but left no lasting legacy on the civilization of the region (Walsh, 2011: 7–42).

The Nanda were overthrown by the Maurya dynasty which is best remembered for the rule of the emperor, Ashoka (269–33 BC), who after a series of military victories early in his reign converted to Buddhism in his later years. In 185 BC, after decline and loss of territory, the Maurya dynasty gave way to the Shunga dynasty which only controlled a small portion of the previous empire controlled by Ashoka. At around the same time there were a number of Indo-Greek kingdoms in Central Asia and, with migration, much of northern India became ruled by small Indo-Greek kingdoms. The Indo-Greek kingdoms were then overrun by the Shakas who were then replaced by the Kushans whose rule would last until the third century AD (Walsh, 2011: 43–54).

Little is known of what is today southern India before the Aryan cultures of the north began filtering south, although it is thought most of the people in these areas before the Mauryan period were nomadic or semi-nomadic who spoke Dravidian languages including Tamil, Telegu and Malayalam. Some urban coastal societies, which were involved in international trade, emerged. Early civilizations in southern India included the Satavahana, Cholas, Cheras and Pandyas (Walsh, 2011: 50–4).

The Gupta period, which lasted from the early fourth century to the middle of the sixth century, is often thought of as a classical period as most of the Sanskrit texts and scriptures used as sacred texts in Vedic Hinduism, Buddhism and Jainism spread throughout India during this era. After the fall of the Gupta, the region faced political fragmentation with only one ruler, Harshavardhana, in the seventh century who was able to consolidate rule over large territories in northern India although his rule did not lead to the establishment of a lasting dynasty (Walsh, 2011, 55–65).

In the eighth century Islam began spreading into Central Asia. In the latter part of the tenth century, Sabuktigin, a Turk, established an Afghan kingdom with the city of Ghazni at its center and Sabuktigin's descendents began launching attacks into Hindu-dominated northern India. The Ghurids took over this kingdom in the middle of the twelfth century and soon conquered most of the northern parts of India. Parts of the southern region of today's India was controlled by the Pallavas who were joined in the early tenth century by a resurgent Cholas dynasty which lasted until the latter years of the thirteenth century (Walsh, 2011: 67–74).

From 1206 to 1526, a series of Islamic dynasties ruled northern India with their capital at Delhi. In the thirteenth and early fourteenth centuries the Mongols controlled most of Central Asia but were never able to venture deep into India itself, while in the south the kingdom of Vijayanagar controlled most of the southern part of the subcontinent from the fourteenth to sixteenth centuries (Walsh, 2011: 78–82).

Babur, the ruler of Kabul, invaded India in 1526 and founded the Mughal Empire; which was expanded greatly under Jalaluddin Muhammad Akbar in the late seventeenth and early eighteenth centuries. The rulers of the Mughal Empire were cultural descendants of the Mongol Empire which had previously controlled all of Central Asia. It was also in the seventeenth and eighteenth centuries that Europeans, including the Portuguese, Dutch, French and British, began setting up trading posts along the Indian coasts. In 1739 the Persian king Nair Shah raided and destroyed much of Delhi which crippled the Mughal Empire to such an extent that it could never recover. In the south, the Maratha Confederacy, controlled by four different families, ruled much of the land (Burgan, 2009; Walsh, 2011: 82–101).

As the Mughal Empire weakened and lost control over the population, the British East India Company filled the power vacuum and began to increase its influence and take direct control over much of India. By 1833, when the company's monopoly on trade ended, it had already gained control, either directly or indirectly, over most of South Asia (Walsh, 2011: 102–6).

The British colonial system brought many changes to India. The British introduced a more rigid legal system, which was mixed with existing local laws and split between one set of laws for Muslims and another for Hindus. This legal division of the population helped shape the social and political future of South Asia. Colonial rule and implementation of colonial legal systems appeared to have ossified the distinction between the Hindu and Muslim populations who were occupying the same lands, although the impact of British legal reforms was not consistent throughout the entire South Asian colonial empire (Denault, 2009; Newbigin, 2009; Sharafi, 2009).

British rule was seriously challenged in the 'mutiny' of 1857–58 which was eventually put down and resulted in control of the colony passing from the British East India Company to direct rule by the British government. The British, who never numbered much above 100,000 in India, were able to put down the uprising and continue to rule the colony due to the British unity of purpose while Indians were divided by religion, caste and other factors. British rule, although leaving much of the rural areas untouched, did bring many new Western ideas and institutions into South Asia (Walsh, 2011: 120–38).

A case could be made that the birth of modern India came in 1885 when 73 men from all over British India met in Bombay (Mumbai) for what was the first meeting of the Indian National Congress. In 1906, 25 delegates met in Dacca and founded the All-India Muslim League. Mohammed Ali Jinnah joined the Muslim League in 1913 and Mohandas Gandhi joined the Indian Congress two years later upon his return from South Africa. Jawaharlal Nehru, a British-educated son of a wealthy lawyer also joined the movement of the Congress and was deeply inspired by Gandhi's philosophy. These three men were to play major roles in the South Asian portion of the British Empire's move towards independence (Walsh, 2011: 167–95).

While divisions between Muslims and Hindus in the independence movement started in the 1920s and 1930s, it was not until 1940 that the Muslim League proposed the idea of separate rule in the Muslim majority regions of northwestern and northeastern parts of British India. The British decision to partition the country came only about two months before independence was formally declared making India and Pakistan separate, independent and sovereign nations on 15 August 1947. This decision left little time for careful planning. Partition of the country resulted in widescale violence and movements of people across borders as chaos reigned in the fall of 1947. It has been estimated that somewhere around 1,000,000 people died in the violence, and abductions of women and rape were also widespread. The violence even resulted in the assassination of Gandhi, the famous advocate of religious unity and non-violence, in January 1948 by a right-wing Hindu extremist (Pandey, 2004).

Nehru became the first prime minister and his family and the Congress Party have been dominant forces in the political scene in independent India ever since. Influenced by the experience of British colonial rule, Nehru followed a path of economic socialism and neutrality between the Communist and capitalist factions in the emerging Cold War. After Nehru's death in 1964, Lal Bahadur Shastri briefly led the country which included conducting a brief, but victorious, war with Pakistan. When Shastri suddenly died of a heart attack in January 1966, Nehru's only child, the politically inexperienced Indira Gandhi, became the country's leader. Indira Gandhi was for most of the time quite popular with the masses, but her continuation of the socialist policies of her father resulted in increases in poverty and poor economic performance and, despite expectations she would be a weak ruler, she showed she was willing to play hardball in the game of politics and used her power as head of state to militarily stifle political dissent in 1975 (Walsh, 2011: 220–40).

Although replaced as prime minister in 1977, after victories by the Congress Party in the elections of 1980 Indira Gandhi returned as prime minister, but in 1984 she was assassinated by two of her Sikh bodyguards and she was succeeded by her son, Rajiv, as prime minister. However, Rajiv was killed by a suicide bomb attack in 1991 while campaigning after the Congress Party lost power in 1989. As the Congress Party returned to power under Prime Minister Narasimha Rao, a change of policy occurred moving the country away from the socialist policies of the past and Rao appointed Manmohan Singh as finance minister and the economy saw its greatest economic growth since independence in the 1990s. Singh later became prime minister, after an interval of rule by the BJP party, and the move towards more market-based economics has continued to some extent (Walsh, 2011: 242–326).

'The Indian political system, the world's largest democracy, still remains today, as it has since independence in 1947, a problematic vehicle for meeting the needs of India's multiple castes, religious minorities, and urban and rural voters' (Walsh, 2011: 334).

Pakistan

Pakistan is only one of two modern countries, Israel being the other, which was founded as a homeland for individuals practicing a particular religion. Pakistan came into existence from the violent and one of the largest two-way migrations in human history that accompanied independence and partition in 1947. Originally, Pakistan was in two parts, East and West Pakistan, but following a bitter civil war and the military intervention of India, which was located between the two parts, East Pakistan became the independent country of Bangladesh in 1971. Pakistan has gone through a series of alternating military and civilian rule since its inception (Burki, 2006). Upon independence, the structures and most of the personnel in the bureaucracy were transferred from the colonial system to the system that developed in the newly independent state (Tomlinson, 2003: 291).

There are more than 150 million people living in Pakistan, and its population continues to grow at a high rate. Six major ethnic groups are recognized; the Punjabis, who speak Punjabi or one of its dialects, are the largest with about 60% of the population. The vast majority of the population follows the Islamic faith with around 75% being Sunni and the other 25% Shia. Urdu is the country's national language, although it is the native language of only a small percentage of the population and is the language used in most schools, although English is often used as the medium of instruction in universities and is the language used in both the government and more modern sectors of the economy (Burki, 2006).

Pakistan's location and history have made stability difficult. Pakistan and India have had numerous military clashes in the past and there is still a dispute between these two South Asian nuclear powers over the Kashmir region. Moreover, due to its border with Afghanistan, Pakistan got involved with the US in being a staging area for covert operations in the 1970s intending to drive out the Soviets. The country has also been dragged into Afghan civil wars and the US-led invasion of Afghanistan after the terrorist attacks in New York in September 2001. It was in Afghanistan US forces found and killed Osama Bin Laden; however, the unilateral nature of the decision and action has resulted in straining the relationship between these two reluctant allies.

Bangladesh

A divided Pakistan with East Pakistan a thousand miles away and having the majority of the population while West Pakistan dominated the economy and political structures was found to be unsustainable. In 1970 Mujibur Rahman and his political party won Pakistan's first parliamentary elections but were blocked by the West Pakistani President Mohammad Yahya Khan from forming a government. The West Pakistan government attempted to impose martial law but East Pakistan led by Mujibur Rahman declared independence for Bangladesh. West Pakistani troops invaded East Pakistan and brutally suppressed the citizens, and around 10 million of its population fled to India. The Indian military came to the assistance of Bangladesh and Indian troops overwhelmed the West Pakistani troops who surrendered in December 1971. This military victory by Indian forces resulted in guaranteeing independence for Bangladesh (Walsh, 2011: 237–8).

Initially, the country took the path of socialism and nationalized industries that had been abandoned by their West Pakistani owners after the nation's separation and independence. But the nation began a privatization program and a form of private sector development occurred during the regime of General Ziaur Rahman, which benefited friends of the general more than it did the general population (Mahmud et al., 2010: 234).

Sri Lanka

The political history of much of the last 3,000 years of Sri Lanka has been the history of various Sinhalese and Tamil kings controlling different and often competing parts of the island. Two of the important early kingdoms were called Anuradhapura and Pollonaruwa, which date back to the third century BC. The Tamil Cola Empire from mainland India began invasions of the island in the tenth century which brought an end to the classical Sinhalese Buddhist civilizations. After the invasions the island fell into a long period of political fragmentation with limited control over outlying regions by the central authorities and political turmoil except during a period in the early to mid-fifteenth century when the island was united under Parakramabahu VI (Gombrich, 2006: 23; Holt, 2006: 50; Obeyesekere, 2006: 137; Van Horen and Pinnawala, 2006: 309).

Sri Lanka fell under colonial rule by the Portuguese and then was controlled by the Dutch before the British added the island to its South

Asian empire. Theravada Buddhism had been suppressed by the colonial invaders. Therefore, in the eighteenth century Kirti Fri Rajasikha sent a mission to Thailand to bring back monks to revive Theravada Buddhist ordination in the country. The country, called Ceylon by the Europeans, received its independence in 1948. Starting in 1983 until very recently the country had suffered from civil war, terrorism and violence between Tamil factions led by the LTTE (Tamil Tigers), who were seeking a homeland and some degree of self-rule in the north, and the Sinhalese (Buddhist) majority who controlled the government (Gombrich, 2006: 24; Gunawardana, 2006: 187; Obeyesekere, 2006; 158; Van Horen and Pinnawala, 2006: 310).

The majority of the island's population is both Sinhalese and Buddhist, while the largest minority are the Tamils who are mostly Hindu (Deegalee, 2006: 2). While Sri Lanka is primarily a Theravada Buddhist country, its culture and religion has been heavily influenced by Hindu values and, therefore, is in some ways closer culturally to India and South Asia than it is to the Theravada Buddhist countries of Southeast Asia (Holt, 2006).

Nepal

While Nepal was never a full colony of the British, it was forced to engage as a subordinate partner in an alliance with the British East India Company in 1816 (Walsh, 2011: 113). In 1962 a new constitution was implemented which moved the country away from having a hereditary prime minister under a king and the first direct elections were held in 1981. The country abandoned the party-less *panchayat* system in 1990 and moved to a multi-party democracy which has led to political instability and frequent changes in political leadership. In 1996 Maoist rebels launched a military campaign to turn the country into a one-party dictatorship. In 2005 the king abolished the government, announced a state of emergency and assumed absolute political control. However, widespread protests forced a reversal of his decisions in 2006. In 2007 the Maoists joined in partnership with the government which appears to have effectively ended the long-running civil war (Asian Development Bank, 2009b).

Business environments

Poverty continues to be a major issue in South Asia. There are more people in South Asia living on less than a $1.25 a day than in sub-

Saharan Africa (Carrasco et al., 2010: 3). The countries of South Asia came to independence at a time when the popularity of centralized economic planning was at its peak, and the countries of the region all have histories of import substitution, protectionism and inward-looking policies (Tomlinson, 2003: 303). In more recent times, more open and outward economic policies have come about and there have been general positive trends in economic growth and reducing levels of poverty, but there are still many challenges to overcome to accelerate economic growth. Despite some market liberalization, throughout the region there are still generally high levels of protectionism, prohibitive tariffs and little intraregional trade between the nations in South Asia (Asian Development Bank, 2009a).

India

'India's market-oriented economic reforms, which were initiated in the 1980s but took full shape in the 1990s, are widely credited with having raised India's rates of economic growth' (Mehta and Hasaon, 2011: 1). Poverty rates in India have significantly decreased as economic growth has increased (Bhagwati, 2005; Walsh, 2011: 332–3). The benefits from this increase in economic development also show up in other quality-of-life statistics with India showing mild increases in life expectancy, substantial decreases in the rate of infant mortality and increases in the literacy rate (Kalirajan et al., 2010: 56), although the downside of economic growth has been increasing income inequality (Mehta and Hasaon, 2011). Increasing income inequality could have a negative effect on the country's future social cohesion and political stability (Ali, 2008).

Business practices in large Indian firms would appear to be quite different from those in smaller firms. In general, larger firms are far more productive and as a result can offer their employees higher salaries and better working conditions than those found in smaller firms (Amoranto and Chun, 2011). It has been found large publicly traded Indian companies generally have pretty open financial disclosures but are less open about sharing their strategic intent (Varghese, 2011). Tripathy and Rath (2011) found that large Indian firms were actively involved in modern corporate social responsibility activities, but did so within a narrow range of activities and public and employee awareness of these activities was limited.

There are also considerable variations in economic growth and poverty reduction across different Indian states. Poverty reduction has been highest in the states of Kerala, Punjab and Andhra Pradesh and lowest in Bihar, Assam and Madhya Pradesh. The states with the most 'pro-worker' regulations have had the lowest rates of economic growth and poverty reduction; and the states with more accountable governments, more pro-investment climates, better access to financial and human capital, better property rights and higher rates of women in the workforce have had more economic growth and poverty reduction (Besley et al., 2007). Kalirajan et al. (2010) reported decentralization of economic and political decisions have had a positive effect on economic and manufacturing growth and advocated further measures to decentralize the country's economic decision making.

India's recent growth has been broad based with the agricultural, manufacturing and service sectors all contributing. In addition, there has been a mix in growth in consumption, investment and exports. Inflation has been a problem but the foreign exchange rate has been fairly stable. The current government has demonstrated monetary discipline and inclinations towards decreasing bureaucratic controls, and therefore prospects for continued high growth look promising. However, continued high growth might rely on additional growth in the service sector where around two thirds of recent growth has come from.

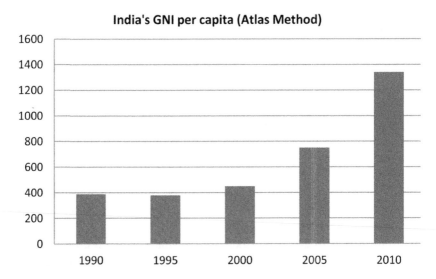

India's GNI per capita (Atlas Method)

Figure 12.1

Source: Asian Development Bank (2011b: 163)

This makes up 55% of the nation's GDP and 25% of the nation's employment. In addition, the large size of the less productive informal sector, reduced public spending on agriculture and continued high levels of regulation despite reforms are all obstacles to continued high levels of growth (Asian Development Bank, 2011a: 155–60).

Pakistan

Since independence Pakistan has seen a major shift from being mostly rural with the majority working in agriculture to more of an urban society. During the time under the country's first military president, Ayub Khan, from 1958 to 1969 there was a big push for industrial development and the country averaged a very respectable 6.4% annual increase in GDP. However, in 1972 under President Zulfikar Ali Bhutto there were moves to nationalize many industries which led to inefficiencies, corruption, stagnation of economic growth and increases in poverty over the next six years. Under the next military ruler, General Zia ul Haq, there was a shift back towards private ownership of industries and increases in economic growth and reduction in poverty (Burki, 2006).

In more recent times, unlike in neighboring India, Pakistan has seen little in the way of economic growth or poverty reduction. Investments have seen a steady decline in recent years due to security concerns. Public debt continues to be a problem which is exacerbated by losses from state-owned industries and paying energy-related subsidies. Inflation continues to rise and current budgetary obligations reduce the availability of funds for badly needed infrastructure projects (Asian Development Bank, 2011a: 168–72).

Bangladesh

Bangladesh has had significant reductions in poverty rates, from as high as 70% of the population living in poverty to less than 40% today. Poverty reduction has been correlated with economic growth, opening of the economy and macroeconomic stability, especially in the 1990s. This economic growth and poverty reduction has come despite a very weak institutional environment (Sen et al., 2007).

The people of Bangladesh have enjoyed some benefits from poverty reduction and economic growth; life expectancy has risen substantially and infant mortality has been more than cut in half. Some liberalization of

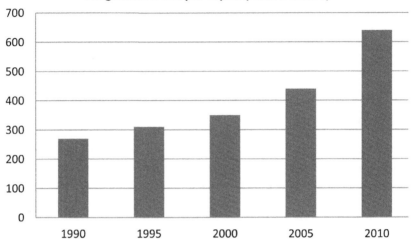

Figure 12.2

Source: Asian Development Bank (2011b: 163)

the economy has helped some small producers import capital equipment and raw materials making the products of these firms more competitive against imported items. However, the majority of the economy is still in the less productive informal sector and Bangladesh is still a very poor country with one of the least open economies in Asia (Mahmud et al., 2010).

In recent years Bangladesh has seen annual GDP growth around the 6% range but the trend has been slowing slightly. Bangladesh has received very limited inward FDI and relies heavily on remittances for consumption. Inflation has been moderately high but growth in garment exports has helped keep the economy growing. Government spending in the form of subsidies continues to crowd out spending for badly needed infrastructure and educational projects (Asian Development Bank, 2011a: 147–52).

Sri Lanka

Upon independence Sri Lanka, like the rest of South Asia, turned to import substitution policies and centralized planning and saw little economic growth or poverty reduction. Starting in 1977, moves began towards a more liberalized economy, but the payoffs have been slow in coming. However, the country's garment industry has profited from this openness and accounts for most of the country's manufactured exports.

Sri Lanka was more affected by the recent global economic downturn than other countries in the region (Van Horen and Pinnawala, 2006: 315; Carrasco et al., 2010; Ranjith and Widner, 2011).

Sri Lanka's economy has rebounded from its recent low point in 2009 and is experiencing increasing investor confidence and numbers of tourists as the long-running civil war has come to an end. Around 60% of the economy is in the service sector, which along with the agriculture sector has shown a good recovery. Inflation has been moderate and while public debt growth has slowed it is still high. Investment, both domestic and foreign, continues to be limited. A major reduction in 'red tape' and a more business-friendly environment along with a more efficient financial sector might be necessary to increase levels of private investment which are needed for increased growth (Asian Development Bank, 2011a: 173–6).

Nepal

Nepal remains the poorest country in the region, as measured by GDP per capita, but has seen some reductions of poverty in recent years although inequality has risen. Despite lackluster economic performance, poverty reduction has been driven by overseas remittances, rural to urban

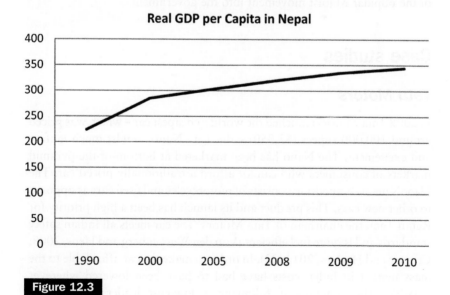

Real GDP per Capita in Nepal

Figure 12.3

Source: UNCTAD (2011: 130)

migration and increases in entrepreneurial activities by those working in the agricultural sector. These are the results of opportunities coming from improved roads and infrastructure, although the overall level of infrastructure in the country remains poor. The cost to the economy of the civil war has been significant and it is hoped the country will experience a peace dividend now the fighting appears to have ended. Nepal suffers from very low labor productivity and there does not appear to have been much improvement in recent years. In addition, the government is small, centralized and not very effective in servicing the needs of outlying rural communities (Asian Development Bank, 2009b).

As a consequence of economic growth remaining slow and the industrial sector being quite small, many Nepalese rely on remittances from family members working abroad, primarily in India. Public debt has been lowered, partially due to prudent monetary decisions and partially due to foreign aid. The percentage of people living below the poverty line has declined to an estimated 25% from approximately 31% in 2004 despite slow economic growth. Much of this decline has been attributed to remittances from abroad. Job creation remains a problem not eased by very rigid labor laws and very poor infrastructure. The lack of jobs pushes nearly half of Nepal's young adults to seek work abroad (Asian Development Bank, 2011a: 164–7). Making many of the needed market reforms may be politically impossible in the near future due to the inclusion of the popular Maoist movement into the government.

Case studies

Tata Motors

In 2008 Tata Motors launched the world's cheapest car – which was priced around 100,000 rupees ($2,350) – the Tata Nano, amidst much fanfare and excitement. The Nano has been marketed at bottom-of-the-pyramid markets of consumers who cannot afford a traditionally priced car. The Nano's main competition consists of motorcycles and used cars as opposed to other new cars. This product and its launch has been a high priority for Ratan Tata, the chairman of Tata Motors. The car meets all Indian safety standards and is quite fuel efficient (Van den Waeyenberg and Hens, 2008; Cromer and Hodges, 2011: 22). In order to make the car affordable to the mass market in India, costs have had to have been lowered wherever possible. The company is following a low-cost leadership strategy, which is being driven by India's relatively low average income and wages. The Nano is a very innovative project, but the innovation is in how to strip down and cut costs in a mature industry to fit the economic environment found in developing economies as opposed to creating a new-product category.

Operating in the automotive industry requires a high level of technical skills; however, as the industry is quite mature much of the knowledge and skills needed to be successful can be transferred and adapted from existing knowledge and procedures. Tata Motors Limited, which was initially incorporated as a public limited company in 1945 as Tata Locomotive and Engineering Company, is the largest automotive manufacturer in India. The company has gained much of its earlier technological skills and experience through joint ventures and other collaborative agreements with foreign automakers. In more recent times Tata Motors has used outward foreign direct investment, such as acquiring Jaguar and Land Rover, to build up its technological skills and abilities (Singh, 2011). The assembly line process used by all auto manufacturers worldwide is mostly an evolution of the original process used by Henry Ford and the transfer of knowledge from Detroit to other locations. Tata Motors has been able to acquire and adapt existing operational technology and knowledge into its operations in India. This acknowledgement of transfer and adaptation does not diminish the innovative thinking of Tata Motors in creating the Nano, but the innovation was based on cutting costs in design while using industry best, most efficient, practices in assembly and operations.

Despite all of the publicity Tata has gotten over this product around the world, sales of the Nano have been quite disappointing. Ramsinghani (2012) believed part of the problem might have been in the marketing of the car. The car was sold in showrooms, in much the same way as cars are normally sold in India and other countries. However, many potential buyers of the Nano would be first-time car buyers who are unfamiliar with the process and often intimidated by Tata's upscale showrooms. Moreover, potential buyers of the Nano are not really part of the bottom-of-the-pyramid market and by Indian standards would be considered middle class; they are often reluctant to be seen driving the world's cheapest car. Being seen with a product using a low-cost leadership strategy might not fit into the image of status many middle-class families want to portray. Chakraverthy and Coughlan (2012) reported Tata has offered cash discounts and reduced down payments for customers buying on credit which, along with other adjustments in its marketing strategy, is hoped will improve the sales of this product – a product that seems to have attracted more media attention than sales.

Hindustan Unilever (HUL)

HUL is the Indian subsidiary of Anglo-Dutch Unilever in which the parent company owns a majority stake. The company is one of the largest and most successful consumer products companies in India (Rohatynskyj, 2011: 66). The company sells a wide variety of consumer products; however, soap and detergents are its biggest sellers. The company sells a variety of products, many with internationally known brand names (Hindustan Unilever Limited, 2011). However, keeping costs and prices at a level affordable to the majority is important in its strategy to reach lower-income and rural consumers; the company has also stressed the importance of its products in maintaining good health (Prahalad, 2005). Therefore, we see HUL uses differentiation strategies with an emphasis on health and reasonable prices for its soaps aimed at low-income rural markets.

In addition to being involved in a number of philanthropic activities, HUL uses a unique program where it partners with local NGOs and government agencies: Project Shakti, designed both to empower poor individuals who become the company's sales representatives in rural villages and to expand the sales of the company. Both the cultural environment and economic conditions make partnership programs with NGOs and local government agencies work in India although they are not widely used in other locations (Kourula and Halme, 2006; Rohatynskyj, 2011). Successful marketing in rural India might require significantly different practices than those usually used in more developed economies.

The company produces its products in a variety of locations throughout the country, and increasing efficiencies and reducing costs are important components in the company's operational practices (Hindustan Unilever Limited, 2011). The company does not need to change operational practices for each location, instead it uses best practices, including those learned in other nations to increase the company's operational efficiencies.

Nabil Bank

Nabil Bank was founded in 1984 as a partnership with Dubai Bank Ltd. Today Nabil Bank is the second largest bank in the country, the largest privately owned bank and one of the country's most respected and profitable banks (De Waal and Frijins, 2011; Nabil Bank, 2011).

The company uses a differentiation strategy with a focus on being a full-service bank that operates in a variety of sectors including corporate banking, infrastructure and project financing, SME banking, microfinance, personal lending as well as providing loans for autos and homes. The bank also has a wider geographical distribution than most other Nepalese banks which is a feature that makes the company stand out from the competition (De Waal and Frijins, 2011; Nabil Bank, 2011). It is likely one of the factors driving the bank's strategic decisions is the relative small size of the economy of Nepal which would make it hard to gain economies of scale for a bank using more of a specialization strategy and focusing mostly on a single target market.

De Waal and Frijins (2011: 12–13) found the bank uses a top-down decision-making style, which is common in the high-power-distance cultures found in Asia. Many decisions, even those that are operational in nature, are often made by the board of directors. The authors also reported that while the company has increased the number of meetings to improve communication, the style of communication at the meetings is often mostly one where information flowed from the management to the employees with little information flowing from the bottom up, which is fairly well aligned with operating in a high-power-distance culture, as opposed to more open two-way communication which is more the norm in cultures with lower levels of power distance.

The company does use a formal annual performance appraisal system (De Waal and Frijins, 2009); however performance appraisal systems are very rare in Nepal (Adhikari, 2010: 314). Employees seem less satisfied with this performance appraisal system than the management (De Waal and Frijins, 2011).

One of the stated goals of Napil Bank is to bring modern banking and modern banking systems to Nepal. The bank uses its partnership with a bank in one of the world's financial centers which has international experience in transferring international best banking operational practices into nations like Nepal in order to improve efficiency. The bank uses modern technology such as ATMs and computer networks linked to global financial markets (Nabil Bank, 2011).

Analysis

In the three companies looked at in South Asia, each uses a strategy influenced by the economic conditions found in the region. The Tata Nano was specifically designed with the purchasing power of Indians in mind. While HUL creates products that appeal to all classes of society, to reach the majority of consumers in India it must ensure its prices are affordable for average families. Nabil Bank's strategy of offering diversified services is probably used to capture the profitable upper-income segments while also attracting enough middle and low-income customers to gain economies of scale.

As is also apparent in each case, interpersonal business practices appear to uniquely fit the cultures of the countries the companies operate in. HUL's unique marketing strategy in rural India is aligned with the specific cultural and institutional environment found in India. While we see Nabil Bank's top-down management style and the reluctance of its workforce to embrace a formal performance appraisal system as being consistent with being a high-power-distance and collectivist Asian culture.

At the operational level all three companies use global technology and other international best practices to improve their operational efficiency.

13

Central Asia: Afghanistan, Kazakhstan, Kyrgyz Republic, Mongolia, Tajikistan, Turkmenistan and Uzbekistan

Abstract: Central Asia is located between Russia, South Asia, the Middle East and East Asia, and the region has been heavily influenced by its neighbors as well as by its location, geographical features and climate. The western parts of Central Asia are primarily populated by Muslim majorities, while in the eastern region Buddhism has had a greater influence. The economies of the region are currently heavily dependent on the extraction of natural resources. Case studies of agribusiness firms in Mongolia are presented.

Key words: Afghanistan, Kazakhstan, Kyrgyz Republic, Mongolia, Tajikistan, Turkmenistan, Uzbekistan, Silk Road, Chinggis Khan.

Area background

Central Asia

There are no clear-cut boundaries that are universally agreed upon which separate Central Asia from East Asia, South Asia and the Middle East. Western Central Asia is often thought of as consisting of the Muslim-dominated regions of the newly independent states of the former Soviet Union: Turkmenistan, Uzbekistan, Kazakhstan, Kyrgyz Republic and Tajikistan. This area has historically been called Western Turkestan. These new states were the invention of the Soviet Union which chose borders for political reasons as well as to group ethno-linguistic groups together. What is often thought of as eastern Central Asia is today mostly Buddhist and consists of Mongolia (both Inner and Outer), Tibet and what has historically been called Manchuria, which today is part of Northeast China (McCauley, 2002: 21; Golden, 2011: 1–2). Afghanistan has also been included as part of Central Asia although it is sometimes classified as being part of South Asia.

Evidence suggests ancestors of modern humans came to Central Asia a very long time ago, possibly as early as 50,000 to 75,000 years (Ranov et al., 1999). Physically, the early inhabitants of much of Central Asia appear to have been more similar to individuals living in Europe or the Middle East at the time as opposed to Asian; therefore it is believed most of the early inhabitants migrated from the west and not the east. The domestication of horses and camels in northern Central Asia appeared to have first occurred around the fifth century BC and early civilizations seemed to have had contacts with Iranian and South Asian civilizations (Dani and Masson, 1999). Local environmental conditions appear to have had a major impact on the evolution of societies in the region and the reliance on nomadic life-styles (Masson, 1999).

International trade and the famous Silk Road have always played important roles in the lives of people in Central Asia. The expansion of the Achaemid Empire of Persia (590–330 BC) drew Central Asia into some of the first global trading networks which brought silk from China to the West and sent Central Asian products into China on the return trips. The major cities of Central Asia were built and mostly populated by Iranian peoples at the time and one of the early major stops on the Silk Road was the city of Samarkand, located in what is now Uzbekistan. During the fourth century BC, Alexander (the Great) brought much of Central Asia under Greco-Macedonian rule (Golden, 2011: 18–25).

All aspects of life in Central Asia were influenced by the nomadic societies which populated the region and political structures were no exception. Prior to importation of the concept of the nation-state into Central Asia, a very flexible concept of tribe which could expand to include or contract to exclude various peoples, depending on the situation, was the dominant form of political organization. Like most types of organizations, this had its strengths and weaknesses but evolved to meet the needs of the people of the region.

One of the earliest famous personages in Central Asian history and lore was Attila (the Hun) who led a tribe referred to in Europe as the Huns. While the Huns as a tribe sprang to life in what is today Kazakhstan, it is likely the tribe has its origins farther east. The Huns were known as fierce enemies of the Roman Empire, but Attila's aims in Eastern Europe were to seek loot and not to conquer lands to control. After Attila's death the Huns as a centrally controlled political unit faded away (Golden, 2011: 33–4).

Around the fifth century AD, on the shores of the Black Sea, there was an increasing influence of Turkic languages and culture which were replacing

Iranian influences. The origins of the Turks and their culture are not well known, but they appear to have come from eastern Central Asia, although some aspects of the language and culture indicate an earlier Iranian influence. In the sixth century, the Turks became heavily involved in the silk trade and worked with the ethnic/political groups called the Sasanids and Sogdians. The Turks were the first to create a transcontinental empire which linked the West with the East (Golden, 2011: 37–49).

There were also important influences coming from the West which would change the region, most specifically Islam. In the early years of the eighth century AD Arab armies and settlers moved across the region and converted many individuals to Islam in important cities of the region including Samarkand. However, Arab fortunes took a turn for the worse when their great general Qutayba withdrew and then died in AD 715 (Bosworth and Bolshakov, 1998).

Political control throughout the region passed through many hands in the next five centuries. In the eighth century AD the Umayyas Caliphate controlled parts of Central Asia. The Chinese were also at the same time expanding their influence westward and a showdown between Muslim forces and those from the Tang dynasty in China occurred near the Talas River in Kazakhstan in AD 751 which resulted in a Muslim victory that opened the door for the spread of Islam throughout the region (Bosworth and Bolshakov, 1998; Golden, 2011: 60–1). In most of the region Sunni Muslims came to dominate (McCauley, 2002: 23).

Through the next few centuries there were many claimants to power in western Central Asia including the Abbasids, the Kimek, the Kipchak, Samanids and Ghaznavids. These political powers were followed by the Seljuqs, Khwarazms and Ghurids (Agajanov, 1998; Bosworth, 1998; Bosworth and Bolshakov, 1998; Negmatov, 1998; Nizami, 1998; Sevim and Bosworth, 1998).

In the thirteenth century all of Central Asia was overrun by the Mongols, led by Chinggis Khan (Genghis Khan) and his descendants. The Mongol Empire would eventually spread from China all the way across Asia to reach the Middle East and Eastern Europe. The Mongols controlled the largest contiguous land empire ever seen in human history and Central Asia was at the center of this empire. However, the size of the empire proved impossible to control from a central base and by the fifteenth century it had splintered. Mongol rulers in much of Central Asia converted to Islam, became defenders of the religion and were assimilated into the local population, much like the Mongol overlords in China were eventually assimilated into Chinese culture (Golden, 2011: 83–93).

In the sixteenth century maritime trade controlled by Europeans began to replace the Silk Road, which had been controlled by Islamic traders, as the main trade route from East to West. Central Asia's economy changed and became less integrated with the world's economy. The groups which evolved into the Uzbek and Kazakh tribes began emerging and taking political control over specific regions in the sixteenth century. At the same time, a resurgent Russia was expanding under Ivan IV (Ivan the Terrible) and was approaching Central Asia (Golden, 2011: 101–8).

By the late eighteenth century the Uzbek state had been split into three components while the Kazakhs for reasons of economics and to increase trade gave up some of their sovereignty to both the Russians and the Ch'ing (Qing), who were then ruling China. This disunity of political power in the region allowed Russia to annex Central Asian territories in the nineteenth century. Some Kyrgyz tribes actually petitioned for Russian control due to Khoqandian misrule. Russia faced little military opposition in acquiring these territories and soon Russian immigrants were pouring into lands which had previously been almost exclusively Muslim (Golden, 2011: 115–28). However, in the early twentieth century, both Kazakhs and Kyrgyz rebelled against Russian rule, but the rebellions were brutally put down by Russian forces (McCauley, 2002: 32). Russian control over Central Asia passed to the Soviet Union after the revolution of 1917.

'Central Asia perceived of itself as Turkestan before 1917. Then Moscow promoted the emergence of separate identities and eventually separate nations so that today one conceives of Kazakhstan, Uzbekistan, Kyrgyzstan, Tajikistan, and Turkmenistan' (McCauley, 2002: xviii).

Unlike what was seen in the Baltic States, there was little appetite for independence in the Central Asian areas that had been under Soviet control. These new countries preferred to retain close military and economic relationships with Russia after independence. Moves in the regions after independence towards becoming open democracies were rather limited (McCauley, 2002: 51–72). 'Most of the current leaders have practiced varying degrees of political repression, familiar to them from the Soviet system in which they were raised' (Golden, 2011: 137).

Saparmurat Niyazov ruled Turkmenistan more like an absolute monarch than a leader of a republic up until his death in 2008, which was a similar approach to the one Islam Karimov has taken in Uzbekistan. While it would be stretching the truth to call Kazakhstan an open democracy, Nursultan Nazarbayev who has been president since independence in 1991 has used less overt political oppression. Although the Kyrgyz Republic operates as a democracy there is considerable ethnic conflict, while Tajikistan continues to try to recover from a devastating civil war which ended in 1997 (Golden, 2011: 137).

Afghanistan

The history of Afghanistan is intertwined with the histories of Central Asia, South Asia and the Middle East. Around four fifths of the landmass of the country are mountainous (Masson, 1999: 35) which has contributed to limiting population density and restricting interaction between different peoples allowing pockets of civilization to grow into separate ethnic identities. Pashtuns make up the largest ethnic group, although they do not constitute an overall majority; other major ethnic groups in the country include members of the Tajik, Hazara, Uzbek, Aimak, Turkmen and Baluchi ethnic groups (Wahab and Youngerman, 2010: 14).

There is evidence of human habitation in present day Afghanistan beginning around 100,000 years ago with signs of the use of stone tools and sizable populations during the Middle and Upper Paleolithic eras (35,000–12,000 years ago). Agriculture may have begun around 9,000 years ago while the Bronze Age civilization of 2000 BC appears to have been linked with civilizations found in South Asia. Is has been suggested Indo-Iranian (Aryan) tribes migrated into the region from around 2000 to 1500 BC. Modern languages used in Afghanistan are more closely related to Iranian languages than those of India (Wahab and Youngerman, 2010: 35–8).

It has been speculated the Assyrians in the eighth century BC ruled over parts of Afghanistan and were followed by the Medes, who ruled over much of Central Asia and who were themselves replaced by the Persians around 550 BC. Alexander (the Great) passed through and controlled Afghanistan during his conquests in the fourth century BC and the rule of his successors was overthrown by the Mauryans who practiced Hinduism. In the second century BC the Kushans, who practiced the Zoroastrianism religion and later Buddhism, began to spread through the area replacing the Mauryans. By the third century AD the Kushans began to lose influence and control over parts of Afghanistan which were taken over by the Sassanian dynasty of Persia. The Ephthalites, or White Huns, briefly and bloodily controlled the area until they were defeated around 565 (Wahab and Youngerman, 2010: 39–51). Soon Islam began to crowd out all previous religions and 'Islam has proven to be the strongest, and at times the only, unifying factor for Afghanistan's varied ethnic groups' (Wahab and Youngerman, 2010: 53).

Around AD 700 Arab armies marched through parts of Afghanistan and took over Herat and Balkh, followed by further Arab advances which conquered Kandahar and Kabul. In the ninth century AD, the devout Muslim Saffari united all of Afghanistan, parts of Iran and the Indus Valley in South Asia. Around AD 900, the Samanids took control of the regime which linked Afghanistan with kingdoms in Central Asia, but the Samanids lost control to the Ilak Khan Turks around 100 years later. In the twelfth century the Kingdom of Ghor expanded and began taking control of many of the lands and peoples of the region. In the thirteenth century, the Mongols on their quest for conquest destroyed all existing civilizations in Afghanistan to such an extent that it can be speculated Afghanistan, even up to the present day, has never been able to fully recover (Wahab and Youngerman, 2010: 55–62).

The Mongol ruler Mahmud Ghazen converted to Islam in 1295, but soon a new leader Timur Lenk (Tamerlane, also Tamburlaine) came to power and his rule reestablished more centralized control and revitalized trade in the region. Babur founded the Mughal Empire that went on to control most of Afghanistan and India in the sixteenth century. The Mughal Empire continued to rule in India, in theory at least, for around 300 more years (Wahab and Youngerman, 2010: 64–8).

It could be claimed the modern Afghan state can trace its foundation back to Durrani Ahmad Shah, a Pashtun, who consolidated power in the mid–eighteenth century. His son moved the capital to Kabul and the Durrani line continued to control Afghanistan until 1973. However, a new power, the British, began applying pressure from their base in the south. In 1836 the British gained control of Peshwar and moved into Kabul in 1838. The British were driven out in 1843. The British returned 35 years later, annexed some parts of southern Afghanistan and forced the Afghan government to accept a permanent embassy and British control over the country's foreign policy (McCauley, 2002: 5–6).

Abdur Rahman Khan ruled from 1880 to 1901 and has been given credit for maintaining the country's independence by effectively using Afghanistan as a buffer state between Russia and British India. In 1919, Afghan military forces attacked British forces while the British were preoccupied with the war in Europe and, as a result, Afghanistan gained full independence (McCauley, 2002: 7–8).

After a series of upheavals and an assassination which removed a number of rulers, Muhammad Zahir came to the throne in 1953 and, although he reigned for 20 years, he left running the government to others. In 1973, Sadar Mohammed Daoud took control over the country in a military coup and curtailed most civil liberties, but his reign was short lived as the Communists – who it is thought helped him to come to power – killed him, took control and aligned the country with the Soviet Union (McCauley, 2002: 15; Wahab and Youngerman, 2010: 113–8).

The Soviet Union began its military adventures in Afghanistan in 1979 to help the Communist Paty retain control against US and Saudi-funded insurgent factions. Approximately 30,000 Arab fighters fought in the *jihad* to drive the Soviets out of the country. The Soviets pulled out in defeat in 1989 after losing around 15,000 soldiers; however, Afghan deaths during the decade of fighting numbered approximately 1.3 million. President Najibullah who was the first leader after the Soviet withdrawal was brutally murdered when his regime was overthrown by insurgents, and he was followed by Burhanuddin Rabbini, a member of the Tajik ethnic minority who had little control over the warlords who actually ran their various regions. In 1994, the Pashtun-led Taliban, with financial backing by Pakistan and Saudi Arabia, began its fight for the country and had taken over most of Afghanistan by 1996 (McCauley, 2002: 16–20, 81–3).

Taliban rule was mostly known in the outside world for its extremely conservative interpretation of Islam and its harsh treatment of women, but initially they received considerable support, mostly from the Pashtun population in the south of the country. It is commonly believed these extreme views mostly arose from the strict and narrow teachings of the madrasas the leaders came from, the influence of Saudi Wahhabi teachings and the fact the rural clerics who led the movement had little experience of female company.

In part, however, the Taliban was merely expressing the century old resentment felt by many members of Afghan tribal society against the centralizing and modernizing programs of the Kabul elites, who sometimes imposed their reforms with insensitivity, arrogance, and even cruelty, particularly during the Communist era. Modern values, especially with regard to gender roles, were also associated with hated foreign imperialists, whether British or Russian.

(Wahab and Youngerman, 2010: 224)

In response to the 11 September 2011 terrorist attacks by al-Qaeda in the USA the US government supplied aid to opponents of the Taliban, called the Northern Alliance, and the regime was toppled. Elections have been held and Hamid Karzai has since held the presidency. However, the long-sought-after peace has proven elusive to achieve, and Afghan, US, British and other international forces have fought an insurgency coming from a reformed Taliban for the last decade or more. Adding to the difficulties is the fact the growing of opium has become a major cornerstone of the nation's economy (Wahab and Youngerman, 2010).

Mongolia

Evidence suggests there have been humans living in Mongolia since the Paleolithic period (35,000–12,000 years ago). It was shortly after this period that the bow and arrow came into use. Cave drawings of animals by early man indicate the climate at one time was considerably warmer in Mongolia than it is now. Archeological evidence suggests the early inhabitants of Mongolia consisted of both nomadic tribes and more settled peoples who relied on agriculture for subsistence. One of the important early tribes of Mongolia were the Xiongnu, also known as the Huns, who were often a military foe of the Chinese during the third and second centuries BC. Turkic tribes became prominent in Mongolia around the sixth century AD and various Turkic tribes competed with the Uighers for control of the eastern part of Central Asia. The Uighers created modern cities and their writing system was used as the foundation for written Mongolian. The Kyrgyz eventually drove out the Uighers and the area fell into a period of decentralized control. In the tenth century the Khitans gained control over much of Mongolia and founded the Liao dynasty in Northern China (Derevyanko and Dorj, 1999; Burgan, 2009: 18–21; May, 2009: 1–5).

In the tenth and eleventh centuries, 'The Mongols were just one of the tribes there, along with other peoples of Mongolian and Turkic ethnic backgrounds. The various tribes often married women from other tribes. This interaction created the Turko-Mongolian culture' (Burgan, 2009: 21).

In the early thirteenth century, a warrior from a humble economic background named Temujin began to make his presence felt. In 1206 he was selected by the other Mongol leaders to become the Great Khan, or Chinggis Khan (Genghis Khan). Chinggis first led his troops into what is now northwest China and the most famous Mongolian of all times started what was to become one of the largest empires the world has ever seen. This initial expansion gave the Mongols control over part of the lucrative trade along the Silk Road. Chinggis' troops continued to move south before switching and heading west. The Mongol conquest and the slaughter after the conquest of the Central Asian kingdom of Khwarazm might have been the bloodiest military conquests in history up until that point. Chinggis Khan died in 1227 and was buried in a secret location and his son Ogedai became the new Great Khan (Burgan, 2009: 27; May, 2009: 6).

Under Ogedai, the Mongols conquered much of modern day Russia and even moved into Poland and Hungary. However, upon hearing of the death of Ogedai, Mongolian troops left Europe and headed home to attend the *quriltai* which would choose the next leader. Guyak, the next leader of the Mongols, was not selected until 1246, but he died shortly afterwards in 1248. In 1251, after much infighting amongst the descendants of Chinggis Khan over control of the empire, Mongke emerged as the new leader of the Mongols. Under Mongke, the Mongol Empire expanded into the Middle East as far as Baghdad and Syria. Mongke died in 1259 and once again Mongol troops returned to Mongolia to engage in political infighting over the selection of a new leader (Burgan, 2009: 29–37; May, 2009: 8).

The next Great Khan was Khubilai (Kublai). Under Khubilai the Mongol Empire reached its largest size and stretched from the Pacific Ocean to the Middle East and Europe; however, during this time the empire also began to fragment and Khubilai only directly controlled China and Mongolia. While the conquest of China began during Mongke's reign, under Khubilai the Mongols continued south and in 1276 brought the Song dynasty to an end and started the Yuan dynasty. The Mongols expanded their influence into Korea and made an ill-fated attempt to subdue Japan. As a result of ruling China, the Mongols, who were few in number, began to adapt Chinese ways; the Chinese system of government probably changed the Mongol rulers to a greater extent than the Mongol rulers changed China (Burgan, 2009: 12, 39–43; May, 2009: 10).

Over time more and more of the Mongols intermarried with locals and converted to Islam in Central Asia. In the middle of the fourteenth century the empire had crumbled and was replaced by a series of local rulers, which included Arabs, Turks, Persians and other Mongols. Although more centralized control of parts of Central Asia returned in the late fourteenth century under Timur Lenk, this revised empire did not last long after Timur Lenk's death. It was at this time that the Mongols were also driven out of China, and most Mongols who remained were absorbed into the Chinese population (Burgan, 2009: 14, 50–74).

The Ming armies from China often attacked Mongolia in the fourteenth and fifteenth centuries, but without completely subduing the Mongolians. In the seventeenth century another power, the Manchus, began to dominate in North Asia, conquered China and incorporated Tibet and Xinjiang into the Ch'ing dynasty (May, 2009: 11–15).

As the Mongol Empire shrank and faded away, Mongolia itself was squeezed by the two emergent powers of Russia and China. By the middle to latter part of the eighteenth century, nearly all Mongolian people had fallen under the rule of the Manchus, who at the time also controlled China under the Ch'ing dynasty (Atwood, 2004: viii).

In the 1920s with direct assistance from the Soviet Union, armies from the northern part of Mongolia drove out the Chinese and declared independence. Mongolia was then split into two parts: Outer Mongolia which was formally independent but in actuality was controlled by the Soviet Union, and Inner Mongolia where the Chinese retained control (Atwood, 2004: viii; Burgan, 2009: 139).

Soviet control brought many changes to Mongolia. The Soviets tried to implement collectivism of agriculture. Although there was no ownership of land in traditional Mongolian nomadic society, the Mongolians had always owned their livestock. Despite resisting collectivist efforts, agricultural production and the economy suffered under central planning. Outer Mongolia remained under the Soviet sphere of influence after World War II but, with the collapse of the Berlin Wall, Soviet and Russian control evaporated and a new era was ushered in with the elections of 1990 (May, 2009: 26–9).

Mongolia of today is shaped by its past and still approximately 40% of the population live a nomadic life-style and about 75% of the landmass continues to be used as pasture for animals. Whether this life-style and use of land can continue as Mongolia moves towards a more modern economy remains uncertain. Buddhism, which became the nation's primary religion during the time of Chinese influence, was suppressed under the Soviets but there has been a revival in the construction of Buddhist temples, and an increase in the influence of Buddhism in daily life has been seen. A somewhat unique feature of life in Mongolia is women make up the majority of urban professionals. In addition, the legacy of Chinggis Khan lives on and his image and name are used to promote an endless variety of products from banks to vodka to energy drinks (Golden, 2011: 139; May, 2009).

Although Mongolia is still struggling after the end of seventy years of Soviet dominance, it remains committed to democracy and a symbol of the successful transition from a one-party system to a democratic government. Whereas most of the former Soviet republics have democracy in name only, Mongolia achieved it early and continues to grow. With a growing interest in Mongolia's mineral and tourism resources, one can only hope that its economy will blossom.

(May, 2009: 31)

Business environments

Afghanistan

The Afghan people and economy have suffered terribly from the country's decades of civil warfare. The total GDP of the nation fell from around $3.7 billion in 1977 to around $2.7 billion in 2000. However, the economy has shown considerable growth since 2000 and reached $13.5 billion in 2009, with approximately another $4 billion from uncounted revenue from the opium trade. The country's banking system consists of private banks, the government's central bank, Da Afghanistan Bank, and Hawala money exchanges (Wahab and Youngerman, 2010: 262).

The main components of the economy of Afghanistan are foreign aid, agriculture (including growing opium) and the informal sector. Despite respectable growth rates in recent years, poverty continues to plague large segments of the population. Mining is an area of the economy which has

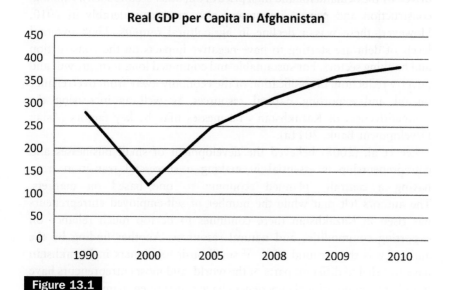

Figure 13.1

Source: UNCTAD (2011: 130)

the potential to create economic growth and new jobs, but the country has many obstacles to overcome to achieve sustainable economic growth and lower levels of poverty. These obstacles include increasing concerns over security, political instability, high levels of corruption, a weak governance system, loss of export competitiveness, new trade barriers and the unreliability of financial aid coming from donor countries in the middle of financial crises (Asian Development Bank, 2011a).

Kazakhstan

Kazakhstan has experienced both significant economic growth and considerable poverty reduction since independence. Much of this growth has been driven by the nation's oil industry and some of the income from the sale of oil has been spent on creating social protection programs. Agrawal (2007) found poverty reduction has been mostly driven by economic growth with provinces experiencing more growth and increased job opportunities also having the largest reductions in poverty. However, Agrawal also suggested government expenditure on social sectors played a role in growing the economy and reducing poverty.

Kazakhstan saw growth slow considerably in 2008 and 2009 before recovering significantly in 2010. While much economic growth has been driven by the demand for and high price of oil, other sectors such as mining, construction and private investment also grew considerably in 2010. However, there was a decline in agricultural outputs. High external levels of debt are starting to have negative impacts on the construction and banking sectors. For sustainable and continued long-term growth and poverty reduction, diversification of the economy away from overreliance on oil and exporting natural resources as well as increasing the competitiveness of Kazakhstan's businesses may be key factors (Asian Development Bank, 2011a).

Lee et al. (2008) believed the development of small businesses and entrepreneurship is essential in making a successful transition from having a centrally planned economy to one based on markets. The authors felt that while the number of self-employed entrepreneurs has risen in Kazakhstan there continues to be too much reliance on exporting commodities and natural resources. Another finding by the authors was that around 85% of small-business owners in Kazakhstan have traveled to different parts of the world, and most entrepreneurs have found these international experiences have contributed to improvement of their businesses.

Kyrgyz Republic

Political upheaval in 2010 had a negative short-term effect on economic growth; however, foreign donors have agreed to supply significant funds for the new government to rebuild the country and its economy. Non-performing loans are a major concern in the banking sector. Gold is the country's biggest export earner, and both increased production and high global gold prices help to maintain the economy. Much of the country's trade is with Russia and Kazakhstan and free flows of trade with and growth in its neighbors will be important for the nation's economic growth. Many citizens of the Kyrgyz Republic work abroad and remittances are another important contributor to the economy (Asian Development Bank, 2011a).

> The country faces huge challenges in economic recovery, reconstruction, and social reconciliation. Success will not be easy given the considerable pressure on public financial resources in a weakened economy. Achieving sustainable robust economic growth remains the major challenge facing the country.
>
> (Asian Development Bank, 2011a: 107)

Mongolia

The Mongolian economy went through considerable strain during the transition from a Soviet-funded socialist economy to a free market economy. Between 1990 and 1994 there was a contraction on a per capita basis of around 30% as the removal of Soviet funding resulted in a drastic reduction in subsidies, welfare programs and the state budget. However, since 1995 when the country made significant market-based reforms, there has been around a 9% annual rate of economic growth that was partly driven by producing and exporting commodities and natural resources (Walker and Hall, 2010).

Agriculture plays a large part in the nation's economy and supports about one third of the population; however, 2010 was a very tough year for the agriculture sector as severe weather prevented high yields of crops and was responsible for the loss of considerable numbers of livestock. The mining sector has prospered with much of its output being exported to the huge and growing economy in China. There is considerable potential for growth in the mining sector and, if global commodity prices stay high, growth prospects look strong. Inflation has been quite high, but due to increases in government revenue the budget has remained balanced.

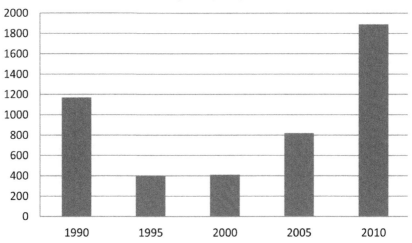

Mongolia's GNI per capita (Atlas Method)

Figure 13.2

Source: Asian Development Bank (2011b)

Diversifying the foundation of the economy, improving the performance of the banking sector and keeping inflation under control can be expected to have a positive impact on economic growth and poverty reduction (Asian Development Bank, 2011a).

Tajikistan

The economy of Tajikistan has had trouble creating enough opportunities for its citizens, which has resulted in around 800,000 Tajiks, or 11% of the population, emigrating and seeking work elsewhere (Riester, 2010). The country experienced over 6% growth in 2010. This was driven by growth in industry, which mostly consists of light industries with food processing and construction being the two largest sectors of the economy. Agricultural production also saw an increase. The banking sector is constrained by a high number of non-performing loans, low levels of deposits and few investment opportunities. Inflation and debt have been on the increase. Aluminum and cotton are the country's two major exports and prices for both have been strong (Asian Development Bank, 2011a).

Tajikistan faces interrelated challenges that hinder reduction of widespread poverty and a move to higher and more sustainable growth. The first is its heavy reliance on remittances, which was keenly felt in 2009's global downturn. The second is its dependence on a few exportable commodities and very narrow production base. The government therefore needs to strengthen infrastructure and services, improve the business and investment climate, and diversify agricultural output.

(Asian Development Bank, 2011a: 110–11)

Turkmenistan

The economy in Turkmenistan is heavily influenced by the production of natural gas and hydrocarbons which make up 90% of the country's exports. The economy has shown considerable growth over recent years and, if plans for new pipelines are realized, growth will be expected to continue. Due to high volumes of natural gas exports, the country is one of the few in the world that has had a governmental budget surplus. The country has used part of its income from exporting natural gas to increase spending on social programs and to develop economic and physical infrastructure. The high reliance on exports has taken some focus away from developing a dynamic private sector. Therefore, to diversify the economy and create conditions for more sustainable long-term growth, more entrepreneurs and the development of a more pro-business environment are expected to be helpful (Asian Development Bank, 2011a).

Uzbekistan

Migration to seek work has become very common in Uzbekistan with somewhere in the neighborhood of 10% of the entire population seeking work outside the country, mostly in low-skilled work in neighboring Russia or Kazakhstan (Riester, 2010). Reported economic growth has been quite high with service and industry being the largest two sectors and driving most of the nation's economic growth. The country has seen some foreign investment, mostly going into the energy, telecommunications and auto-manufacturing sectors. Inflation has been running in double digits for a number of years. The government has been able to balance its budget and has decided to lower tax rates to encourage development of a more dynamic private sector. The country's main exports are cotton, gas and gold, all of which have been experiencing historically high prices. There are a number of factors indicating that there are opportunities for continued positive growth in the coming years (Asian Development Bank, 2011a).

Case studies

Mongolian Produce

In the town of Mandakh Soum there is a small business which operates out of the northern province of Selenge in Mongolia next to the Russian border. Mongolian Produce (a pseudonym) has been in business for seven years, has around a dozen employees and grows and sells fresh potatoes, vegetables and wheat for the retail market.

From a strategic standpoint, the company mostly focuses on maintaining a cost leadership position and often is willing to give discounts for bulk purchases. While customers in Mongolia prefer fresh to frozen or canned foods and good quality is expected, the average income in the country dictates price to be a dominant factor in making purchasing decisions for most consumers and therefore maintaining reasonable prices and lowering overhead costs are of primary concern for the company.

From the interpersonal perspective, the company mostly operates informally with relaxed hiring practices, on-the-job training, few written instructions and a paternalistic management style.

From the operational standpoint, the company has incorporated some international best agricultural practices, buys high-quality seeds from international suppliers and uses irrigation practices which help to ensure a consistent supply of fresh food for its customers.

Agro Alpha LLC

Directly south of Selenge Province lies Tuv Province where Agro Alpha LLC operates. The company has around 20 employees, grows and sells potatoes, and distributes milk, agricultural products, pesticides and herbicides. With higher-than-average prices, the company's operates a differentiation strategy, yet the range of prices the company can charge is limited due to the low level of income in the region. One feature the company uses to differentiate itself is through the use of environmentally friendly packaging.

At the interpersonal level, the firm mostly uses informal instructions, on-the-job training and informal recruitment practices, as would be expected in most small firms in LDCs.

At the operational level, the company tries to use modern agricultural techniques and purchases imported seeds and other agricultural products from Europe and Japan. However, for spare parts and other items of a non-technical nature the firm buys from local suppliers.

Delger Uyanga LLC

Another small agricultural company in Mongolia is Delger Uyanga LLC. The company produces both fresh and seed potatoes as well as wheat. The company has around ten employees and has been in business for over 20 years. As the company is primarily in a commodity industry, it keeps its prices competitive while trying to differentiate itself through improved service. It would appear the company's strategy would straddle the line between being classified as low-cost and low-cost/differentiation.

As in the other agricultural companies looked at in Mongolia, the company uses mostly informal hiring and training practices. The company's turnover is small and its small size and cultural preferences indicate the company does not have a formal hierarchy beyond separation between the owners and the employees.

In its operations in the field, the company uses foreign seeds and agricultural equipment to maximize productivity.

Elite Seed LLC

Elite Seed LLC is a new agribusiness company located in the Selenge Province of Mongolia. The company has been in business for around one year and focuses on producing seed potatoes as well as growing some wheat. The company employs around a dozen individuals. The company uses a differentiation strategy as its prices are higher than the average but its quality is considered higher as well. As with other firms operating as industrial or agribusiness suppliers, low price is not automatically associated with low cost or economic efficiency for the purchasers. If farmers can produce more efficiently from using quality seeds, the motivation for purchasing the higher priced differentiated product is not actual price but price per unit of output.

At the interpersonal level the firm operates quite informally with few written rules or regulations. However, it does pay higher-than-average wages and provides additional benefits to its employees, in alignment with its differentiation strategy. At the operational level the firm uses imported strains of potatoes from Europe and agricultural machinery from China.

New Crop LLC

New Crop LLC is another agribusiness located in the Selenge Province of Mongolia. The company produces both new and seed potatoes and employs around a dozen workers. The company uses a low-cost strategy and offers its customers a low and steady price that does not fluctuate very much between the seasons.

As seen in the other cases of agribusinesses examined in Mongolia, the company uses interpersonal business practices which are aligned with the cultural environment. It also makes uses of technology and ideas created outside of Mongolia.

Analysis

The choice of crops produced by the agribusinesses examined is influenced by the land, weather and food preferences of the people of the region. We see different companies use different types of strategies, although price and costs are significant factors in all strategic choices.

At the interpersonal level we see more processes that are informal than bureaucratic, although this is probably due as much to the size of the organizations as it is to the cultural environment.

At the operational level, we see the companies using technology and best practices imported from other areas of the world where there are more resources available for agricultural research. While foreign technologies often have to be adapted to, or specifically selected for, local environmental conditions, the use of these international best practices has greatly improved agricultural productivity in the country.

14

Myanmar/Burma

Abstract: The country of Myanmar/Burma has had one of the least successful economies in the world and poverty is widespread. Economic sanctions have been imposed on the country by many Western countries which has contributed to limiting integration of the country's economy with the global economy. Many changes are currently happening in the country which leads to optimism for the future and may create new business opportunities.

Key words: Burma, Myanmar, Theravada Buddhism, Aung San Suu Kyi, U Nu, Ne Win, economic sanctions.

Country background

Morck and Yeung (2007: 354) proposed the idea that in order to find success in Asia foreign business practitioners need to understand Asia as it is, and not only in comparison to Western culture; 'Asia must be understood on its own terms. This requires a deep respect for, and understanding of, Asian history.' This sentiment may apply to working and investing in Myanmar/Burma as much as it does for any other country in the region.

One of the first civilizations to emerge in the territories that today comprise Myanmar/Burma was the Pyu who appeared to have evolved from a pre-existing Iron Age culture. The Pyu dominated the region from around 200 BC to AD 900. By the fourth or fifth century AD the Pyu adopted Buddhism as their religion and spoke a language from the Sino-Tibetan family while using a written language based on scripts borrowed from India. Beikthano, Sri Ksetra and Halin, all located alongside tributaries of the Irrawaddy River, were the major centers of population of the Pyu (Higham, 2001).

Burmese legends place the origins of the Burmese civilization in Tagaung, north of present day Mandalay, where a kingdom was founded by immigrants from India, although there is little archeological evidence to support these legends. The evidence suggests there had been a continuously evolving society in Upper Burma beginning shortly before the end of the Bagan (Pagan) period in the thirteenth and fourteenth centuries AD and continuing up until today. Foreign and colonial scholars of the region tended to reject Burmese legends and believed the ancestors of the Burmese were a mix of peoples moving southward from present day Tibet and immigrants from India (Dautremer, 1913: 35; Hudson, 2006; Myint-U, 2006: 42–7).

By the early eighth century political rivalry between the Kingdom of Nan Chao and the Mon people began in much of the Irrawaddy Valley. Around the middle of the ninth century, the Kingdom of Bagan (Pagan) arose which was controlled by the 'Burmese' who were recent immigrants into the region and were culturally distinct from the Mon and Pyu who previously held political control (Taylor, 1992: 165; Myint-U, 2006: 48–57).

Anawrahta became the new leader in Bagan and ruled from around 1044 to 1077; he is responsible for transforming the region (Hall, 1992: 240). 'The Burmese people traditionally saw Anawrathta [Anawrahta] as the "founder" of the first Burmese empire and the one who established Buddhism as the national religion' (Goh, 2007: 1). Anawrahta has been thought of as being heavily influenced by Buddhist values and his conquests were believed to have been motivated by the desire to spread Theravada Buddhism and obtain Buddhist relics. Along with Theravada Buddhism, other aspects of Mon culture were adapted by the Burmese during the Bagan era. In addition, Bagan had frequent contacts with China in which goods, religious practices and political support were exchanged. Moreover, it is believed Bagan maintained contacts with other centers of Theravada Buddhism which at the time included Sri Lanka and newly formed kingdoms in present day Thailand. Buddhism and the Burmese language spread widely during the Bagan era and most people in Myanmar/Burma believe the country and its culture have evolved from the Kingdom of Bagan and the rule of Anawrahta (Taylor, 1992: 165; Myint-U, 2006: 52–62; Goh, 2007).

Theravada Buddhism arrived and became established in Myanmar/Burma before spreading across mainland Southeast Asia (Stuart-Fox, 2003: 69). There are Burmese legends stating the Buddha traveled to areas now identified as being part of Myanmar/Burma (Bode, 1898: 21), and others claim Buddhism arrived when King Asoka from India sent monks to spread the religion in the third century BC (Carbine, 2004: 101). However, it would seem more likely the introduction and spread of Buddhism happened gradually beginning in the early centuries AD. Buddhism was well established in the region by the beginning of the era of King Anawrahta, although there is some debate over whether Anawrahta was an actual historical figure or a literary device used by Buddhist scholars to convey Buddhist values to the population throughout the region. In the twelfth century, there were three branches of Burmese Buddhism vying for supremacy, Mahayana, Theravada and Sarvastivadin. However, around 1180 an elderly monk and a novice have been recorded as making a pilgrimage to Sri Lanka and bringing back four additional monks who helped to institutionalize the Sinhalese (Theravada) form of Buddhism (Goh, 2007).

Armies of the Mongol (Yuan) dynasty from China attached Yunnan and then pressed on towards Bagan after the King of Bagan refused to pay tribute to the rulers of the Yuan Empire. The Yuan forces eventually captured the Bagan capital in 1287. However, Bagan proved a difficult area to control and the Mongol/Chinese forces withdrew in 1303 and Bagan regained its sovereignty (Dai, 2004).

Bagan's position was greatly weakened by the invasion and others, particularly the Shan – a group classified as part of the Tai people – began to compete for political power and control. A number of new kingdoms arose with the richest and most powerful being the Mon-speaking Kingdom of Pegu which was located near present day Yangon (Rangoon). Other kingdoms of the post-Bagan period included Ava, Prome, Arakan and Toungoo; Burmese society became both fragmented politically and more isolated from the outside world after the decline of Bagan power (Taylor, 1992: 167; Myint-U, 2006: 64–5; Goh, 2007: 37).

The Kingdom of Ava which sprang up after the decline of Bagan has traditionally been considered a Shan kingdom because the initial leaders were thought to be Shan; this has been considered a time of decline and warfare (Taylor, 1992: 167). However, Aung Thwin (1996) showed Burmese language was the primary form of communication in Ava. A continuation of the styles of arts and economic activities from the Bagan period as well as its political cooperation with other Burmese-speaking areas suggests Ava was actually a Burmese-dominated realm. The chaotic and politically fragmented nature of the period may well have been overstated.

Under the leadership of Tabinshweti and his successor Bayinnaung, who came from the Burmese-speaking kingdom of Toungoo, the country was politically reunited in the sixteenth century. Portuguese mercenaries and modern weaponry played an important role in Bayinnaung's military which was used to consolidate power within Burma and also invade and devastate the Thai kingdoms of Lannathai and Ayutthaya. In addition, the Shan were subdued and brought into the nation under Burmese leadership at this time. These sixteenth-century military victories continue to inspire the nation's military and are used to remind the people that the country was not always a less developed nation; rather, it has a powerful and glorious past when previously ruled by military strongmen (Chanthanom, 1998: 39; Myint-U, 2006: 63–71).

After the death of Bayinnaung, another period of political fragmentation ensued but a new consolidated power arose under the leadership of Alaungpaya, who founded the Konbaung dynasty in 1752. The city of Pegu was conquered in 1759 and Alaungpaya personally led an attack on the Thai kingdom of Ayutthaya in 1750 and again in 1760, but the assault in 1760 was abandoned when Alaungpaya fell ill. However, the Burmese regrouped and overran Lannathai in 1763 and then sacked Ayutthaya which brought the Thai kingdom to an end in 1776 (Dai, 2004: 154; Myint-U, 2006: 97–9).

However, the armies of the Ch'ing (Manchu) dynasty started invading northern Burma from China. As a consequence, the attention of the leaders turned from controlling Thailand to protecting its northern borders in a battle for survival. The Manchu-led Ch'ing forces were eventually repulsed by a combination of the Burmese army and tropical diseases. Eventually, the Ch'ing withdrew after a face-saving agreement was reached in which the Burmese agreed to send tribute to China so the Ch'ing could claim a victory in order to end the war (Dai, 2004).

Feeling confident after victories against the Ch'ing and the Thais, the Burmese military initiated campaigns to the west. The Burmese military became involved in Arakan and Assam. As a result these moves were interpreted by the British as threats against the British Empire's own interests in South Asia. The British and Burmese engaged in a bloody confrontation from 1822 to 1824, which resulted in a British victory forcing Burma to cede some of its territory, agree to cease military activities in Assam, Jaintia and Cachar and pay a huge indemnity. A second brief war was fought between the British and Burmese in 1852, one outcome of which was an internal split in the Burmese royal family which ended up with King Mindon ascending to the throne (Myint-U, 2006: 113–34).

During the reign of King Mindon (1852–78), a devout Buddhist, peace between the British and the Burmese held. However, there was some serious fighting over his succession, and eventually King Thibaw rose to power but over a nation that had been greatly weakened by the internal fight for succession. The British saw the weakened state of Burma as an opportunity and gave as justification for the invasion the immorality, ineffectiveness and cruelty of the Burmese ruler. The British also claimed the invasion helped to protect British interests in India. Other similarities between the British, in addition to using removal of a cruel tyrant as justification for the attack, and the more recent US-led invasion of Iraq was the relative ease of initial victory upon arriving in Mandalay in 1855 and the ensuing difficulties in subduing an insurrection which was opposed to foreign forces controlling the country (Dautremer, 1913).

A case can be made that some of Myanmar/Burma's problems of today can trace their roots to colonial times. The use of ethnic minorities in the British army created a division between many ethnic minority groups and the majority Burmese population that continues to this day. This has been especially true of the ethnic Karen peoples, who previously had many of its people converted to Christianity and heavily recruited into British military and police forces, which resulted in the Karens having trouble integrating into the greater Burmese society (Smeaton, 1920). Although the fighting between Karen nationalists and the Burmese government has lessened in recent years, there continues to be distrust and unwillingness on both sides to integrate their cultural differences within a single political union. Other impacts of the colonial period include large Indian immigration and the dominance of ethnic Indians in commerce during the colonial era, the increased importance of secular education, the diminishing role of Buddhist monasteries and their schools in the country, the elimination of the monarchy and limiting the power of local and traditional elites (Carbine, 2004: 131; Kaw, 2005; Myint-U, 2006: 186–7).

As in much of Asia, the beginning of the end of the colonial system was initiated by the Japanese invasion during World War II, where British troops retreated and 'sacrificed' Burma to attempt to regroup and hold Singapore which was overlooking the strategically important Straits of Malacca. Aung San, Ne Win and others in support of Burmese nationalism returned from training in Japan to help lead the 'liberalization' of the country and a declaration of independence was made in 1943 with Dr. Ba Maw serving as the first prime minister. However, it did not take long to realize 'independence' under the Japanese was neither preferable nor freer than being a colony of the British. The Burmese quickly realized they had traded a European colonial master for an Asian one. The tide of war turned after a massive counterattack the British launched from India drove out the Japanese. This counterattack resulted in large-scale engagements in the mountainous region of Manipur killing approximately 80,000 of the 200,000 Japanese troops who were engaged in the actions. Aung San, Ne Win and many others switched sides and the Anti-Fascist People's Party was formed to oppose Japanese rule. The British retook Rangoon on 3 May 1945 without any significant resistance and Japanese colonial control over Burma was ended (Myint-U, 2006: 220–41).

British control after the war did not last long and in early 1948 a delegation of Burmese leaders in London, under the leadership of Aung San, negotiated a deal for independence but the joy and promise of independence was soon shattered as, within months of the British withdrawal, fighting over the Karen's demand for an independent state broke out and the country fell into a long period of violence and bloodshed (Myint-U, 2006: 248–55; Min, 2009: 1061).

Conflicts between minority non-Burmese ethnic groups and the Burmese majority have plagued the country since independence. However, initially there were some indications of the possibility of peaceful coexistence between the different ethnic groups. In 1947, an agreement with the backing of Aung San and the leaders of a number of ethnic groups was signed in Panglong which might have set the stage for peaceful coexistence; however, while the leaders of the Shan, Kachin and Chin signed the agreement, the leaders of some of the largest ethnic minority populations, in particular the Karen and Karenni, did not show up for the conference. The lack of participation of some of the major ethnic groups in the conference and future events – including the death of Aung San, a leading supporter of negotiating with ethnic minority groups; the continued Karen struggle for independence; and the Communist rebellion which dragged many ethnic minority groups into clashes with the government – killed the spirit of the Panglong conference and an opportunity to evolve into a peaceful multiethnic political union was missed (Walton, 2008).

On the morning of 19 July 1947, gunmen broke into a meeting of the interim government's executive council and shot and killed Aung San, who was one of the most influential politicians in the country at the time, and wounded four others. It came out later the killings were orchestrated by U Saw, a bitter rival of Aung San, along with some rogue elements of the British Officer Corps (Myint-U, 2006: 54–5).

In the early years of independence the country ran under a parliamentary democracy and the government, for all but one year of the country's democratic experiment, was led by U Nu. U Nu was born in Wakema, about 50 miles outside Rangoon, into a moderately wealthy family. He attended Rangoon University, taught English and history, and when returning to the university to earn a graduate degree in law he met and became good friends with Aung San. U Nu was something of an idealist and his vision for Burma was a country governed according to a mixture of socialist and Buddhist values. U Nu was popular with the voters and he became the first prime minister of the country after independence and remained in the position, except for a brief period where U Nu, in an attempt to stave off a military coup, appointed a caretaker government led by Ne Win. While U Nu easily returned to power on the strength of the 1960 elections, the cohesion of his political party soon began to disintegrate and the lack of economic progress during his administration caused some dissatisfaction throughout the population (Myint-U, 2006: 265–87; Hlaing, 2008).

Ne Win – bolstered by praise for the way in which his caretaker military government had previously been more effective than U Nu's democratically elected government – in cahoots with the military seized power in a military coup on 2 March 1962. U Nu was arrested, but released in 1966, and Burma's experiment with democratic rule and U Nu's idealistic vision of a socialist society guided by Buddhist values came to an end. Democratic institutions were replaced by military dictatorship and the 'Burmese Way to Socialism' doctrine. Ne Win created the Burma Socialist Programme Party (BSPP). In 1974 it was announced that power was to be transferred from the state, headed by Ne Win, to the party, also headed by Ne Win, which was claimed to represent the people. Ne Win felt military rule was necessary to keep united a country with such a diverse population. Despite numerous challenges to his authority from different factions within the military, Ne Win was able to remain in power until 1988 (Myint-U, 2006: 290–309; Hlaing, 2008; Min, 2008).

Without explanation, on 23 July 1988 Ne Win called for a return to multiparty elections, resigned and named Sein Lwin, known for being a military hardliner, as his successor. On 8 August 1988, student-led demonstrations calling for democratic change began. The protests led to a violent crackdown on dissent by the military, the sacking of Sein Lwin, further protests and the rise of Aung San Suu Kyi, daughter of national hero Aung San, as the leader of the movement towards democracy. The military regrouped under the banner of the State Law and Order Restoration Council (SLORC), led by General Saw Maung, and brutally crushed demonstrations, jailed dissidents, put Aung San Suu Kyi under house arrest and took firm control of the country (Myint-U, 2006: 31–6). After military control was restored, the government decided to change the official name of the country from Burma to Myanmar. However, opponents to the military regime have continued to use Burma as the name of the country; whichever name is used can have political implications (Dittmer, 2008).

Than Shwe took over leadership of SLORC in 1992, and the military junta changed its name to the State Peace and Development Council (SPDC). After eliminating from office his main rival, Prime Minister Khin Nyunt, Than Shwe consolidated his hold over power (Hlaing, 2008). The country was given a new capital and the government moved from Yangon (Rangoon) to the remote area now called Naypyidaw. While no rational explanation has ever been given for this huge expenditure and disruption, it has been reported it was due to Than Shwe following the advice of his personal astrologer (Seekins, 2009: 173). More likely the motivation was for security reasons and moving the government away from a major population center made it less vulnerable to popular protests (Wilson and Skidmore, 2008: 1).

In 2007, there emerged another protest movement often called the Saffron Rebellion due to the color of the robes worn by the Buddhist monks who joined it. Initially, protests were sparked by the removal of subsidies on consumer goods and rising prices, but soon the tone of the protests became more political and renewed calls for democratic change emerged. There was a lot of excitement amongst the opposition in and outside of the country and among democratic activists. But in the end the government used its military might to once again quell the protests and calls for change (Horsey, 2008).

However, times are changing and the country appears to be at a crossroads with opportunities for change. There is expected to be a generational shift in the leadership of the military and the government over the next few years, and the country has both agreed to hold elections and make constitutional changes which guarantee the military's dominance over the civilian component of future governments (Horsey, 2011). At the time of writing, the first round of elections have been held and it appears the National League for Democracy and Aung San Suu Kyi have won resounding victories and democracy remains the choice of the people of Myanmar/Burma as opposed to continued military rule. Whether these reforms are just for show to appease international critics or are the first steps towards gradual but fundamental change are not at this time obvious.

Reform has been made more difficult by the exodus of much of the country's most talented human resources and moves by the citizens away from using government institutions to alternative options in education, health and employment, as the population has no faith in the government to improve its performance (Wilson and Skidmore, 2008). Moreover, the extremely poor and deteriorating education system will have a negative impact on the country's ability to develop the human capital needed to grow economically and develop politically (Lall, 2008; Lorch, 2008; Tin, 2008).

As Myanmar/Burma's relations with the West have worsened, the country has developed more economic and political connections with China. However, relationships between the two countries since Myanmar/Burma's independence have not always been completely harmonious. During the early years of Communist rule in China, Chinese-backed Communist parties and other left-leaning organizations sought to overthrow various governments in Myanmar/Burma. What is more, remnants of the Kuomintang (KMT), who had fled after the Chinese civil war, operated out of areas inside Burma's borders in the 1950s, with some support from the governments of Taiwan and the USA before most were finally repatriated to Taiwan in 1961 (Aung Myoe, 2011).

In more recent times the two non-elected governments of Myanmar/ Burma and China have relied on each other for political support. However, because there are vast differences in population size, military strength and overall economies, the relationship is of far more strategic importance to Myanmar/Burma than it is to China. Opponents of the regime in Myanmar/Burma often claim China's support adds strength to the military dictators, but there is also considerable anti-Chinese sentiment amongst the population within the country. China has become a major supplier of military equipment, investment and development assistance. Although the leaders of Myanmar/Burma always keep in mind the potential threat coming from China's power and size and its location on the country's northern border, it is generally felt Western economic and diplomatic sanctions have pushed the government of Myanmar/Burma deeper into the sphere of Chinese interests (Aung Myoe, 2011).

Business environment

Myanmar's economy has not kept pace with the growth seen in other economies in Southeast Asia; as a result poverty continues to be a major problem for many people living in the country. Many workers have been forced to cross the border and attempt to find work in Thailand, but the remittances sent back are mostly used for survival purposes for those who stay behind and are not driving domestic economic growth (Turnell et al., 2008). The Burmese Way to Socialism has worked better in maintaining the continuation of the regime than it has in spurring economic growth and poverty reduction. 'An evaluation of the government's policy reforms on subsidies reveals a continuing preoccupation with regime survival over economic efficiencies' (Thawnghmung, 2008: 282).

Thailand and China are the country's two largest trading partners. However, Myanmar/Burma's trade with China is very lopsided with imports far exceeding exports. Most exports from Myanmar/Burma are of natural resources while imports are primarily manufactured goods. Most of the trade with China is cross-border and, while overall trade with Myanmar/Burma is a tiny percentage of China's overall trade, this cross-border trade is important for businesses located in China's Yunnan province (Kudo, 2008; Aung Myoe, 2011). Because of the nature of trade with China, it has been questioned whether exporting a few raw materials while importing large quantities of finished products has proven to be substantially beneficial to the economy and people of Myanmar/Burma. 'The lop-sided trade with China has, however, failed to have a substantial impact on Myanmar's broad-based economic and industrial development' (Kudo, 2008: 103).

In the 1950s, Myanmar/Burma was not considered one of the world's least developed economies, but 'in the next two decades (the 1960s and 1970s), as a consequence of command-style economic management under military rule, self-imposed isolation and the "Burmese way to socialism", the economy deteriorated' (Myint-U, 2008: 53).

Recent annual economic growth and forecasts for the future range between 5 and 6%, although these figures might not be an accurate reflection of overall economic health as much of this growth in statistics is from construction of the new capital city and the roads to and from it. How effective spending on this particular type of infrastructure by the government will be in improving the lives of the people is debatable. Inflation has been an issue, although the rate has not been outside a reasonable range. The country continues to have lots of room to improve economically if it is expected to meet its full potential, grow its economy and reduce poverty. Current obstacles that need to be overcome in order to grow the economy include an inefficient and expensive banking system, an unrealistic exchange rate which is circumvented through the black market, an overreliance on inefficient state-owned enterprises and a lack of availability of credit for the agricultural sector (Asian Development Bank, 2011a: 198–200). Moreover, as trade statistics and economic growth data are known to be very unreliable (Myint-U, 2008: 51; Aung

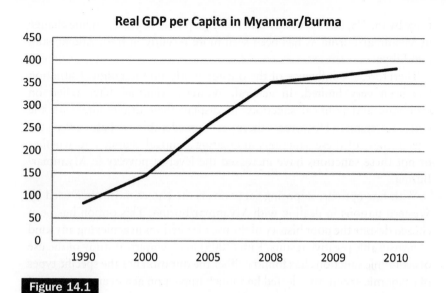

Figure 14.1

Source: UNCTAD (2011: 130)

Myoe, 2011: 153) it is difficult to feel confident about current trends in the economy based on reported information and data.

Studies of actual business practices in the country are very scarce and, due to the political climate, most business owners contacted showed reluctance to share information or ideas with outsiders.

Economic sanctions

The military-led government of Myanmar/Burma has little international support and has been the object of fairly intense criticism in the Western media. The government has been harshly criticized for its suppression of democracy, violent crackdowns against peaceful street protests, the imprisonment of Nobel Laureate Aung San Suu Kyi and its use of extremely harsh tactics in its attempts to suppress movements for political self-rule by various groups in ethnic minority areas. After the end of American involvement in the war in Vietnam, the attention of most Western nations towards Southeast Asia greatly decreased. Economically and strategically Myanmar/Burma is not a foreign policy priority for most Western nations and it is highly unlikely there has ever been, or will be in the near future, serious consideration of using military force by the US, NATO or any other foreign power to create regime change in Myanmar/Burma as has been seen more recently in Iraq, Afghanistan and Libya.

Therefore, the influence of the outside world on the political situation has been very limited. In general, Western countries have relied on economic and political sanctions to display their displeasure with the current regime. However, there is considerable debate over the effectiveness of these sanctions in creating political change and whether or not these sanctions have increased the level of poverty in Myanmar/Burma.

With few options, imposing sanctions is the choice most often used by Western nations in dealing with Myanmar/Burma. This option has been chosen despite the poor history of the use of sanctions in achieving any kind of measurable positive results. Kim (2009) in an empirical study of the use of economic sanctions has found neither the duration nor the specific types of economic sanctions selected had much impact on achieving any type of measurable success, and economic sanctions imposed for human rights violations, such as seen in Myanmar/Burma, had a worse record than sanctions imposed over other issues. Kim (2009: 41) also found it is often impossible for sanctions to succeed as in many cases sanctions were never actually intended to succeed; instead, they were often merely symbolic. Hipsher (2010a: 93) felt sanctions are often used in democracies as a way for Western politicians to prove they are 'doing something' to appease public pressure when atrocities and repression in distant lands make the headlines. What is more, after a specific crisis passes and the headlines fade from the public's memory there is little political price to pay if the forgotten sanctions did not achieve stated goals. Lektzian and Souva (2007) reported economic sanctions are more likely to be effective when used against a democratic country than a non-democratic one. In fact, sanctions often result in economic gains for corrupt government officials and provide both an excuse for economic failure and a nationalistic rallying cry for a regime to use to prove it is protecting the sovereignty of the nation against imperialist foreign forces. For example, an argument can be made that the 50 years of economic sanctions by the USA against Cuba in hoping for regime change has not only not achieved its goal but may have contributed to the survival of the Communist government of Cuba despite poor economic performance.

The issue of Myanmar and support for Suu Kyi has been a 'boutique' issue in the United States, and one that requires no real investment in time, energy or resources. Strong statements against unpopular and unlikeable generals at critical moments have, to date, served everybody's interests well.

(Yawnghwe, 2010: 429)

The primary argument against the use of economic sanctions is, in an attempt to punish the guilty few, the innocent many are the ones who actually experience the most negative effects of withholding trade and other international exchanges from a country. Alamgir (2008) felt economic sanctions imposed by Western countries have resulted in preventing the emergence of a class of traders and business operators in Myanmar/Burma who are independent of the government. This class of independent traders would be the people expected to lead movements for political and economic reform; therefore, economic sanctions may be having the opposite of the intended effect and sanctions might actually be lengthening military rule in the country. The wisdom and effectiveness of the use of economic sanctions in Myanmar/Burma have often been questioned (James, 2004; Steinberg, 2004; Hlaing, 2005; Roberts, 2006). On the other hand, Ewing-Chow (2007: 177) has pointed out not all countries have engaged in imposing sanctions on Myanmar/ Burma but trade with India, China and Thailand has done little to lessen poverty as the government has been able to control most of the rents that come from this trade.

Another result of Western economic sanctions has been to have the military junta in Myanmar/Burma seek closer economic and political ties with China (Alamgir, 2008; Clapp, 2010: 416). It is unlikely an unelected government in China will put substantial pressure on the government of Myanmar/Burma to make changes to a more democratic system.

Relationships between Myanmar/Burma and the USA have been strained and little progress towards coming to common agreement has been made (Clapp, 2010) although more recent events may provide a window of opportunity. Yawnghwe (2010) believed there were two major obstacles preventing better relationships over the long term between Myanmar/Burma and the USA. First is the almost exclusive focus of US policy on the personal leadership of Aung San Suu Kyi. While there are few people in the world more respected than Daw Aung San Suu Kyi, it is questioned whether concern for the good of a single person should override consideration for the millions currently living in poverty in the country. The second obstacle is the fact the leadership of the military government places its survival as a higher priority than improving relationships with the US, UN or any other foreign entity. Therefore, the military regime has been unwilling to make any concessions it feels will put its position as the ruling power in jeopardy.

There is a faction of the ruling SPDC who are 'quite content with Western economic sanctions, because they prevent Western domination of the country's economy and influence in the country's internal affairs. The sanctions have also provided them a convenient scapegoat for explaining Myanmar's woeful economic conditions' (Clapp, 2010: 422).

A lot has been happening recently in Myanmar/Burma, with the results of limited elections – which appear to represent the will of the people – being allowed to stand, the release of Aung San Suu Kyi from house arrest and some significant moves towards making peace in some of the regions where the ethnic non-Burmese are the majority give room for optimism. Whether these events will lead to major political or economic reforms in the country is uncertain. However, these changes do provide an opportunity to reevaluate the existing policies and practices of foreign governments in their dealings with Myanmar/Burma. Years of economic and political isolation have left millions of people in Myanmar/Burma in poverty although it is most likely the policies of the military regime have contributed to a greater extent to the misery than have foreign sanctions. Recently, some economic sanctions have been lifted by some

Figure 14.2 Ethnic minority (Karen) refugees from Myanmar/ Burma living in Thailand

parties and there are now more opportunities for private businesses to invest in and trade with Myanmar/Burma.

Good intentions do not always lead to good results and the outcomes of actions are only obvious in hindsight. Nevertheless, there may be many opportunities for international businesses to now engage in economic activities within Myanmar/Burma. These economic activities and investments have the potential to spur economic growth, promote job creation and increase purchasing options, all of which are important components of poverty reduction. Isolation and disengagement by governments and private industry from developed economies have not lessened poverty or improved the quality of life for millions of people living in the country. Maybe it is time to give engagement, investment and trade a try. Engaging in economic activities in Myanmar/Burma, with or without economic sanctions, will be filled with difficulties and obstacles, which will be very difficult to overcome. In addition, the existing poverty and low-skilled labor force in the country limits the potential profitability of operations in the country. However, without the innovation, technologies, capital and experience of international businesses it is unlikely the country will be able to quickly create the conditions needed for significant and sustainable reductions in poverty. Firms willing to accept the challenge of trying to create win–win business activities in Myanmar/Burma have the potential to have a major impact on reducing poverty in this mostly forgotten corner of Southeast Asia.

15

Creating sustainable win–win situations

Abstract: The private sector has an important role to play in poverty reduction. Business transactions are voluntary in nature and therefore are likely to result in win–win situations for all parties involved. Lessons concerning poverty reduction and wealth creation from various parts of the world are examined, and recommendations for both the public and private sectors are made. In addition, non-financial benefits of the private sector and voluntary business transactions are identified.

Key words: Africa, South America, poverty reduction, wealth creation, Asia, private sector.

Poverty worldwide

Asia is the continent where the majority of the world's poor live and also the area which has seen the greatest success in poverty reduction. However, Asia has neither a monopoly on poverty nor a monopoly on success in fostering poverty reduction. Lessons from Asia can be useful in other locations, and the reverse is also true as lessons from other areas can help in understanding poverty reduction within Asia.

Sub-Saharan Africa

Although recognizing sub-Saharan African economic successes is often ignored and the problems of the continent are often overemphasized, poverty is still a major concern in the region. While much is made of globalization, African companies and societies have generally been excluded from global value chain networks. Africa's share of global trade has fallen from around 4% in the 1990s to less than 2% today (Kigabo, 2010: 87). Experience has shown trade and development go together and the lack of international trade and limited large-scale private business involvement in the economy have been factors in the slow economic growth and limited amounts of poverty reduction seen in sub-Saharan Africa. 'Globalisation began later in Africa than elsewhere and has been less advanced' (Tsikata, 2003: 54).

> The debate on whether Africa needs FDI for its development has long ended among serious people. African leaders must now accept that attracting and retaining FDI must be an integral part of efforts and policies to engender economic growth, social development, and poverty reduction ... Africa simply does not have the capital and technology necessary to produce sustainable growth, and hence to make a decisive impact on poverty. Any discussion of African economic growth and poverty reduction must, therefore, include a discussion of the important role of private investment capital, mostly FDI.
>
> (Mkapa, 2010: 55)

Ghana is one country that has experienced respectable average annual growth of around 4.5% or 2% per capita, for over two decades. This growth has been accompanied by significant reductions in poverty. Prior to the period of high growth which started in 1985, Ghana's government used many central planning policies such as import substitutions and high taxes on exports. These policies created many market distortions, particularly in the cocoa industry, which were accompanied by changes in production which were driven by government policies – not the market. Therefore, the industry did not reach its full potential. However, since 1985 the fairly stable political environment, market liberalization, investments in education and infrastructure, and public spending supported by international foreign aid have produced moderate success in fostering economic growth and poverty reduction. Despite the success, Ghana remains a fairly poor country with structural problems. Private investment and formal sector employment have lagged what is needed for more rapid growth (Aryeetey and McKay, 2007).

Uganda is often associated with the misrule and cruelty of Idi Amin in the 1970s, whose policies included driving out most ethnic Asian entrepreneurs which the economy had previously relied upon. However, the country has changed dramatically since that time. Uganda has liberalized its markets, privatized many state-owned businesses and encouraged foreign investment. In response to these policy changes, the country saw substantial economic growth and poverty reduction in the early 1990s, although growth has substantially slowed since that time. In the early 1990s pro-market changes in government policy were accompanied by favorable external conditions. While increases in foreign trade played a role in the country's economic growth and poverty reduction, integration with the global economy was limited and growth in employment in the formal sector was stagnant, yet a thriving group of entrepreneurs in the informal sector of the economy have emerged (Okidi et al., 2007).

Mugerwa (2003) felt there are lessons to learn from the successes of Uganda and Ghana. The pro-market political policies in both countries arose in the aftermath of a period of political mismanagement and chaos. These changes were associated in the minds of the public with creating conditions for social development and some quick successes. Having 'benevolent dictatorships' at the early stages allowed the policies to take hold and become sustainable.

On the other hand, Nigeria has the largest population of any nation in sub-Saharan Africa, a coastal location, large oil reserves and revenues from oil exports, and a large number of English-speaking workers. Yet, despite all these apparent advantages the country has seen little integration with the world economy, slow economic growth and little progress in poverty reduction. Between 1960 and 2000 Nigeria saw a decrease in per capita income which resulted in large increases in poverty in the country. During this period a succession of inefficient governments placed a higher priority on redistributing the existing wealth based on tribal and political loyalty as opposed to promoting policies designed to grow the economy. Since 2000, the country has made some limited moves towards liberalizing its economy, but the success of these moves has been limited by the legacy of corruption; ethnic, religious and tribal rivalries; and poor infrastructure (Iyzoha, 2010).

Coquery-Vidrovitch (2003) made two important points: first, the colonial legacy of the region is likely a source of many of sub-Saharan Africa's problems and, second, there is a negative world view of sub-Saharan Africa where average Africans are often thought of as victims and unable to manage their own affairs. Private firms can do little about the former but can be influential in changing the later. Until a time machine is invented, we will have to live with our history; however, private trade is between parties who have an equal ability to voluntarily decide to engage in a transaction or not. For example, while the average consumer may not have the financial strength of a major corporation, no trade between any consumer and McDonald's, Coca-Cola or Wal-mart happens without the consumer's consent. Likewise, trade between African individuals and companies and individuals and companies from the rest of the world will have to be voluntary in nature. The voluntary nature of business transactions can help to change the world view of the average sub-Saharan African away from victim and charity recipient to one of consumer, employee, investor or manager.

A healthy economy usually has private firms coming in a variety of sizes. In some markets, economies of scale or other factors give large firms an advantage, while in other markets, because of the need for flexibility or local responsiveness, SMEs have the advantage. However, in sub-Saharan Africa, one sees mostly either large firms or microenterprises operating in the informal economy with fewer firms in 'the middle'. Small local markets, weak regional integration, an abundance of red tape, corruption, lack of access to financial resources and high taxes encourage many firms to stay small and informal. On the other hand, large firms have the resources and often the government contacts and connections to overcome these obstacles (Wegner, 2007). Small microenterprises don't achieve the economies of scale to become efficient producers while the near monopoly positions of large companies reduces incentives to innovate and improve processes; therefore, this missing middle section of economies likely slows the productivity gains needed for economic growth.

Growth in agriculture productivity is often associated with pro-poor economic growth as most of the world's poor work in the agricultural sector. Agriculture is a sector that has underperformed in many of the economies of sub-Saharan Africa. Only a small fraction of the continent's arable land is under cultivation. Much of the soil found in sub-Saharan Africa is not very fertile, therefore the use of fertilizers has a substantial impact on the productivity of the land. Yet, fertilizer use is limited and much of the land farmed is done for subsistence purposes (Bonaglia, 2007). While agricultural subsidies in Europe and the USA make it more difficult for large-scale agricultural production to take place in sub-Saharan Africa, 'bottlenecks created by the institutions that govern or impact upon sub-Saharan Africa's agricultural development play an important role, but are often overlooked' (Laoglesia, 2007: 139). Conditions may indicate small subsistence farming will have a difficult time becoming productive enough to make a significant impact on reducing poverty on the continent. Yet, there may be opportunities for large-scale labor-intensive agricultural production which could help improve productivity, grow the economies and reduce poverty in sub-Saharan Africa if locally made investments, reductions in subsidies in developed countries and financial support to these farming communities are made.

Investments in public infrastructure, private enterprises and human capital are all important in combating poverty, but investment in all three areas is lacking in sub-Saharan Africa. The transportation infrastructure is very weak in the region, even when compared to other developing regions of the world (Goldstein, 2007). Investment in the productive base of some of the economies in the region has actually decreased (Dasgupta, 2007: 10) and investment in education in order to provide the human capital needed for a modern economy has not been adequate (Tsikata, 2003: 54). In addition, legal and bureaucratic barriers have kept the level of formal trade between African countries very low (Okogbule, 2008: 224) which restricts the ability of African companies to develop the economies of scale and experience needed to become globally competitive.

While corruption is a problem in sub-Saharan Africa, Sachs (2005: 191) rejected the assumption corruption is the primary factor slowing growth. Sachs cites the example that in Asia some countries with reputations for high levels of corruption have economically performed better than some fairly well-governed countries in Africa such as Ghana, Mali, Malawi and Senegal. While corruption is a problem and steps to reduce it are always welcome, its elimination is not necessarily a precondition for economic growth and poverty reduction.

If we accept the assumption that engaging in the international trading system is preferred to isolation and is an ingredient in substantial poverty reduction systems, the biggest obstacles to overcome to seeing increased investment in and trade with African nations may be in our minds. When thinking of Africa, many in the outside world conjure up images of starving children, as seen on TV commercials presented by international aid organizations aimed at pulling at heart strings and increasing donations, or images from the news of civil war and gun-toting youths. While these images may not be false, they are not the whole story. Throughout the countries of sub-Saharan Africa there are hundreds of millions of individuals who each day go to work, to the fields, to school or take care of children, much as seen in the rest of the world.

Sub-Saharan Africa has many individual and group success stories to tell, but too often these successes are overlooked and only the negative images remain. Foreign aid given with the best of intentions has also often resulted in competition by the best and brightest over getting a piece of the distribution of this unearned wealth, as opposed to more productive competition over creating and earning wealth. Moreover, there is the cottage academic industry which seeks to link all of Africa's problems with its past colonial history and more recent exploitation by former colonial powers. While there is undoubtedly a significant linkage between the past and present, this focus on blaming others subtly creates an image of Africans as victims needing the help of others and of being incapable of creating anything without Western influence, even their own problems and current situations.

Private business transactions and trade, on the other hand, are voluntary and investing and trading with companies and individuals from the many diverse countries of sub-Saharan Africa can assist in replacing the image of victim. Instead, these actions can help to create images of shrewd and demanding customers, productive workers, good managers and sought-after trading partners.

Central and South America

While each country has unique features, the majority of countries of Central and South America share many characteristics, which include having a history of being colonies of European powers, going through wars of independence, and having a 'Roman Catholic tradition that pervades not only their history, but also their ways of life and thinking' (Moran et al., 2007: 367).

Upon independence, many of the South American countries were not thought of as being members of the group of least developed economies. Economically, socially and culturally most of the living standards of the majority of citizens of these countries would have been closer to what was seen in Europe than in Asia or Africa at that time. Yet, despite the head start Central and South America have fallen far behind Asia in terms of economic growth and poverty reduction. In addition, income inequality is extremely high in the region with Brazil having the most unequal distribution of income in the world (Moran et al., 2007: 375).

Attempts to emulate the success of East Asia in South America have generally not been very successful and many South American countries have discovered that reliance on export-led growth can turn into export-led decline when overseas demand slackens (Morley, 2003: 68). Morley (2003: 69) also reported 'Latin America is hostage to past policy failures that will take a long time to correct.' Although some countries such as Brazil and Mexico have gone through periods of respectable economic growth, these growth periods have generally not been sustainable or evenly distributed enough to have the kind of success in poverty reduction as has been seen in East Asia.

Income inequality, which is the main source of poverty in Central and South America, appears to have many causes. Historically, many countries in the region have gone through alternating periods of military rule and democracy. When looking at the histories of Brazil, Chile, Argentina and Colombia, one sees inequality generally increasing under military rule but decreasing under democratic rule (Robinson, 2003). However, in more recent times democracy has become the norm in the region and inequality continues to plague the region.

Marichal and Topik (2003) took a historical look at the economies of Mexico and Brazil. During the period from 1870 to 1910, both countries followed policies based on free market principles and experienced considerable economic growth during that time period. From 1888 to 1910 the per capita average incomes of Brazil doubled and at that time were considerably higher than the per capita income in Mexico. Brazil was then heavily involved in international trade while Mexico was much less so. Although Brazil has always used some protectionist and import substitution policies since its independence, the use of these policies increased in the twentieth century which had the effect of decreasing the percentage of imported goods (Giroletti, 2003). These protectionist policies did not help grow the economy or decrease the ever widening gap between the haves and have nots. While Brazil looked inward, Mexico eventually became more connected economically to the USA and today the positions have reversed, with Mexico having much higher standards of living, less inequality and a lower percentage of people living in poverty.

Brazil has seen reductions in poverty during times of economic growth. In the 1970s the percentage of people living in extreme poverty went from 68% to 35%; however, in the 1980s poverty actually increased, before declines in the poverty rate returned in the 1990s (Menezes-Filho and Vasconcellos, 2007).

Anti-globalization and anti-capitalist feelings are strongly held by a significant portion of the population in Central and South America, and the economies of the region have not integrated in the global trading system to the same extent as the economies of East Asia. At the end of World War II, Central and South America had much higher average incomes than those in Asia; today the reverse is true. Many of the economies of Asia have engaged in connecting to global value chains while most economies of Central and South America have seen much less integration. Protectionism has enriched the few in the region apparently at the expense of the many. Protectionists and anti-globalization policies have not resulted in either significant economic growth or poverty reduction, but have gone hand in hand with increasing levels of inequality.

The rest of the world

Poverty and attempts at poverty reduction have always been major concerns in all locations around the world. In the Middle East and Northern Africa, poverty continues to affect a large number of people, but there have also been some success stories in reducing poverty. For example, in Tunisia from 1980 to 2000 poverty dropped by 16% while per capita incomes rose by 50% (Lahouel, 2007). Lahouel (2007) also reported, 'growth has been essential in providing job opportunities and higher income for the poor.'

Relative poverty is not unknown in developed economies, but in general there is little absolute poverty. However, this near absence of extreme poverty in developed economies is a relatively recent phenomenon. Acemoglu and Robinson (2010: 143) pointed out it was the private sector and international trade which drove major changes in political institutions in seventeenth-century England which set the conditions necessary for long-term economic growth and the reductions in poverty that accompanied that growth. The dynamic shifts that led to economic growth in Europe, and locations that were culturally European, happened when there were moves away from mercantilist attitudes and policies to attitudes and policies more aligned with free market–based thought (Williamson, 2005: 140). Sachs (2005: 20) made the case the vast majority of poverty seen in developed economies is of a moderate or relative nature, while extreme poverty, where survival is threatened, is mostly only seen in LDCs.

Some opponents to globalization have claimed the developed economies of the world got rich from exploiting workers from LDCs and used military force to extract wealth from their colonies. However, Sachs (2005: 31) claimed this would be a false interpretation as the entire world's economy grew at a remarkable rate following the Industrial Revolution and the expansion of European influence into other regions and, while the whole world benefited from this growth, it was not evenly distributed. The wealth enjoyed by developed economies was created and it was increases in worldwide wealth that have driven high living standards in developed economies and not wealth transferred from one location to another. In the past as today, economic growth and poverty reduction have come more from creation of wealth as opposed to the redistribution of wealth.

Economic success is generally associated with four features. First, today most areas of the world where incomes are high and poverty is low – with oil-rich Saudi Arabia, Kuwait and the UAE being major exceptions – are democracies. Second, wealthier countries tend to trade internationally more than poorer countries and, third, have domestic business environments where winners and losers are determined through competition. Fourth, wealthy countries always have some government involvement in regulating business activities.

Democracy can take many different forms and include many different practices. The parliamentary system used in Japan is significantly different from the system used in the United States in both form and practice. However, democratic systems normally (and imperfectly) reflect the will of the people, provide accountability for leaders and provide a correction mechanism when results do not live up to expectations. In developed economies, there is near universal agreement in relying on the market as the foundation for the economy. Although there are intense political debates over how and how much the government should regulate the market, nearly everyone in wealthier societies agrees the government does have a role to play in regulating it. Therefore, the combination of democracy, international trade and regulated market-based economies, in a variety of specific forms, has proven to be a most successful formula for economic growth and poverty reduction. Claiming a nation can achieve a high standard of living for its citizens – unless the country has a relatively small population and huge amounts of oil – without these four fundamental building blocks remains mostly an unproven hypothesis.

Recommendations for governments

While there are many different views on specific policy initiatives any individual country should take, there are many general principles experience shows a country should follow to achieve economic growth and poverty reduction. Yet, many (all?) governments often follow some policies which contradict these general principles. Advisors and academics can easily prescribe general policy directions, but government officials and leaders must also consider the political implications of each policy decision.

Basically, all government leaders, politicians and political parties have two primary goals. First, make the country 'better' and, second, retain political power. Even the best intentioned politician or leader knows his or her policies will only help the country if the leadership stays in power and well-intentioned policies are allowed to continue and take hold. Moreover, as any policy initiative is likely to be opposed by someone, trade-offs between policies aimed at remaining in power and those aimed at improving the country often have to be made. Many general policies to improve competition and make markets more open take many years to pay off and the improvements are not always directly attributed to the specific policies, while the costs of more open policies are often paid upfront and any negative consequences are easy to identify and attribute to the policies. Protectionism and other interference in the market often directly benefit specific special interest groups in the short term and the benefits can easily be attributed to specific policies. On the other hand, negative impacts, such as higher prices for consumers, are more indirect and not easily attributed to specific policies. It is often politically difficult for the leadership of a government to sacrifice short-term political gain for long-term economy gains the leadership may not be around long enough to take credit for.

Everyone enjoys being a consumer in markets where competition is constantly forcing companies to improve the quality and lower the price of their offerings. Yet, many individuals – whether auto workers in the USA, farmers in France or telecommunication managers in a state-owned enterprise in Vietnam – want their sector of the economy shielded from competition to preserve their own individual jobs and profits even when it drives up prices and reduces choices for all consumers. What is more, these specific interests often have political clout which is exerted to protect their own individual sector at the expense of overall economic growth.

Therefore, it is realized any policy implementation requires a government to have enough political capital and support from the general population to overcome the intense pressure it will receive from special interest groups. Yet, in the long term the two goals are not mutually exclusive and the way to retain political power is often to improve the overall conditions of the area being governed.

Sustained growth often requires trading short-term pain for long-term gain. The end point of growth and development – the well-being of a nation's people – will thus be meaningful only to a people united on the purpose and destiny of their country and who have an entrenched stake in the country.

(Ying et al., 2010: 110)

It is not only LDCs which have implemented protectionist policies, these policies are also seen in developed economies. This is especially true in policies to protect farmers and agricultural industries. 'For many decades agricultural protection and subsidies in high-income (and some middle-income) countries have been depressing international prices of farm products, which lowers the earnings of farmers and associated rural businesses in developing countries' (Anderson, 2010: 80). Anderson (2010: 88) estimated that 'agricultural price and trade reduced earnings of farmers in developing Asia on average by more than 20 percent' as a result of these policies. In addition, many developed economies use a tariff escalation policy which allows unproduced raw materials to be imported without unduly increasing costs while tariffs increase on higher value-added processed goods which discourages global value chains from engaging in more profitable and value-adding activities inside the borders of LDCs (Srinivasan, 2009: 14).

As the majority of the poor in Asia and around the world live in rural areas and work in the agricultural sector (OECD, 2011: 39), reducing and eventually eliminating protectionist agricultural policies in developed economies would be expected to raise prices and incomes in many of the areas where poverty continues to lower the standards of living of the population. Although it is realized these policies will be difficult politically because the political systems in many developed democratic economies tend to overrepresent rural areas where most of those who benefit from these protectionist measures live.

It is recommended all governments, both developed and in LDCs, engage in policies designed to link their economies with international markets. There is very convincing evidence from multiple studies that openness to trade and free trade policies have had a significant and positive effect on economic growth (Williamson, 2005). It is sometimes argued that globalization and exploitation by developed economies is the cause of much of the poverty in the world, but evidence shows most international trade takes place between developed nations and 'there is also surprisingly little trade between rich and poor countries' (Beattie, 2009: 193).

International trade helps a country improve its economic performance in many ways. Openness brings in new sources of capital, labor and raw materials. Openness also accelerates the efficient allocation of resources and allows the global spread of innovation (Srinivasan, 2009: 12–13). Evidence overwhelmingly suggests governments should make moves towards more open economies to achieve economic growth and poverty reduction.

The extent of benefits gained from openness to foreign trade will depend to a considerable degree on domestic conditions. Lack of infrastructure and capacity constraints often prevent openness to trade from actually increasing economic growth (OECD, 2011: 64). Therefore, to maximize the benefits from international trade, governments also need to look at how to prepare the domestic environment to take advantage of new opportunities. Internal military conflicts and external market conditions have major impacts on the effectiveness of openness policies on poverty reduction (Cord, 2007: 4). Srinivasan (2009) reported research showing countries which made domestic reforms, such as reducing support for capital-intensive industries and overhauling dysfunctional land and labor policies, were more likely to turn openness and increases in trade into economic growth and poverty reduction.

Governments should put most of their resources into investment policies and not redistribution policies. Governments, like all organizations, have a limited supply of resources to use. Resources used for one purpose cannot be used for others. Redistribution policies are often popular with the general public and are often used to repay political favors or reward loyalty. Resources used for redistribution policies cannot be used for investment purposes. Moreover, redistribution policies are often hijacked by the non-poor and encourage engaging in non-productive activities (Srinivasan, 2009: 13). Instead of redistribution of resources, Cord (2007: 17) believed poverty reduction policies should attempt to improve the investment climate, create labor regulations that make offering employment attractive to companies, expand access to secondary education by ensuring girls go to school and increase access to public infrastructure.

The paths used to achieve openness and a competitive business environment can vary. 'Institutions and policies that work in one country will not necessarily work in another' (OECD, 2011: 48). For example, while the successful economies in Asia generally moved from import substitution policies to export-driven ones, the use of export promotion of the production of local firms was widely used and successful in northeast Asia while in Southeast Asia most exports were created by investments made by international firms (Jomo, 2003). While the policies and practices differed, both paths had the result of linking local economies with the international trading system. The principles of increasing trade and linking a single economy to the international system may be universal, yet the practices to achieve the ends will often have to be tailored to local political, economic and social conditions.

Government policies, like most human actions, often have unintended consequences (North, 2005: 7). Basu (2005: 175) believed rushing into action without understanding the underlying implications and theories on which the actions are built can sometimes cause more harm than good. Before putting large amounts of resources into specific programs, especially those based on new concepts (e.g., microfinance), it is a good idea to reflect on both the direct and indirect impact of the programs.

While implementing pro-growth policies should be the top priority for a government interested in poverty reduction, incorporating safety nets and other policies for individuals who find themselves excluded from the benefits of economic growth should also be used. In East Asia, from 1975 to 1995, poverty rates fell by an astounding two thirds, life expectancy increased, infant mortality decreased and more people gained access to education. However, as evidenced by the economic crisis of 1997–98, without some social safety nets previous gains in the region can be lost during the inevitable periods of economic slowdown (Pangestu, 2003: 83).

While there is intense political debate over how much and which kind of involvement governments have in the running of an economy, it is generally agreed governments do have a role to play. Today most experts agree governments should mostly play an indirect role and allow markets to primarily make decisions about what to produce and what prices to charge. Economic growth is driven by increases in productivity. While government regulations can cause market distortions and inefficiencies, at times government regulations can also improve competitiveness (Hasan et al., 2007). Government involvement in regulating business should primarily be concerned with reducing transaction costs and correcting market failures which will improve productivity and provide incentives for productivity. To drive economic growth and reduce poverty, firms should be making decisions based on improving productivity and sound business principles instead of working to find ways to lower taxes or comply with market-distorting government rules.

Human capital – the result of having an educated population as well as a transportation and energy infrastructure – is important for economic growth and often this areas can be better managed by governments than the private sector. Therefore, it is recommended governments make the long-term investments in roads, electricity, ports and other physical infrastructure projects which assist in reducing transaction costs for all companies. Moreover, investments in human resources through education and health are recommended (Pangestu, 2003; Menezes-Filho and Vasconcellos, 2007). Furthermore, it should not be forgotten that a 'brain drain' can be a major problem for LDCs, and therefore countries should explore ways to provide opportunities locally for the country's most educated and talented workers.

In examining poverty reduction and economic development there is often an assumption the role of government is central to success. However, governments are not the sole actors involved in poverty reduction and economic success. Rodrik (2005) pointed out trade and investment increased considerably in China, India, Uganda and Vietnam despite the existence of policies which put up many obstacles to free trade. Private enterprises seem to be endlessly innovative and are often able to trade profitably despite government interference. Acemoglu and Robinson (2010) made the case policies and institutional changes will have little impact unless there are changes in the underlying political systems which support the policies and institution. Yet, quality of governments and choice of government policies do have major impacts on long-term economic growth and poverty reduction. The choice of following the common belief of the time of pursuing import substitution policies had a negative impact on economic growth and poverty reduction in most of the newly independent countries of South Asia and Africa in the post–World War II era. The choice of turning from centrally planned economies to economies that are more market based in China and Vietnam was followed by the fastest and largest reductions in poverty the world has ever seen. Governments in general do not drive the economic growth which is needed for poverty reduction, the private sector does. But governments do greatly influence the environment in which the private sector operates and some environments have proven much better than others in allowing the private sector to flourish and have a positive impact.

As most 'bad' economy policy decisions come from choosing policies designed to retain political power, creating a better alignment between retaining power and reducing poverty would be expected to result in better policies. At the risk of being considered utopian, the final three recommendations are directed at 'countries' as opposed to individual governments. First, attempt to achieve peace. Resources used in civil wars cannot be used for other purposes. Many countries around the world such as Nepal, Sri Lanka and Angola have seen some of their peace dividends after years of fighting come in the form of economic growth and poverty reduction. Second, have a government that is accountable to the people. While democracy with free and fair elections is generally considered the gold standard of accountability in government, many observers claim other countries, in particular China, have seen systems evolve to where an unelected government needs to be responsive to the will of the people in order to retain power. Third, improve and encourage education in economics and increase the understanding of the long-term consequences of economic choices in the population. Many economic principles run counter to intuition and, with a better understanding of the issues, populations will hopefully be less likely to pressure their governments to choose policies that are against the long-term interests of the country.

Recommendations for private companies and individuals

'Broad-based growth is critical to accelerating poverty reduction' (Cord, 2007: 1). However, without a dynamic, efficient and innovative private sector it is very difficult, if not impossible, to achieve broad-based growth. For example, while China retains public ownership of many of the factors of production, 'Unambiguously, the private sector has become the engine driving China's growth' (Kuhn, 2010: 253).

However, running a successful business in an LDC is not an easy task. Business environments in LDCs often hinder as opposed to facilitate the emergence of dynamic private enterprises which provide employment, drive economic growth and produce valuable goods and services.

Taking up the challenge of starting and/or operating a business in the LDCs in Asia is a way for private citizens to get directly involved in poverty reduction. Governments have a role to play, but aid given by wealthier countries has not proven effective as most governments in LDCs are constrained by budgets and politics. Despite less-than-perfect environments we have seen both local entrepreneurs and international businesses innovatively find ways to create sustainable and profitable businesses throughout developing Asia and these successful businesses have been the foundation for some of the world's greatest successes in reducing poverty. But, there is still much work to be done and far too many individuals have not been able to reach their potential due to poverty and lack of opportunities.

Firms and individuals from developed economies wishing to expand or start operations in an LDC will face many challenges one would not expect to find in more developed economies. In developing economies, operations are less predictable and managers working in these environments need to be more flexible and develop 'exception handling' skills (Orr and Scott,

2008). Negotiating business deals in developing economies often involves operating within unknown languages, cultures, tax regimes and labor laws while having to consider the desires of government bureaucracies (Hurn, 2007: 354). Foreign firms integrating workers or managers from developed countries into operations in LDCs has been found to be a challenge (Brett et al., 2006).

Running overseas business operations is complex, contextual and there is no shortage of advice given to managers originating from developed economies for running international operations. For example, Luo and Shenkar (2006) suggest firms make the choice of operational language based on the company's overall strategy. Existing advice can be supplemented by following the three-level framework introduced in Chapter 4 which can be used as a foundation for international managers designing operations in LDCs.

Business principles are fairly universal but specific practices are mostly contextual. Strategic decisions will often be driven by the economic conditions because the level of purchasing power in LDCs is generally low. Some international firms will continue to use similar strategic practices as deployed in developed economies and attempt to skim off some of the cream at the top of the market. However, to more deeply engage in LDC markets international firms will normally have to adjust their strategic approach to local economic conditions.

Interpersonal business practices normally need to be adjusted when a business expands into a new cultural environment. Brett et al. (2006: 88) pointed out decision-making practices can vary considerably from culture to culture and while American managers are known for making quick decisions in other cultures these same American managers are likely to experience frustration over the slower pace of decision making. Taylor (2007) made the case that business relationship in individualistic or 'highly specific oriented societies', such as found in most Western societies, tend to be more unifaceted, focusing on work only, while relationships between co-workers and between a supervisor and subordinate in collectivist or 'diffuse oriented societies', such as are the norm in LDCs, are usually more multifaceted, focusing on work as well as personal relationships.

At the operational level, firms from developed economies can often implement processes across cultures with little need for adapting to local conditions. In examining Japanese firms operating in Thailand, Swierczek and Onishi (2003: 188) observed:

Machines and tools can be transferred easily. Standardized technical skills can also be taught, although with somewhat more difficulty. In transferring a system for managing workers, however, it is necessary to take the cultural conditions in the host country into account.

To summarize, international firms and managers, while operating in LDCs, can use the same universal principles of strategic management as used in developed countries, although it is likely strategic practices will have to be adjusted to local economic conditions. Interpersonal business practices will most likely have to use both principles and practices aligned with local cultural environments. For many operational business practices, existing principles and practices can often be transferred to the new location without much need for major adjustments to local conditions.

Although foreign investment and trade are useful in creating the conditions needed for economic growth and poverty reduction, the bulk of the private sector in any LDC will be home grown, and therefore local businesses will have the most impact on driving economic growth and poverty reduction. While businesses originating in LDCs often have many disadvantages in comparison to large multinational corporations, they also have advantages which include local knowledge, connections and no need to satisfy foreign stakeholders. Local businesses should not only think of foreign companies as competitors, but also as potential suppliers, buyers and sources of knowledge transfers.

Often companies originating from one LDC can expand and operate successfully in other LDCs. Specific skills and knowledge are often gained from working in the environments typically found in an LDC and these skills and knowledge are often useful when operating in other LDCs (Cuervo-Cazurra and Genc, 2008).

Wherever they operate in the world, all firms – small and large, foreign or domestic, publically or privately owned – should be good 'corporate citizens'. While in most cases acting ethically and legally are fully compatible with maximizing long-term profits, there are cases where there are choices to be made between short-term profits and doing the right thing. Firms require profits to create increased economic growth and new job opportunities. Seeking profits results in firms seeking to continuously improve their operations. Seeking profits should be encouraged, but not seeking profits at any cost. Seeking profits through excessive pollution, using unsafe work practices or producing, selling and marketing unsafe or dangerous products is inexcusable in any location. Finally, international firms should make attempts to hire and train local managers and allow knowledge transfers to encourage further growth and improvements in the private sector.

Indirect benefits of the private sector

There are many indirect benefits, mostly unintended but nevertheless important, the private sector provides society.

The private sector helps to combat corruption. Corruption is only possible in situations where an individual controls resources he or she does not own. In a pure market transaction where the buyer is buying for himself and the seller is selling products or services he or she owns with no government regulations or taxes, there are no opportunities for corruption. Each party can voluntarily accept and reject any offer and the attractiveness of an offer is not affected by whether it is given in the open or under the table.

However, with government involvement, opportunities for corruption increase. Government officials involved in either running or regulating business activities have authority over the use of resources, such as license approvals or even sales or purchases, they do not own and the objectives of government officials are not always perfectly aligned with the goals of maximizing profits for the firm or increasing efficiency.

Corruption is of course possible in purely private sector transactions as employees often control resources they do not own. However, in market transactions corruption is inefficient and raises costs, which puts any company with employees engaging in corruption in market transactions at a competitive disadvantage. Therefore, the profit motive encourages companies to police themselves. However, corruption though bribery of government officials in non–market based transactions can offer a company a distinct competitive advantage. No matter how much it is wished every company executive and government official be perfectly ethical and honest, the temptation of gain is bound to attract some individuals to engage in corruption. Removing the temptation by having more transactions between two willing partners in the private sector, without significant government interference, will reduce opportunities for corruption.

The private sector can increase non-material benefits for individuals. Money does not automatically bring happiness and there is little evidence wealthier individuals are significantly happier than the average person. Happiness is not something one can receive from others, but comes from within. However, extreme poverty lessens opportunities for individuals to live full lives. Poverty is highly associated with poor health, and good health is the foundation for a happy and productive life. Moreover, extreme poverty often removes opportunities for leisure, education and other pursuits which are only possible when one's survival is assumed. In driving economic growth and poverty reduction, the private sector helps individuals to have access not only to material possessions, but also to non-material benefits which come from having the time and energy to engage in activities which are not directly related to one's survival and safety needs.

Poverty reduction improves the world's human resources which benefits all mankind. Much of the world's human potential is wasted by poverty. Many individuals with the potential to be great writers, philosophers, musicians, entrepreneurs, government leaders, artists and other useful professionals, never get the chance to achieve their potential due to lives born into and lived in poverty. All of us are poorer from not having our lives enriched by the efforts these individuals had the potential to accomplish. The first step towards reaching one's potential is education, and Basu (2005: 182) finds the evidence very convincing that poverty increases the use of child labor which robs children of an opportunity for education.

Final thoughts

Private enterprises and the voluntary transactions they engage in encourage respect and dignity and help change the image of the poor. 'If we stop thinking of the poor as victims or a burden and start recognizing them as resilient and creative entrepreneurs and value-conscious consumers, a whole new world of opportunity will open up' (Prahalad, 2005). The private sector is the best source of a job, or better yet choices of jobs, business opportunities and products one can voluntary choose to purchase in hopes of improving one's life. With opportunities, the poor can make their own choices on how to earn a living and what type of lifestyle to lead. In a vibrant market economy, companies have to compete for employees, business partners and customers, and to retain any individual, wealthy or poor, as a customer, business partner or employee in an environment where choices are available requires treating the individual with respect and dignity.

We should also throw out any romantic notions about the nobility of the poor or assume all the world's poor are victims of exploitation by greedy individuals or the system. Each individual living in poverty, like the rest of us, is an imperfect human who often makes poor choices. Domestic violence, drug abuse, alcoholism, and poor time and resource management can all be both the results and causes of poverty. No poverty reduction program ever designed has been able to prevent individuals from making poor choices. The poor should neither be completely blamed for their condition nor absolved of all responsibility for their condition. While the private sector has little direct control over the choices individuals make, it can provide additional career and purchasing options for individuals. Experience teaches us individuals when given additional choices are more likely to choose options which will help them achieve their life goals than to make 'bad' decisions. As long as individuals have free choice some will choose paths the majority of society feel are the wrong ones.

Poverty reduction should not become a political issue driven by political ideology, the issue is too important. Both the left and the right have at times pushed for protectionism or other misguided policies which have limited

Figure 15.1 Children begging at the Thailand–Cambodia border crossing

Figure 15.2 **Woman finding a way to make a living in Siem Reap, Cambodia**

the poor from having opportunities to improve their lives. Poverty reduction should be an issue individuals from all political backgrounds can work together to achieve. Policies and ideas that have proven to be successful should be followed, regardless of their conformity to any particular political ideology.

One of the possible obstacles in developing conditions which can drive growth and poverty reduction in LDCs is fear. There are some factions in the developed world who are concerned 'we' and 'our' jobs are under threat from 'them' in the LDCs and 'their' low wages (Sachs, 2005). This attitude can lead to pressure to implement protectionist policies in developed economies. Moreover, this danger intensifies during economic downturns where scapegoats are sought by individuals and governments. However, history and academic research have consistently shown that economic success in the world is not a zero sum gain and that growth in LDCs can in fact help to drive growth in the developed world.

Private sector–driven poverty reduction can be a win–win situation for the poor and the rest alike.

References

Abbasi, S.M., Hollman, K.W. and Murrey, J.H. (1989) 'Islamic economics: Foundations and practices', *International Journal of Social Economics*, **16**(5): 5–17.

Abinales, P. (2011) 'Political outlook: Philippines,' in M. Montesano and L.P. Onn (Eds.), *Regional Outlook; Southeast Asia: 2010–2011*, Singapore: Institute of Southeast Asian Studies, pp. 46–50.

Abinales, P.N. and Amoroso, D.J. (2005) *State and Society in the Philippines*, Lanham, MD: Rowman & Littlefield.

Acemoglu, D. and Robinson, J. (2010) 'The role of institutions in growth and development,' in D. Brady and M. Spence (Eds.), *Leadership and Growth*, Washington, D.C.: World Bank, pp. 135–64.

Adams, W.H.D. (1879) *In the Far East: A Narrative of Exploration and Adventure in Cochin-China, Cambodia, Laos and Siam*, London: Thomas Nelson & Sons.

Adhikari, D.R. (2010) 'Human resource development (HRD) for performance management,' *International Journal of Productivity and Performance Management*, **59**(4): 306–24.

Agajanov, S.G. (1998) 'The states of the Oghuz, the Kimek and the Kipchak,' in M.S. Asimov and C.E. Bosworth (Eds.), *History of Central Asia, Volume IV*, Paris: UNESCO, pp. 66–82.

Agrawal, P. (2007) 'Economic growth and poverty reduction: Evidence from Kazakhstan,' *Asian Development Review*, **24**(2), 90–115.

Alamgir, J. (2008) 'Myanmar's foreign trade and its political consequences,' *Asian Survey*, **48**(6): 977–96.

Ali, A.J. and Al-Owaihan, A. (2008) 'Islamic work ethic: A critical review,' *Cross Cultural Management*, **15**(1): 5–19.

Ali, A.J. and Gibbs, M. (1998) 'Foundations of business ethics in contemporary religious thought: The Ten Commandments perspective,' *International Journal of Social Economics*, **25**(10): 1552–62.

Ali, I. (2007) 'Inequality and the imperative for inclusive growth in Asia,' *Asian Development Review*, **24**(2): 1–16.

Ali, I. (2008) 'Inequality in developing Asia,' *Asian Development Review*, **25**(1/2): 15–21.

Ali, I. and Son, H.H. (2007) 'Measuring inclusive growth,' *Asian Development Review*, **24**(2): 11–31.

Allen, R.S., Helms, M.M., Takeda, M.B., White, C.S. and White, C. (2006) 'A comparison of competitive strategies in Japan and the United States,' *SAM Advanced Management Journal*, **71**(1): 24–34.

Alley, L. and Stanley, T. (1993) 'San Miguel's expansion in Southeast Asia,' *Journal of Asian Business*, **9**(3): 71–92.

Amine, L. and Chao, M. (2005) 'Managing country image to long-term advantage: The case of Taiwan and Acer,' *Place Branding*, **1**(2): 187–204.

Amoranto, G. and Chun, N. (2011) 'Quality employment and firm performance: Evidence from Indian firm-level data,' *Asian Development Bank Economics Working Paper Series*, No. 277.

Anantarangsi, S. (2011) 'Study of cross-border trading of Myanmar and Thailand: Reviewing the unseen importance of Maw Danung and Dan Singkorn checkpoints,' *Shinawatra International University Journal of Management*, **1**(1): 41–57.

Andaya, B.W. (1992) 'Political development between the sixteenth and eighteenth centuries,' in N. Tarling (Ed.), *The Cambridge History of Southeast Asia, Volume 1*, Cambridge, UK: Cambridge University Press, pp. 402–59.

Andaya, L.Y. (1992) 'Interactions with the outside world and adaptation in Southeast Asian society, 1500–1800,' in N. Tarling (Ed.), *The Cambridge History of Southeast Asia, Volume 2*, Cambridge, UK: Cambridge University Press, pp. 345–401.

Anderson, A.R., Drakopoulou-Dodd, S.L. and Scott, M.G. (2000) 'Religion as an environmental influence on enterprise culture: The case of Britain in the 1980s,' *International Journal of Entrepreneurial Behaviour and Research*, **6**(1): 5–20.

Anderson, J. and Billou, N. (2007) 'Serving the world's poor: Innovation at the base of the economic pyramid,' *Journal of Business Strategy*, **28**(2): 14–21.

Anderson, K. (2005) 'On the virtues of multilateral trade negotiations,' *Economic Record*, **81**(255): 414–38.

Anderson, K. (2010) 'Government distortions of agricultural prices: Lessons from rich and emerging economies,' in K. Otsuka and K. Kalirajan (Eds.), *Community, Market and State in Development*, London: Palgrave Macmillan, pp. 80–102.

Angeles, F.M. (2005) 'Emerging paradigm of internationalization by two leading firms from a third world country: Profile of indigenous MNEs from Philippines,' paper presented at the *Academy of International Business Southeast Asia Regional Conference in Manila, Philippines, November*.

Angelini, P. and Generale, A. (2008) 'On the evolution of firm size distributions,' *American Economic Review*, **98**(1): 426–38.

Aoki, S., Esteban-Pretel, J., Okazaki, T. and Sawada, Y. (2010) 'The role of the government in facilitating TFP growth during Japan's rapid-growth era,' in K. Otsuka and K. Kalirajan (Eds.), *Community, Market and State in Development*, London: Palgrave Macmillan, pp. 21–44.

Areethamsirikul, S. (2008) 'The impact of ASEAN enlargement on economic integration: Successes and impediments under ASEAN political institution,' doctoral dissertation, University of Wisconsin-Madison.

Aribarg R. (2005) 'Thai border town businessmen and the state: An examination of their influence on Thai foreign policy toward Burma,' doctoral dissertation, Boston University.

Aroca, P., Guo, D. and Hewings, G. (2008) 'Spatial convergence in China: 1952–99 China,' in G. Wan (Ed.), *Inequality and Growth in Modern China*, New York: Oxford University Press, pp. 125–43.

Arora, V. and Varnvakidis, A. (2005) 'How much do trading partners matter for economic growth?' *IMF Staff Papers*, **52**(1): 24–40.

Aryeetey, E. and McKay, A. (2007) 'Ghana: The challenge of translating sustained growth into poverty reduction,' in T. Besley and L.J. Cord (Eds.), *Delivering on the Promise of Pro-poor Growth: Insights and Lessons from Country Experiences*, New York: World Bank/Palgrave Macmillan, pp. 147–68.

Asher, M.G. (2010) 'The global economic crisis: Can Asia grasp the opportunity to strengthen social protection systems?' in A. Bauer and M. Thant (Eds.), *Poverty and Sustainability Development in Asia: Impacts and Responses to the Global Economic Crisis*, Mandaluyong City, Philippines: Asian Development Bank, pp. 319–40.

Asian Development Bank (2009a) *Study on Intraregional Trade and Investment in South Asia*, Mandaluyong City, Philippines: Asian Development Bank.

Asian Development Bank (2009b) *Nepal: Critical Development Constraints*, Mandaluyong City, Philippines: Asian Development Bank.

Asian Development Bank (2010) *Outlook 2008: Macroeconomic Management, Beyond the Crisis*, Mandaluyong City, Philippines: Asian Development Bank.

Asian Development Bank (2011a) *Asian Development Outlook 2011*, Mandaluyong City, Philippines: Asian Development Bank.

Asian Development Bank (2011b) *Key Indicators for Asian and the Pacific*, 42nd Edition, Mandaluyong City, Philippines: Asian Development Bank.

Atwood, C. (2004) *Encyclopedia of Mongolia and the Mongol Empire*, New York: Facts on File.

Aung Myoe, M. (2011) *In the Name of Pauk-Phaw: Myanmar's China Policy since 1948*, Singapore: Institute of Southeast Asia Studies.

Aung Thwin, M. (1996) 'The myth of the "Three Shan Brothers" and the Ava period in Burmese history,' *The Journal of Asian Studies*, **55**(4): 881–901.

Bach, D. and Allen, D.B. (2010) 'What every CEO needs to know about nonmarket strategy,' *MIT Sloan Management Review*, **51**(3): 41–8.

Baird, I.G. (2010) 'Land, rubber and people: Rapid agrarian changes and responses in Southern Laos,' *Journal of Lao Studies*, **1**(1), 1–47.

Barro, R.J. and McCleary, R.M. (2003) 'Religion and economic growth across countries,' *American Sociological Review*, **68**(5): 760–81.

Bass, B.M. and Avolio, B.J. (1993) 'Transformational leadership and organizational culture,' *Public Administration Quarterly*, **17**(1): 112–21.

Bass, B.M. and Steidlmeier, P. (1999) 'Ethics, character, and authentic transformational leadership behavior,' *Leadership Quarterly*, **10**(2): 281–317.

Basu, K. (2005) 'Global labour standards and local freedoms,' in A. Shorrocks (Ed.), *Wider Perspectives in Global Development*, New York: Palgrave Macmillan, pp. 175–200.

Bauer, A. and Thant, M. (2010) 'Overview,' in A. Bauer and M. Thant (Eds.), *Poverty and Sustainability Development in Asia: Impacts and Responses to the Global Economic Crisis*, Mandaluyong City, Philippines: Asian Development Bank, pp. 1–12.

Beamish, P. (1999) 'Sony's Yoshihide Nakamura on structure and decision making,' *The Academy of Management Perspectives*, **13**(4): 12–16.

Beattie, A. (2009) *False Economy: A Surprising Economic History of the World*, New York: Riverhead Books.

Beaudoin, S.M. (2007) *Poverty in World History*, London: Routledge.

Beer, M. and Katz, N. (2003) 'Do incentives work? The perceptions of a worldwide sample of senior executives,' *HR: Human Resource Planning*, **6**(3): 30–44.

Befus, D.R., Mescon, T.S., Debbie L. and Vozikis, G.S. (1988) 'International investment of expatriate entrepreneurs: The case of Honduras,' *Journal of Small Business Management*, **26**(3): 40–7.

Bellwood, P. (1992) 'Southeast Asia before history,' in N. Tarling (Ed.), *The Cambridge History of Southeast Asia, Volume 1*, Cambridge, UK: Cambridge University Press, pp. 55–136.

Berggren, N. and Jordahl, H. (2005) 'Does free trade really reduce growth? Further testing using the Economic Freedom Index,' *Public Choice*, **122**(1/2): 99–114.

Besley, T., Burgess, R. and Esteve-Volart, B. (2007) 'The policy origins of poverty and growth in India,' in T. Besley and L.J. Cord (Eds.), *Delivering on the Promise of Pro-poor Growth: Insights and Lessons from Country Experiences*, New York: World Bank/Palgrave Macmillan, pp. 59–78.

Bhagwati, J. (2005) 'Globalization and appropriate governance,' in A. Shorrocks (Ed.), *Wider Perspectives in Global Development*, New York: Palgrave Macmillan, pp. 74–100.

Bhakti, I. (2004) 'Transition to democracy in Indonesia: Some outstanding problems,' in J. Rolfe (Ed.), *The Asia Pacific: A Region in Transition*, Honolulu, HI: Asia-Pacific Center for Security Studies, pp. 207–18.

Bjerke, B.V. (2000) 'A typified, culture-based, interpretation of management of SMEs in Southeast Asia,' *Asia Pacific Journal of Management*, **17**(1): 103–32.

Bode, M.H. (1898) 'A Burmese historian of Buddhism', doctoral dissertation, University of Berne.

Bonaglia, F. (2007) 'Agriculture in Africa: Open for business?' in *Business and Development: Fostering the Private Sector*, Paris: Development Centre of the Organisation for Economic Co-operation and Development, pp. 109–38.

Bosworth, C.E. (1998) 'The Ghaznavids,' in M.S. Asimov and C.E. Bosworth (Eds.), *History of Central Asia, Volume IV*, Paris: UNESCO, pp. 102–24.

Bosworth, C.E. and Bolshakov, O.G. (1998) 'Central Asia under the Umayyads and the early Abbasids,' in M.S. Asimov and C.E. Bosworth (Eds.), *History of Central Asia, Volume IV*, Paris: UNESCO, pp. 27–46.

Bourguignon, F. and Verdier, T. (2003) 'Globalisation and endogenous educational responses: The main economic transmission channels,' in R. Kohl (Ed.), *Globalisation, Poverty and Inequality*, Paris: Organisation for Economic Co-operation and Development, pp. 19–44.

Brackney, K.S. and Witmer, P.R. (2005) 'The European Union's role in international standards setting,' *The CPA Journal*, **75**(11): 18–27.

Brady, D and Spence, M. (2010) 'Leadership and politics: A perspective from the commission on growth and development,' in D. Brady and M. Spence (Eds.), *Leadership and Growth*, Washington, D.C.: World Bank, pp. 1–14.

Breazeale, K. (2002) 'The Lao–Tay–Son alliance, 1792 and 1793,' in M. Ngaosrivathana and K. Breazeale (Eds.), *Breaking New Ground in Lao History: Essays on the Seventh to Twentieth Centuries*, Chiang Mai, Thailand: Silkworm Books, pp. 261–80.

Brett, J., Behfar, K. and Kern, M.C. (2006) 'Managing multicultural teams,' *Harvard Business Review*, **83**(11): 84–91.

Brooks, D.H. and Stone, S.F. (2010) 'Infrastructure and trade facilitation in Asian APEC,' *Asian Development Review*, **27**(1): 135–59.

Bui, T. and Perez, G. (2010) 'Destination branding: The comparative case of Guam and Vietnam,' *Journal of International Business Research*, **9** (Special Issue 2): 95–111.

Burgan, M. (2009) *Empire of the Mongols*, Revised Edition, New York: Chelsea House.

Burki, S. (2006) *Historical Dictionary of Pakistan*, Lanham, MD: The Scarecrow Press.

Burusphat, S., Deepadung, S., Suraratdecha, S., Ardsamiti, N., Patpong, P. and Setapong, P. (2011) 'Language vitality and the ethnic tourism development of the Lao ethnic groups in the western region of Thailand,' *Journal of Lao Studies*, **2**(2): 23–46.

Carbine, J. (2004) 'An ethic of continuity: Shwegyin monks and the Sasana in contemporary Burma/Myanmar,' doctoral dissertation, University of Chicago.

Cardoso, F.H. and Graeff, E. (2010) 'Political leadership and economic reform: The Brazilian experience in the context of Latin America,' in D. Brady and M. Spence (Eds.), *Leadership and Growth*, Washington, D.C.: World Bank, pp. 195–226.

Carrasco, B., Hayashi, T. and Mukhopadhyay, H. (2010) 'The impact of the global crisis on South Asia,' *Asian Development Bank South Asia Working Paper Series*, No. 1.

Caspary, G. (2008) 'Tackling opposition to implementing fiscal reform in developing countries,' *International Journal of Emerging Markets*, **3**(1): 87–103.

Chakraverthy, B. and Coughlan, S. (2012) 'Emerging market strategy: Innovating both products and delivery systems,' *Strategy and Leadership*, **40**(1): 27–32.

Chan, S.H. (2010) 'Microfinance–microenterprise relationship: The Malaysian growth experience,' in J.M. Munoz (Ed.), *Contemporary Microenterprise: Concepts and Cases*, Cheltenham, UK: Edward Elgar, pp. 180–92.

Chandler, D. (2000) *A History of Cambodia*, Third Edition, Chiang Mai, Thailand: Silkworm Books.

Chang, H. (2007) 'Globalization, global standards, and the future of East Asia,' in J. Shin (Ed.), *Global Challenges and Local Responses*, New York: Routledge, pp. 14-30.

Chang, S. (2006) 'Business groups in East Asia: Post-crisis restructuring and new growth,' *Asia Pacific Journal of Management*, **23**(4): 407–17

Chanthanom, S. (1998) 'Globalization of the Golden Triangle: Cultural transformation in Burma, Laos and Thailand,' doctoral dissertation, University of Pittsburgh.

Chapuis, O. (2000) *The Last Emperors of Vietnam: From Tu Duc to Bao Dai*, Greenwood, CT: Greenwood Press.

Charmes, J. (2009) 'Concepts, measures and trends,' in J. Jutting and J.R. de Laiglesia (Eds.), *Is Informal Normal?: Towards More and Better Jobs in Developing Countries*, Paris: Organisation for Economic Cooperation and Development, pp. 27-62.

Chattananon, A. and Trimetsoontorn, J. (2009) 'Relationship marketing: A Thai case,' *International Journal of Emerging Markets*, **4**(3): 252–74.

Chen, J. (2006) 'China, the Vietnam War and the Sino-American rapprochement, 1968–1973,' in O.A. Westad and S. Quinn-Judge (Eds.), *The Third Indochina*

War: Conflict between China, Vietnam and Cambodia, 1972–79, London: Routledge, pp. 33–64.

Chen, J. (2009) 'The practice of the Mean: China's soft power cultivation,' in M. Li (Ed.), *Soft Power: China's Emerging Strategy in International Politics*, Lanham, MD: Lexington Books, pp. 83–102.

Chen, K.C. (1987) *China's War with Vietnam, 1979*, Stanford, CA: Hoover Press.

Chen, S. and Wilson, M. (2003) 'Standardization and localization of human resource management in Sino-joint ventures,' *Asia-Pacific Journal of Management*, 20(3): 397–408.

Cheong, Y.M. (1992) 'The political structures of the independent states,' in N. Tarling (Ed.), *The Cambridge History of Southeast Asia, Volume 2*, Cambridge, UK: Cambridge University Press, pp. 387–466.

Chew, I. and Goh, M. (1997) 'Some future directions of human resources practices in Singapore,' *Career Development International*, 2(5): 238–53.

China Daily (2012) 'Give workers their due,' *China Daily*, 13 February 2012 Edition, p. 8.

Chino, T. (2004) 'President's address,' *Asian Development Bank Review*, 36(4): 9–12.

Choi, C.J., Kim, S.W. and Kim, J.B. (2010) 'Globalizing business ethics research and the ethical need to include the bottom-of-the-pyramid countries: Redefining the global triad as business systems and institutions,' *Journal of Business Ethics*, 94: 299–306.

Choi, J.P. and Cowing, T.G. (1999) 'Firm behavior and group affiliation: The strategic role of corporate grouping for Korean firms,' *Journal of Asian Economics*, 10(2): 195–209.

Chong, L.M. and Thomas, D.C. (1997) 'Leadership perceptions in cross-cultural context: Pakeha and Pacific islanders in New Zealand,' *Leadership Quarterly*, 8(3): 275–93.

Choo, S. and Wong, M. (2006) 'Entrepreneurial intention: Triggers and barriers to new venture creation in Singapore,' *Singapore Management Review*, 28(2): 47–64.

Chu, P., Teng, M., Lee, C. and Chiu, H. (2010) 'Spin-off strategies and performance: A case study of Taiwan's Acer group,' *Asian Business and Management*, 9(1): 101–25.

Chu, T.C. and MacMurray, T. (1993) 'The road ahead of Asia's leading conglomerates,' *McKinsey Quarterly*, 3: 117–26.

Clapp, P. (2010) 'Prospects for rapprochement between the United States and Myanmar,' *Contemporary South East Asia*, 32(3): 409–26.

Claus, L. and Hand, M.L. (2009) 'Customization decisions regarding performance management systems of multinational companies: An empirical view of Eastern European Firms,' *International Journal of Cross Cultural Management*, 9(2): 237–58.

Clymner, K. (2004) *The United States and Cambodia, 1969–2000: A Troubled Relationship*, London: RoutledgeCurzon.

CNN Money (2011) Global 500, 2011, available from *http://money.cnn.com/magazines/fortune/global500/2011/index.html*, accessed 12 September 2011.

Coquery-Vidrovitch (2003) 'Nation without a state and a state without a nation: The case of Africa south of the Sahara,' in A. Teichiva and H. Matis (Eds.), *Nation,*

State and the Economy in History, Cambridge, UK: Cambridge University Press, pp. 239–50.

Cord, L.J. (2007) 'Overview,' in T. Besley and L.J. Cord (Eds.), *Delivering on the Promise of Pro-poor Growth: Insights and Lessons from Country Experiences*, New York: World Bank/Palgrave Macmillan (co-publishers), pp. 1–28.

Cornwell, B., Cui, C.C., Mitchell, V., Schlegelmilch, B., Dzulkifee, A. and Chan J. (2005) 'A cross-cultural study of the role of religion in consumers' ethical positions,' *International Marketing Review*, 22(5): 531–46.

Creak, S. (2011) 'Muscular Buddhism for modernizing Laos,' *Journal of Lao Studies*, 2(1): 1–22.

Cromer, C. and Hodges, S. (2011) 'Analysis of the microcar market in the United States and India: Impact of macroeconomic forces and cultural factors,' *Journal of Applied Business and Economics*, 12(5): 21–34.

Crossley, P.K. (2010) *The Wobbling Pivot: China since 1800*, Chichester, UK: Wiley–Blackwell.

Cuervo-Cazurra, A and Genc, M. (2008) 'Transforming disadvantages into advantages: Developing-country MNEs in the least developed countries,' *Journal of International Business Studies*, 30(6): 957–79.

Curtis, L.J. (1903) *The Laos of Northern Thailand*, Philadelphia: The Westminster Press.

Daft, R.L. and Marcic, D. (2004) *Understanding Management*, Fourth Edition, Mason, OH: Thomson South-Western.

Dai, Y. (2004) 'A disguised defeat: The Myanmar campaign of the Qing dynasty,' *Modern Asian Studies*, 38(1): 145–89.

Dana, L.P. and Barthman, S. (2009) 'Laos,' in L.P. Dana, M. Han, V. Ratten, and I.M. Welpe (Eds.), *Handbook of Research on Asian Entrepreneurship*, Cheltenham, UK: Edward Elgar, pp. 168–71.

Dani, A.H. and Masson, V.M. (1999) 'Introduction,' in A.H. Dani and V.M. Masson (Eds.), *History of Civilization of Central Asia, Volume 1*, Delhi: UNESCO, pp. 19-28

Danis, W.M., Chiaburu, D.S. and Lyles, M.A. (2010) 'The impact of managerial networking intensity and market-based strategies on firm growth during institutional upheaval: A study of small and medium-sized enterprises in a transition economy,' *Journal of International Business Studies*, 41(2): 387–407.

Dasgupta, P. (2007) 'Measuring sustainable development: Theory and application,' *Asian Development Review*, 24(1): 1–10.

Dasgupta, S. and Williams, D. (2010) 'Women facing the economic crisis: The garment sector in Cambodia,' in A. Bauer and M. Thant (Eds.), *Poverty and Sustainability Development in Asia: Impacts and Responses to the Global Economic Crisis*, Mandaluyong City, Philippines: Asian Development Bank, pp. 149–68.

Dautremer, J. (1913) *Burma under British Rule*, translated by George Scott, London: T. Fisher Unwin.

Davidson, K. (2009) 'Ethical concerns at the bottom of the pyramid: Where CSR meets BOP,' *Journal of International Business Ethics*, 2(1): 22–32.

De Casparis, J.G. and Mabbett, I.W. (1992) 'Religion and popular beliefs in Southeast Asia before c. 1500,' in N. Tarling (Ed.), *The Cambridge History of Southeast Asia, Volume 1*, Cambridge, UK: Cambridge University Press, pp. 276–339.

Dedoussis, V. (2001) 'Keiretsu and management practices in Japan: Resilience amid change,' *Journal of Managerial Psychology*, **16**(2): 173–88.

Deegalee, M. (2006) 'Introduction: Buddhism, conflict and violence,' in M. Deegalle (Ed.), *Buddhism, Conflict and Violence in Modern Sri Lanka*, London: Routledge, pp. 1–21.

Denault, L. (2009) 'Partition and the politics of the joint family in nineteenth-century north India,' *The Indian Economic and Social History Review*, **46**(1): 27–55.

Deng, K.G. (2003) 'State transformation, reforms and economic performance in China, 1840–1910,' in A. Teichiva and H. Matis (Eds.), *Nation, State and the Economy in History*, Cambridge, UK: Cambridge University Press, pp. 308–31.

Dent, C.M. (1998) 'Regionalism in Southeast Asia: Opportunities and threats for the European Union,' *European Business Review*, **98**(4): 184–95.

Derevyanko, A.P. and Dorj, D. (1999) 'Neolithic tribes in northern parts of Central Asia,' in A.H. Dani and V.M. Masson (Eds.), *History of Civilization of Central Asia, Volume 1*, New Delhi: UNESCO, pp. 169–89.

De Valk, P. (2003) 'How do firms learn? With case studies from Lao PDR,' *Working Paper Series, Institute of Social Studies, The Hague*, No. 385.

De Waal, A. and Frijins, M. (2009) 'Working on high performance in Asia: The case of Nabil Bank,' *Measuring Business Excellence*, **13**(3): 29–38.

De Waal, A. and Frijins, M. (2011) 'Longitudinal research into factors of high performance: The follow-up case of Nabil Bank,' *Measuring Business Excellence*, **15**(1): 4–19.

Dieleman, M. and Sachs, W. (2006) 'Oscillating between a relationship-based and a market-based model: The Salim Group,' *Asia Pacific Journal of Management*, **23**(2): 521–36.

Dikova, D., Sahib, P.R. and van Wittloostujin, A. (2010) 'Cross-border acquisition abandonment and completion: The effect of institutional differences and organizational learning in the international business service industry, 1981–2001,' *Journal of International Business Studies*, **41**(2): 223–45.

Dittmer, L. (2008) 'Burma vs. Myanmar: What's in a name?' *Asian Survey*, **48**(6): 885–8.

Dougherty, S.M. and McGuckin, R.H. (2008) 'The effects of federalism on productivity in Chinese firms,' *Management and Organization Review*, **4**(1): 39–61.

Downie, S. and Kingsbury, D. (2001) 'Political development and the re-emergence of civil society in Cambodia,' *Contemporary Southeast Asia*, **23**(1): 43–64.

Dror, O. (2007) *Cult, Culture and Authority: Princess Lieu Hanh in Vietnamese History*, Honolulu, HI: University of Hawai'i Press.

Dutton, G. (2006) *Tay Son Uprising: Society and Rebellion in Eighteenth-Century Vietnam*, Honolulu, HI: University of Hawai'i Press.

Dyer, J.H. (1996) 'Does governance matter? Keiretsu alliances and asset specificity as sources of Japanese competitive advantage,' *Organization Science*, **7**(6): 649–66.

Eanes, J. (2002) 'The rise and fall of the Khmer Rouge', master's thesis, California State University, Fresno.

Ear, S. (1995) 'The Khmer Rouge canon 1975–1979: The standard academic view on Cambodia,' undergraduate political science honors thesis, University of California, Berkeley.

Ear, S. (2009) 'Sowing and sewing growth: The political economy of rice and garments in Cambodia,' *Stanford Center for International Development Working Paper*, No. 384.

Easterly, W. (2007) 'The ideology of development,' *Foreign Policy*, **161**: 31–5.

Easterly, W. (2009) 'The poor man's burden,' *Foreign Policy*, **170**: 77–81.

Easterly, W. (2010) 'Democratic accountability in development: The double standard,' *Social Research*, **77**(4): 1074–104.

Elson, R.E. (1992) 'International commerce, the state and society: Economic and social change,' in N. Tarling (Ed.), *The Cambridge History of Southeast Asia, Volume 2*, Cambridge, UK: Cambridge University Press, pp. 131–96.

Ensign, P.C. (2008) 'Small business strategy as a dynamic process: Concepts, controversies and implications,' *Journal of Business and Entrepreneurship*, **20**(2): 25–43.

Epstein, M.J., Buhovac, A.R. and Yuthas, K. (2010) 'Implementing sustainability: The role of leadership and organizational culture,' *Strategic Finance*, **91**(10): 41–8.

Evans, G. (2002) *A Short History of Laos: A Land in Between*, Crows Nest, Australia: Allen & Unwin.

Ewing-Chow, M. (2007) 'First do no harm: Myanmar trade sanctions and human rights,' *Northwestern Journal of International Human Rights*, **5**(2): 153–80.

Fairbanks, J.K., Reischauer, E.O. and Craig, A.M. (1989) *East Asia: Traditions and Transformation*, Revised Edition, Boston: Houghton Mifflin.

Fan, P. and Wan, G. (2008) 'China's regional inequality in innovation: 1995–2004,' in G. Wan (Ed.), *Inequality and Growth in Modern China*, New York: Oxford University Press, pp. 144–62.

Farrell, D. (2004) 'The case for globalization,' *The International Economy*, **18**(1): 52–5.

Faulkner, F. (2011) 'Strictly in confidence: Thai economic virility, internal angst and the market: Problems, perceptions, prognoses,' *Shinawatra International University Journal of management*, **1**(1): 105–24.

Fenby, J. (2008) *Modern China: The Fall and Rise of a Great Power, 1850 to the Present*, New York: Ecco (HarperCollins).

Ford, R. (2011) 'Memories of Chao Anu: New history and post-socialist ideology,' *Journal of Lao Studies*, **2**(2): 104–26.

Forsyth, D.R., O'Boyle, E.H. and McDaniel, M.A. (2008) 'East meets West: A meta-analytic investigation of cultural variations in idealism and relativism,' *Journal of Business Ethics*, **83**: 813–33.

Foster, J. (2011) 'Evolutionary macroeconomics: A research agenda,' *Journal of Evolutionary Economics*, **21**(1): 5–28.

Franke, R.H., Mento, A.J., Prumo, S.M. and Edlund, T.W. (2007) 'General Electric performance over a half century: Evaluation of effects of leadership and other strategic factors by quantitative case analysis,' *International Journal of Business*, **12**(1): 137–51.

Frantzen, D. (2004) 'Technological diffusion and productivity convergence: A study for manufacturing in the OECD,' *Southern Economic Journal*, **71**(2): 352–76.

Freeman, J.H. (1910) *An Oriental Land of the Free: or, Life and Mission Work among the Laos of Siam, Burma, China and Indo-China*, Philadelphia: The Westminster Press.

Friedman, E. (1994) 'Reconstructing China's national identity: A southern alternative to Mao-era anti-imperialistic nationalism,' *Journal of Asian Studies*, **53**(1): 67–91.

Friedman, T.L. (2005) *The World Is Flat: A Brief History of the Twenty-first Century*, New York: Farrar, Straus & Giroux.

Fukasaku, K. (2007) 'Introduction and overview,' in *Business and Development: Fostering the Private Sector*, Paris: Development Centre of the Organisation for Economic Co-operation and Development, pp. 11–20.

Gagnon, J. (2009). 'Moving out of bad jobs: More mobility, more opportunity,' in J. Jutting and J.R. de Laiglesia (Eds.), *Is Informal Normal?: Towards More and Better Jobs in Developing Countries*, Paris: Organisation for Economic Cooperation and Development, pp. 115–42.

Gallo, F.T. (2011) *Business Leadership in China: How to Blend Best Western Practices with Chinese Wisdom*, Revised Edition, Singapore: John Wiley & Sons.

Gay, B. (2002) 'Millenarian movements in Laos, 1895–1936: Depictions by modern Lao historians,' in M. Ngaosrivathana and K. Breazeale (Eds.), *Breaking New Ground in Lao History: Essays on the Seventh to Twentieth Centuries*, Chiang Mai, Thailand: Silkworm Books, pp. 281–97.

Gilson, R. and Roe, M. (1993) 'Understanding the Japanese keiretsu: Overlaps between corporate governance and industrial organization,' *Yale Law Journal*, **102**(4): 871–906.

Giroletti, D.A. (2003) 'Building the Brazilian nation-state: From colony to globalization,' in A. Teichiva and H. Matis (Eds.), *Nation, State and the Economy in History*, Cambridge, UK: Cambridge University Press, pp. 373–86.

Godo, Y. (2010) 'The human capital basis of the Japanese miracle: A historical perspective,' in K. Otsuka and K. Kalirajan (Eds.), *Community, Market and State in Development*, London: Palgrave Macmillan, pp. 103–22.

Goh, G.Y. (2007) 'Cakkrvatiy Anuruddha and the Buddhist Oikoumene: Historical narratives of kingship and religious networks in Burma, Northern Thailand and Sri Lanka (11th–14th centuries),' doctoral dissertation, University of Hawaii.

Golden, P. (2011) *Central Asia in World History*, Oxford, UK: Oxford University Press.

Goldstein, A. (2007) 'Transport infrastructure in Africa,' in *Business and Development: Fostering the Private Sector*, Paris: Development Centre of the Organisation for Economic Co-operation and Development, pp. 145–48.

Gombrich, R. (2006) 'Is the Sri Lankan war a Buddhist fundamentalism,' in M. Deegalle (Ed.), *Buddhism, Conflict and Violence in Modern Sri Lanka*, London: Routledge, pp. 22–37.

Gouillart, E. (2008) 'An interview with C.K. Prahalad,' *Journal of International Affairs*, **62**(1): 215–27.

Grabowsky, V. and Tappe, O. (2011) 'Important kings of Laos: Translation and analysis of a Lao cartoon pamphlet,' *Journal of Laos Studies*, **2**(1): 1–44.

Greco, J. (1999) 'Akio Morita (b. 1921): A founder of Japan Inc.' *The Journal of Business Strategy*, **20**(5): 38–8.

Griffin, R.W. and Putsay, M.W. (2005) *International Business*, Fourth Edition, Upper Saddle River, NJ: Pearson Education.

Guillermo, A.R. and Win, M.K. (2005) *Historical Dictionary of the Philippines*, Second Edition, Lanham, MA: Scarecrow Press.

Gunawardana, R. (2006) 'Roots of the conflict and the peace process problem in Buddhist history,' in M. Deegalle (Ed.), *Buddhism, Conflict and Violence in Modern Sri Lanka*, London: Routledge, pp. 177–201.

Gunn, G.C. (2008) 'Laos in 2007: Regional integration and international fallout,' *Asian Survey*, **48**(1): 62–8.

Habib, M. and Zurawicki, L. (2010) 'The bottom of the pyramid: Key roles for businesses,' *Journal of Business and Economics Research*, **8**(5): 23–32.

Hagan, A.F. and Amin, S.G. (1995) 'Corporate executives and environmental scanning activities: An empirical investigation,' *SAM Advanced Management Journal*, **60**(2): 41–8.

Hall, E.T. (1976) *Beyond Culture*, New York: Doubleday.

Hall, J.L. and Leidecker, J.K (1981) 'Is Japanese-style management anything new? A comparison of Japanese-style management with US participative models,' *Human Resource Management*, **20**(4): 14–21.

Hall, K.R. (1992) 'Economic history of early Southeast Asia: Early economic development,' in N. Tarling (Ed.), *The Cambridge History of Southeast Asia, Volume 2*, Cambridge, UK: Cambridge University Press, pp. 185–275.

Hallen, L and Johanson, M. (2004) 'Integration of relationships and business network development in the Russian transition economy,' *International Marketing Review*, **21**(2): 151–71.

Han, S., Kang, T., Salter, S. and Yoo, Y.K. (2010) 'A cross-country study on the effects of national culture on earnings management,' *Journal of International Business Studies*, **41**(1): 123–41.

Hanlon, J., Barrientos, A. and Hulme, D. (2010) *Just Give Money to the Poor: The Development Revolution from the Global South*, Sterling, VA: Kumarian Press.

Harley, G.T. and Tan, C.T. (1999) 'East vs West: strategic marketing management meets the Asian networks,' *Journal of Business and Industrial Marketing*, **14**(2): 91–101.

Hasan, R. and Jandoc, K.B. (2010) 'Trade liberalization and wage inequality in the Philippines,' *Asia Development Bank Economics Working Paper Series*, No. 195.

Hasan, R., Mitra, D. and Ulubasoglu, M. (2007) 'Institutions and policies for growth and poverty reduction: The role of private sector development,' *Asian Development Review*, **24**(1): 69–116.

Hatcher, C. and Terjesen, S. (2007) 'Towards a new theory of entrepreneurship in culture and gender: A grounded study of Thailand's most successful female entrepreneurs,' paper presented at the *Fourth AGSE International Entrepreneurship Research Exchange, 6–9 February, Brisbane, Australia*.

Hawks, V.D. (2005) 'Observations of small manufacturing enterprise owners in Phnom Penh, Cambodia,' doctoral dissertation, Gonzaga University.

Header, S. (2005) 'Hun Sen's consolidation: Death or beginning of reform?' in *Southeast Asian Affairs 2005*, Singapore: Institute for Southeast Asian Studies, pp. 113–30.

Hengkietisak, K. (2008) 'PPP must step carefully,' *Bangkok Post*, 26 January 2008 Edition, Section 1, p. 10.

Herrmann, D. and Hague, I. (2006) 'Convergence: In search of the best,' *Journal of Accountancy*, **201**(1): 69–73.

Higham, C.F.W. (2001) '(Commentary) Archaeology in Myanmar: Past, present and future,' *Asian Perspectives*, **40**(1): 127–38.

Hill, H. and Jongwanich, J. (2009) 'Outward foreign direct investment and the financial crisis in East Asia,' *Asian Development Review*, **26**(2): 1–25.

Hill, R. (2002) *Southeast Asia: People, Land and Economy*, Crows Nest, Australia: Allen & Unwin.

Hindustan Unilever Limited (2011) Annual Report, 2010–2011, available from *http://www.hul.co.in/Images/HUL_Annual%20Report_%202010-11_tcm114 -268010_tcm114-268010.pdf*

Hipsher, S. (2007) 'Creating market size: Regional strategies for the world's least developed areas,' in J. Stoner and C. Wankel (Eds.), *Innovative Approaches to Reducing Global Poverty*, Charlotte, NC: Information Age Publishing, pp. 58–71.

Hipsher, S. (2009) 'Thailand,' in L.P. Dana, M. Han, V. Ratten, and I.M. Welpe (Eds.), *Handbook of Research on Asian Entrepreneurship*, Cheltenham, UK: Edward Elgar, pp. 331–8.

Hipsher, S. (2010a) *Business Practices in Southeast Asia: An Interdisciplinary Analysis of Theravada Buddhist Countries*, Oxford, UK: Routledge Publishing.

Hipsher, S. (2010b). 'Transfer or adapt: Evidence from the Theravada Buddhist countries of Southeast Asia,' *Global Business and Organizational Excellence*, **29**(3): 35–43.

Hipsher, S. (2010c) 'Theoretical view on microenterprise entrepreneurial motivators,' in J.M. Munoz (Ed.), *Contemporary Micro-enterprise: Concepts and Cases*, Northampton, MA: Edward Elgar.

Hipsher, S. (2011) 'The impact of Theravada Buddhist values on work practices in Southeast Asia,' *Shinawatra International University Journal of Management*, **1**(1): 76–100.

Hipsher, S., Hansanti, S. and Pomsuwan, S. (2007) *The Nature of Asian Firms: An Evolutionary Perspective*, Oxford, UK: Chandos Publishing.

Hitt, M.A., Lee, H. and Yucel, E. (2002) 'The importance of social capital to the management of multinational enterprises: relational networks among Asian and Western firms,' *Asia Pacific Journal of Management*, **19**(2/3): 353–72.

Hitt, M.A., Ireland, R.D. and Hoskisson, R.E. (2005) *Strategic Management: Competitiveness and Globalization*, Sixth Edition, Mason, OH: Thomson.

Hlaing, K.Y. (2005) 'Myanmar in 2004: Why military rule continues,' *Southeast Asian Affairs*, **2005**: 231–56.

Hlaing, K.Y. (2008) 'Power and factional struggles in post-independence Burmese governments,' *Journal of Southeast Asian Studies*, **39**(1): 149–77.

Hofstede, G. (1980) 'Motivation, leadership, and organization: Do American theories apply abroad?' *Organizational Dynamics*, **9**(1): 42–63.

Hofstede, G. (1983) 'The cultural relativity of organizational practices and theories,' *Journal of International Business Studies*, **14**(1): 75–89.

Hofstede, G. (1994) 'Management scientists are human,' *Management Science*, **40**(1): 4–13

Hofstede, G. (2002) 'Dimensions do not exist: A reply to Brendan McSweeny,' *Human Relations*, **55**(11): 1355–61.

Hofstede, G. (2007) Asian management in the 21st century,' *Asia Pacific Journal of Management*, **24**(4), 411–20.

Hofstede, G. and Bond, M.H. (1988) 'The Confucius connection: From cultural roots to economic growth,' *Organizational Dynamics*, **16**(4): 4–21.

Holmes, H., Tangtongtavy, S. and Tomizawa, R. (1996) *Working with the Thais: A Guide to Managing in Thailand*, Third Edition, Bangkok: White Lotus.

Holt, J.C. (2006) 'Hindu influences on medieval Sri Lankan Buddhist culture,' in M. Deegalle (Ed.), *Buddhism, Conflict and Violence in Modern Sri Lanka*, London: Routledge, pp. 38–66.

Hon, J.S., Tarng, M.Y. and Chu, P.Y. (2000) 'A case study exploring Acer's global logistics and innovation,' *Management International*, **5**(1): 21–30.

Horn, Z. (2010) 'No cushion to fall back on: The impact of the global recession on women in the informal economy in four Asian countries,' in A. Bauer and M. Thant (Eds.), *Poverty and Sustainability Development in Asia: Impacts and Responses to the Global Economic Crisis*, Mandaluyong City, Philippines: Asian Development Bank, pp. 169–86.

Horsey, R. (2008) 'The dramatic events of 2007 in Myanmar: Domestic and international implications,' in M. Skidmore and T. Wilson (Eds.), *Dictatorship, Disorder and Decline*, Canberra: ANU E Press, pp. 13–28.

Horsey, R. (2011) 'Political outlook: Myanmar,' in M. Montesano and L.P. Onn (Eds.), *Regional Outlook; Southeast Asia: 2010–2011*, Singapore: Institute of Southeast Asian Studies, pp. 42–6.

Horstmann, C.A. (2005) 'Playing a leadership role in international convergence,' *Journal of Accountancy*, **200**(4): 98–9.

Hoshino, T. (2002) 'Wen Dan and its neighbors: The Central Mekong Valley in the seventh and eighth centuries,' in M. Ngaosrivathana and K. Breazeale (Eds.), *Breaking New Ground in Lao History: Essays on the Seventh to Twentieth Centuries*, Chiang Mai, Thailand: Silkworm Books, pp. 25–72.

Huang, X., Shi, K., Zhang, Z. and Cheung, Y.L. (2006) 'The impact of participative leadership behavior on psychological empowerment and organizational commitment in Chinese state-owned enterprises: The moderating role of organizational tenure,' *Asia Pacific Journal of Management*, **23**(3): 345–67.

Hucker, C.O. (1975) *China's Imperial Past: An Introduction to Chinese History and Culture*, Stanford, CA: Stanford University Press.

Hudson, B. (2006) 'The origins of Bagan: The archaeological landscape of Upper Burma to ad 1300,' doctotal dissertation, University of Sydney Digital Theses, available from *http://hdl.handle.net/2123/638*

Hui, M.K., Au, K. and Fock, H. (2004) 'Empowerment effects across cultures,' *Journal of International Business Studies*, **35**(1): 41–60.

Hurn, B.J. (2007) 'The influence of culture on international business negotiations,' *Industrial and Commercial Training*, **39**(7): 354–60.

Hurst, R., Buttle, M. and Sandars, J. (2010) 'The impact of the global economic slowdown on value chain labor markets in Asia,' in A. Bauer and M. Thant (Eds.), *Poverty and Sustainability Development in Asia: Impacts and Responses to the Global Economic Crisis*, Mandaluyong City, Philippines: Asian Development Bank, pp. 113–30.

Hwang, I. and Seo, J. (2000) 'Corporate governance and chaebol reform in Korea,' *Seoul Journal of Economics*, **13**(3): 361–89.

Ileto, R. (1992) 'Religion and anti-colonial movements,' in N. Tarling (Ed,) *The Cambridge History of Southeast Asia, Volume 2*, Cambridge, UK: Cambridge University Press, pp. 197–248.

Inglehart, R. and Welzel, C. (2009) 'How development leads to democracy,' *Foreign Affairs*, 88(2): 33–48.

Ito, K. (1995) 'Japanese spinoffs: Unexplored survival strategies,' *Strategic Management Journal*, 16(6): 431–46.

Ito, K. and Rose, E.L. (2005) 'An emerging structure of corporations,' *Multinational Business Review*, 12(13): 63–83.

Ivarsson, S. and Goscha, C.E. (2007) 'Prince Phetsarath (1890–1959): Nationalism and royalty in the making of modern Laos,' *Journal of Southeast Asian Studies*, 38(1): 55–81.

Iyoha, M. (2010) 'Leadership, policy making and economic growth in African countries: The case of Nigeria,' in D. Brady and M. Spence (Eds.), *Leadership and Growth*, Washington, D.C.: World Bank, pp. 165–93.

James, H. (2004) 'King Solomon's judgment,' *NBR Analysis*, 15(1): 55–66.

Javidan, M. and Carl, D.E. (2005) 'Leadership across cultures: A study of Canadian and Taiwanese executives,' *Management International Review*, 45(1): 23–44.

Jeldres, J.A. (1993) 'The UN and the Cambodian transition,' *Journal of Democracy*, 4(4): 104–16.

Jomo, K.S. (2003) 'Globalisation, liberalisation, poverty and income inequality in Southeast Asia,' in R. Kohl (Ed.), *Globalisation, Poverty and Inequality*, Paris: Organisation for Economic Co-operation and Development, pp. 91–8.

Jongwanich, J., James, W.E., Minor, P.J. and Greenbaum, A. (2009) 'Trade structure and the transmission of economic distress in the high-income OECD countries to developing Asia,' *Asian Development Review*, 26(1), 48–102.

Jumsai, M. (2000) *History of Laos*, Bangkok: Chalermnit.

Jumsai, M. (2001) *History of Thailand and Cambodia*, Bangkok: Chalermnit.

Jung, J., Su, X., Baeza, M. and Hong, S. (2008) 'The effect of organizational culture stemming from national culture towards quality management deployment,' *TQM Journal*, 20(6): 622–27.

Jutting, J. and de Laiglesia, J.R. (2009) 'Employment, poverty reduction and development', in J. Jutting and J.R. de Laiglesia (Eds.), *Is Informal Normal?: Towards More and Better Jobs in Developing Countries*, Paris: Organisation for Economic Cooperation and Development, pp. 17–26.

Kalirajan, K., Bhide, S. and Singh, K. (2010) 'Development performance across Indian States and the role of government,' in K. Otsuka and K. Kalirajan (Eds.), *Community, Market and State in Development*, London: Palgrave Macmillan, pp. 45-63.

Kanungo, R.N. and Wright, R.W. (1983) 'A cross-cultural comparative study of managerial job attitudes,' *Journal of International Business Studies*, 14(2): 115–29.

Kao, C., Wu, W.Y., Hsieh, W.J., Wang, T.Y., Lin, C. and Chen, L.H. (2008) 'Measuring the national competitiveness of Southeast Asian countries,' *European Journal of Operational Research*, 187: 613–28.

Karnani, A. (2010) 'Failure of the libertarian approach to reducing poverty,' *Asian Business and Management*, 9(1): 5–21.

Karnow, S. (1985) *Vietnam: A History*, New York: Penguin Books.

Kathirithamby-Wells, J. (1992) 'The age of transition: The mid-eighteenth to the early nineteenth centuries,' in N. Tarling (Ed.), *The Cambridge History of Southeast Asia, Volume 1*, Cambridge, UK: Cambridge University Press, pp. 572–609.

Kaw, E. (2005) 'Buddhism and education in Burma: Varying conditions for a social ethos in the path to "Nibbana",' doctoral dissertation, Princeton University.

Keller, G.F. and Kronstedt, C.R. (2005) 'Connecting Confucianism, communism, and the Chinese culture of commerce,' *Journal of Language for International Business*, 16(1): 60–75.

Kelly, L., MacNab, B. and Worthley, R. (2006) 'Crossvergence and cultural tendencies: Longitudinal test of the Hong Kong, Taiwan and United States banking sectors,' *Journal of International Management*, 12: 67–84.

Keyes, C. (2002) 'Presidential address: "The peoples of Asia"—science and politics in the classification of ethnic groups in Thailand, China, and Vietnam,' *Journal of Asian Studies*, 61(4): 1163–203.

Kienzle, R. and Shadur, M. (1997) 'Developments in business networks in East Asia,' *Management Decision*, 35(1): 23–32.

Kigabo, T.T. (2010) 'Leadership, policy making, quality of economic policies, and their inclusiveness: The case of Rwanda,' in D. Brady and M. Spence (Eds.), *Leadership and Growth*, Washington, D.C.: World Bank, pp. 81–97.

Kihara, T. (2012) 'Effective development aid: Selectivity, proliferation and fragmentation, and the growth impact of development assistance,' *ADBI Working Paper*, No. 342.

Kim, A.M. (2008) *Learning to be Capitalists: Entrepreneurs in Vietnam's Transition Economy*, New York: Oxford University Press.

Kim H. (2009) 'Determinants of the success of economic sanctions: An empirical analysis,' *Journal of International and Area Studies*, 16(1): 27–51.

Kim, H., Hoskisson, R.E., Tihanyi, L. and Hong, J. (2004) 'The evolution and restructuring of diversified business groups in emerging markets: The lessons from chaebols in Korea,' *Asia Pacific Journal of Management*, 21(1/2): 25–48.

Kim, W.Y. (1982) 'Discoveries of rice in prehistoric sites in Korea,' *Journal of Asian Studies*, 41(3): 513–18.

Kim, Y. (2006) 'Do South Korean companies need to obscure their country-of-origin image?: A case of Samsung,' *Corporate Communications*, 11(2): 126–37.

Kingston, W. (2006) 'Schumpeter, business cycles and co-evolution,' *Industry and Innovation*, 13(1): 97–106.

Kipping, M. and Cailluet, L. (2010) 'Mintzberg's emergent and deliberate strategies: Tracking Alcan's activities in Europe, 1928–2007,' *Business History Review*, 84(1): 79–95.

Klein, A., Waxin, M.F. and Radnell, E. (2009) 'The impact of the Arab national culture on the perception of ideal organizational culture in the United Arab Emirates; An empirical study of 17 firms,' *Education, Business and Society: Contemporary Middle Eastern Issues*, 2(1): 44–56.

Klump, R. (2007) 'Pro-poor growth in Vietnam: Miracle or model?' in T. Besley and L.J. Cord (Eds.), *Delivering on the Promise of Pro-poor Growth: Insights and Lessons from Country Experiences*, New York: World Bank/Palgrave Macmillan, pp. 119–46.

Koh, D. (2011) 'Political outlook: Cambodia,' in M. Montesano and L.P. Onn (Eds.), *Regional Outlook; Southeast Asia: 2010–2011*. Singapore: Institute of Southeast Asian Studies, pp. 58–61.

Kourula, A. and Halme, M. (2006) 'Types of corporate social responsibility and engagement with NGOs: An exploration of business and societal outcomes,' *Corporate Governance*, 8(4): 557–70.

Kratoska, P. and Batson, B. (1992) 'Nationalism and modernist reform,' in N. Tarling (Ed.), *The Cambridge History of Southeast Asia, Volume 2*, Cambridge, UK: Cambridge University Press, pp. 249–324.

Kucera, D. and Xenogiani, T. (2009) 'Women in informal employment: What do we know and what can we do?' in J. Jutting and J.R. de Laiglesia (Eds.), *Is Informal Normal?: Towards More and Better Jobs in Developing Countries*, Paris: Organisation for Economic Cooperation and Development, pp. 89–114.

Kudo, T. (2008) 'Myanmar's economic relations with China: Who benefits and who pays?' in M. Skidmore and T. Wilson (Eds.), *Dictatorship, Disorder and Decline*, Canberra: ANU E Press, pp. 87–109.

Kuhn, R.K. (2010) *How China's Leaders Think: The Inside Story of China's Reform and What This Means for the Future*, Singapore: John Wiley & Sons.

Kurlantzick, J. (2005) 'Laos: Still communist after all these years,' *Current History*, 104(680): 114–19.

Lahouel, M.H. (2007) 'The success of pro-poor growth in rural and urban Tunisia,' in T. Besley and L.J. Cord (Eds.), *Delivering on the Promise of Pro-poor Growth: Insights and Lessons from Country Experiences*, New York: World Bank/ Palgrave Macmillan, pp. 199–218.

Laird, M (2007) 'Private sector development in a pro-poor growth context: The role of donors,' in *Business and Development: Fostering the Private Sector*, Paris: Development Centre of the Organisation for Economic Co-operation and Development, pp. 54–8.

Lall, M. (2008) 'Evolving education in Myanmar: The interplay of state, business and the community,' in M. Skidmore and T. Wilson (Eds.), *Dictatorship, Disorder and Decline*, Canberra: ANU E Press, pp. 127–49.

Langenfeld, J. and Nieberding, J. (2005) 'The benefits of free trade to US consumers business,' *Business Economics*, 4(3): 41–51.

Laoglesia, J.D (2007) 'Institutional bottlenecks in agricultural development in Africa in developing countries,' in *Business and Development: Fostering the Private Sector*, Paris: Development Centre of the Organisation for Economic Co-operation and Development, pp. 139–44.

Laplante, B. (2010) 'Poverty, climate change, and the economic recession,' in A. Bauer and M. Thant (eds.), *Poverty and Sustainability Development in Asia: Impacts and Responses to the Global Economic Crisis*, Mandaluyong City, Philippines: Asian Development Bank, pp. 507–20.

Lau, C.M. (2006) 'Achievements, challenges and research agendas for Asian management research studies,' *Asian Business and Management*, 5(1): 53–66.

Lederman, D. (2010) 'An international multilevel analysis of product innovation,' *Journal of International Business Studies*, 41(4): 606–19.

Lee, J., Brahmasrene, T. and Tai, S. (2008) 'Recent evidence of small business development in CIS transition economies,' *International Journal of Entrepreneurship*, 12: 71–85.

Lee, J.W. (2002) 'The nature of chaebol restructuring: Two lessons from Professor Coase,' *Journal of International and Area Studies*, **9**(2): 23–41.

Lee, K. and Kim, S. (2000) 'Characteristics and economic efficiency of the venture companies in Korea: Comparisons with chaebols and other traditional firms,' *Seoul Journal of Economics*, **13**(3): 335–60.

Lee, M.P. (2008) 'Widening gap of educational opportunity? A study of the changing patterns of educational attainment in China,' in G. Wan (Ed.), *Inequality and Growth in Modern China*, New York: Oxford University Press, pp. 163–83.

Lee, S.J. and Han, T.J. (2006) 'The demise of "Korea Inc.": Paradigm shift in Korea's development state,' *Journal of Contemporary Asia*, **36**(3): 305–26.

Legge, J.D. (1992) 'The writing of Southeast Asian history,' in N. Tarling (Ed.), *The Cambridge History of Southeast Asia, Volume 1*, Cambridge, UK: Cambridge University Press, pp. 1–50.

Lektzian, D. and Souva, M. (2007) 'An institutional theory of sanctions onset and success,' *Journal of Conflict Resolution*, **51**(6): 848–71.

Lerpold, L. and Romani L. (2010) 'Social capital and cross-cultural model replication: The case of hand in hand in India and South Africa,' in J.S. Munoz (Ed.), *Contemporary Microenterprise: Concepts and Cases*, Cheltenham, UK: Edward Elgar, pp. 221–33.

Li, J. and Harrison, R. (2008) 'Corporate governance and national culture: A multi-country study,' *Corporate Governance*, **8**(5): 607–21.

Li, M. (2009) 'Soft power in Chinese discourse: Popularity and prospect,' in M. Li (Ed.), *Soft Power: China's Emerging Strategy in International Politics*, Lanham, MD: Lexington Books, pp. 21–44.

Li, W. and Yang, D.T. (2005) 'The Great Leap Forward: Anatomy of a central planning disaster,' *Journal of Political Economy*, **113**(4): 840–77.

Li, Y., Zhou, N. and Si, Y. (2010) 'Exploratory innovation and exploitative innovation, and performance,' *Nankai Business Review International*, **1**(3): 297–316.

Liang, Z. (2008) 'Financial development, growth and regional disparity in post-reform China,' in G. Wan (Ed.), *Inequality and Growth in Modern China*, New York: Oxford University Press, pp. 112–24.

Lien-Hang, N.T. (2006) 'The Sino-Vietnamese split and the Indochina War, 1968–1975,' in O.A. Westad and S. Quinn-Judge (Eds.), *The Third Indochina War: Conflict between China, Vietnam and Cambodia, 1972–79*, London: Routledge, pp. 12–32.

Lin, J. and Liu, P. (2008) 'Development strategies and regional income disparities in China,' in G. Wan (Ed.), *Inequality and Growth in Modern China*, New York: Oxford University Press, pp. 56–78.

Lin, J., Zuang, J., Tang, M. and Lin, T. (2008) 'Inclusive growth toward a harmonious society in the People's Republic of China: An overview,' *Asian Development Review*, **25**(1/2): 1–14.

Lin, J.F., Zhuang, J., Tang, M. and Lin, T. (2008) 'Inclusive growth toward a harmonious society in the People's Republic of China: An overview,' *Asian Development Review*, **25**(1): 1–14.

Lin, J.Y. and Liu, P. (2008) 'Achieving equity and efficiency simultaneously in the primary distribution stage in the People's Republic of China,' *Asian Development Review*, **25**(1): 34–57.

London, T. and Hart, S.T. (2004) 'Perspective: reinventing strategies for emerging markets: Beyond the transnational model,' *Journal of International Business Studies*, **35**(5): 350–70.

Lorch, J. (2008) 'The (re)-emergence of civil society in areas of state weakness: The case of education in Burma/Myanmar,' in M. Skidmore and T. Wilson (Eds.), *Dictatorship, Disorder and Decline*, Canberra: ANU E Press, pp. 151–76.

Lu, D. (2007) 'The Chinese response to globalization: Accession to the WTO and its challenges,' in J. Shin (Ed.), *Global Challenges and Local Responses*, New York: Routledge, pp. 95–115.

Lu, L.T. and Lee, Y.H. (2005) 'The effect of culture on the management style and performance of international joint ventures in China: The perspective of foreign parent firms,' *International Journal of Management*, **22**(3): 452–63.

Lu, Y., Zhou, L., Bruton, G. and Li, W. (2010) 'Capabilities as a mediator linking resources and international performance of entrepreneurial firms in an emerging economy,' *Journal of International Business Studies*, **41**(3): 419–36.

Luk, C., Yau, O., Sin, L., Tse, A., Chow, R. and Lee, J. (2008) 'The effects of social capital and organizational innovativeness in different institutional contexts,' *Journal of International Business Studies*, **39**(4): 589–612.

Luo, Y. and Shenkar, O. (2006) 'The multinational corporation as a multilingual community: Language and organization in a global context,' *Journal of International Business Studies*, **37**(3): 321–39.

Luthans, F. and Ibrayeva, E.S. (2006) 'Entrepreneurial self-efficacy in Central Asian transition economies: Quantitative and qualitative analysis,' *Journal of International Business Studies*, **37**(1): 92–110.

Ma, D. (2011) 'The role of traditional Chinese state and the origin of modern East Asia,' in K. Otsuka and K. Kalirajan (Eds.), *Community, Market and State in Development*, London: Palgrave Macmillan, pp. 64–79.

Ma, Z. (2007) 'Chinese conflict management styles and negotiation behaviors,' *International Journal of Cross Cultural Management*, **7**(1): 101–19.

Mahmood, M. (2005) 'Getting decent work for poverty reduction for Cambodia,' *International Labour Organization (Geneva) Working Paper*, 48.

Mahmud, W., Ahmed, C. and Mahajan, S. (2010) 'Economic reforms, growth, and governance: The political economy aspects of Bangladesh's development surprise,' in D. Brady and M. Spence (Eds.), *Leadership and Growth*, Washington, D.C.: World Bank, pp. 227–54.

Marichal, C. and Topik, S. (2003) 'The state and economic growth in Latin America: Brazil and Mexico, nineteenth and early twentieth centuries,' in A. Teichiva and H. Matis (Eds.), *Nation, State and the Economy in History*, Cambridge, UK: Cambridge University Press, pp. 349–72.

Martinez, R. (2011) 'Remembering within a sacred space in Vientiane,' *Journal of Lao Studies*, **2**(1): 75–103.

Masson, P. (2001) 'Globalization: Facts and figures,' *IMF Policy Discussion Paper*, PDP/01/04.

Masson, V.H. (1999) 'The environment,' in A.H. Dani and V.M. Masson (Eds.), *History of Civilization of Central Asia, Volume 1*, New Delhi: UNESCO, pp. 29–44.

Mathews, J.A. (2006) 'Dragon multinationals: New players in 21st century globalization,' *Asia Pacific Journal of Management*, **23**(1): 5–27.

Mathews, V.E. (2000) 'Management in a developing nation: And we thought American managers had it tough,' *Multinational Business Review*, 8(2): 10–15.

May, T.M. (2009) *Culture and Customs of Mongolia*, Westport, CT: Greenwood Press.

Mayrhofer, W., Muller-Camen, M., Ledolter, J., Strunk, G. and Erten, C. (2004) 'Devolving responsibilities for human resources to line management? An empirical study about convergence in Europe,' *Journal for East European Management Studies*, 9(2): 123–46.

McCargo, D. (2008) 'Thailand: State of anxiety,' *Southeast Asian Affairs*, 2008: 333–56.

McCargo, D. (2011) 'Political outlook: Thailand,' in M. Montesano and L.P. Onn (Eds.), *Regional Outlook; Southeast Asia: 2010–2011*, Singapore: Institute of Southeast Asian Studies, pp. 54–8.

McCauley, M. (2002) *Afghanistan and Central Asia: A Modern History*, London: Longman.

McCleary, R.M. and Barro, R.J. (2006) 'Religion and political economy in an international panel,' *Journal of the Scientific Study of Religion*, 45(2): 149–75.

McCulloch, N., Winters, L.A. and Cirera, X. (2001) *Trade Liberalization and Poverty: A Handbook*, London: Centre for Economic Policy Research.

McGrath-Champ, S. and Carter, S. (2001) 'The art of selling corporate culture: Management and human resources in Australian construction companies operating in Malaysia,' *International Journal of Manpower*, 22(4): 349–68.

Mehta, A and Hasaon, R. (2011) 'Effects of trade and services liberalization on wage inequality in India,' *Asian Development Bank (ADB) Economics Working Paper Series*, No. 268.

Menezes-Filho, N. and Vasconcellos, L. (2007) 'Human capacity, inequality, and pro-poor growth in Brazil,' in T. Besley and L.J. Cord (Eds.), *Delivering on the Promise of Pro-poor Growth: Insights and Lessons from Country Experiences*, New York: World Bank/Palgrave Macmillan, pp. 219–43.

Menon, J. (2011) 'Economic outlook: Cambodia,' in M. Montesano and L.P. Onn (Eds.), *Regional Outlook; Southeast Asia: 2010–2011*, Singapore: Institute of Southeast Asian Studies, pp. 101–8.

Metcalf, L.E., Shankarmahesh, M., Bird, A., Lituchy, T.R. and Peterson, M.F. (2007) 'Cultural influences in negotiations: A four country comparative analysis,' *International Journal of Cross Cultural Management*, 7(2): 147–68.

Meyer, K. (2004) 'Perspectives on multinational enterprises in emerging economies,' *Journal of International Business Studies*, 35(4): 259–76.

Min, W. (2008) 'Internal dynamics of the Burmese military: Before, during and after the 2007 demonstrations,' in M. Skidmore and T. Wilson (Eds.), *Dictatorship, Disorder and Decline*, Canberra: ANU E Press, pp. 29–47.

Min, W. (2009) 'Looking inside the Burmese military,' *Asian Survey*, 48(6): 1018–37.

Mirrlees, J. (2011) 'Poverty and redistribution in emerging economies,' *Asian Development Review*, 28(2): 1–10.

Miwa, Y. and Ramseyer, J.M. (2006) *The Fable of Keiretsu: Urban Legends of the Japanese Economy*, Chicago: University of Chicago Press.

Mizuno, N. (2010) 'Inequality and sequence of economic liberalization,' *Journal of Economic Development*, 35(1): 1–13.

Mkapa, B.J. (2010) 'Leadership for growth, development and poverty reduction: An African viewpoint and experience,' in D. Brady and M. Spence (Eds.), *Leadership and Growth*, Washington, D.C.: World Bank, pp. 19–79.

Montesano, M. (2005) 'Beyond the assimilation fixation: Skinner and the possibility of a spatial approach to twentieth-century Thai history,' *Journal of Chinese Overseas*, **1**(2): 184–216.

Montreevat, S. (2011) 'Economic outlook: Thailand,' in M. Montesano and L.P. Onn (Eds.), *Regional Outlook; Southeast Asia: 2010–2011*, Singapore: Institute of Southeast Asian Studies, pp. 159–63.

Moon, H. and Lee, D. (2004) 'The competitiveness of multinational firms: A case study of Samsung and Sony,' *Journal of International and Area Studies*, **11**(1): 1–21.

Moran, R.T., Harris, P.R, and Moran, S.V. (2007) *Managing Cultural Differences: Global Leadership Strategies for the 21st Century*, Seventh Edition, Burlington, MA: Butterworth-Heinemann.

Morck, R. and Yeung, B. (2007) 'History in perspective: Comment on Jones and Khanna "Bringing history (back) into international business",' *Journal of International Business Studies*, **38**(3): 357–60.

Morden, T. and Bowles, D. (1998) 'Management in South Korea: A review,' *Management Decision*, **36**(5): 316–30.

Morley, S.A. (2003) 'Distribution and growth in Latin America in an era of structural reform: The impact of globalization,' in R. Kohl (Ed.), *Globalisation, Poverty and Inequality*, Paris: Organisation for Economic Co-operation and Development, pp. 63–70.

Moy, J., Vivienne, W.M. and Wright, P.C. (2003) 'Perceptions of entrepreneurship as a career: Views of young people in Hong Kong,' *Equal Opportunities International*, **22**(4): 16–40.

Mroczkowski, T. and Hanaoka, M. (1998) 'The end of Japanese management: How soon?' *HR: Human Resource Planning*, **21**(3): 20–30.

Mugerwa, S.K. (2003) 'Globalisation, growth and income inequality: The African experience,' in R. Kohl (Ed.), *Globalisation, Poverty and Inequality*, Paris: Organisation for Economic Co-operation and Development, pp. 45–52.

Myint-U, T. (2006) *The River of Lost Footprints: A History of Burma*, New York: Farrar, Straus & Giroux.

Myint-U, T. (2008) 'Myanmar's GDP growth and investment: Lessons from a historical perspective,' in M. Skidmore and T. Wilson (Eds.), *Dictatorship, Disorder and Decline*, Canberra: ANU E Press, pp. 51–61.

Nabil Bank (2011) Annual Report 2010–11, available from *http://www.nabilbank. com/uploads/financial/file/AR_201011_20120315121117.pdf*

Neelankavil, J.P., Mathur, A. and Zhang, Y. (2000) 'Determinants of managerial performance: A cross-cultural comparison of the perceptions of middle-level managers in four countries,' *Journal of International Business Studies*, **31**(1): 121–40.

Negmatov, N.N. (1998) 'The Samanid state,' in M.S. Asimov and C.E. Bosworth (Eds.), *History of Central Asia, Volume IV*, Paris: UNESCO, pp. 83–101.

Newa, F.O. (2010) 'Microfinance and the growth of micro and small enterprises (MSEs) in sub-Saharan Africa: The case of Faulu Kenya,' in J.M. Munoz (Ed.),

Contemporary Microenterprise: Concepts and Cases, Cheltenham, UK: Edward Elgar, pp. 87–101.

Newbigin, E. (2009) 'The codification of personal law and secular citizenship: Revisiting the history of law reform in late colonial India,' *Indian Economic and Social History Review*, 46(1): 83–104.

Newburry, W. and Yakova, N. (2006) 'Standardized preferences: A function of national culture, work interdependence and local embeddedness,' *Journal of International Business Studies*, 37(1): 44–60.

Ngaosrivathana, M. and Ngaosrivathana, P. (2002) 'Early European impression of the Lao,' in M. Ngaosrivathana and K. Breazeale (Eds.), *Breaking New Ground in Lao History: Essays on the Seventh to Twentieth Centuries*, Chiang Mai, Thailand: Silkworm Books, pp. 95–150.

Ngo, L.V. (2006) 'The socialization of South Vietnam,' in O.A. Westad and S. Quinn-Judge (Eds.), *The Third Indochina War: Conflict between China, Vietnam and Cambodia, 1972–79*, London: Routledge, pp. 126–51.

Nguyen, T.V., Weinstein, M. and Meyer, A.D. (2005) 'Development of trust of interfirm relationships in Vietnam,' *Asia Pacific Journal of Management*, 22(3): 211–31.

Nizami, K.A. (1998) 'The Ghurids,' in M.S. Asimov and C.E. Bosworth (Eds.), *History of Central Asia, Volume IV*, Paris: UNESCO, pp. 182–95.

North, D.C. (2005) 'The contribution of the new institutional economic to an understanding of the transition problem,' in A. Shorrocks (Ed.), *Wider Perspectives in Global Development*, New York: Palgrave Macmillan, pp. 1–15.

O'Brien, P.K. (2003) 'Political structures and grand strategies for the growth of the British economy, 1688–1815,' in A. Teichiva and H. Matis (Eds.), *Nation, State and the Economy in History*, Cambridge, UK: Cambridge University Press, pp. 11–33.

O'Bryan, S. (2009) *The Growth Idea: Purpose and Prosperity in Postwar Japan*, Honolulu, HI: University of Hawai'i Press.

O'Connor, R.A. (1995) 'Agricultural change and ethnic succession in Southeast Asian states: A case for regional anthropology,' *Journal of Asian Studies*, 54(4): 968–96.

Obeyesekere, G. (2006) 'Buddhism, ethnicity, and identity: A problem in Buddhist history,' in M. Deegalle (Ed.), *Buddhism, Conflict and Violence in Modern Sri Lanka*, London: Routledge, pp. 134–62.

OECD (2006) *Promoting Private Investment for Development: The Role of ODA*, Paris: Organisation for Economic Cooperation and Development.

OECD (2010) *Perspectives on Global Development 2010: Shifting Wealth*, Paris: Organisation for Economic Cooperation and Development.

OECD (2011) *Trade for Growth and Poverty Reduction: How Aid for Trade Can Help the Development Dimension*, Paris: Organisation for Economic Co-operation and Development.

Okidi, J.A., Ssewanyana, S., Betegeka, L. and Muhumuza, F. (2007) 'Uganda's experience with operationalizing pro-poor growth, 1992–2003,' in T. Besley and L.J. Cord (Eds.), *Delivering on the Promise of Pro-poor Growth: Insights and Lessons from Country Experiences*, New York: World Bank/Palgrave Macmillan, 169-98.

Okogbule, N.S. (2008) 'Globalization, economic sovereignty and African Development: From Principles to Realities,' *Journal of Third World Studies*, 25(1): 213–31.

Orr, R.J. and Scott, W.R (2008) 'Institutional exceptions on global projects: A process model,' *Journal of International Business Studies*, 39(4): 562–88.

Ospina, S. and Schiffbaer, M. (2010) 'Competition and firm productivity: Evidence from firm level data,' *IMF Working Paper*, WP/10/67.

Owen, N.G. (1992) 'Economic and social change,' in N. Tarling (Ed.), *The Cambridge History of Southeast Asia, Volume 2*, Cambridge, UK: Cambridge University Press, pp. 467–528.

Pagell, M., Katz, J.P. and Shen, C. (2005) 'The importance of national culture in operations management research,' *International Journal of Operational and Production Management*, 25(3/4): 371–94.

Pandey, G. (2004) *Remembering Partition: Violence, Nationalism and History in India*, Cambridge, UK: Cambridge University Press.

Pangestu, M. (2003) 'The social impact of globalization in Southeast Asia,' in R. Kohl (Ed.), *Globalisation, Poverty and Inequality*, Paris: Organisation for Economic Co-operation and Development, pp. 83-90.

Papanek, G.F., Basri, M.C. and Schydlowsky, D.M. (2010) 'The impact of the world recession on Indonesia and an appropriate policy response: Some lessons for Asia,' in A. Bauer and M. Thant (Eds.), *Poverty and Sustainability Development in Asia: Impacts and Responses to the Global Economic Crisis*, Mandaluyong City, Philippines: Asian Development Bank, pp. 13–50.

Park, B. (2007) 'Globalization and local political economy: The multi-scalar approach,' in J. Shin (Ed.), *Global Challenges and Local Responses*, New York: Routledge, pp. 50–69.

Paulson, A.L. and Townsend, R.M. (2005) 'Financial constraints and entrepreneurship: Evidence from the Thai financial crisis,' *Economic Perspectives*, **Third Quarter**: 34–48.

Pellicer, E., Yepes, V., and Rojas, R.J. (2010) 'Innovation and competitiveness in construction companies: A case study,' *Journal of Management Research*, 10(2): 103–15.

Peng, M.W. (2002) 'Towards an institution-based view of business strategy,' *Asia Pacific Journal of Management*, 19(2/3): 251–67.

Peng, M.W. and Zhou, J.Q. (2005) 'How network strategies and institutional transitions evolve in Asia,' *Asia Pacific Journal of Management*, 22(4): 321–36.

Peng, M.W., Lee, S.H. and Wang, D.Y. (2005) 'What determines the scope of the firm over time?' *Academy of Management Review*, 30(3): 622–33.

Peng, M.W., Wang, D. and Jiang, Y. (2008) 'An institution-based view of international business strategy: A focus on emerging economies,' *Journal of International Business Studies*, 39(5): 920–36.

Penny, D., Hua, Q., Pottier, C., Fletcher, R. and Barbetti, M. (2007) 'The use of AMS ^{14}C dating to explore issues of occupation and demise at the medieval city of Angkor, Cambodia,' *Nuclear Instruments and Methods in Physics Research*, **B** 259: 388–94.

Persons, L.S. (2008) 'Face dynamics, social power and virtue among Thai leaders: A cultural analysis,' doctoral dissertation, Fuller Graduate School, School of Intercultural Studies.

Peterson, P. (2001) 'Akio Morita,' *Proceedings of the American Philosophical Society*, **145**(2): 213–20.

Phannalangsi, N. (2011) 'Impact of global financial crisis on economic growth in Lao PDR,' *International Journal of Business and Social Science*, **2**(22): 236–42.

Pholsena, V. (2004) 'The changing historiographies of Laos: A focus on the early period,' *Journal of Southeast Asian Studies*, **35**(2): 235–59.

Pholsena, V. (2010) 'US rapprochement with Laos and Cambodia: A response,' *Contemporary Southeast Asia*, **32**(3): 460–6.

Phongpaichit, P. and Baker, C. (2008) '(Commentary) Thailand: Fighting over democracy,' *Economic and Political Weekly*, 13 December 2008 Edition, pp. 18–21.

Phothisane, S. (2002) 'Evolution of the chronicle of Luang Prabang: A comparison of sixteen versions,' in M. Ngaosrivathana and K. Breazeale (Eds.), *Breaking New Ground in Lao History: Essays on the Seventh to Twentieth Centuries*, Chiang Mai, Thailand: Silkworm Books, pp. 73–93.

Phouphet, K. (2011) 'Economic outlook: Laos,' in M. Montesano and L.P. Onn (Eds.), *Regional Outlook; Southeast Asia: 2010–2011*, Singapore: Institute of Southeast Asian Studies, pp. 114–19.

Pietrobelli, C. (2007) 'Private sector development: Concepts and practices,' in *Business and Development: Fostering the Private Sector*, Paris: Development Centre of the Organisation for Economic Co-operation and Development, pp. 21–53.

Pinaud, N. (2007) 'Public–private dialogue in developing countries,' in *Business and Development: Fostering the Private Sector*, Paris: Development Centre of the Organisation for Economic Co-operation and Development, pp. 59–64.

Pinfold, J.F. (2001) 'The expectations of new business founders: The New Zealand case,' *Journal of Small Business Management*, **39**(3): 279–85.

Platzdasch, B. (2011) 'Political outlook: Indonesia,' in M. Montesano and L.P. Onn (Eds.), *Regional Outlook; Southeast Asia: 2010–2011*, Singapore: Institute of Southeast Asian Studies, pp. 29–33.

Poletti, M.J., Engelland, B.T. and Ling, H.G. (2011) 'An empirical study of declining lead times: Potential ramifications on the performance of early market entrants,' *Journal of Marketing Theory and Practice*, **19**(1): 27–38.

Porter, M.E. (1980) *Competitive Strategy*, New York: Free Press.

Porter, M.E. (1990) *The Competitive Advantage of Nations*, New York: Free Press.

Porter, M.E. (1996) 'What is strategy?', Harvard Business Review, 74(6): 61-78.

Porter, M.E. and Stern S. (2001) 'Innovation matters,' *MIT Sloan Management Review*, **42**(4): 28–36.

Postma, T. (2002) 'The adaptability of corporate governance,' *East Asian Economic Perspectives*, **13**: 97–110.

Prahalad, C.K. (2005) *Fortune at the Bottom of the Pyramid: Eradicating Poverty through Profits*, Philadelphia: Wharton School Publishing.

Prahalad, C.K. and Hart, S.L. (2002) 'The fortune at the bottom of the pyramid,' *Strategy and Business*, **26**(1): 54–67.

Prasnikar, J., Pahor, M. and Svetlik, J.V. (2008) 'Are national cultures still important in international business? Russia, Serbia and Slovenia in comparison,' *Journal of Contemporary Management Issues*, **13**(2): 1–26.

Pribbenow, M.L. (2006) 'Vietnam's invasion of Cambodia,' *The Journal of Military History*, **70**(2): 459–86.

Pucik, V. (1984) 'White-collar human resource management in large Japanese manufacturing firms,' *Human Resource Management*, **23**(3): 257–76.

Pudelko, M. (2004) 'HRM in Japan and the West: What are the lessons to be learnt from each other?' *Asian Business and Management*, **3**(3): 337–61.

Quy, T.V. (2002) 'The Quy Hop archive: Vietnamese–Lao relations reflected in border-post documents dating from 1619–1880,' in M. Ngaosrivathana and K. Breazeale (Eds.), *Breaking New Ground in Lao History: Essays on the Seventh to Twentieth Centuries*, Chiang Mai, Thailand: Silkworm Books, pp. 239–60.

Rahman, Z. and Bhattacharyya, S.K. (2003) 'Sources of first mover advantages in emerging market: An Indian perspective,' *European Business Review*, **15**(6): 361–71.

Ramamurti, R. (2004) '(Commentary) Developing countries and MNEs: Extending and enriching the research agenda,' *Journal of International Business Studies*, **35**(4): 277–83.

Ramsinghani, M. (2012) 'The trouble with India's people's car,' *Technology Review*, **115**(1): 69–70.

Ranjith, J. and Widner, B. (2011) 'Sri Lanka's garment industry: Prospects for agglomeration, challenges and implications for regional development,' *South Asian Journal of Management*, **18**(4): 7–22.

Ranov, V.A., Dorj, D. and Lu, Z. (1999) 'Lower Palaeolithic cultures,' in A.H. Dani and V.M. Masson (Eds.), *History of Civilization of Central Asia, Volume 1*, New Delhi: UNESCO, pp. 45–63.

Rasiah, R. (2007) 'Globalization and the Malaysian response: Trade-related investment liberalization under the WTO,' in J. Shin (Ed.), *Global Challenges and Local Responses*, New York: Routledge, pp. 140–60.

Ravallion, M. (2009) 'A comparative perspective on poverty reduction in Brazil, China and India,' *World Bank Policy Research Working Paper*, No. 5080.

Rehbein, B. (2007a) *Globalization, Culture and Society in Laos*, Oxford, UK: Routledge.

Rehbein, B. (2007b) 'Configurations of globalization in Laos and Cambodia,' *Internationales Asienforum*, **38**(1/2): 67–85.

Reid, A. (1992) 'Economic and social change, c. 1400–1800,' in N. Tarling (Ed.), *The Cambridge History of Southeast Asia, Volume 1*, Cambridge, UK: Cambridge University Press, pp. 460–507.

Reid, D.M. (2011) 'China: The elephant in every room,' *Shinawatra International University Journal of Management*, **1**(1): 8–40.

Reynolds, E.B. (2004) *Thailand's Secret War: The Free Thai, OSS, and SOE during World War II*, Cambridge, UK: Cambridge University Press.

Ricart, J.E., Enright, M.J., Ghemaway, P., Hart, S.L. and Khanna, T. (2004) 'Perspective: New frontiers in international strategy,' *Journal of International Business Studies*, **35**(3): 175–200.

Riester, A. (2010) 'Impact of the global recession on international labor migration and remittances: Implications for poverty reduction and development in Nepal, Philippines, Tajikistan, and Uzbekistan,' in A. Bauer and M. Thant (Eds.), *Poverty and Sustainability Development in Asia: Impacts and Responses to the Global Economic Crisis*, Mandaluyong City, Philippines: Asian Development Bank, pp. 239–56.

Rigg, J. (2005) *Living with Transition in Laos: Market Integration in Southeast Asia*, London: Routledge.

Robbins, S.P. and Coulter, M. (2005) *Management*, Eighth Edition, International Edition, Upper Saddle River, NJ: Pearson Education.

Roberts, C. (2006) 'Myanmar and the argument for engagement: A clash of contending moralities,' *East Asia*, **23**(2): 34–62.

Robinson, J.A. (2003) 'Where does inequality come from? Ideas and implication for Latin America,' in R. Kohl (Ed.), *Globalisation, Poverty and Inequality*, Paris: Organisation for Economic Co-operation and Development, pp. 71–6.

Rodrik, D. (2005) 'Rethinking growth strategies,' in A. Shorrocks (Ed.), *Wider Perspectives in Global Development*, New York: Palgrave Macmillan, pp. 201–23.

Rohatynskyj, M. (2011) 'Development discourse and selling soap in Madhya Pradesh, India,' *Human Organization*, **70**(1): 63–73.

Romani, L. and Lerpold, L. (2010) 'Microfinance and poverty alleviation: Underlying values and assumptions,' in J.M. Munoz (Ed.), *Contemporary Microenterprise: Concepts and Cases*, Cheltenham, UK: Edward Elgar, pp. 276–87.

Sachs, J. (2005) *The End of Poverty: Economic Possibilities for Our Time*, New York: The Penguin Press.

Sachs, J. and Yang, X. (1999) 'Gradual spread of market led industrialization,' *Center for International Development (Harvard University) Working Paper*, No. 11.

Saeed, M.K. and Shahbaz, N. (2011) 'Employees' perceptions about the effectiveness of performance appraisals: The case of Pakistan,' *Shinawatra International University Journal of Management*, **1**(1): 58–75.

Salvatore, D. (2007) *Managerial Economics in a Global Economy*, Sixth Edition, New York: Oxford University Press.

San Miguel (2010) San Miguel Annual Report.

San Miguel Corp (2006) *Wall Street Journal (Eastern Edition)*, 12 July 2006 Edition.

Sato, Y. (1993) 'The Salim Group in Indonesia: The development and behavior of the largest conglomerate in Southeast Asia,' *The Developing Economies*, **41**(4): 408–41.

Scholz, W., Bonnet, F. and Ehmke, E. (2010) 'Income support in times of global crisis: An assessment of the role of unemployment insurance and options for coverage extension in Asia,' in A. Bauer and M. Thant (Eds.), *Poverty and Sustainability Development in Asia: Impacts and Responses to the Global Economic Crisis*, Mandaluyong City, Philippines: Asian Development Bank, pp. 341–66.

Seekins, D.M. (2009) 'Myanmar in 2008: Hardship, compounded,' *Asian Survey*, **49**(1): 166–73.

Sejersted, F. (2003) 'Nationalism in the epoch of organised capitalism: Norway and Sweden choose different paths,' in A. Teichiva and H. Matis (Eds.), *Nation, State and the Economy in History*, Cambridge, UK: Cambridge University Press, pp. 96–112.

Sekiguchi, T. (2006) 'How organizations promote person–environment fit: Using the case of Japanese firms to illustrate institutional and cultural influences,' *Asia Pacific Journal of Management*, **23**(1): 47–69.

Sen, A. (2002) 'Globalization, inequality and global protest,' *Development*, **45**(2): 11–16.

Sen, B., Mujeri, M.K. and Shahabuddin, Q. (2007) 'Explaining pro-poor growth in Bangladesh: Puzzles, evidence and implications,' in T. Besley and L.J. Cord (Eds.), *Delivering on the Promise of Pro-poor Growth: Insights and Lessons from Country Experiences*, New York: World Bank/Palgrave Macmillan, pp. 79–115.

Setboonsarng, S. (2008) 'Global partnership in poverty reduction: Contract farming and regional cooperation,' *Asian Development Bank Institute Discussion Paper*, No. 89.

Sevim, A. and Bosworth, C.E. (1998) 'The Seljuqs and the Khwarazm Shahs,' in M.S. Asimov and C.E. Bosworth (Eds.), *History of Central Asia, Volume IV*, Paris: UNESCO, pp. 151–81.

Shao, B. (2011) 'First mover advantages: Flexible or not?' *Journal of Management and Marketing Research*, **7**(1): 1–13.

Shapiro, D.M., Gedaijlovis, E. and Erdener, C. (2003) 'The Chinese family firm as a multinational enterprise,' *International Journal of Organizational Analysis*, **11**(2): 105–22.

Sharafi, M. (2009) 'The semi-autonomous judge in colonial India: Chivalric imperialism meets Anglo-Islamic dower and divorce law,' *Indian Economic and Social History Review*, **46**(1): 57–81.

Sharma, S., Deller, J., Biswal, R. and Mandal, M.K. (2009) 'Emotional intelligence: Factorial structure and construct validity across cultures,' *International Journal of Cross Cultural Management*, **9**(2): 217–36.

Sharrock, P.D. (2009) 'Garuda, Vajrapani and religious change in Jayavarman VII's Angkor,' *Journal of Southeast Asian Studies*, **40**(1): 111–51.

Shenkar, O. (2009) 'Becoming multinational: Challenges for Chinese firms,' *Journal of Chinese Economic and Foreign Trade Studies*, **2**(3): 149–62.

Shin, J. (2007) 'Globalization and challenges to the development state: A comparison between South Korea and Singapore,' in J. Shin (Ed.), *Global Challenges and Local Responses*, New York: Routledge, pp. 31–49.

Shin, K. (2002) 'The treatment of market power in Korea,' *Review of Industrial Organization*, **21**(2): 113–28.

Shinkle, G.A. and Kriauciunas, A.P. (2010) 'Institutions, size, and age in transition economies: Implications for export growth,' *Journal of International Business Studies*, **41**(2): 267–86.

Singh, N. (2011) 'Emerging economy multinationals: The role of business groups,' *Economics, Management, and Financial Markets*, **6**(1): 142–82.

Sinha, A. (2010) 'Global meltdown and informality: An economy wide analysis for India – Policy research brief,' in A. Bauer and M. Thant (Eds.), *Poverty and Sustainability Development in Asia: Impacts and Responses to the Global Economic Crisis*, Mandaluyong City, Philippines: Asian Development Bank, pp. 131–40.

Skarbek, D.B. and Leeson, P.T. (2009) 'What can aid do?' *Cato Journal*, **29**(3): 391–97.

Smeaton, D.M. (1920) *Loyal Karens of Burma*, Second Edition, London: Kegan Paul, Trench, Trubner & Co.

Smith-Speck, S.K. and Roy, A. (2008) 'The relationship between television viewing, values and perceived well being: A global perspective,' *Journal of International Business Studies*, **39**(7): 197–219.

So, S. (2011) 'Political outlook: Cambodia,' in M. Montesano and L.P. Onn (Eds.), *Regional Outlook; Southeast Asia: 2010–2011*, Singapore: Institute of Southeast Asian Studies, pp. 25–9.

Son, H.H. (2007) 'Interrelationship between growth, inequality and poverty: The Asian experience,' *Asian Development Review*, **24**(2): 37–63.

Son, H.H. (2010) 'A multi-country analysis of achievements and inequalities in economic growth and standards of living,' *Asian Development Review*, **27**(1): 1–42.

Southiseng, N. and Walsh, J. (2008) 'Competition and management issues in SEM entrepreneurs in Laos: Evidence from empirical studies in Vientiane Municipality, Savannakhet and Luang Prabang,' *Proceedings of the Second International Colloquium on Business and Management (ICBM)*.

Southiseng, N. and Walsh, J. (2010) 'Competition and management issues of SME entrepreneurs in Laos: Evidence from empirical studies in Vientiane Municipality, Savannakhet and Luang Prabang,' *Asian Journal of Business Management*, **2**(3): 57–72

Southiseng, N. and Walsh, J. (2011) 'Study of tourism and labour in Luang Prabang Province,' *Journal of Lao Studies*, **2**(1): 45–65.

Srinivasan, T.N. (2009) *Trade, Growth and Poverty Reduction: Least-developed Countries, Landlocked Developing Countries and Small States in the Global Economic System*, New Delhi: Commonwealth Secretariat/London: Academic Foundation.

Stark, J. (2005) 'The state of globalization,' *The International Economy*, **19**(2): 52–6.

Steinberg, D.I. (2004) 'A guide for the perplexed?' *NBR Analysis*, **15**(1): 41–54.

Steward, F. (2005) 'Horizontal inequalities: A neglected dimension of development,' in A. Shorrocks (Ed.), *Wider Perspectives in Global Development*, New York: Palgrave Macmillan, pp. 101–35.

Stiglitz, J.E. (2005) 'More instruments and broader goals: Moving toward the post-Washington consensus,' in A. Shorrocks (Ed.), *Wider Perspectives in Global Development*, New York: Palgrave Macmillan, pp. 16–48.

Stockwell, A.J. (1992) 'Southeast Asia in war and peace: The end of European colonial empires', in N. Tarling (Ed.), *The Cambridge History of Southeast Asia, Volume 2*, Cambridge, UK: Cambridge University Press, pp. 329–86.

Strauss, J., Qian, E., Shen, M., Liu, D., Majbouri, M., Sun, A. et al. (2010) 'Private-sector industrialization in China: Evidence from Wenzhou,' in K. Otsuka and K. Kalirajan (Eds.), *Community, Market and State in Development*, London: Palgrave Macmillan, pp. 262–91.

Stuart-Fox, M. (2002) 'On writing of Lao history: Continuities and discontinuities,' in M. Ngaosrivathana and K. Breazeale (Eds.), *Breaking New Ground in Lao History: Essays on the Seventh to Twentieth Centuries*, Chiang Mai, Thailand: Silkworm Books, pp. 1–24.

Stuart-Fox, M. (2003) *A Short History of China and Southeast Asia: Tribute, Trade and Influence*, Crows Nest, Australia: Allen & Unwin.

Stuart-Fox, M. (2011) 'Political outlook: Laos,' in M. Montesano and L.P. Onn (Eds.), *Regional Outlook; Southeast Asia: 2010–2011*, Singapore: Institute of Southeast Asian Studies, pp. 33–7.

Subrahmanya, M. (2009) 'Case study: Nature and strategy of product innovations in SMEs: A case study-based comparative perspective of Japan and India,' *Innovation: Management, Policy and Practice*, **11**(1): 104–13.

Suehiro, A. and Wailerdsak, N. (2004) 'Family business in Thailand: Its management, governance, and future challenges,' *ASEAN Economic Bulletin*, **21**(1): 81–93.

Suh, T. and Kwon, I.G. (2002) 'Globalization and reluctant buyers,' *International Marketing Review*, **19**(6): 663–80.

Suutari, V., Raharjo, K. and Riikkila, T. (2002) 'The challenge of cross-cultural leadership interaction: Finnish expatriates in Indonesia,' *Career Development International*, **7**(6/7): 415–29.

Swierczek, F.W. and Onishi, J. (2003) 'Culture and conflict: Japanese managers and Thai subordinates,' *Personnel Review*, **32**(1/2): 187–210.

Syamananda, R. (1993) *A History of Thailand*, Bangkok: Thai Watana Panich.

Takamiya, H. (2001) 'Introductory routes of rice to Japan: An examination of the southern route hypothesis,' *Asian Perspectives: Journal of Archeology for Asia and the Pacific*, **40**(2): 209–26.

Tan, C. (2007) 'Education reforms in Cambodia: Issues and concerns,' *Educational Research for Policy and Practice*, **6**(1): 5–24.

Tan, K.Y. (1997) 'East Asia as an independent engine of growth: Prospects and implications for managers,' *Management Decision*, **35**(8): 574–86.

Tang, L. and Koveos, P.E. (2004) 'Venture entrepreneurship, innovation entrepreneurship, and economic growth,' *Journal of Development Entrepreneurship*, **9**(2): 161–71.

Tarling, N. (1992) 'The establishment of the colonial regimes,' in N. Tarling (Ed.), *The Cambridge History of Southeast Asia, Volume 2*, Cambridge, UK: Cambridge University Press, pp. 5–78.

Taylor, K.W. (1992) 'The early kingdoms,' in N. Tarling (Ed.), *The Cambridge History of Southeast Asia, Volume 1*, Cambridge, UK: Cambridge University Press, pp. 137–82.

Taylor, S. (2007) 'Creating social capital in MNCs: The international human resource management challenge,' *Human Resource Management Journal*, **17**(4): 336–64.

Tedeschi, G. (2010) 'Microfinance: Assessing its impact on microenterprises,' in J.M. Munoz (Ed.), *Contemporary Microenterprise: Concepts and Cases*, Cheltenham, UK: Edward Elgar, pp. 116–28.

Thai, M. and Agrawal, N.M. (2009) 'Vietnam,' in L.P. Dana, M. Han, V. Ratten and I.M. Welpe (Eds.), *Handbook of Research on Asian Entrepreneurship*, Cheltenham, UK: Edward Elgar, pp. 377–86.

Thai, M and Ngoc, H. (2010) 'Micro entrepreneurship in a transitional economy: Evidence from Vietnam,' in J.M. Munoz (Ed.), *Contemporary Micro-enterprise: Concepts and Cases*, Northampton, MA: Edward Elgar, pp. 32–48.

Thawnghmung, A.M. (2008) 'Responding to strategies and programmes of Myanmar's military regime: An economic viewpoint,' *Southeast Asian Affairs*, **2008**: 274–90.

Thayer, C.A. (2010) 'US rapprochement with Laos and Cambodia,' *Contemporary Southeast Asia*, **32**(3): 442–59.

Timmer, C.P. (2007) 'How Indonesia connected the poor to rapid growth,' in T. Besley and L.J. Cord (Eds.), *Delivering on the Promise of Pro-poor Growth: Insights and Lessons from Country Experiences*, New York: World Bank/Palgrave Macmillan, pp. 29–58.

Tin, H. (2008) 'Myanmar education: Challenges, prospects and options,' in M. Skidmore and T. Wilson (Eds.), *Dictatorship, Disorder and Decline*, Canberra: ANU E Press, pp. 113–26.

Tokoro, M. (2005) 'The shift towards American-style human resource management systems and the transformation of workers' attitudes at Japanese firms,' *Asian Business and Management*, 4: 23–44.

Tomlinson, B.R. (2003) 'Economic change and the formulation of states and nations in South Asia, 1941–1947: India and Pakistan,' in A. Teichiva and H. Matis (Eds.), *Nation, State and the Economy in History*, Cambridge, UK: Cambridge University Press, pp. 291–307.

Tong, K. (2010) 'The social impact of the global recession on Cambodia: How the crisis impacts on poverty,' in A. Bauer and M. Thant (Eds.), *Poverty and Sustainability Development in Asia: Impacts and Responses to the Global Economic Crisis*, Mandaluyong City, Philippines: Asian Development Bank, pp. 141–48.

Torrisi, C.R. and Uslu, G. (2010) 'Transitioning economics: A calculus of competitiveness,' *Journal of Applied Business and Economics*, 11(3): 39–54.

Tripathy, S. and Rath, N. (2011) 'Practice of corporate social responsibility in NALCO and the perceptions of employees and the public: A case study,' *South Asian Journal of Management*, 18(4): 44–61.

Trocki, C.A. (1992) 'Political structures in the nineteenth and early twentieth centuries,' in N. Tarling (Ed.) *The Cambridge History of Southeast Asia, Volume 2*, Cambridge, UK: Cambridge University Press, pp. 79–130.

Troilo, M. (2010) 'Microenterprise start-up: A cross cultural comparison,' in J.M. Munoz (Ed.), *Contemporary Micro-enterprise: Concepts and Cases*, Northampton, MA: Edward Elgar, pp. 9–19.

Tsang, E. (2001) 'Internationalizing the family firm: A case study of a Chinese family business,' *Journal of Small Business Management*, 39(2): 88–94.

Tsikata, Y.M. (2003) 'The political economy of globalization, poverty and inequality in sub-Saharan Africa,' in R. Kohl (Ed.), *Globalisation, Poverty and Inequality*, Paris: Organisation for Economic Co-operation and Development, pp. 53–8.

Tsui, K. (2008) 'Forces shaping China's interprovincial inequality,' in G. Wan (Ed.), *Inequality and Growth in Modern China*, New York: Oxford University Press, 79–111.

Tudor, T.R., Trumble, R.R. and George, G. (1996) 'Significant historic origins that influenced the team concept in major Japanese companies,' *Journal of Applied Business Research*, 12(4): 115–28.

Tully, J. (2005) *A Short History of Cambodia: From Empire to Survival*, Crows Nest, Australia: Allen & Unwin.

Tung, R.L. (1984) 'Human resource planning in Japanese multinationals: A model for U.S. firms?' *Journal of International Business Studies*, 15(2): 139–49.

Turk, C. and Mason, A. (2010) 'Impacts of the economic crisis in East Asia: Findings from qualitative monitoring in five countries,' in A. Bauer and M. Thant (Eds.), *Poverty and Sustainability Development in Asia: Impacts and Responses to the*

Global Economic Crisis, Mandaluyong City, Philippines: Asian Development Bank, pp. 51–76.

Turnbull, A.M. (1992) 'Regionalism and nationalism,' in N. Tarling (Ed.), *The Cambridge History of Southeast Asia, Volume 2*, Cambridge, UK: Cambridge University Press, pp. 585–646.

Turnell, S., Vicary, A. and Bradford, W. (2008) 'Migrant-workers remittances and Burma: An economic analysis of survey results,' in M. Skidmore and T. Wilson (Eds.), *Dictatorship, Disorder and Decline*, Canberra: ANU E Press, pp. 63–86.

Ty, M., Walsh, J. and Anurit, P. (2010) 'An empirical assessment of the relationship between national culture and learning capability in organizations in Cambodia,' *International Business Research*, 3(4): 81–90.

UNCTAD (2011) *The Least Developed Countries Report: The Potential Role of South–South Cooperation for Inclusive and Sustainable Development*, Geneva/New York: United Nations.

Ungpakorn, G.J. (2007) *A Coup for the Rich: Thailand's Political Crisis*, Bangkok: Workers Democracy Publishing.

Van Ark, B. and Piatkowski, M. (2004) 'Productivity, innovation and ICT in old and new Europe,' *International Economics and Economic Policy*, 1(2/3): 215–46.

Van Beuningen, C. (2007) 'Democracy and development,' *Development*, 50(1), 50–5.

Vandenberg, P. (2006) 'Poverty reduction through small enterprises: Emerging consensus, unresolved issues and ILO activities,' *SEED Working Paper (International Labour Organization), Geneva, Switzerland*, No. 75.

Van den Waeyenberg, S. and Hens, L. (2008) 'Crossing the bridge to poverty, with low-cost cars,' *Journal of Consumer Marketing*, 25(7): 439–45.

Van de Ven, A.H. (2004) 'The context-specific nature of competence and corporate development,' *Asia Pacific Journal of Management*, 21(1/2): 123–47.

Van de Vliert, E., Einarsen, S., Euwema, M.C. and Janssen, O. (2009) 'Ecological limits to globalization of managerial situations,' *International Journal of Cross Cultural Management*, 9(2): 185–98.

Van Horen, B. and Pinnawala, S. (2006) 'Sri Lanka,' in B. Roberts and T. Kanaley (Eds.), *Urbanization and Sustainability in Asia: Case Studies of Good Practices*, Mandaluyong City, Philippines: Asian Development Bank, pp. 309–40.

Van Praag, C.M. and Versloot, P.H. (2007) 'What is the value of entrepreneurship,' *Small Business Economics*, 29(4): 351–82.

Varghese, R. (2011) 'Voluntary annual report disclosures of manufacturing companies in India and their linkage with organisational demographics,' *South Asian Journal of Management*, 18(4): 23–43.

Varma, A., Pichler, S., Budhwar, P. and Biswas, S. (2009) 'Chinese host country nationals' willingness to support expatriates: The role of collectivism, interpersonal affect and guanxi,' *International Journal of Cross Cultural Management*, 9(2): 199–216.

Vickery, M. (2004) 'Cambodia and its neighbors in the 15th century,' *Asia Research Institute Working Paper Series*, No. 27.

Vinten, G. (2000) 'Business theology,' *Management Decisions*, 38(3): 209–15.

Wad, P. (2007) 'Transformation of automobile trade unions in Korea and Malaysia,' in J. Shin (Ed.), *Global Challenges and Local Responses*, New York: Routledge, pp. 164–83.

Wahab, S. and Youngerman, B. (2010) *A Brief History of Afghanistan*, Second Edition, New York: Facts on File.

Wakeman, F. (1975) *The Fall of Imperial China*, New York: Free Press.

Walde, K. and Wood, C. (2004) 'The empirics of trade and growth: Where are the policy recommendations?' *International Economics and Economic Policy*, 1(2/3): 275–92.

Walker, W. and Hall, D. (2010) 'Reforming social protection systems when commodity prices collapse: The experience of Mongolia,' in A. Bauer and M. Thant (Eds.), *Poverty and Sustainability Development in Asia: Impacts and Responses to the Global Economic Crisis*, Mandaluyong City, Philippines: Asian Development Bank, pp. 389–403.

Walsh, J.E. (2011) *A Brief History of India*, Second Edition, New York: Facts on File.

Walsh, K. (2004) 'Interpreting the impact of culture on structure: The role of change processes,' *The Journal of Applied Behavioral Science*, 40(3): 302–22.

Walton, M.J. (2008) 'Ethnicity, conflict, and history in Burma: The myths of Panglong,' *Asian Survey*, 48(6): 889–910.

Wan, G., Lu, M. and Chen, Z. (2010) 'The inequality–growth nexus in the short and long run: Empirical evidence from China,' in G. Wan (Ed.), *Inequality and Growth in Modern China*, New York: Oxford University Press, pp. 1–17.

Wang, M.C. (2004) 'Greater China: Powerhouse of East Asian regional cooperation,' *East Asia*, 21(4): 38–63.

Wang, T. and Chien, S. (2007) 'The influences of technology development on economic performance: The example of ASEAN countries,' *Technovation*, 27(8): 471–88.

Wang, X. (2008) 'Income inequality in China and its influencing factors,' in G. Wan (Ed.), *Inequality and Growth in Modern China*, New York: Oxford University Press, pp. 18–32.

Warr, P. (2007) 'Long-term economic performance in Thailand,' *Asian Economic Bulletin*, 24(1): 138–63.

Warr, P. and Sarntisart, I. (2005) 'Poverty targeting in Thailand,' in J. Weiss (Ed.), *Poverty Targeting in Asia*, Cheltenham, UK: Edward Elgar, pp. 186–218.

Watanabe, T. (2003) 'Recent trends in Japanese human resource management: The introduction of a system of individual and independent career choice,' *Asian Business and Management*, 2: 111–41.

Weber, A. and Piechulek, H. (2010) 'The impact of the global recession on the poor and vulnerable in the Philippines and on the social health insurance system,' in A. Bauer and M. Thant (Eds.), *Poverty and Sustainability Development in Asia: Impacts and Responses to the Global Economic Crisis*, Mandaluyong City, Philippines: Asian Development Bank, pp. 425–39.

Wegner, L. (2007) 'Financing SME development in Africa in developing countries,' in *Business and Development: Fostering the Private Sector*, Paris: Development Centre of the Organisation for Economic Co-operation and Development, pp. 97–100.

Wennekers, S. and Thurik, R. (1999) 'Linking entrepreneurship and economic growth,' *Small Business Economics*, 13(1): 27–55.

Werlin, H.H. (2009) 'The poverty of nations: The impact of foreign aid,' *The Journal of Social, Political and Economic Studies*, 34(4): 480–510.

Wheeler, W.R. (1919) *China and the World War*, New York: Macmillan.

Widyono, B. (2008) *Dancing in Shadows*, Lanham, MD: Rowman & Littlefield.

Williamson, J. (2005) 'Winners and losers over two centuries of globalization,' in A. Shorrocks (Ed.), *Wider Perspectives in Global Development*, New York: Palgrave Macmillan, pp. 136–74.

Wilson, T. and Skidmore, M. (2008) 'Overview,' in M. Skidmore and T. Wilson (Eds.), *Dictatorship, Disorder and Decline*, Canberra: ANU E Press, pp. 1–9.

Winters, A.L. (2006) 'International trade and poverty: Cause or cure?' *Australian Economic Review*, 39(4): 347–58.

Wong, Y.U. and Maher, T.E. (1998) 'Doing business with dragons of different breeds: Some important differences between China and Japan,' *Management Research News*, 21(4): 45–54.

Woodward, M. (2011) *Java, Indonesia and Islam*, New York: Springer-Verlag.

Wooten, L.P., Parmigiani, A. and Lahiri, N. (2005) 'CK Prahalad's passions: Reflections on his scholarly journey as a researcher, teacher and management guru,' *Journal of Management Inquiry*, 14(2): 168–75.

World Bank (2010) 'Gross national income per capita [data file]', available from *http://siteresources.worldbank.org/DATASTATISTICS/Resources/GNIPC.pdf*

WIPO (World Intellectual Property Organization) (2008) *World Patent Report: A Statistical Review*, available from *http://www.wipo.int/ipstats/en/statistics/patents/pdf/wipo_pub_ 931.html*

Wright, G. (2003) 'The role of nationhood in the economic development of the USA,' in A. Teichiva and H. Matis (Eds.), *Nation, State and the Economy in History*, Cambridge, UK: Cambridge University Press, pp. 387–403.

Wu, F., Webster, C., He, S. and Liu Y. (2010) *Urban Poverty in China*, Cheltenham, UK: Edward Elgar.

Wu, W.P. and Choi, W.L. (2004) 'Transaction cost, social capital and firms' synergy creation in Chinese business networks,' *Asia Pacific Journal of Management*, 21(3): 325–44.

Wyatt, D.K. (2003) *Thailand: A Short History*, Second Edition, Chiang Mai, Thailand: Silkworm Books.

Yamano, T., Kijima, Y., Matsumoto, T. and Muto, M. (2010) 'Recent developments of agricultural markets in East Africa,' in K. Otsuka and K. Kalirajan (Eds.), *Community, Market and State in Development*, London: Palgrave Macmillan, pp. 245–61.

Yan, J. and Sorenson, R.L. (2004) 'The influence of Confucian ideology on conflict in Chinese family business,' *International Journal of Cross Cultural Management*, 4(1): 5–17.

Yao, S. (2006) 'On economic growth, FDI and exports in China,' *Applied Economics*, 38(3): 339–51.

Yawnghwe, H. (2010) 'United States–Myanmar relations: On the threshold of rapprochement? A response,' *Contemporary Southeast Asia*, 32(3): 427–33.

Ying, T.Y., Eng, A., and Robinson, E. (2010) 'Perspectives on growth: A political-economy framework: Lessons from the Singapore experience,' in D. Brady and M. Spence (Eds.), *Leadership and Growth*, Washington, D.C.: World Bank, pp. 99–128.

Yip, G.S. (1996) 'Global strategy as a factor in Japanese success,' *International Executive*, 38(1): 145–67.

Yip, G.S., Johansson, J.K. and Roos, J. (1997) 'Effects of nationality on global strategy,' *Management International Review*, 37(4): 365–85.

Young, C.S. (2005) 'Top management teams' social capital in Taiwan: The impact on firm value in an emerging economy,' *Journal of Intellectual Capital*, 6(2): 177–90.

Young, E. (1900) *The Kingdom of the Yellow Robe*, Second Edition, Westminster, UK: Archibald Constable & Co.

Yu, J. and Zaheer, S. (2010) 'Building a process model of local adaptation of practices: Study of six sigma implementation in Korean and US firms,' *Journal of International Business Studies*, 41(3): 475–99.

Yu, S. (1999) 'The growth pattern of Samsung electronics: A strategy perspective,' *International Studies of Management and Organization*, 28(4): 57–72.

Yunus, M. and Weber, K. (2007) *Creating a World without Poverty: Social Business and the Future of Capitalism*, New York: Public Affairs.

Zagorsek, H., Jaklic, M. and Stough, S.J. (2004) 'Comparing leadership practices between the United States, Nigeria, and Slovenia: Does culture matter?' *Cross Cultural Management*, 11(2): 16–34.

Zhang, L.J. and Jeckle, M. (2004) 'Convergence of web services and grid computing,' *International Journal of Web Services Research*, 1(3): 1–4.

Zhang, X. (2002) 'China's involvement in Laos during the Vietnam War, 1963–1975,' *The Journal of Military History*, 66(4): 1141–66.

Zhang, X. and Lin, S. (2010) 'The impact of the global slowdown on the People's Republic of China's rural migrants: Empirical evidence from a 12 city survey,' in A. Bauer and M. Thant (Eds.), *Poverty and Sustainability Development in Asia: Impacts and Responses to the Global Economic Crisis*, Mandaluyong City, Philippines: Asian Development Bank, pp. 203–18.

Zhang, Y. (2009) 'The discourse of China's soft power and its discontents,' in M. Li (Ed.), *Soft Power: China's Emerging Strategy in International Politics*, Lanham, MD: Lexington Books, pp. 45–60.

Zhang, Y. (2010) 'The impact of free trade agreements on business activity: A survey of firms in the People's Republic of China,' *Asian Development Bank Institute Working Paper*, No. 251.

Zhang, Y. and Wan, G. (2008) 'Poverty reduction in China: Trends and causes,' in G. Wan (Ed.), *Inequality and Growth in Modern China*, New York: Oxford University Press, pp. 33–55.

Zhu, Z. (2006) *US–China Relations in the 21st Century: Power Transition and Peace*, London: Routledge.

Zhuang, J. (2008) 'Inclusive growth toward a harmonious society in the People's Republic of China: Policy implications,' *Asian Development Review*, 25(1/2): 22–33.

Zou, H. and Adams, M.B. (2008) 'Corporate ownership, equity risk and return in the People's Republic of China,' *Journal of International Business Studies*, 39(7): 1149–68.

Index

Printed and bound by CPI Group (UK) Ltd, Croydon, CR0 4YY

08/05/2025

01864968-0002